CONFLICT

&

COURAGE

In ancient times, Abraham, Isaac, Jacob, Moses with his meekness and wisdom, and Joshua with his varied capabilities, were all enlisted in God's service. The music of Miriam, the courage and piety of Deborah, the filial affection of Ruth, the obedience and faithfulness of Samuel, the stern fidelity of Elijah, the softening, subduing influence of Elisha—all were needed. So now all upon whom God's blessing has been bestowed are to respond by actual service; every gift is to be employed for the advancement of His kingdom and the glory of His name. —Christ's Object Lessons, *p. 301.*

The greatest want of the world is the want of men—men who will not be bought or sold, men who in their inmost souls are true and honest, men who do not fear to call sin by its right name, men whose conscience is as true to duty as the needle to the pole, men who will stand for the right though the heavens fall. —Education, *p. 57.*

CONFLICT
&
COURAGE

Compiled from the writings of Ellen G. White

ELLEN G. WHITE

"For whatever was written in former days was written for our instruction, that by steadfastness and by the encouragement of the scriptures we might have hope." Romans 15:4, RSV.

REVIEW AND HERALD® PUBLISHING ASSOCIATION
HAGERSTOWN, MD 21740

Texts credited to ARV are from *The Holy Bible,* edited by the American Revision Committee, Thomas Nelson and Sons, 1901.

Texts credited to NEB are from *The New English Bible.* © The Delegates of the Oxford University Press and the Syndics of the Cambridge University Press 1961, 1970. Reprinted by permission.

Bible texts credited to Phillips are from J. B. Phillips: *The New Testament in Modern English,* Revised Edition. © J. B. Phillips 1958, 1960, 1972. Used by permission of Macmillan Publishing Co.

Bible texts credited to RSV are from the Revised Standard Version of the Bible, copyright © 1946, 1952, 1971, by the Division of Christian Education of the National Council of the Churches of Christ in the U.S.A. Used by permission.

Texts credited to RV are from *The Holy Bible,* Revised version, Oxford University Press, 1911.

PRINTED IN THE U.S.A.

Cover design by Leumas Design/Willie Duke
Cover photo by Getty Images/Alan Pappe

ISBN 0-8280-1825-1

FOREWORD

The Bible record of men and women of ancient times presents backgrounds so broad and diverse that every modern person may identify with someone portrayed therein. All who are wise will gain from a study of this record that which will direct, enrich, and guard their own personal life. They will draw courage from those who triumphed, learn from the mistakes of others, and hopefully will be spared the heartaches of those who made unwise choices.

The Word of God treats only briefly the exploits, failures, and successes of the characters it portrays. More detailed accounts are given to us by Ellen G. White in her inspired writings. In a rare manner she catches and applies, with sensitive, divinely guided insight, relevant lessons from the lives of saints and sinners depicted in sacred history. From this voluminous and rich source of materials the 365 brief sketches that comprise this devotional volume have been selected. Obviously there could not be reproduced here full biographies of the many characters mentioned in the Bible. These may be pursued in the five volumes of the Conflict of the Ages Series, the *Testimonies,* other Ellen G. White books, and in the Ellen G. White supplement to *The Seventh-day Adventist Bible Commentary.* Rather, the lessons from their lives have been set forth here by incidents, in their biographical setting. They appear in roughly chronological order, but without a tight sequence of events; nor has it been possible to be exhaustive even in this selective area.

The Scripture reference at the top of many of the pages will guide to the Bible account of the experience from which the lesson has been drawn.

Credit is given for each item appearing in these pages. A close look at the listing at the back of this volume will reveal that the prime source has been the familiar books of the Conflict Series, which in general present the fullest and richest accounts.

The task of selecting and arranging these sketches has been undertaken in the office of the Ellen G. White Estate. May they accomplish the purpose for which they are intended—to bring courage to God's people for the trials of earth's closing days.

THE TRUSTEES OF THE ELLEN G. WHITE ESTATE

THAT WE MAY BE ENCOURAGED

For all those words which were written long ago are meant to teach us today; that when we read in the scriptures of the endurance of men and of all the help that God gave them in those days, we may be encouraged to go on hoping in our own time. Rom. 15:4, Phillips.

The lives recorded in the Bible are authentic histories of actual individuals. From Adam down through successive generations to the times of the apostles we have a plain, unvarnished account of what actually occurred and the genuine experience of real characters. It is a subject of wonder to many that inspired history should narrate in the lives of good men facts that tarnish their moral characters. . . . The inspired writers did not testify to falsehoods to prevent the pages of sacred history being clouded by the record of human frailties and faults. . . .

It is one of the best evidences of the authenticity of the Scriptures that the truth is not glossed over nor the sins of its chief characters suppressed. . . . How many biographies have been written of faultless Christians, who, in their ordinary home life and church relations, shone as examples of immaculate piety. . . . Yet had the pen of inspiration written their histories, how different would they have appeared. There would have been revealed human weaknesses, struggles with selfishness, bigotry, and pride, hidden sins, perhaps, and the continual warfare between the spirit and the flesh. . . .

Had our good Bible been written by uninspired persons, it would have presented quite a different appearance and would have been a discouraging study to erring mortals, who are contending with natural frailties and the temptations of a wily foe. But as it is, we have a correct record of the religious experience of marked characters in Bible history. Men whom God favored, and to whom He entrusted great responsibilities, were sometimes overcome by temptation and committed sins, even as we of the present day strive, waver, and frequently fall into error. But it is encouraging to desponding hearts to know that through God's grace they could gain fresh vigor to again rise above their evil natures; and, remembering this, we are ready to renew the conflict ourselves.[1]

THERE'S HOPE

Now these things which happened to our ancestors are illustrations of the way in which God works, and they were written down to be a warning to us who are the heirs of the ages which have gone before us. 1 Cor. 10:11, Phillips.

The murmurings of ancient Israel and their rebellious discontent, as well as the mighty miracles wrought in their favor and the punishment of their idolatry and ingratitude, are recorded for our benefit. The example of ancient Israel is given as a warning to the people of God, that they may avoid unbelief and escape His wrath. If the iniquities of the Hebrews had been omitted from the Sacred Record, and only their virtues recounted, their history would fail to teach us the lesson that it does. . . .

If God's people would recognize His dealings with them and accept His teachings, they would find a straight path for their feet and a light to guide them through darkness and discouragement. David learned wisdom from God's dealings with him and bowed in humility beneath the chastisement of the Most High. The faithful portrayal of his true state by the prophet Nathan made David acquainted with his own sins and aided him to put them away. He accepted counsel meekly and humiliated himself before God. "The law of the Lord," he exclaims, "is perfect, converting the soul."

Repentant sinners have no cause to despair because they are reminded of their transgressions and warned of their danger. These very efforts in their behalf show how much God loves them and desires to save them. They have only to follow His counsel and do His will, to inherit eternal life. God sets the sins of His erring people before them, that they may behold them in all their enormity under the light of divine truth. It is then their duty to renounce them forever.

God is as powerful to save from sin today as He was in the times of the patriarchs, of David, and of the prophets and apostles. The multitude of cases recorded in sacred history where God has delivered His people from their own iniquities should make the Christian of this time eager to receive divine instruction and zealous to perfect a character that will bear the close inspection of the judgment.[2]

A PLACE IN LINE

The lips of the righteous feed many. Prov. 10:21.

Notwithstanding the prevailing iniquity, there was a line of holy men who, elevated and ennobled by communion with God, lived as in the companionship of heaven. They were men of massive intellect, of wonderful attainments. They had a great and holy mission— to develop a character of righteousness, to teach a lesson of godliness, not only to the men of their time, but for future generations. Only a few of the most prominent are mentioned in the Scriptures; but all through the ages God had faithful witnesses, true-hearted worshipers.[3]

How often those who trusted the word of God, though in themselves utterly helpless, have withstood the power of the whole world—Enoch, pure in heart, holy in life, holding fast his faith in the triumph of righteousness against a corrupt and scoffing generation; Noah and his household against the men of his time, men of the greatest physical and mental strength and the most debased in morals; the children of Israel at the Red Sea, a helpless, terrified multitude of slaves, against the mightiest army of the mightiest nation on the globe; David, a shepherd lad, having God's promise of the throne, against Saul, the established monarch, bent on holding fast his power; Shadrach and his companions in the fire, and Nebuchadnezzar on the throne; Daniel among the lions, his enemies in the high places of the kingdom; Jesus on the cross, and the Jewish priests and rulers forcing even the Roman governor to work their will; Paul in chains led to a criminal's death, Nero the despot of a world empire.

Such examples are not found in the Bible only. They abound in every record of human progress. The Vaudois and the Huguenots, Wycliffe and Huss, Jerome and Luther, Tyndale and Knox, Zinzendorf and Wesley, with multitudes of others have witnessed to the power of God's word against human power and policy in support of evil. These are the world's true nobility. This is its royal line. In this line the youth of today are called to take their places.[4]

WHAT FRUIT?

They that plow iniquity, and sow wickedness, reap the same.
Job 4:8.

As an educator no part of the Bible is of greater value than are its biographies. These biographies differ from all others in that they are absolutely true to life. It is impossible for any finite mind to interpret rightly, in all things, the workings of another. None but He who reads the heart, who discerns the secret springs of motive and action, can with absolute truth delineate character, or give a faithful picture of a human life. In God's word alone is found such delineation.

No truth does the Bible more clearly teach than that what we do is the result of what we are. To a great degree the experiences of life are the fruition of our own thoughts and deeds.

"The curse causeless shall not come" (Prov. 26:2). "Say ye to the righteous, that it shall be well with him. . . . Woe unto the wicked! it shall be ill with him: for the reward of his hands shall be given him" (Isa. 3:10, 11). "Hear, O earth: behold, I will bring evil upon this people, even the fruit of their thoughts" (Jer. 6:19). Terrible is this truth, and deeply should it be impressed. Every deed reacts upon the doer. Never a human being but may recognize, in the evils that curse his life, fruitage of his own sowing. Yet even thus we are not without hope. . . .

Jacob resorted to fraud, and he reaped the harvest in his brother's hatred. Through twenty years of exile he was himself wronged and defrauded. . . . But God says: ". . . I have seen his ways, and will heal him. . . ." (Isa. 57:18). Jacob in his distress was not overwhelmed. He had repented, he had endeavored to atone for the wrong to his brother. And when threatened with death through the wrath of Esau, he sought help from God. . . . "He wept, and made supplication" (Hosea 12:4). "And he blessed him there" (Gen. 32:29). . . . The power of evil in his own nature was broken; his character was transformed. . . .

God does not annul His laws. He does not work contrary to them. The work of sin He does not undo. But He transforms. Through His grace the curse works out blessing.[5]

10

IN GOD'S IMAGE

So God created man in his own image, in the image of God created he him; male and female created he them. Gen. 1:27.

After the earth with its teeming animal and vegetable life had been called into existence, man, the crowning work of the Creator, and the one for whom the beautiful earth had been fitted up, was brought upon the stage of action. To him was given dominion over all that his eye could behold. . . .

God created man in His own image. Here is no mystery. There is no ground for the supposition that man was evolved by slow degrees of development from the lower forms of animal or vegetable life. Such teaching lowers the great work of the Creator to the level of man's narrow, earthly conceptions. Men are so intent upon excluding God from the sovereignty of the universe that they degrade man and defraud him of the dignity of his origin. He who set the starry worlds on high and tinted with delicate skill the flowers of the field, who filled the earth and the heavens with the wonders of His power, when He came to crown His glorious work, to place one in the midst to stand as ruler of the fair earth, did not fail to create a being worthy of the hand that gave him life. The genealogy of our race, as given by inspiration, traces back its origin, not to a line of developing germs, mollusks, and quadrupeds, but to the great Creator. Though formed from the dust, Adam was "the son of God." . . .

His nature was in harmony with the will of God. His mind was capable of comprehending divine things. His affections were pure; his appetites and passions were under the control of reason. He was holy and happy in bearing the image of God and in perfect obedience to His will.[6]

He [Adam] was more than twice as tall as men now living upon the earth, and was well proportioned. His features were perfect and beautiful. . . . Eve was not quite as tall as Adam. Her head reached a little above his shoulders. She, too, was noble, perfect in symmetry, and very beautiful.

This sinless pair wore no artificial garments. They were clothed with a covering of light and glory, such as the angels wear.[7]

11

EDEN

And the Lord God took the man, and put him into the garden of Eden to dress it and to keep it. Gen. 2:15.

Although everything God had made was in the perfection of beauty, and there seemed nothing wanting upon the earth which God had created to make Adam and Eve happy, yet He manifested His great love to them by planting a garden especially for them. A portion of their time was to be occupied in the happy employment of dressing the garden, and a portion in receiving the visits of angels, listening to their instruction, and in happy meditation. Their labor was not wearisome but pleasant and invigorating. This beautiful garden was to be their home.

In this garden the Lord placed trees of every variety for usefulness and beauty. There were trees laden with luxuriant fruit, of rich fragrance, beautiful to the eye, and pleasant to the taste, designed of God to be food for the holy pair. There were the lovely vines which grew upright, laden with their burden of fruit, unlike anything man has seen since the fall. The fruit was very large and of different colors; some nearly black, some purple, red, pink, and light green. This beautiful and luxuriant growth of fruit upon the branches of the vine was called grapes. They did not trail upon the ground, although not supported by trellises, but the weight of the fruit bowed them down. It was the happy labor of Adam and Eve to form beautiful bowers from the branches of the vine and train them, forming dwellings of nature's beautiful, living trees and foliage, laden with fragrant fruit.[8]

It was the design of God that man should find happiness in the employment of tending the things He had created, and that his wants should be met with the fruits of the trees of the garden. . . .

Had happiness consisted in doing nothing, man, in his state of holy innocence, would have been left unemployed. But He who created man knew what would be for his happiness; and no sooner had He created him than He gave him his appointed work. The promise of future glory, and the decree that man must toil for his daily bread, came from the same throne.[9]

A CHANCE TO CHOOSE

But of the tree of the knowledge of good and evil, thou shalt not eat of it: for in the day that thou eatest thereof thou shalt surely die. Gen. 2:17.

Our first parents, though created innocent and holy, were not placed beyond the possibility of wrongdoing. . . . They were to enjoy communion with God and with holy angels; but before they could be rendered eternally secure, their loyalty must be tested. At the very beginning of man's existence a check was placed upon the desire for self-indulgence, the fatal passion that lay at the foundation of Satan's fall. The tree of knowledge, which stood near the tree of life in the midst of the garden, was to be a test of the obedience, faith, and love of our first parents. While permitted to eat freely of every other tree, they were forbidden to taste of this, on pain of death. They were also to be exposed to the temptations of Satan; but if they endured the trial, they would finally be placed beyond his power, to enjoy perpetual favor with God. . . .

God might have created man without the power to transgress His law; He might have withheld the hand of Adam from touching the forbidden fruit; but in that case man would have been, not a free moral agent, but a mere automaton. Without freedom of choice, his obedience would not have been voluntary, but forced. There could have been no development of character. . . . It would have been unworthy of man as an intelligent being, and would have sustained Satan's charge of God's arbitrary rule.

God made man upright; He gave him noble traits of character, with no bias toward evil. He endowed him with high intellectual powers, and presented before him the strongest possible inducements to be true to his allegiance. Obedience, perfect and perpetual, was the condition of eternal happiness. On this condition he was to have access to the tree of life. . . .

So long as they remained loyal to the divine law, their capacity to know, to enjoy, and to love would continually increase. They would be constantly gaining new treasures of knowledge, discovering fresh springs of happiness, and obtaining clearer and yet clearer conceptions of the immeasurable, unfailing love of God.[10]

SOMEONE TO SHARE

It is not good that the man should be alone; I will make him an help meet for him. Gen. 2:18.

After the creation of Adam every living creature was brought before him to receive its name; he saw that to each had been given a companion, but among them "there was not found an help meet for him." Among all the creatures that God had made on the earth, there was not one equal to man. And God said, "It is not good that the man should be alone; I will make him an help meet for him." Man was not made to dwell in solitude; he was to be a social being. Without companionship the beautiful scenes and delightful employments of Eden would have failed to yield perfect happiness. Even communion with angels could not have satisfied his desire for sympathy and companionship. There was none of the same nature to love and to be loved.

God Himself gave Adam a companion. He provided "an help meet for him"—a helper corresponding to him—one who was fitted to be his companion, and who could be one with him in love and sympathy. Eve was created from a rib taken from the side of Adam, signifying that she was not to control him as the head, nor to be trampled under his feet as an inferior, but to stand by his side as an equal, to be loved and protected by him. A part of man, bone of his bone, and flesh of his flesh, she was his second self; showing the close union and the affectionate attachment that should exist in this relation. "For no man ever yet hated his own flesh; but nourisheth and cherisheth it" (Eph. 5:29). "Therefore shall a man leave his father and his mother, and shall cleave unto his wife: and they shall be one" (Gen. 2:24).

God celebrated the first marriage. Thus the institution has for its originator the Creator of the universe. "Marriage is honorable" (Heb. 13:4); it was one of the first gifts of God to man, and it is one of the two institutions that, after the Fall, Adam brought with him beyond the gates of Paradise. When the divine principles are recognized and obeyed in this relation, marriage is a blessing; it guards the purity and happiness of the race, it provides for man's social needs, it elevates the physical, the intellectual, and the moral nature.[11]

14

DECEIVED!

And he said unto the woman, Yea, hath God said, Ye shall not eat of every tree of the garden? Gen. 3:1.

To man, the crowning work of creation, God has given power to understand His requirements, to comprehend the justice and beneficence of His law, and its sacred claims upon him; and of man unswerving obedience is required.

Like the angels, the dwellers in Eden had been placed upon probation; their happy estate could be retained only on condition of fidelity to the Creator's law. They could obey and live, or disobey and perish. . . .

The angels had cautioned Eve to beware of separating herself from her husband while occupied in their daily labor in the garden; with him she would be in less danger from temptation than if she were alone. But absorbed in her pleasing task, she unconsciously wandered from his side. . . . She soon found herself gazing with mingled curiosity and admiration upon the forbidden tree. The fruit was very beautiful, and she questioned with herself why God had withheld it from them. Now was the tempter's opportunity. As if he were able to discern the workings of her mind, he addressed her: "Yea, hath God said, Ye shall not eat of every tree of the garden?" . . .

The tempter intimated that the divine warning was not to be actually fulfilled; it was designed merely to intimidate them. . . .

Such has been Satan's work from the days of Adam to the present, and he has pursued it with great success. He tempts men to distrust God's love and to doubt His wisdom. He is constantly seeking to excite a spirit of irreverent curiosity, a restless, inquisitive desire to penetrate the secrets of divine wisdom and power. In their efforts to search out what God has been pleased to withhold, multitudes overlook the truths which He has revealed, and which are essential to salvation. . . .

Eve really believed the words of Satan, but her belief did not save her from the penalty of sin. She disbelieved the words of God, and this was what led to her fall. In the judgment men will not be condemned because they conscientiously believed a lie, but because they did not believe the truth, because they neglected the opportunity of learning what is truth.[12]

USED BY SATAN

She took of the fruit thereof, and did eat, and gave also unto her husband with her; and he did eat. Gen. 3:6.

Having herself transgressed, she [Eve] became the agent of Satan working the ruin of her husband. In a state of strange, unnatural excitement, with her hands filled with the forbidden fruit, she sought his presence, and related all that had occurred.

An expression of sadness came over the face of Adam. He appeared astonished and alarmed. To the words of Eve he replied that this must be the foe against whom they had been warned; and by the divine sentence she must die. In answer she urged him to eat, repeating the words of the serpent, that they should not surely die. She reasoned that this must be true, for she felt no evidence of God's displeasure, but on the contrary realized a delicious, exhilarating influence, thrilling every faculty with new life, such, she imagined, as inspired the heavenly messengers.

Adam understood that his companion had transgressed the command of God, disregarded the only prohibition laid upon them as a test of their fidelity and love. There was a terrible struggle in his mind. He mourned that he had permitted Eve to wander from his side. But now the deed was done; he must be separated from her whose society had been his joy. How could he have it thus? Adam had enjoyed the companionship of God and of holy angels. He had looked upon the glory of the Creator. He understood the high destiny opened to the human race should they remain faithful to God. Yet all these blessings were lost sight of in the fear of losing that one gift which in his eyes outvalued every other. Love, gratitude, loyalty to the Creator— all were overborne by love to Eve. She was a part of himself, and he could not endure the thought of separation. . . . He resolved to share her fate; if she must die, he would die with her. After all, he reasoned, might not the words of the wise serpent be true? Eve was before him, as beautiful and apparently as innocent as before this act of disobedience. She expressed greater love for him than before. No sign of death appeared in her, and he decided to brave the consequences. He seized the fruit and quickly ate.[13]

WHEN IT'S BETTER NOT TO KNOW

And I gave my heart to know wisdom, and to know madness and folly. Eccl. 1:17.

Adam and Eve both ate of the fruit, and obtained a knowledge which, had they obeyed God, they would never have had—an experience in disobedience and disloyalty to God—the knowledge that they were naked. The garment of innocence, a covering from God, which surrounded them, departed; and they supplied the place of this heavenly garment by sewing together fig-leaves for aprons.

This is the covering that the transgressors of the law of God have used since the days of Adam and Eve's disobedience. . . . The fig-leaves represent the arguments used to cover disobedience. . . .

But the nakedness of the sinner is not covered. . . .

Had Adam and Eve never disobeyed their Creator, had they remained in the path of perfect rectitude, they could have known and understood God. But when they listened to the voice of the tempter, and sinned against God, the light of the garments of heavenly innocence departed from them; and in parting with the garments of innocence, they drew about them the dark robes of ignorance of God. The clear and perfect light that had hitherto surrounded them had lightened everything they approached; but deprived of that heavenly light, the posterity of Adam could no longer trace the character of God in His created works.[14]

If Adam and Eve had never touched the forbidden tree, the Lord would have imparted to them knowledge—knowledge upon which rested no curse of sin, knowledge that would have brought them everlasting joy. . . .

Age after age, the curiosity of men has led them to seek for the tree of knowledge; and often they think they are plucking fruit most essential, when, like Solomon's research, they find it altogether vanity and nothingness in comparison with that science of true holiness which will open to them the gates of the city of God. The human ambition has been seeking for that kind of knowledge that will bring to them glory and self-exaltation and supremacy. Thus Adam and Eve were worked upon by Satan.[15]

CURSED!

Unto the woman he said, I will greatly multiply thy sorrow and thy conception; . . . and thy desire shall be to thy husband, and he shall rule over thee. And unto Adam he said, . . . cursed is the ground for thy sake; in sorrow shalt thou eat of it all the days of thy life. Gen. 3:16, 17.

Eve was told of the sorrow and pain that must henceforth be her portion. . . . In the creation God had made her the equal of Adam. Had they remained obedient to God—in harmony with His great law of love—they would ever have been in harmony with each other; but sin had brought discord, and now their union could be maintained and harmony preserved only by submission on the part of the one or the other. Eve had been the first in transgression; and she had fallen into temptation by separating from her companion, contrary to the divine direction. It was by her solicitation that Adam sinned, and she was now placed in subjection to her husband. . . .

Eve had been perfectly happy by her husband's side in her Eden home; but, like restless modern Eves, she was flattered with the hope of entering a higher sphere than that which God had assigned her. In attempting to rise above her original position, she fell far below it. A similar result will be reached by all who are unwilling to take up cheerfully their life duties in accordance with God's plan. In their efforts to reach positions for which He has not fitted them, many are leaving vacant the place where they might be a blessing. . . .

When God made man, He made him ruler over the earth and all living creatures. So long as Adam remained loyal to Heaven, all nature was in subjection to him. But when he rebelled against the divine law, the inferior creatures were in rebellion against his rule. Thus the Lord, in His great mercy, would show men the sacredness of His law, and lead them, by their own experience, to see the danger of setting it aside, even in the slightest degree.

And the life of toil and care which was henceforth to be man's lot was appointed in love. It was a discipline rendered needful by his sin, to place a check upon the indulgence of appetite and passion, to develop habits of self-control. It was a part of God's great plan for man's recovery from the ruin and degradation of sin.[16]

TAUGHT BY NATURE

But ask now the beasts, and they shall teach thee; and the fowls of the air, and they shall tell thee: or speak to the earth, and it shall teach thee: and the fishes of the sea shall declare unto thee. Who knoweth not in all these that the hand of the Lord hath wrought this? Job 12:7-9.

Although the earth was blighted with the curse, nature was still to be man's lesson book. It could not now represent goodness only; for evil was everywhere present, marring earth and sea and air with its defiling touch. . . .

In drooping flower and falling leaf Adam and his companion witnessed the first signs of decay. Vividly was brought to their minds the stern fact that every living thing must die. Even the air, upon which their life depended, bore the seeds of death.

Continually they were reminded also of their lost dominion. Among the lower creatures Adam had stood as king, and so long as he remained loyal to God, all nature acknowledged his rule; but when he transgressed, this dominion was forfeited. The spirit of rebellion, to which he himself had given entrance, extended throughout the animal creation. . . .

But man was not abandoned to the results of the evil he had chosen. In the sentence pronounced upon Satan was given an intimation of redemption. . . . This sentence, spoken in the hearing of our first parents, was to them a promise. Before they heard of the thorn and the thistle, of the toil and sorrow that must be their portion, or of the dust to which they must return, they listened to words that could not fail of giving them hope. All that had been lost by yielding to Satan could be regained through Christ.[17]

After the transgression of Adam, God might have destroyed every opening bud and blooming flower, or He might have taken away their fragrance, so grateful to the senses. In the earth seared and marred by the curse, in the briers, the thistles, the thorns, the tares, we may read the law of condemnation; but in the delicate color and perfume of the flowers, we may learn that God still loves us, that His mercy is not wholly withdrawn from the earth.[18]

BETWEEN GOD AND MAN

Wherefore he is able also to save them to the uttermost that come unto God by him, seeing he ever liveth to make intercession for them. Heb. 7:25.

The Lord did not place in Adam fallen and disobedient the confidence He placed in Adam loyal and true. . . . The rewards of heaven are not granted to transgressors. . . .

The eyes of Adam and Eve were indeed opened, but to what? To see their own shame and ruin, to realize that the garments of heavenly light which had been their protection were no longer around them as their safeguard. Their eyes were opened to see that nakedness was the fruit of transgression. As they heard God in the garden, they hid themselves from Him; for they anticipated that which till their fall they had not known—the condemnation of God. . . .

God has declared that man's only means of safety is entire obedience to all His words. We are not to make the experiment of testing the evil course, with all its results. This will bring weakness through disobedience. God's plan was to give man clear-sightedness in all his work. . . .

There was to be co-operation between man and God. But this plan was greatly interfered with by Adam's transgression. Satan led him to sin, and the Lord would not communicate with him after he had sinned as he did when he was without sin.

After the fall Christ became Adam's instructor. He acted in God's stead toward humanity, saving the race from immediate death. He took upon him the office of mediator. Adam and Eve were given a probation in which to return to their allegiance, and in this plan all their posterity were embraced.[19]

Without the atonement of the Son of God there could have been no communication of blessing or salvation from God to man. God was jealous for the honor of His law. The transgression of that law had caused a fearful separation between God and man. To Adam in his innocence was granted communion, direct, free, and happy, with his Maker. After his transgression, God would communicate to man only through Christ and angels.[20]

ONE EXPENSIVE MISTAKE

God hath made man upright; but they have sought out many inventions. Eccl. 7:29.

The book of Genesis gives quite a definite account of social and individual life, and yet we have no record of an infant's being born blind, deaf, crippled, deformed, or imbecile. There is not an instance upon record of a natural death in infancy, childhood, or early manhood. There is no account of men and women dying of disease. Obituary notices in the book of Genesis run thus: "And all the days that Adam lived were nine hundred and thirty years: and he died." "And all the days of Seth were nine hundred and twelve years: and he died." . . .

God endowed man with so great vital force that he has withstood the accumulation of disease brought upon the race in consequence of perverted habits, and has continued for six thousand years. This fact of itself is enough to evidence to us the strength and electrical energy that God gave to man at his creation. . . . If Adam, at his creation, had not been endowed with twenty times as much vital force as men now have, the race, with their present habits of living in violation of natural law, would have become extinct. . . .

God did not create the race in its present feeble condition. This state of things is not the work of Providence, but the work of man; it has been brought about by wrong habits and abuses, by violating the laws that God has made to govern man's existence.[21]

God created man for His own glory, that after test and trial the human family might become one with the heavenly family. It was God's purpose to re-populate heaven with the human family, if they would show themselves obedient to His every word.[22]

To Eve it seemed a small thing to disobey God by tasting the fruit of the forbidden tree, and to tempt her husband also to transgress; but their sin opened the floodgates of woe upon the world. Who can know, in the moment of temptation, the terrible consequences that will result from one wrong step?[23]

BY WORD OF MOUTH

And all the days that Adam lived were nine hundred and thirty years: and he died. Gen. 5:5.

Adam's life was one of sorrow, humility, and continual repentance. As he taught his children and grandchildren the fear of the Lord, he was often bitterly reproached for the sin which had resulted in so much misery to his posterity. When he left beautiful Eden, the thought that he must die thrilled him with horror. He looked upon death as a dreadful calamity. . . . Most bitterly did he reproach himself for his first great transgression. He entreated pardon from God through the promised Sacrifice. Deeply had he felt the wrath of God for his crime committed in Paradise. He witnessed the general corruption which finally provoked God to destroy the inhabitants of the earth by a flood. Though the sentence of death pronounced upon him by his Maker at first appeared so terrible to him, yet after he had lived some hundreds of years, it looked just and merciful in God, thus to bring to an end a miserable life.

As Adam witnessed the fast signs of decay in the falling leaf and in the drooping flowers, he mourned more deeply than men now mourn over their dead. The dying flowers were not so great a cause of grief, because they were more tender and delicate; but when the tall stately trees cast off their leaves to decay, it presented before him the general dissolution of beautiful nature, which God had created for the especial benefit of man.

To his children, and to their children, to the ninth generation, Adam delineated the perfections of his Eden home; and also his fall and its dreadful results. . . . He declared to them that sin would be punished, in whatever form it existed; and he entreated them to obey God, who would deal mercifully with them if they should love and fear Him.

Adam was commanded to teach his descendants the fear of the Lord, and, by his example of humble obedience, lead them to highly regard the offerings which typified a Savior to come. Adam carefully treasured what God had revealed to him, and handed it down by word of mouth to his children and children's children. By this means the knowledge of God was preserved.[24]

22

HOME AGAIN!

For as in Adam all die, even so in Christ shall all be made alive. But every man in his own order: Christ the firstfruits; afterward they that are Christ's at his coming. 1 Cor. 15:22, 23.

Amid the reeling of the earth, the flash of lightning, and the roar of thunder, the voice of the Son of God calls forth the sleeping saints. . . . The dead shall hear that voice, and they that hear shall live. And the whole earth shall ring with the tread of the exceeding great army of every nation, kindred, tongue, and people. . . .

All come forth from their graves the same in stature as when they entered the tomb. Adam, who stands among the risen throng, is of lofty height and majestic form, in stature but little below the Son of God. He presents a marked contrast to the people of later generations; in this one respect is shown the great degeneracy of the race. But all arise with the freshness and vigor of eternal youth. . . .

All blemishes and deformities are left in the grave. Restored to the tree of life in the long-lost Eden, the redeemed will "grow up" to the full stature of the race in its primeval glory. . . .

As the ransomed ones are welcomed to the City of God, there rings out upon the air an exultant cry of adoration. The two Adams are about to meet. The Son of God is standing with outstretched arms to receive the father of our race—the being whom He created, who sinned against his Maker, and for whose sin the marks of the crucifixion are borne upon the Savior's form. As Adam discerns the prints of the cruel nails, he does not fall upon the bosom of his Lord, but in humiliation casts himself at His feet, crying: "Worthy, worthy is the Lamb that was slain!" Tenderly the Savior lifts him up and bids him look once more upon the Eden home from which he has so long been exiled. . . .

This reunion is witnessed by the angels who wept at the fall of Adam and rejoiced when Jesus, after His resurrection, ascended to heaven, having opened the grave for all who should believe on His name. Now they behold the work of redemption accomplished, and they unite their voices in the song of praise.[25]

23

IT'S UP TO YOU

By faith Abel offered unto God a more excellent sacrifice than Cain, by which he obtained witness that he was righteous, God testifying of his gifts: and by it he being dead yet speaketh. Heb. 11:4.

Cain and Abel, the sons of Adam, differed widely in character. Abel had a spirit of loyalty to God; he saw justice and mercy in the Creator's dealings with the fallen race, and gratefully accepted the hope of redemption. But Cain cherished feelings of rebellion, and murmured against God because of the curse pronounced upon the earth and upon the human race for Adam's sin. He permitted his mind to run in the same channel that led to Satan's fall—indulging the desire for self-exaltation and questioning the divine justice and authority. . . .

These two brothers erected their altars alike, and each brought an offering. Abel presented a sacrifice from the flock, in accordance with the Lord's directions. "And the Lord had respect unto Abel and to his offering." Fire flashed from heaven and consumed the sacrifice. But Cain, disregarding the Lord's direct and explicit command, presented only an offering of fruit. There was no token from heaven to show that it was accepted. . . .

Abel grasped the great principles of redemption. He saw himself a sinner, and he saw sin and its penalty, death, standing between his soul and communion with God. He brought the slain victim, the sacrificed life, thus acknowledging the claims of the law that had been transgressed. Through the shed blood he looked to the future sacrifice, Christ dying on the cross of Calvary; and trusting in the atonement that was there to be made, he had the witness that he was righteous, and his offering accepted.

Cain had the same opportunity of learning and accepting these truths as had Abel. He was not the victim of an arbitrary purpose. One brother was not elected to be accepted of God, and the other to be rejected. Abel chose faith and obedience; Cain, unbelief and rebellion. Here the whole matter rested.[26]

TWO WAYS TO GO

And the Lord had respect unto Abel and to his offering: but unto Cain and to his offering he had not respect. And Cain was very wroth, and his countenance fell. Gen. 4:4, 5.

Cain came before God with murmuring and infidelity in his heart in regard to the promised sacrifice and the necessity of the sacrificial offerings. His gift expressed no penitence for sin. He felt, as many now feel, that it would be an acknowledgement of weakness to follow the exact plan marked out by God, of trusting his salvation wholly to the atonement of the promised Savior. He chose the course of self-dependence. He would come in his own merits. He would not bring the lamb, and mingle its blood with his offering, but would present *his* fruits, the products of *his* labor. He presented his offering as a favor done to God, through which he expected to secure the divine approval. Cain obeyed in building an altar, obeyed in bringing a sacrifice, but he rendered only a partial obedience. The essential part, the recognition of the need of a Redeemer, was left out. . . .

Cain and Abel represent two classes that will exist in the world till the close of time. One class avail themselves of the appointed sacrifice for sin; the other venture to depend upon their own merits; theirs is a sacrifice without the virtue of divine mediation, and thus it is not able to bring man into favor with God. It is only through the merits of Jesus that our transgressions can be pardoned. . . .

It is claimed by some that the human race is in need, not of redemption, but of development—that it can refine, elevate, and regenerate itself. As Cain thought to secure the divine favor by an offering that lacked the blood of a sacrifice, so do these expect to exalt humanity to the divine standard, independent of the atonement. This history of Cain shows what must be the result. It shows what man will become apart from Christ. Humanity has no power to regenerate itself. It does not tend upward, toward the divine, but downward, toward the satanic. Christ is our only hope. "There is none other name under heaven given among men, whereby we must be saved." "Neither is there salvation in any other" (Acts 4:12).[27]

YOUR FACE IS TELLING

And the Lord said unto Cain, Why art thou wroth? and why is thy countenance fallen? If thou doest well, shalt thou not be accepted? and if thou doest not well, sin lieth at the door. Gen. 4:6, 7.

The Lord saw the wrath of Cain. He saw the falling of his countenance. Thus is revealed how closely the Lord marks every action, all the intents and purposes, yes, even the expression of the countenance. This, though man may say nothing, expresses his refusal to do the way and will of God.[28]

Mark the words of the Lord. . . . This question may be addressed to every young man and young woman who, like Cain, reveal their passion . . . when acting out the promptings of Satan, which are in direct opposition to the requirements of God.[29]

If you choose to throw off the sacred, restraining influence of the truth, Satan will lead you captive at his will. You will be in danger of giving scope to your appetites and passions, giving loose rein to lusts, to evil and abominable desires. Instead of bearing in your countenance a calm serenity under trial and affliction, like faithful Enoch, having your face radiant with hope and that peace which passeth understanding, you will stamp your countenance with carnal thoughts, with lustful desires. You will bear the impress of the satanic instead of the divine.[30]

Many children and youth have their characters imprinted on their countenances. Their life's history they carry in the features of the face. . . . If Christ is the abiding principle in the heart, you may read purity, refinement, peace, and love in the features. In other countenances, an evil character hangs out the sign; selfishness, cunning, deceit, falsehood, enmity, and jealousy are expressed there. How difficult it is for truth to impress the hearts and countenances of such characters! . . .

All spiritual culture Christ has provided for His children. If Jesus is abiding in the soul, the heart is filled with the holy graces of His Spirit, which makes itself manifest in the transforming of the features. If you would have beauty and loveliness of character, the divine law must be written upon the heart and carried out in the life.[31]

CAIN "WENT OUT"

And Cain went out from the presence of the Lord. Gen. 4:16.

God had given Cain an opportunity to confess his sin. . . . He knew the enormity of the deed he had done, and of the falsehood he had uttered to conceal it; but he was rebellious still, and sentence was no longer deferred. . . .

Notwithstanding that Cain had by his crimes merited the sentence of death, a merciful Creator still spared his life, and granted him opportunity for repentance. But Cain lived only to harden his heart, to encourage rebellion against the divine authority, and to become the head of a line of bold, abandoned sinners. This one apostate, led on by Satan, became a tempter to others; and his example and influence exerted their demoralizing power, until the earth became so corrupt and filled with violence as to call for its destruction. . . .

Upon receiving the curse of God, Cain had withdrawn from his father's household. . . . He had gone out from the presence of the Lord, cast away the promise of the restored Eden, to seek his possessions and enjoyment in the earth under the curse of sin, thus standing at the head of that great class of men who worship the god of this world. In that which pertains to mere earthly and material progress, his descendants became distinguished. But they were regardless of God, and in opposition to His purposes for man.[32]

In sparing the life of Cain the murderer, God gave the world an example of what would be the result of permitting the sinner to live to continue a course of unbridled iniquity. Through the influence of Cain's teaching and example, multitudes of his descendants were led into sin, until "the wickedness of man was great in the earth," and "every imagination of the thoughts of his heart was only evil continually."[33]

As Cain went out from the presence of the Lord to seek his home; as the prodigal wandered into the "far country," so do sinners seek happiness in forgetfulness of God.[34]

HE WALKED WITH GOD

Enoch lived sixty and five years, and begat Methuselah: and Enoch walked with God after he begat Methuselah three hundred years. Gen. 5:21, 22.

Of Enoch it is written that he lived sixty-five years, and begat a son. . . . During these earlier years Enoch had loved and feared God and had kept His commandments. . . . But after the birth of his first son, Enoch reached a higher experience; he was drawn into a closer relationship with God. He realized more fully his own obligations and responsibility as a son of God. And as he saw the child's love for its father, its simple trust in his protection; as he felt the deep, yearning tenderness of his own heart for that firstborn son, he learned a precious lesson of the wonderful love of God to men in the gift of His Son, and the confidence which the children of God may repose in their heavenly Father. The infinite, unfathomable love of God through Christ became the subject of his meditation day and night; and with all the fervor of his soul he sought to reveal that love to the people among whom he dwelt.

Enoch's walk with God was not in a trance or a vision, but in all the duties of his daily life. He did not become a hermit, shutting himself entirely from the world; for he had a work to do for God in the world. In the family and in his intercourse with men, as a husband and father, a friend, a citizen, he was the steadfast, unwavering servant of the Lord. . . . And this holy walk was continued for three hundred years. There are few Christians who would not be far more earnest and devoted if they knew that they had but a short time to live, or that the coming of Christ was about to take place. But Enoch's faith waxed the stronger, his love became more ardent, with the lapse of centuries.[35]

He [Enoch] was of one mind with God. . . . If we are of one mind with God, our will will be swallowed up in God's will, and we shall follow wherever God leads the way. As a loving child places his hand in that of his father, and walks with him in perfect trust whether it is dark or bright, so the sons and daughters of God are to walk with Jesus through joy or sorrow.[36]

GOD TOOK HIM

*Enoch walked with God: and he was not; for God took him.
Gen. 5:24.*

Enoch, we read, walked with God three hundred years. That was a long time to be in communion with Him. . . . He communed with God because it was agreeable to him, . . . and he loved the society of God.[37]

Enoch was a marked character. Many look upon his life as something above what the generality of mortals can ever reach. But Enoch's life and character . . . represent what the lives and characters of all must be if, like Enoch, they are subjects to be translated when Christ shall come. His life was what the life of every individual may be if he closely connects with God. We should remember that Enoch was surrounded with influences so depraved that God brought a flood of waters on the world to destroy its inhabitants for their corruption.[38]

We are living in an evil age. The perils of the last days thicken around us. Because iniquity abounds, the love of many waxes cold. . . .

Enoch's case is before us. . . . He lived in a corrupt age, when moral pollution was teeming all round him; yet he trained his mind to devotion, to love purity. His conversation was upon heavenly things. He educated his mind to run in this channel, and he bore the impress of the divine. His countenance was lighted up with the light which shineth in the face of Jesus.

Enoch had temptations as well as we. He was surrounded with society no more friendly to righteousness than is that which surrounds us. The atmosphere he breathed was tainted with sin and corruption, the same as ours; yet he lived a life of holiness. He was unsullied with the prevailing sins of the age in which he lived. So may we remain pure and uncorrupted. He was a representative of the saints who live amid the perils and corruptions of the last days. For his faithful obedience to God he was translated. So, also, the faithful, who are alive and remain, will be translated. They will be removed from a sinful and corrupt world to the pure joys of heaven.[39]

Our present work is to come out from the world and be separate. This is the only way we can walk with God, as did Enoch.[40]

LOOKING AT CHRIST

*But we all, with open face beholding as in a glass the glory of
the Lord, are changed into the same image from glory to glory,
even as by the Spirit of the Lord. 2 Cor. 3:18.*

In the midst of a life of active labor, Enoch steadfastly maintained
his communion with God. The greater and more pressing his labors,
the more constant and earnest were his prayers. He continued to exclude himself at certain periods from all society. After remaining for
a time among the people, laboring to benefit them by instruction and
example, he would withdraw, to spend a season in solitude, hunger-
ing and thirsting for that divine knowledge which God alone can impart. Communing thus with God, Enoch came more and more to
reflect the divine image. His face was radiant with a holy light, even
the light that shineth in the face of Jesus. As he came forth from these
divine communings, even the ungodly beheld with awe the impress
of heaven upon his countenance.[41]

Enoch kept the Lord ever before him. . . . He made Christ his constant companion. He was in the world, and performed his duties to
the world; but he was ever under the influence of Jesus. He reflected
Christ's character, exhibiting the same qualities of goodness, mercy,
tender compassion, sympathy, forbearance, meekness, humility, and
love. His association with Christ day by day transformed him into the
image of Him with whom he was so intimately connected. Day by day
he was growing away from his own way into Christ's way, the heavenly, the divine, in his thoughts and feelings.[42]

If we keep the Lord ever before us, allowing our hearts to go out
in thanksgiving and praise to Him, we shall have a continual freshness
in our religious life. Our prayers will take the form of a conversation
with God as we would talk with a friend. He will speak His mysteries
to us personally. Often there will come to us a sweet, joyful sense of
the presence of Jesus. Often our hearts will burn within us as He draws
nigh to commune with us as He did with Enoch. When this is in truth
the experience of the Christian, there is seen in his life a simplicity, a
humility, meekness, and lowliness of heart, that show to all with whom
he associates that he has been with Jesus and learned of Him.[43]

AN OPEN DOOR

By faith Enoch was translated that he should not see death; and was not found, because God had translated him: for before his translation he had this testimony, that he pleased God. Heb. 11:5.

When we learn to walk by faith and not by feeling, we shall have help from God just when we need it, and His peace will come into our hearts. It was this simple life of obedience and trust that Enoch lived. If we learn this lesson of simple trust, ours may be the testimony that he received, that he pleased God.[44]

In every phase of your character building you are to please God. This you may do; for Enoch pleased Him though living in a degenerate age. And there are Enochs in this our day.[45]

For three hundred years Enoch had been seeking purity of heart, that he might be in harmony with heaven. For three centuries he had walked with God. Day by day he had longed for a closer union; nearer and nearer had grown the communion, until God took him to Himself. He had stood at the threshold of the eternal world, only a step between him and the land of the blest; and now the portals opened, the walk with God, so long pursued on earth, continued, and he passed through the gates of the holy city—the first from among men to enter there.[46]

With the word of God in his hands, every human being, wherever his lot in life may be cast, may have such companionship as he shall choose. In its pages he may hold converse with the noblest and best of the human race, and may listen to the voice of the Eternal as He speaks with men. . . . He may dwell in this world in the atmosphere of heaven, imparting to earth's sorrowing and tempted ones thoughts of hope and longings for holiness; . . . like him of old who walked with God, drawing nearer and nearer the threshold of the eternal world, until the portals shall open, and he shall enter there. He will find himself no stranger. The voices that will greet him are the voices of the holy ones, who, unseen, were on earth his companions— voices that here he learned to distinguish and to love. He who through the word of God has lived in fellowship with heaven will find himself at home in heaven's companionship.[47]

31

GOD OR IDOLS?

Their idols are silver and gold, the work of men's hands. . . .
They that make them are like unto them; so is every one that
trusteth in them. Ps. 115:4-8.

In the days of Noah a double curse was resting upon the earth in consequence of Adam's transgression and of the murder committed by Cain. Yet this had not greatly changed the face of nature. . . . The human race yet retained much of its early vigor. But a few generations had passed since Adam had access to the tree which was to prolong life; and man's existence was still measured by centuries. Had that long-lived people with their rare powers to plan and execute devoted themselves to the service of God, they would have made their Creator's name a praise in the earth. . . . But they failed to do this. . . .

Not desiring to retain God in their knowledge, they soon came to deny His existence. They adored nature in place of the God of nature. . . . Extensive groves, that retained their foliage throughout the year, were dedicated to the worship of false gods. . . . Men put God out of their knowledge and worshiped the creatures of their own imagination; and as the result, they became more and more debased.[48]

The men of that generation were not all, in the fullest acceptation of the term, idolaters. Many professed to be worshipers of God. They claimed that their idols were representations of the Deity and that through them the people could obtain a clearer conception of the divine Being. This class were foremost in rejecting the preaching of Noah. As they endeavored to represent God by material objects, their minds were blinded to His majesty and power; they ceased to realize the holiness of His character, or the sacred, unchanging nature of His requirements.[49]

Man will rise no higher than his conceptions of truth, purity, and holiness. If the mind is never exalted above the level of humanity, if it is not uplifted by faith to contemplate infinite wisdom and love, the man will be constantly sinking lower and lower. The worshipers of false gods clothed their deities with human attributes and passions, and thus their standard of character was degraded to the likeness of sinful humanity.[50]

GIANTS IN THE LAND

There were giants in the earth in those days. Gen. 6:4.

The first people upon the earth received their instructions from that infinite God who created the world. Those who received their knowledge direct from infinite wisdom were not deficent in knowledge. . . .

There are many inventions and improvements, and labor-saving machines now that the ancients did not have. They did not need them. . . .

Men before the Flood lived many hundreds of years, and when one hundred years old were considered but youths. Those long-lived men had sound minds in sound bodies. . . . They came upon the stage of action from the ages of sixty to one hundred years, about the time those who now live the longest have acted their part in their little short life time, and have passed off the stage.[51]

There were many giants, men of great stature and strength, renowned for wisdom, skillful in devising the most cunning and wonderful works; but their guilt in giving loose rein to iniquity was in proportion to their skill and mental ability.

God bestowed upon these antediluvians many and rich gifts; but they used His bounties to glorify themselves, and turned them into a curse by fixing their affections upon the gifts instead of the Giver. They employed the gold and silver, the precious stones and the choice wood, in the construction of habitations for themselves, and endeavored to excel one another in beautifying their dwellings with the most skillful workmanship. They sought only to gratify the desires of their own proud hearts, and reveled in scenes of pleasure and wickedness.[52]

They became corrupt in their imagination, because they left God out of their plans and councils. They were wise to do what God had never told them to do, wise to do evil. . . . They used the probation so graciously granted them in ridiculing Noah. They caricatured him and criticized him. They laughed at him for his peculiar earnestness and intense feeling in regard to the judgments which he declared God would surely fulfill. They talked of science and of the laws controlling nature. Then they held a carnival over the words of Noah, calling him a crazy fanatic.[53]

ABUSED TALENTS

And his brother's name was Jubal: he was the father of all such as handle the harp and organ. And Zillah, she also bare Tubal-cain, an instructor of every artificer in brass and iron. Gen. 4:21, 22.

There perished in the Flood greater inventions of art and human skill than the world knows of today. The arts destroyed were more than the boasted arts of today. . . .

Looking upon the world, God saw that the intellect He had given man was perverted, that the imagination of his heart was evil and that continually. God had given these men knowledge. He had given them valuable ideas, that they might carry out His plan. But the Lord saw that those whom He designed should possess wisdom, tact, and judgment, were using every quality of the mind to glorify self. By the waters of the Flood, He blotted this long-lived race from the earth, and with them perished the knowledge they had used only for evil. When the earth was repeopled, the Lord trusted His wisdom more sparingly to men, giving them only the ability they would need in carrying out His great plan.[54]

The world today takes much satisfaction in talking of the progress of the age. But in this God does not delight. It may be said of the men of this time, as of those before the Flood, They have sought out many inventions. In the antediluvian world there were many wonderful works of art and science. These descendants of Adam, fresh from the hand of God, possessed capabilities and powers that we never now look upon.[55]

Those who lived before the Flood were only a few steps from God, the Creator of the world and its inhabitants. The long life and large intellect given to these men might have been used in God's service. But their intellectual strength, that mighty power, was perverted to dishonor God. . . .

When men separate from God, they place themselves under the control of Satan. Talents have been given to men that they may be used in God's service. . . . There is only one safe way for any man, and that is the way of obedience to a "Thus saith the Lord."[56]

34

AN AFFLUENT SOCIETY

In the days that were before the flood they were eating and drinking . . . and knew not until the flood came and took them all away. Matt. 24:38, 39.

The sin of the Noatic world was intemperance, and today the sin exhibited by intemperance in eating and drinking is so marked that God will not always tolerate it. . . . Man carries to excess that which is lawful, and his whole being suffers the result of the violation of the laws which the Lord has established.

Intemperance in eating and drinking is on the increase. Tables are spread with all kinds of food with which to satisfy the epicurean appetite. Suffering must follow this course of action. The vital force of the system cannot bear up under the tax placed on it, and it finally breaks down.

God . . . will not work a miracle to counteract a perverse violation of the laws of health and life. . . . Man should estimate himself by the price which has been paid for him. When he places this value upon himself, he will not knowingly abuse one of his physical or mental faculties. It is an insult to the God of heaven for man to abuse his precious powers by placing himself under the control of satanic agencies, and besotting himself by indulging in that which is ruinous to health, to piety, and to spirituality.[57]

Though the wickedness of the world was so great, yet the Lord gave men one hundred and twenty years of probation, in which, if they would, they could repent. But notwithstanding the forbearance of a good and merciful God, the people did not improve their opportunities. For a little time they were awed, and afraid to go on as recklessly as they had done. Then, depraved habits prevailed over restraint. In proportion as the people resisted conviction, their discernment was clouded, and their desire to follow a course of ungodliness strengthened.[58]

It is necessary for us to eat and to drink that we may have physical strength to serve the Lord, but when we carry our eating to gluttony, without a thought of pleasing our heavenly Father, eating just that which is pleasing to our taste, we are doing just as they did in the days of Noah.[59]

MARRYING AND GIVING IN MARRIAGE

In the days that were before the flood they were . . . marrying and giving in marriage, until the day that Noe entered into the ark. Matt. 24:38.

In Noah's day brute force was the prevailing influence in the world. By threatened punishment, men intimidated other men.[60]

Instead of doing justice to their neighbors, they carried out their own unlawful wishes. They had a plurality of wives, which was contrary to God's wise arrangement. In the beginning God gave to Adam one wife—showing, to all who should live upon the earth, his order and law in that respect. The transgression and fall of Adam and Eve brought sin and wretchedness upon the human race, and man followed his own carnal desires, and changed God's order. The more men multiplied wives to themselves, the more they increased in wickedness and unhappiness. If one chose to take the wives, or cattle, or anything belonging to his neighbor, he did not regard justice or right, but if he could prevail over his neighbor by reason of strength, or by putting him to death, he did so, and exulted in his deeds of violence. They loved to destroy the lives of animals. They used them for food, and this increased their ferocity and violence, and caused them to look upon the blood of human beings with astonishing indifference.[61]

The descendants of Seth were called the sons of God; the descendants of Cain, the sons of men. As the sons of God mingled with the sons of men, they became corrupt and, by intermarriage with them, lost, through the influence of their wives, their peculiar, holy character, and united with the sons of Cain in their idolatry. Many cast aside the fear of God and trampled upon His commandments. But there were a few that did righteousness, who feared and honored their Creator. Noah and his family were among the righteous few.[62]

Polygamy was practiced at an early date. It was one of the sins that brought the wrath of God upon the antediluvian world. . . . It was Satan's studied effort to pervert the marriage institution, to weaken its obligations and lessen its sacredness; for in no surer way could he deface the image of God in man and open the door to misery and vice.[63]

UNTIL THE DAY . . .

And spared not the old world, but saved Noah the eighth person, a preacher of righteousness, bringing in the flood upon the world of the ungodly. 2 Peter 2:5.

God warned the inhabitants of the old world of what He purposed to do in cleansing the earth of its impurity. But they laughed to scorn what they regarded as a superstitious prediction.[64]

Many at first appeared to receive the warning; yet they did not turn to God with true repentance. They were unwilling to renounce their sins. During the time that elapsed before the coming of the Flood, their faith was tested, and they failed to endure the trial. Overcome by the prevailing unbelief, they finally joined their former associates in rejecting the solemn message. Some were deeply convicted, and would have heeded the words of warning; but there were so many to jest and ridicule that they partook of the same spirit, . . . and were soon among the boldest and most defiant scoffers; for none are so reckless and go to such lengths in sin as do those who have once had light but have resisted the convicting Spirit of God.[65]

They continued their festivities and their gluttonous feasts; they ate and drank, planted and builded, laying their plans in reference to advantages they hoped to gain in the future; and they went to greater lengths in wickedness, and in defiant disregard of God's requirements, to testify that they had no fear of the Infinite One. . . .

Had the antediluvians believed the warning, and repented of their evil deeds, the Lord would have turned aside His wrath, as He afterward did from Nineveh. But by their obstinate resistance to the reproofs of conscience and the warnings of God's prophet, that generation filled up the measure of their iniquity, and became ripe for destruction.[66]

The Lord has sent us, by His ambassadors, messages of warning, declaring that the end of all things is at hand. Some will listen to these warnings, but by the vast majority they will be disregarded.

Thus will it be when Christ comes. Farmers, merchants, lawyers, tradesmen, will be wholly engrossed in business, and upon them the day of the Lord will come as a snare.[67]

BUILD AN ARK

And God said unto Noah, The end of all flesh is come before me; for the earth is filled with violence through them; and, behold, I will destroy them with the earth. Make thee an ark. Gen. 6:13, 14.

God gave Noah the exact dimensions of the ark and explicit directions in regard to its construction in every particular. Human wisdom could not have devised a structure of so great strength and durability. God was the designer, and Noah the master builder. It was constructed like the hull of a ship, that it might float upon the water, but in some respects it more nearly resembled a house. . . . The material employed in the construction of the ark was the cypress, or gopher wood, which would be untouched by decay for hundreds of years. The building of this immense structure was a slow and laborious process.[1]

The race of men then living were of very great stature, and possessed wonderful strength. The trees were vastly larger, and far surpassing in beauty and perfect proportions anything mortals can now look upon. The wood of these trees was of fine grain and hard substance—in this respect more like stone. It required much more time and labor, even of that powerful race, to prepare the timber for building, than it requires in this degenerate age to prepare trees that are now growing upon the earth, even with the present weaker strength men now possess.[2]

Every piece of timber was closely fitted, and every seam covered with pitch. All that men could do was done to make the work perfect; yet, after all, God alone could preserve the building upon the angry, heaving billows, by His miraculous power.[3]

Methuselah and his sons, and grandsons, lived in the time of the building of the ark. They, with some others, received instruction from Noah, and assisted him in building the ark.[4]

While Noah was giving his warning message to the world, his works testified of his sincerity. It was thus that his faith was perfected and made evident. He gave the world an example of believing just what God says. All that he possessed, he invested in the ark. . . . Every blow struck upon the ark was a witness to the people.[5]

SAFE INSIDE

And the Lord said unto Noah, Come thou and all thy house into the ark; for thee have I seen righteous before me in this generation. Gen. 7:1.

Noah had faithfully followed the instructions which he had received from God. The ark was finished in every part as the Lord had directed, and was stored with food for man and beast. And now the servant of God made his last solemn appeal to the people. With an agony of desire that words cannot express, he entreated them to seek a refuge while it might be found. Again they rejected his words, and raised their voices in jest and scoffing. Suddenly a silence fell upon the mocking throng. Beasts of every description, the fiercest as well as the most gentle, were seen coming from mountain and forest and quietly making their way toward the ark. A noise as of a rushing wind was heard, and lo, birds were flocking from all directions, their numbers darkening the heavens, and in perfect order they passed to the ark. Animals obeyed the command of God, while men were disobedient.[6]

When they saw the beasts come from the forests to the door of the ark, and Noah take them in, they had so long resisted, so long denied the message that God had given them, that . . . conscience had become unimpressible.[7]

Mercy had ceased its pleadings for the guilty race. The beasts of the field and the birds of the air had entered the place of refuge. Noah and his household were within the ark, "and the Lord shut him in." . . . The massive door, which it was impossible for those within to close, was slowly swung to its place by unseen hands. Noah was shut in, and the rejecters of God's mercy were shut out. The seal of Heaven was on that door; God had shut it, and God alone could open it. So when Christ shall cease His intercession for guilty men, before His coming in the clouds of heaven, the door of mercy will be shut. Then divine grace will no longer restrain the wicked, and Satan will have full control of those who have rejected mercy. They will endeavor to destroy God's people; but as Noah was shut into the ark, so the righteous will be shielded by divine power.[8]

AFTER SEVEN DAYS

And it came to pass after seven days, that the waters of the flood were upon the earth. Gen. 7:10.

For seven days after Noah and his family entered the ark, there appeared no sign of the coming storm. During this period their faith was tested. It was a time of triumph to the world without. The apparent delay confirmed them in the belief that Noah's message was a delusion, and that the Flood would never come. Notwithstanding the solemn scenes which they had witnessed . . . they still continued their sport and revelry, even making a jest of these signal manifestations of God's power. They gathered in crowds about the ark, deriding its inmates with a daring violence which they had never ventured upon before.[9]

At the end of seven days clouds began to gather. This was a new sight; for the people had never seen clouds. . . . Soon rain began to fall. Still the people tried to think that this was nothing very alarming. . . . For a time the ground drank up the rain; but soon the water began to rise, and day by day it rose higher and higher. Each morning as the people found the rain still falling they looked at one another in despair, and each night they repeated the words, "Raining still!"[10]

The people first beheld the destruction of the works of their own hands. Their splendid buildings, and the beautiful gardens and groves where they had placed their idols, were destroyed by lightning from heaven, and the ruins were scattered far and wide. . . . The terror of man and beast was beyond description. Above the roar of the tempest was heard the wailing of a people that had despised the authority of God. . . . In that terrible hour they saw that the transgression of God's law had caused their ruin. Yet while, through fear of punishment, they acknowledged their sin, they felt no true contrition, no abhorrence of evil. They would have returned to their defiance of Heaven, had the judgment been removed. So when God's judgments shall fall upon the earth before its deluge by fire, the impenitent will know just where and what their sin is—the despising of His holy law. Yet they will have no more true repentance than did the old-world sinners.[11]

AS IT WAS IN THE DAYS OF NOAH

And as it was in the days of Noe, so shall it be also in the days of the Son of man. They did eat, they drank, they married wives, they were given in marriage, until the day that Noe entered into the ark, and the flood came, and destroyed them all. Luke 17:26, 27.

God did not condemn the antediluvians for eating and drinking; He had given them the fruits of the earth in great abundance to supply their physical wants. Their sin consisted in taking these gifts without gratitude to the Giver, and debasing themselves by indulging appetite without restraint. It was lawful for them to marry. Marriage was in God's order; it was one of the first institutions which He established. He gave special directions concerning this ordinance, clothing it with sanctity and beauty; but these directions were forgotten, and marriage was perverted and made to minister to passion.

A similar condition of things exists now. That which is lawful in itself is carried to excess. Appetite is indulged without restraint. . . . Multitudes feel under no moral obligation to curb their sensual desires, and they become the slaves of lust. Men are living for the pleasures of sense; for this world and this life alone. . . . The picture which Inspiration has given of the antediluvian world represents too truly the condition to which modern society is fast hastening. . . .

As the time of their probation was closing, the antediluvians gave themselves up to exciting amusements and festivities. Those who possessed influence and power were bent on keeping the minds of the people engrossed with mirth and pleasure, lest any should be impressed by the last solemn warning.[12]

Before the Flood God sent Noah to warn the world, that the people might be led to repentance, and thus escape the threatened destruction. As the time of Christ's second appearing draws near, the Lord sends His servants with a warning to the world to prepare for that great event. Multitudes have been living in transgression of God's law, and now He in mercy calls them to obey its sacred precepts. All who will put away their sins by repentance toward God and faith in Christ are offered pardon.[13]

GOD COMES DOWN TO SEE

Then they said, "Come, let us build ourselves a city, and a tower with its top in the heavens, and let us make a name for ourselves, lest we be scattered abroad upon the face of the whole earth." Gen. 11:4, RSV.

For a time the descendants of Noah continued to dwell among the mountains where the ark had rested. As their numbers increased, apostasy soon led to division. Those who desired to forget their Creator and to cast off the restraint of His law felt a constant annoyance from the teaching and example of their God-fearing associates, and after a time they decided to separate from the worshipers of God. Accordingly they journeyed to the plain of Shinar, on the banks of the river Euphrates. . . . Here they decided to build a city, and in it a tower of such stupendous height as should render it the wonder of the world. . . .

The dwellers on the plain of Shinar disbelieved God's covenant that He would not again bring a flood upon the earth. Many of them denied the existence of God and attributed the Flood to the operation of natural causes. Others believed in a Supreme Being, and that it was He who had destroyed the antediluvian world; and their hearts, like that of Cain, rose up in rebellion against Him. One object before them in the erection of the tower was to secure their own safety in case of another deluge. By carrying the structure to a much greater height than was reached by the waters of the Flood, they thought to place themselves beyond all possibility of danger. And as they would be able to ascend to the region of the clouds, they hoped to ascertain the cause of the Flood. . . .

There are tower builders in our time. Infidels construct their theories from the supposed deductions of science, and reject the revealed word of God. . . . In the professedly Christian world many turn away from the plain teachings of the Bible and build up a creed from human speculations and pleasing fables, and they point to their tower as a way to climb up to heaven. . . .

The time of God's investigation is at hand. The Most High will come down to see that which the children of men have builded. His sovereign power will be revealed; the works of human pride will be laid low.[14]

CONFUSED AND SCATTERED

So the Lord scattered them abroad from thence upon the face of all the earth: and they left off to build the city. Gen. 11:8.

The dwellers on the plain of Shinar established their kingdom for self-exaltation, not for the glory of God. Had they succeeded, a mighty power would have borne sway, banishing righteousness and inaugurating a new religion. The world would have been demoralized. . . . But God never leaves the world without witnesses for Him. At this time there were men who humbled themselves before God and cried unto Him. "O God," they pleaded, "interpose between Thy cause, and the plans and methods of men." [15]

When the tower had been partially completed, a portion of it was occupied as a dwelling place for the builders; other apartments, splendidly furnished and adorned, were devoted to their idols. . . .

Suddenly the work that had been advancing so prosperously was checked. Angels were sent to bring to naught the purpose of the builders. The tower had reached a lofty height, and it was impossible for the workmen at the top to communicate directly with those at the base; therefore men were stationed at different points, each to receive and report to the one next below him the orders for needed material or other directions concerning the work. As messages were thus passing from one to another the language was confounded, so that material was called for which was not needed, and the directions delivered were often the reverse of those that had been given. Confusion and dismay followed. All work came to a standstill. . . .

Up to this time all men had spoken the same language; now those that could understand one another's speech united in companies; some went one way, and some another. "The Lord scattered them abroad from thence upon the face of all the earth." This dispersion was the means of peopling the earth, and thus the Lord's purpose was accomplished through the very means that men had employed to prevent its fulfillment. [16]

In our day the Lord desires that His people shall be dispersed throughout the earth. They are not to colonize. Jesus said: "Go ye into all the world, and preach the gospel to every creature" (Mark 16:15). [17]

43

NO QUESTIONS ASKED

By faith Abraham, when he was called to go out into a place which he should after receive for an inheritance, obeyed; and he went out, not knowing whither he went. Heb. 11:8.

Abraham had grown up in the midst of superstition and heathenism. Even his father's household, by whom the knowledge of God had been preserved, were yielding to the seductive influences surrounding them, and they "served other gods" than Jehovah. . . .

The message of God came to Abraham, "Get thee out of thy country, and from thy kindred, and from thy father's house, unto a land that I will show thee." In order that God might qualify him for his great work as the keeper of the sacred oracles, Abraham must be separated from the associations of his early life. . . . Abraham's unquestioning obedience is one of the most striking evidences of faith to be found in all the Bible. . . .

It was no light test that was thus brought upon Abraham, no small sacrifice that was required of him. There were strong ties to bind him to his country, his kindred, and his home. But he did not hesitate to obey the call. He had no question to ask concerning the land of promise—whether the soil was fertile and the climate healthful; whether the country afforded agreeable surroundings and would afford opportunities for amassing wealth. God had spoken, and His servant must obey; the happiest place on earth for him was the place where God would have him to be.

Many are still tested as was Abraham. . . . They may be required to abandon a career that promises wealth and honor, to leave congenial and profitable associations, and separate from kindred, to enter upon what appears to be only a path of self-denial, hardship, and sacrifice. God has a work for them to do. . . .

Who is ready at the call of Providence to renounce cherished plans and familiar associations? Who will accept new duties and enter untried fields . . . ? He who will do this has the faith of Abraham, and will share with him that "far more exceeding and eternal weight of glory," with which "the sufferings of this present time are not worthy to be compared" (2 Cor. 4:17; Rom. 8:18).[18]

THERE'S A REASON

That the trial of your faith, being much more precious than of gold that perisheth, though it be tried with fire, might be found unto praise and honour and glory at the appearing of Jesus Christ. 1 Peter 1:7.

Abraham continued to journey southward, and again his faith was tested. The heavens withheld their rain, the brooks ceased to flow in the valleys, and the grass withered on the plains. The flocks and herds found no pasture, and starvation threatened the whole encampment. Did not the patriarch now question the leadings of Providence? Did he not look back with longing to the plenty of the Chaldean plains? All were eagerly watching to see what Abraham would do, as trouble after trouble came upon him. So long as his confidence appeared unshaken, they felt that there was hope. . . .

Abraham could not explain the leadings of Providence; he had not realized his expectations; but he held fast the promise, "I will bless thee, and make thy name great; and thou shalt be a blessing." With earnest prayer he considered how to preserve the life of his people and his flocks, but he would not allow circumstances to shake his faith in God's word. To escape the famine he went down into Egypt. He did not forsake Canaan, or in his extremity turn back to the Chaldean land from which he came, where there was no scarcity of bread; but he sought a temporary refuge as near as possible to the Land of Promise, intending shortly to return where God had placed him.

The Lord in His providence had brought this trial upon Abraham to teach him lessons of submission, patience, and faith. . . .

God permits trials to assail His people, that by their constancy and obedience they themselves may be spiritually enriched, and that their example may be a source of strength to others. "I know the thoughts that I think toward you, saith the Lord, thoughts of peace, and not of evil" (Jer. 29:11). The very trials that task our faith most severely and make it seem that God has forsaken us are to lead us closer to Christ, that we may lay all our burdens at His feet and experience the peace which He will give us in exchange.[19]

GOD PROTECTS HIS OWN

He suffered no man to do them wrong: yea, he reproved kings for their sakes; saying, Touch not mine anointed, and do my prophets no harm. Ps. 105:14, 15.

It is by close, testing trials that God disciplines His servants. He sees that some have powers which may be used in the advancement of His work, and He puts these persons upon trial; in His providence He brings them into positions that test their character and reveal defects and weaknesses that have been hidden from their own knowledge. He gives them opportunity to correct these defects and to fit themselves for His service. He shows them their own weakness, and teaches them to lean upon Him; for He is their only help and safeguard. Thus His object is attained. They are educated, trained, and disciplined, prepared to fulfill the grand purpose for which their powers were given them. . . .

During his stay in Egypt, Abraham gave evidence that he was not free from human weakness and imperfection. In concealing the fact that Sarah was his wife, he betrayed a distrust of the divine care, a lack of that lofty faith and courage so often and nobly exemplified in his life. . . . He reasoned that he was not guilty of falsehood in representing Sarah as his sister, for she was the daughter of his father, though not of his mother. But this concealment of the real relation between them was deception. No deviation from strict integrity can meet God's approval. Through Abraham's lack of faith, Sarah was placed in great peril. The king of Egypt, being informed of her beauty, caused her to be taken to his palace, intending to make her his wife. But the Lord, in His great mercy, protected Sarah by sending judgments upon the royal household. . . .

The warning that had been given to Pharaoh proved a protection to Abraham in his after-intercourse with heathen peoples; . . . it was seen that the God whom Abraham worshiped would protect His servant, and that any injury done him would be avenged. It is a dangerous thing to wrong one of the children of the King of heaven.[20]

KEEPING THE PEACE

Let there be no strife, I pray thee, between me and thee, and between my herdmen and thy herdmen; for we be brethren. Is not the whole land before thee? separate thyself, I pray thee, from me: if thou wilt take the left hand, then I will go to the right; or if thou depart to the right hand, then I will go to the left. Gen. 13:8, 9.

Abraham returned to Canaan "very rich in cattle, in silver and in gold." Lot was still with him and again they came to Bethel, and pitched their tents by the altar which they had before erected. They soon found that increased possessions brought increased trouble. In the midst of hardships and trials they had dwelt together in harmony, but in their prosperity there was danger of strife between them. The pasturage was not sufficient for the flocks and herds of both. . . . It was evident that they must separate. Abraham was Lot's senior in years, and his superior in relation, in wealth, and in position; yet he was the first to propose plans for preserving peace. Although the whole land had been given him by God Himself, he courteously waived his right. . . .

Here the noble, unselfish spirit of Abraham was displayed. How many under similar circumstances would, at all hazards, cling to their individual rights and preferences! How many households have thus been rent asunder! How many churches have been divided, making the cause of truth a byword and a reproach among the wicked! "Let there be no strife between me and thee," said Abraham, "for we be brethren;" not only by natural relationship, but as worshipers of the true God. The children of God the world over are one family, and the same spirit of love and conciliation should govern them. "Be kindly affectioned one to another with brotherly love; in honor preferring one another" (Rom. 12:10) is the teaching of our Savior. The cultivation of a uniform courtesy, a willingness to do to others as we would wish them to do to us, would annihilate half the ills of life. The spirit of self-aggrandizement is the spirit of Satan; but the heart in which the love of Christ is cherished will possess that charity which seeketh not her own. Such will heed the divine injunction, "Look not every man on his own things, but every man also on the things of others" (Phil. 2:4).[21]

TOWARD SODOM

Abram dwelled in the land of Canaan, and Lot dwelled in the cities of the plain, and pitched his tent toward Sodom. But the men of Sodom were wicked and sinners before the Lord exceedingly. Gen. 13:12, 13.

The most fertile region in all Palestine was the Jordan valley. . . . There were cities also, wealthy and beautiful, inviting to profitable traffic in their crowded marts. Dazzled with visions of worldly gain, Lot overlooked the moral and spiritual evils that would be encountered there. . . . He "chose him all the plain of Jordan," and "pitched his tent toward Sodom." How little did he foresee the terrible results of that selfish choice![22]

Lot chose Sodom for his home because he saw that there were advantages to be gained there from a worldly point of view. But after he had established himself, and grown rich in earthly treasure, he was convinced that he had made a mistake in not taking into consideration the moral standing of the community in which he was to make his home.

The dwellers in Sodom were corrupt; vile conversation greeted his ears daily, and his righteous soul was vexed by the violence and crime he was powerless to prevent. His children were becoming like these wicked people, for association with them had perverted their morals. Taking all these things into consideration, the worldly riches he had gained seemed small and not worth the price he had paid for them. His family connections were extensive, his children having married among the Sodomites. The Lord's anger was finally kindled against the wicked inhabitants of the city, and angels of God visited Sodom to bring forth Lot, that he should not perish in the overthrow of the city.[23]

The influence of his wife and the associations of that wicked city would have led him to apostatize from God had it not been for the faithful instruction he had early received from Abraham. The marriage of Lot and his choice of Sodom for a home were the first links in a chain of events fraught with evil to the world for many generations.[24]

It is Satan's purpose to attract men and women to the cities, and to gain his object he invents every kind of novelty and amusement, every kind of excitement. And the cities of the earth today are becoming as were the cities before the Flood.[25]

A HOME GOD CAN BLESS

For I know him, that he will command his children and his household after him, and they shall keep the way of the Lord, to do justice and judgment. Gen. 18:19.

In God's sight, a man is just what he is in his family. The life of Abraham, the friend of God, was signalized by a strict regard for the word of the Lord. He cultivated home religion. The fear of God pervaded his household. He was the priest of his home. He looked upon his family as a sacred trust. His household numbered more than a thousand souls, and he directed them all, parents and children, to the divine Sovereign. He suffered no parental oppression on the one hand or filial disobedience on the other. By the combined influence of love and justice, he ruled his household in the fear of God, and the Lord bore witness to his faithfulness.[26]

He "will command . . . his household." There would be no sinful neglect to restrain the evil propensities of his children, no weak, unwise, indulgent favoritism, no yielding of his conviction of duty to the claims of mistaken affection. Abraham would not only give right instruction, but he would maintain the authority of just and righteous laws.

How few there are in our day who follow this example. On the part of too many parents there is a blind and selfish sentimentalism, which is manifested in leaving children, with their unformed judgment and undisciplined passions, to the control of their own will. This is the worst cruelty to the youth and a great wrong to the world. Parental indulgence causes disorder in families and in society. It confirms in the young the desire to follow inclination, instead of submitting to the divine requirements.[27]

Parents and children alike belong to God to be ruled by Him. By affection and authority combined, Abraham ruled his house. God's word has given us rules for our guidance. These rules form the standard from which we cannot swerve if we would keep the way of the Lord. God's will must be paramount. The question for us to ask is not: What have others done? What will my relatives think? or, What will they say of me if I pursue this course? but, What has God said? Neither parent nor child can truly prosper in any course excepting in the way of the Lord.[28]

ENTERTAINING STRANGERS

Be not forgetful to entertain strangers: for thereby some have entertained angels unawares. Heb. 13:2.

God conferred great honor upon Abraham. Angels of heaven walked and talked with him as friend with friend. When judgments were about to be visited upon Sodom, the fact was not hidden from him, and he became an intercessor with God for sinners. His interview with the angels presents also a beautiful example of hospitality.[29]

In the records of Genesis we see the patriarch at the hot summer noontide resting in his tent door under the shadow of the oaks of Mamre. Three travelers are passing near. They make no appeal for hospitality, solicit no favor; but Abraham does not permit them to go on their way unrefreshed. He is a man full of years, a man of dignity and wealth, one highly honored, and accustomed to command; yet on seeing these strangers he "ran to meet them from the tent door, and bowed himself toward the ground." Addressing the leader, he said: "My Lord, if now I have found favor in thy sight, pass not away, I pray thee, from thy servant" (Gen. 18:2, 3). With his own hands he brought water that they might wash the dust of travel from their feet. He himself selected their food; while they were at rest under the cooling shade, Sarah his wife made ready for their entertainment, and Abraham stood respectfully beside them while they partook of his hospitality. This kindness he showed them simply as wayfarers, passing strangers, who might never come his way again. But, the entertainment over, his guests stood revealed. He had ministered not only to heavenly angels, but to their glorious Commander, his Creator, Redeemer, and King. And to Abraham the counsels of heaven were opened, and he was called "the friend of God.". . .

The privilege granted Abraham and Lot is not denied to us. By showing hospitality to God's children we, too, may receive His angels into our dwellings. Even in our day, angels in human form enter the homes of men and are entertained by them. And Christians who live in the light of God's countenance are always accompanied by unseen angels, and these holy beings leave behind them a blessing in our homes.[30]

COUNTDOWN FOR SODOM

And Abraham drew near, and said, Wilt thou also destroy the righteous with the wicked? . . . That be far from thee to do after this manner, to slay the righteous with the wicked:. . . Shall not the Judge of all the earth do right? Gen. 18:23-25.

Abraham had honored God, and the Lord honored him, taking him into His counsels, and revealing to him His purposes. "Shall I hide from Abraham that thing which I do?" said the Lord. . . .

And the man of faith pleaded for the inhabitants of Sodom. Once he had saved them by his sword, now he endeavored to save them by prayer. . . . With deep reverence and humility he urged his plea. . . . Himself a sinner, he pleaded in the sinner's behalf. Such a spirit all who approach God should possess. Yet Abraham manifested the confidence of a child pleading with a loved father. He came close to the heavenly Messenger, and fervently urged his petition.

Though Lot had become a dweller in Sodom, he did not partake in the iniquity of its inhabitants. Abraham thought that in that populous city there must be other worshipers of the true God. . . . Abraham asked not once merely, but many times. Waxing bolder as his requests were granted, he continued until he gained the assurance that if even ten righteous persons could be found in it, the city would be spared.

Love for perishing souls inspired Abraham's prayer. While he loathed the sins of that corrupt city, he desired that the sinners might be saved. His deep interest for Sodom shows the anxiety that we should feel for the impenitent. We should cherish hatred of sin, but pity and love for the sinner.

All around us are souls going down to ruin as hopeless, as terrible, as that which befell Sodom. Every day the probation of some is closing. Every hour some are passing beyond the reach of mercy. And where are the voices of warning and entreaty to bid the sinner flee from this fearful doom? Where are the hands stretched out to draw him back from death? Where are those who with humility and persevering faith are pleading with God for him? [31]

UNSAFE STREETS

And there came two angels to Sodom at even: and Lot sat in the gate of Sodom: and Lot seeing them rose up to meet them; . . . and he said, Behold now, my lords, turn in, I pray you, into your servant's house, and tarry all night. Gen. 19:1, 2.

Lot, Abraham's nephew, though he had made his home in Sodom, was imbued with the patriarch's spirit of kindness and hospitality. Seeing at nightfall two strangers at the city gate, and knowing the dangers sure to beset them in that wicked city, Lot insisted on bringing them to his home. To the peril that might result to himself and his household he gave no thought. It was a part of his lifework to protect the imperiled and to care for the homeless, and the deed performed in kindness to two unknown travelers brought angels to his home. Those whom he sought to protect protected him. At nightfall he had led them for safety to his door; at the dawn they led him and his household forth in safety from the gate of the doomed city.[32]

Lot did not know their true character, but politeness and hospitality were habitual with him; they were a part of his religion—lessons that he had learned from the example of Abraham. Had he not cultivated a spirit of courtesy, he might have been left to perish with the rest of Sodom. Many a household, in closing its doors against a stranger, has shut out God's messenger, who would have brought blessing and hope and peace.

Every act of life, however small, has its bearing for good or for evil. Faithfulness or neglect in what are apparently the smallest duties may open the door for life's richest blessings or its greatest calamities. It is little things that test the character. It is the unpretending acts of daily self-denial, performed with a cheerful, willing heart, that God smiles upon. We are not to live for self, but for others. And it is only by self-forgetfulness, by cherishing a loving, helpful spirit, that we can make our life a blessing. The little attentions, the small, simple courtesies, go far to make up the sum of life's happiness, and the neglect of these constitutes no small share of human wretchedness.[33]

THAT LAST NIGHT

And turning the cities of Sodom and Gomorrha into ashes condemned them with an overthrow, making them an ensample unto those that after should live ungodly. 2 Peter 2:6.

The flames that consumed the cities of the plain shed their warning light down even to our time. We are taught the fearful and solemn lesson that while God's mercy bears long with the transgressor, there is a limit beyond which men may not go on in sin. When that limit is reached, then the offers of mercy are withdrawn, and the ministration of judgment begins.

The Redeemer of the world declares that there are greater sins than that for which Sodom and Gomorrah were destroyed. Those who hear the gospel invitation calling sinners to repentance, and heed it not, are more guilty before God than were the dwellers in the vale of Siddim. And still greater sin is theirs who profess to know God and to keep His commandments, yet who deny Christ in their character and their daily life. In the light of the Savior's warning, the fate of Sodom is a solemn admonition . . . to all who are trifling with Heaven-sent light and privileges.[34]

The judgments of God are soon to be poured out upon the earth. "Escape for thy life" is the warning from the angels of God. Other voices are heard saying: "Do not become excited; there is no cause for special alarm." Those who are at ease in Zion cry "Peace and safety," while heaven declares that swift destruction is about to come upon the transgressor. The young, the frivolous, the pleasure loving, consider these warnings as idle tales and turn from them with a jest. Parents are inclined to think their children about right in the matter, and all sleep on at ease. Thus it was at the destruction of the old world and when Sodom and Gomorrah were consumed by fire. On the night prior to their destruction the cities of the plain rioted in pleasure. Lot was derided for his fears and warnings. But it was these scoffers that perished in the flames. That very night the door of mercy was forever closed to the wicked, careless inhabitants of Sodom.[35]

The same voice that warned Lot to leave Sodom bids us, "Come out from among them, and be ye separate, . . . and touch not the unclean" (2 Cor. 6:17). Those who obey this warning will find a refuge.[36]

DON'T FORGET

Remember Lot's wife. Luke 17:32.

One of the fugitives ventured to cast a look backward to the doomed city, and she became a monument of God's judgment. If Lot himself had manifested no hesitancy to obey the angels' warning, but had earnestly fled toward the mountains, without one word of pleading or remonstrance, his wife also would have made her escape. The influence of his example would have saved her from the sin that sealed her doom. But his hesitancy and delay caused her to lightly regard the divine warning. While her body was upon the plain, her heart clung to Sodom, and she perished with it. She rebelled against God because His judgments involved her possessions and her children in the ruin. Although so greatly favored in being called out from the wicked city, she felt that she was severely dealt with, because the wealth that it had taken years to accumulate must be left to destruction. Instead of thankfully accepting deliverance, she presumptuously looked back to desire the life of those who had rejected the divine warning. Her sin showed her to be unworthy of life, for the preservation of which she felt so little gratitude.

We should beware of treating lightly God's gracious provisions for our salvation. There are Christians who say, "I do not care to be saved unless my companion and children are saved with me." They feel that heaven would not be heaven to them without the presence of those who are so dear. But have those who cherish this feeling a right conception of their own relation to God, in view of His great goodness and mercy toward them? Have they forgotten that they are bound by the strongest ties of love and honor and loyalty to the service of their Creator and Redeemer? The invitations of mercy are addressed to all; and because our friends reject the Savior's pleading love, shall we also turn away?

The redemption of the soul is precious. Christ has paid an infinite price for our salvation, and no one who appreciates the value of this great sacrifice or the worth of the soul will despise God's offered mercy because others choose to do so.[37]

A BETTER COUNTRY

Now they desire a better country, that is, an heavenly: wherefore God is not ashamed to be called their God: for he hath prepared for them a city. Heb. 11:16.

When Lot entered Sodom he fully intended to keep himself free from iniquity and to command his household after him. But he signally failed. . . .

Many are still making a similar mistake. . . . Their children are surrounded by temptation, and too often they form associations that are unfavorable to the development of piety and the formation of a right character. The atmosphere of lax morality, of unbelief, of indifference to religious things, has a tendency to counteract the influence of the parents. Examples of rebellion against parental and divine authority are ever before the youth; many form attachments for infidels and unbelievers, and cast in their lot with the enemies of God.

In choosing a home, God would have us consider, first of all, the moral and religious influences that will surround us and our families. We may be placed in trying positions, for many cannot have their surroundings what they would; and whenever duty calls us, God will enable us to stand uncorrupted, if we watch and pray, trusting in the grace of Christ. But we should not needlessly expose ourselves to influences that are unfavorable to the formation of Christian character. . . .

Those who secure for their children worldly wealth and honor at the expense of their eternal interests will find in the end that these advantages are a terrible loss. Like Lot, many see their children ruined, and barely save their own souls. Their lifework is lost; their life is a sad failure. Had they exercised true wisdom, their children might have had less of worldly prosperity, but they would have made sure of a title to the immortal inheritance.

The heritage that God has promised to His people is not in this world. . . .

We must dwell as pilgrims and strangers here if we would gain "a better country, that is, an heavenly." [38]

NOTHING TOO PRECIOUS

By faith Abraham when he was tried, offered up Isaac; and he that had received the promises offered up his only begotten son, . . . accounting that God was able to raise him up, even from the dead. Heb. 11:17-19.

God had called Abraham to be the father of the faithful, and his life was to stand as an example of faith to succeeding generations. But his faith had not been perfect. He had shown distrust of God in concealing the fact that Sarah was his wife, and again in his marriage with Hagar. That he might reach the highest standard, God subjected him to another test, the closest which man was ever called to endure.[39]

The Lord spoke unto him, saying: "Take now thy son, thine only son Isaac, whom thou lovest," "and offer him . . . for a burnt offering." The heart of the old man stood still with horror. The loss of such a son by disease would have been most heartrending to the fond father, it would have bowed his whitened head with sorrow; but now he is commanded to shed the precious blood of that son with his own hand. It seemed to him a fearful impossibility. Yet God had spoken, and His word must be obeyed. Abraham was stricken in years, but this did not excuse him from duty. He grasped the staff of faith and in dumb agony took by the hand his child, beautiful in the rosy health of youth, and went out to obey the word of God. . . .

Abraham did not stop to question how God's promises could be fulfilled if Isaac were slain. He did not stay to reason with his aching heart, but carried out the divine command to the very letter, till, just as the knife was about to be plunged into the quivering flesh of the child, the word came: "Lay not thine hand upon the lad;" "for now I know that thou fearest God, seeing thou hast not withheld thy son, thine only son from me."[40]

This act of faith in Abraham is recorded for our benefit. It teaches the great lesson of confidence in the requirements of God, however close and cutting they may be; and it teaches children perfect submission to their parents and to God. By Abraham's obedience we are taught that nothing is too precious for us to give to God.[41]

CHOOSING A WIFE

Thou shalt not take a wife unto my son of the daughters of the Canaanites, among whom I dwell: but thou shalt go unto my country, and to my kindred, and take a wife unto my son Isaac. Gen. 24:3, 4.

Abraham's habitual faith in God and submission to His will were reflected in the character of Isaac; but the young man's affections were strong, and he was gentle and yielding in disposition. If united with one who did not fear God, he would be in danger of sacrificing principle for the sake of harmony. In the mind of Abraham, the choice of a wife for his son was a matter of grave importance; he was anxious to have him marry one who would not lead him from God. . . .

Abraham had marked the result of the intermarriage of those who feared God and those who feared Him not, from the days of Cain to his own time. The consequences of his own marriage with Hagar, and of the marriage connections of Ishmael and Lot, were before him. The lack of faith on the part of Abraham and Sarah had resulted in the birth of Ishmael, the mingling of the righteous seed with the ungodly. The father's influence upon his son was counteracted by that of the mother's idolatrous kindred and by Ishmael's connection with heathen wives. . . .

The wife of Lot was a selfish, irreligious woman, and her influence was exerted to separate her husband from Abraham. But for her, Lot would not have remained in Sodom, deprived of the counsel of the wise, God-fearing patriarch. . . .

No one who fears God can without danger connect himself with one who fears Him not. "Can two walk together, except they be agreed?" (Amos 3:3). The happiness and prosperity of the marriage relation depends upon the unity of the parties; but between the believer and the unbeliever there is a radical difference of tastes, inclinations, and purposes. They are serving two masters, between whom there can be no concord. However pure and correct one's principles may be, the influence of an unbelieving companion will have a tendency to lead away from God. . . . The Lord's direction is, "Be ye not unequally yoked together with unbelievers" (2 Cor. 6:14, 17, 18).[42]

A HAPPY MARRIAGE

The Lord God of heaven, which took me from my father's house, and from the land of my kindred, and which spake unto me, and that sware unto me, saying, Unto thy seed will I give this land; he shall send his angel before thee, and thou shalt take a wife unto my son from thence. Gen. 24:7.

Isaac was highly honored by God in being made inheritor of the promises through which the world was to be blessed; yet when he was forty years of age he submitted to his father's judgment in appointing his experienced, God-fearing servant to choose a wife for him. And the result of that marriage, as presented in the Scriptures, is a tender and beautiful picture of domestic happiness: "Isaac brought her into his mother Sarah's tent, and took Rebekah, and she became his wife; and he loved her: and Isaac was comforted after his mother's death."

What a contrast between the course of Isaac and that pursued by the youth of our time, even among professed Christians! Young people too often feel that the bestowal of their affections is a matter in which self alone should be consulted—a matter that neither God nor their parents should in any wise control. Long before they have reached manhood or womanhood they think themselves competent to make their own choice, without the aid of their parents. . . . Many have thus wrecked their happiness in this life and their hope of the life to come. . . .

Parents should never lose sight of their own responsibility for the future happiness of their children. Isaac's deference to his father's judgment was the result of the training that had taught him to live a life of obedience. While Abraham required his children to respect parental authority, his daily life testified that the authority was not a selfish or arbitrary control, but was founded in love, and had their welfare and happiness in view.[43]

If there is any subject which should be carefully considered and in which the counsel of older and more experienced persons should be sought, it is the subject of marriage; if ever the Bible was needed as a counselor, if ever divine guidance should be sought in prayer, it is before taking a step that binds persons together for life.[44]

LET YOUR RELIGION SHOW

That ye may be blameless and harmless, the sons of God, without rebuke, in the midst of a crooked and perverse nation, among whom ye shine as lights in the world. Phil. 2:15.

Abraham was honored by the surrounding nations as a mighty prince and a wise and able chief. He did not shut away his influence from his neighbors. His life and character, in their marked contrast with those of the worshipers of idols, exerted a telling influence in favor of the true faith. His allegiance to God was unswerving, while his affability and benevolence inspired confidence and friendship and his unaffected greatness commanded respect and honor.

His religion was not held as a precious treasure to be jealously guarded and enjoyed solely by the possessor. True religion cannot be thus held, for such a spirit is contrary to the principles of the gospel. While Christ is dwelling in the heart it is impossible to conceal the light of His presence, or for that light to grow dim. On the contrary, it will grow brighter and brighter as day by day the mists of selfishness and sin that envelop the soul are dispelled by the bright beams of the Sun of Righteousness.

The people of God are His representatives upon the earth, and He intends that they shall be lights in the moral darkness of this world. Scattered all over the country, in the towns, cities, and villages, they are God's witnesses, the channels through which He will communicate to an unbelieving world the knowledge of His will and the wonders of His grace. It is His plan that all who are partakers of the great salvation shall be missionaries for Him. The piety of the Christian constitutes the standard by which worldlings judge the gospel. Trials patiently borne, blessings gratefully received, meekness, kindness, mercy, and love, habitually exhibited, are the lights that shine forth in the character before the world, revealing the contrast with the darkness that comes of the selfishness of the natural heart.[45]

NONIDENTICAL TWINS

*And the boys grew: and Esau was a cunning hunter, a man of
the field; and Jacob was a plain man, dwelling in tents. Gen. 25:27.*

Jacob and Esau, the twin sons of Isaac, present a striking contrast,
both in character and in life. . . . Esau grew up loving self-gratification
and centering all his interest in the present. Impatient of restraint, he
delighted in the wild freedom of the chase, and early chose the life of
a hunter. Yet he was the father's favorite. The quiet, peace-loving
shepherd was attracted by the daring and vigor of this elder son, who
fearlessly ranged over mountain and desert, returning home with
game for his father and with exciting accounts of his adventurous life.

Jacob, thoughtful, diligent, and care-taking, ever thinking more of
the future than the present, was content to dwell at home, occupied
in the care of the flocks and the tillage of the soil. His patient perseverance, thrift, and foresight were valued by the mother. His affections were deep and strong, and his gentle, unremitting attentions
added far more to her happiness than did the boisterous and occa-
sional kindnesses of Esau. . . .

Jacob had learned from his mother of the divine intimation that
the birthright should fall to him, and he was filled with an unspeak-
able desire for the privileges which it would confer. It was not the
possession of his father's wealth that he craved; the spiritual
birthright was the object of his longing. To commune with God as did
righteous Abraham, to offer the sacrifice of atonement for his family,
to be the progenitor of the chosen people and of the promised
Messiah, and to inherit the immortal possessions embraced in the
blessings of the covenant—here were the privileges and honors that
kindled his most ardent desires. . . .

But while he thus esteemed eternal above temporal blessings,
Jacob had not an experimental knowledge of the God whom he
revered. His heart had not been renewed by divine grace. He believed
that the promise concerning himself could not be fulfilled so long as
Esau retained the rights of the first-born, and he constantly studied to
devise some way whereby he might secure the blessing which his
brother held so lightly, but which was so precious to himself.[46]

TWISTED VALUES

Thus Esau despised his birthright. Gen. 25:34.

Esau had no love for devotion, no inclination to a religious life. The requirements that accompanied the spiritual birthright were an unwelcome and even hateful restraint to him. The law of God, which was the condition of the divine covenant with Abraham, was regarded by Esau as a yoke of bondage. Bent on self-indulgence, he desired nothing so much as liberty to do as he pleased. To him power and riches, feasting and reveling, were happiness. He gloried in the unrestrained freedom of his wild, roving life.[47]

There are very many who are like Esau. He represents a class who have a special, valuable blessing within their reach—the immortal inheritance, life that is as enduring as the life of God, the Creator of the universe, happiness immeasurable, and an eternal weight of glory—but who have so long indulged their appetites, passions, and inclinations that their power to discern and appreciate the value of eternal things is weakened.

Esau had a special, strong desire for a particular article of food, and he had so long gratified self that he did not feel the necessity of turning from the tempting, coveted dish. He thought upon it, making no special effort to restrain his appetite, until the power of appetite . . . controlled him, and he imagined that he would suffer great inconvenience, and even death, if he could not have that particular dish. The more he thought upon it, the more his desire strengthened, until his birthright, which was sacred, lost its value and its sacredness.[48]

Esau passed the crisis of his life without knowing it. What he regarded as a matter worthy of scarcely a thought was the act which revealed the prevailing traits of his character. It showed his choice, showed his true estimate of that which was sacred and which should have been sacredly cherished. He sold his birthright for a small indulgence to meet his present wants, and this determined the after course of his life.[49]

Esau represents those who have not tasted of the privileges which are theirs, purchased for them at infinite cost, but have sold their birthright for some gratification of appetite, or for the love of gain.[50]

BARTERED BIRTHRIGHT

Commit thy way unto the Lord; trust also in him; and he shall bring it to pass. Ps. 37:5.

Isaac loved Esau better than Jacob. And when he thought that he was about to die he requested Esau to prepare him meat, that he might bless him before he died. . . . Rebekah heard the words of Isaac, and she remembered the words of the Lord, "The elder shall serve the younger," and she knew that Esau had lightly regarded his birthright and sold it to Jacob. . . .

Rebekah was acquainted with Isaac's partiality for Esau, and was satisfied that reasoning would not change his purpose. Instead of trusting in God, the Disposer of events, she manifested her lack of faith by persuading Jacob to deceive his father. . . .

If Esau had received the blessing of his father, which was bestowed upon the first-born, his prosperity could have come from God alone; and He would have blessed him with prosperity, or brought upon him adversity, according to his course of action. If he should love and reverence God, like righteous Abel, he would be accepted and blessed of God. If, like wicked Cain, he had no respect for God nor for His commandments, but followed his own corrupt course, he would not receive a blessing from God but would be rejected of God, as was Cain. If Jacob's course should be righteous, if he should love and fear God, he would be blessed of God, and the prospering hand of God would be with him, even if he did not obtain the blessings and privileges generally bestowed upon the first-born.[51]

Jacob and Rebekah succeeded in their purpose, but they gained only trouble and sorrow by their deception. God had declared that Jacob should receive the birthright, and His word would have been fulfilled in His own time had they waited in faith for Him to work for them. But like many who now profess to be children of God, they were unwilling to leave the matter in His hands. Rebekah bitterly repented the wrong counsel she had given her son; it was the means of separating him from her, and she never saw his face again.[52]

A BITTER PRICE

He found no place of repentance, though he sought it carefully with tears. Heb. 12:17.

No sooner had Jacob left his father's tent than Esau entered. Though he had sold his birthright, and confirmed the transfer by a solemn oath, he was now determined to secure its blessings, regardless of his brother's claim. With the spiritual was connected the temporal birthright, which would give him the headship of the family and possession of a double portion of his father's wealth. These were blessings that he could value. . . .

Esau had lightly valued the blessing while it seemed within his reach, but he desired to possess it now that it was gone from him forever. All the strength of his impulsive, passionate nature was aroused, and his grief and rage were terrible. He cried with an exceeding bitter cry, "Bless me, even me also, O my father!". . .

The birthright which he had so carelessly bartered he could not now regain. "For one morsel of meat," for a momentary gratification of appetite that had never been restrained, Esau sold his inheritance; but when he saw his folly, it was too late to recover the blessing. . . .

Esau was not shut out from the privilege of seeking God's favor by repentance, but he could find no means of recovering the birthright. His grief did not spring from conviction of sin; he did not desire to be reconciled to God. He sorrowed because of the results of his sin, but not for the sin itself.[53]

Repentance includes sorrow for sin, and a turning away from it. We shall not renounce sin unless we see its sinfulness; until we turn away from it in heart, there will be no real change in the life.

There are many who fail to understand the true nature of repentance. Multitudes sorrow that they have sinned, and even make an outward reformation, because they fear that their wrongdoing will bring suffering upon themselves. But this is not repentance in the Bible sense. They lament the suffering, rather than the sin. Such was the grief of Esau when he saw that the birthright was lost to him forever.[54]

HOPE FOR A FUGITIVE

And he dreamed, and behold a ladder set up on the earth, and the top of it reached to heaven: and behold the angels of God ascending and descending on it. Gen. 28:12.

Threatened with death by the wrath of Esau, Jacob went out from his father's home a fugitive; but he carried with him the father's blessing; Isaac had renewed to him the covenant promise, and had bidden him, as its inheritor, to seek a wife of his mother's family in Mesopotamia. Yet it was with a deeply troubled heart that Jacob set out on his lonely journey. With only his staff in his hand he must travel hundreds of miles through a country inhabited by wild, roving tribes. In his remorse and timidity he sought to avoid men, lest he should be traced by his angry brother. He feared that he had lost forever the blessing that God had purposed to give him; and Satan was at hand to press temptations upon him. . . .

The darkness of despair pressed upon his soul, and he hardly dared to pray. But he was so utterly lonely that he felt the need of protection from God as he had never felt it before. With weeping and deep humiliation he confessed his sin, and entreated for some evidence that he was not utterly forsaken. . . . God did not forsake Jacob. His mercy was still extended to His erring, distrustful servant. The Lord compassionately revealed just what Jacob needed—a Savior. . . .

Wearied with his journey, the wanderer lay down upon the ground, with a stone for his pillow. As he slept he beheld a ladder, bright and shining, whose base rested upon the earth, while the top reached to heaven. Upon this ladder angels were ascending and descending; above it was the Lord of glory. . . .

Jacob awoke from his sleep in the deep stillness of night. The shining forms of his vision had disappeared. Only the dim outline of the lonely hills, and above them the heavens bright with stars, now met his gaze. But he had a solemn sense that God was with him. An unseen presence filled the solitude. "Surely the Lord is in this place," he said, "and I knew it not. . . . This is none other but the house of God, and this is the gate of heaven."[55]

RETURN TO GOD HIS OWN

And this stone, which I have set for a pillar, shall be God's house: and of all that thou shalt give me I will surely give the tenth unto thee. Gen. 28:22.

In accordance with the custom of commemorating important events, Jacob set up a memorial of God's mercy, that whenever he should pass that way he might tarry at this sacred spot to worship the Lord. . . . With deep gratitude he repeated the promise that God's presence would be with him; and then he made the solemn vow, "If God will be with me, and will keep me in this way that I go, and will give me bread to eat, and raiment to put on, so that I come again to my father's house in peace; then shall the Lord be my God: and this stone, which I have set for a pillar, shall be God's house: and of all that thou shalt give me I will surely give the tenth unto thee."

Jacob was not here seeking to make terms with God. The Lord had already promised him prosperity, and this vow was the outflow of a heart filled with gratitude for the assurance of God's love and mercy. Jacob felt that God had claims upon him which he must acknowledge, and that the special tokens of divine favor granted him demanded a return. So does every blessing bestowed upon us call for a response to the Author of all our mercies. The Christian should often review his past life and recall with gratitude the precious deliverances that God has wrought for him, supporting him in trial, opening ways before him when all seemed dark and forbidding, refreshing him when ready to faint. He should recognize all of them as evidences of the watchcare of heavenly angels. In view of these innumerable blessings he should often ask, with subdued and grateful heart, "What shall I render unto the Lord for all his benefits toward me?" (Ps. 116:12).

Our time, our talents, our property, should be sacredly devoted to Him who has given us these blessings in trust. Whenever a special deliverance is wrought in our behalf, or new and unexpected favors are granted us, we should acknowledge God's goodness, not only by expressing our gratitude in words, but, like Jacob, by gifts and offerings to His cause. As we are continually receiving the blessings of God, so we are to be continually giving.[56]

SEVEN SHORT YEARS

And Jacob served seven years for Rachel; and they seemed unto him but a few days, for the love he had to her. Gen. 29:20.

How different his [Jacob's] arrival from that of Abraham's messenger nearly a hundred years before! The servant had come with a train of attendants riding upon camels, and with rich gifts of gold and silver; the son was a lonely, footsore traveler, with no possession save his staff. Like Abraham's servant, Jacob tarried beside a well, and it was here that he met Rachel, Laban's younger daughter. . . . Though he came portionless and unattended, a few weeks showed the worth of his diligence and skill, and he was urged to tarry. It was arranged that he should render Laban seven years' service for the hand of Rachel.

In early times custom required the bridegroom, before the ratification of a marriage engagement, to pay a sum of money or its equivalent in other property, according to his circumstances, to the father of his wife. This was regarded as a safeguard to the marriage relation. . . . But provision was made to test those who had nothing to pay for a wife. They were permitted to labor for the father whose daughter they loved, the length of time being regulated by the value of the dowry required. When the suitor was faithful in his services, and proved in other respects worthy, he obtained the daughter as his wife; and generally the dowry which the father had received was given her at her marriage. . . .

The ancient custom, though sometimes abused, as by Laban, was productive of good results. When the suitor was required to render service to secure his bride, a hasty marriage was prevented, and there was opportunity to test the depth of his affections, as well as his ability to provide for a family. In our time many evils result from pursuing an opposite course. It is often the case that persons before marriage have little opportunity to become acquainted with each other's habits and disposition, and, so far as everyday life is concerned, they are virtually strangers when they unite their interests at the altar. Many find, too late, that they are not adapted to each other, and lifelong wretchedness is the result of their union.[1]

A LIFE-AND-DEATH MATTER

And he said, Let me go, for the day breaketh. And he said, I will not let thee go, except thou bless me. Gen. 32:26.

Jacob, in the great crisis of his life, turned aside to pray. He was filled with one overmastering purpose—to seek for transformation of character.[2]

It was in a lonely, mountainous region, the haunt of wild beasts and lurking place of robbers and murderers. Solitary and unprotected, Jacob bowed in deep distress upon the earth. . . . With earnest cries and tears he made his prayer before God. Suddenly a strong hand was laid upon him. He thought that an enemy was seeking his life, and he endeavored to wrest himself from the grasp of his assailant.

In the darkness the two struggled for the mastery. Not a word was spoken, but Jacob put forth all his strength, and did not relax his efforts for a moment. While he was thus battling for his life, the sense of his guilt pressed upon his soul; his sins rose up before him, to shut him out from God. But in his terrible extremity he remembered God's promises, and his whole heart went out in entreaty for His mercy. The struggle continued until near the break of day, when the stranger placed his finger upon Jacob's thigh, and he was crippled instantly. The patriarch now discerned the character of his antagonist. He knew that he had been in conflict with a heavenly messenger, and this was why his almost superhuman effort had not gained the victory. It was Christ, "the Angel of the covenant," who had revealed Himself to Jacob. The patriarch was now disabled and suffering the keenest pain, but he would not loosen his hold. . . .

He urged, "Let me go, for the day breaketh;" but Jacob answered, "I will not let thee go, except thou bless me." Had this been a boastful, presumptuous confidence, Jacob would have been instantly destroyed; but his was the assurance of one who confesses his own unworthiness, yet trusts the faithfulness of a covenant-keeping God.[3]

That for which Jacob had vainly wrestled in his own strength was won through self-surrender and steadfast faith.[4]

THE TIME OF JACOB'S TROUBLE

Alas! for that day is great, so that none is like it: it is even the time of Jacob's trouble; but he shall be saved out of it. Jer. 30:7.

When Christ shall cease His work as mediator in man's behalf, then this time of trouble will begin. Then the case of every soul will have been decided, and there will be no atoning blood to cleanse from sin. . . .

Then the restraining Spirit of God is withdrawn from the earth. As Jacob was threatened with death by his angry brother, so the people of God will be in peril from the wicked who are seeking to destroy them. And as the patriarch wrestled all night for deliverance from the hand of Esau, so the righteous will cry to God day and night for deliverance from the enemies that surround them. . . .

When in his distress Jacob laid hold of the Angel, and made supplication with tears, the heavenly Messenger, in order to try his faith, also reminded him of his sin, and endeavored to escape from him. But Jacob would not be turned away. He had learned that God is merciful, and he cast himself upon His mercy. He pointed back to his repentance for his sin, and pleaded for deliverance. As he reviewed his life, he was driven almost to despair; but he held fast the Angel, and with earnest, agonizing cries urged his petition until he prevailed.

Such will be the experience of God's people in their final struggle with the powers of evil. God will test their faith, their perseverance, their confidence in His power to deliver them. Satan will endeavor to terrify them with the thought that their cases are hopeless; that their sins have been too great to receive pardon. They will have a deep sense of their shortcomings, and as they review their lives their hopes will sink. But remembering the greatness of God's mercy, and their own sincere repentance, they will plead His promises made through Christ to helpless, repenting sinners. Their faith will not fail because their prayers are not immediately answered. They will lay hold of the strength of God, as Jacob laid hold of the Angel, and the language of their souls will be, "I will not let thee go, except thou bless me." [5]

POWER GUARANTEED

As a prince hast thou power with God and with men, and hast prevailed. Gen. 32:28.

Had not Jacob previously repented of his sin in obtaining the birthright by fraud, God could not have heard his prayer and mercifully preserved his life. So in the time of trouble, if the people of God had unconfessed sins to appear before them while tortured with fear and anguish, they would be overwhelmed; despair would cut off their faith, and they could not have confidence to plead with God for deliverance. But while they have a deep sense of their unworthiness, they will have no concealed wrongs to reveal. Their sins will have been blotted out by the atoning blood of Christ, and they cannot bring them to remembrance. . . .

All who endeavor to excuse or conceal their sins, and permit them to remain upon the books of heaven, unconfessed and unforgiven, will be overcome by Satan. The more exalted their profession, and the more honorable the position which they hold, the more grievous is their course in the sight of God, and the more certain the triumph of the great adversary.

Yet Jacob's history is an assurance that God will not cast off those who have been betrayed into sin, but who have returned unto Him with true repentance. It was by self-surrender and confiding faith that Jacob gained what he had failed to gain by conflict in his own strength. God thus taught His servant that divine power and grace alone could give him the blessing he craved. Thus it will be with those who live in the last days. As dangers surround them, and despair seizes upon the soul, they must depend solely upon the merits of the atonement. . . . None will ever perish while they do this. . . .

Jacob prevailed because he was persevering and determined. . . . It is now that we are to learn this lesson of prevailing prayer, of unyielding faith. The greatest victories to the church of Christ or to the individual Christian are not those that are gained by talent or education, by wealth or the favor of men. They are those victories that are gained in the audience chamber with God, when earnest, agonizing faith lays hold upon the mighty arm of power.[6]

REUNION

And be ye kind one to another, tenderhearted, forgiving one another, even as God for Christ's sake hath forgiven you. Eph. 4:32.

While Jacob was wrestling with the Angel, another heavenly messenger was sent to Esau. In a dream, Esau beheld his brother for twenty years an exile from his father's house; he witnessed his grief at finding his mother dead; he saw him encompassed by the hosts of God. This dream was related by Esau to his soldiers, with the charge not to harm Jacob, for the God of his father was with him.

The two companies at last approached each other, the desert chief leading his men of war, and Jacob with his wives and children, attended by shepherds and handmaidens, and followed by long lines of flocks and herds. Leaning upon his staff, the patriarch went forward to meet the band of soldiers. He was pale and disabled from his recent conflict, and he walked slowly and painfully, halting at every step; but his countenance was lighted up with joy and peace.

At sight of that crippled sufferer, "Esau ran to meet him, and embraced him, and fell on his neck, and kissed him: and they wept." As they looked upon the scene, even the hearts of Esau's rude soldiers were touched. Notwithstanding he had told them of his dream, they could not account for the change that had come over their captain. Though they beheld the patriarch's infirmity, they little thought that this his weakness had been made his strength.

In his night of anguish beside the Jabbok, when destruction seemed just before him, Jacob had been taught how vain is the help of man, how groundless is all trust in human power. He saw that his only help must come from Him against whom he had so grievously sinned. Helpless and unworthy, he pleaded God's promise of mercy to the repentant sinner. That promise was his assurance that God would pardon and accept him. Sooner might heaven and earth pass than that word could fail; and it was this that sustained him through that fearful conflict.[7]

SEPARATE WAYS

He that believeth on the Son hath everlasting life: and he that believeth not the Son shall not see life. John 3:36.

Jacob and Esau met at the deathbed of their father. Once the elder brother had looked forward to this event as an opportunity for revenge, but his feelings had since greatly changed. And Jacob, well content with the spiritual blessings of the birthright, resigned to the elder brother the inheritance of their father's wealth—the only inheritance that Esau sought or valued. . . .

Esau and Jacob had alike been instructed in the knowledge of God, and both were free to walk in His commandments and to receive His favor; but they had not both chosen to do this. The two brothers had walked in different ways, and their paths would continue to diverge more and more widely.

There was no arbitrary choice on the part of God by which Esau was shut out from the blessings of salvation. The gifts of His grace through Christ are free to all. There is no election but one's own by which any may perish. . . . Every soul is elected who will work out his own salvation with fear and trembling. He is elected who will put on the armor and fight the good fight of faith. He is elected who will watch unto prayer, who will search the Scriptures, and flee from temptation. He is elected who will have faith continually, and who will be obedient to every word that proceedeth out of the mouth of God. The *provisions* of redemption are free to all; the *results* of redemption will be enjoyed by those who have complied with the conditions.

Esau had despised the blessings of the covenant. He had valued temporal above the spiritual good, and he had received that which he desired. It was by his own deliberate choice that he was separated from the people of God. Jacob had chosen the inheritance of faith. He had endeavored to obtain it by craft, treachery, and falsehood; but God had permitted his sin to work out its correction. . . . The baser elements of character were consumed in the furnace fire, the true gold was refined, until the faith of Abraham and Isaac appeared undimmed in Jacob.[8]

A HOME IN TROUBLE

And when his brethren saw that their father loved him more than all his brethren, they hated him. Gen. 37:4.

The sin of Jacob, and the train of events to which it led, had not failed to exert an influence for evil—an influence that revealed its bitter fruit in the character and life of his sons. As these sons arrived at manhood they developed serious faults. The results of polygamy were manifest in the household. This terrible evil tends to dry up the very springs of love, and its influence weakens the most sacred ties. The jealousy of the several mothers had embittered the family relation, the children had grown up contentious and impatient of control, and the father's life was darkened with anxiety and grief.

There was one, however, of a widely different character—the elder son of Rachel, Joseph, whose rare personal beauty seemed but to reflect an inward beauty of mind and heart. Pure, active, and joyous, the lad gave evidence also of moral earnestness and firmness. He listened to his father's instructions, and loved to obey God. . . . His mother being dead, his affections clung the more closely to the father, and Jacob's heart was bound up in this child of his old age. He "loved Joseph more than all his children."

But even this affection was to become a cause of trouble and sorrow. Jacob unwisely manifested his preference for Joseph, and this excited the jealousy of his other sons. . . . The father's injudicious gift to Joseph of a costly coat, or tunic, . . . excited a suspicion that he intended to pass by his elder children, to bestow the birthright upon the son of Rachel. Their malice was still further increased as the boy one day told them of a dream that he had had. . . .

As the lad stood before his brothers, his beautiful countenance lighted up with the Spirit of Inspiration, they could not withhold their admiration; but they did not choose to renounce their evil ways, and they hated the purity that reproved their sins. The same spirit that actuated Cain was kindling in their hearts.[9]

AN INSPIRED RESOLUTION

Joseph is a fruitful bough, even a fruitful bough by a well; whose branches run over the wall. Gen. 49:22.

Joseph regarded his being sold into Egypt as the greatest calamity that could have befallen him; but he saw the necessity of trusting in God as he had never done when protected by his father's love.[10]

As the caravan journeyed southward toward the borders of Canaan, the boy could discern in the distance the hills among which lay his father's tents. Bitterly he wept at thought of that loving father in his loneliness and affliction. Again the scene at Dothan came up before him. He saw his angry brothers and felt their fierce glances bent upon him. The stinging, insulting words that had met his agonized entreaties were ringing in his ears. With a trembling heart he looked forward to the future. What a change in situation—from the tenderly cherished son to the despised and helpless slave! . . .

But, in the providence of God, even this experience was to be a blessing to him. He had learned in a few hours that which years might not otherwise have taught him. His father, strong and tender as his love had been, had done him wrong by his partiality and indulgence. This unwise preference had angered his brothers and provoked them to the cruel deed that had separated him from his home. Its effects were manifest also in his own character. Faults had been encouraged that were now to be corrected. . . .

His thoughts turned to his father's God. In his childhood he had been taught to love and fear Him. Often in his father's tent he had listened to the story of the vision that Jacob saw as he fled from his home an exile and a fugitive. . . . His soul thrilled with the high resolve to prove himself true to God—under all circumstances to act as became a subject of the King of heaven. He would serve the Lord with undivided heart; he would meet the trials of his lot with fortitude and perform every duty with fidelity. One day's experience had been the turning point in Joseph's life. Its terrible calamity had transformed him from a petted child to a man, thoughtful, courageous, and self-possessed.[11]

A BLESSED PARTNERSHIP

And the Lord was with Joseph, and he was a prosperous man. . . . And his master saw that the Lord was with him, and that the Lord made all that he did to prosper in his hand. Gen. 39:2, 3.

Arriving in Egypt, Joseph was sold to Potiphar, captain of the king's guard, in whose service he remained for ten years. He was here exposed to temptations of no ordinary character. He was in the midst of idolatry. The worship of false gods was surrounded by all the pomp of royalty, supported by the wealth and culture of the most highly civilized nation then in existence. Yet Joseph preserved his simplicity and his fidelity to God. The sights and sounds of vice were all about him, but he was as one who saw and heard not. His thoughts were not permitted to linger upon forbidden subjects. The desire to gain the favor of the Egyptians could not cause him to conceal his principles. Had he attempted to do this, he would have been overcome by temptation; but he was not ashamed of the religion of his fathers, and he made no effort to hide the fact that he was a worshiper of Jehovah. . . . Potiphar's confidence in Joseph increased daily, and he finally promoted him to be his steward, with full control over all his possessions. . . .

The marked prosperity which attended everything placed under Joseph's care was not the result of a direct miracle; but his industry, care, and energy were crowned with the divine blessing. Joseph attributed his success to the favor of God and even his idolatrous master accepted this as the secret of his unparalleled prosperity. Without steadfast, well-directed effort, however, success could never have been attained. God was glorified by the faithfulness of His servant. It was His purpose that in purity and uprightness the believer in God should appear in marked contrast to the worshipers of idols—that thus the light of heavenly grace might shine forth amid the darkness of heathenism.

Joseph's gentleness and fidelity won the heart of the chief captain, who came to regard him as a son rather than a slave. The youth was brought in contact with men of rank and learning, and he acquired a knowledge of science, of languages, and of affairs—an education needful to the future prime minister of Egypt.[12]

HOW CAN I DO IT?

*How then can I do this great wickedness, and sin against God?
Gen. 39:9.*

It is always a critical period in a young man's life when he is separated from home influences and wise counsels and enters upon new
scenes and trying tests. But if he does not of his own accord place
himself in these positions of danger and remove himself from
parental restraint; if, without will or choice of his own, he is placed
in dangerous positions and relies upon God for strength—cherishing
the love of God in his heart—he will be kept from yielding to temptation by the power of God who placed him in that trying position.
God will protect him from being corrupted by the fierce temptation.
God was with Joseph in his new home. He was in the path of duty,
suffering wrong but not doing wrong. He therefore had the love and
protection of God, for he carried his religious principle into everything he undertook.[13]

Joseph's faith and integrity were to be tested by fiery trials. His
master's wife endeavored to entice the young man to transgress the
law of God. Heretofore he had remained untainted by the corruption
teeming in that heathen land; but this temptation, so sudden, so
strong, so seductive—how should it be met? Joseph knew well what
would be the consequence of resistance. On the one hand were concealment, favor, and rewards; on the other, disgrace, imprisonment,
perhaps death. His whole future life depended upon the decision of
the moment. Would principle triumph? Would Joseph still be true to
God? With inexpressible anxiety, angels looked upon the scene.

Joseph's answer reveals the power of religious principle. He
would not betray the confidence of his master on earth, and, whatever the consequences, he would be true to his Master in heaven.
Under the inspecting eye of God and holy angels many take liberties
of which they would not be guilty in the presence of their fellow
men, but Joseph's first thought was of God. "How can I do this great
wickedness, and sin against God?" he said.

If we were to cherish an habitual impression that God sees and
hears all that we do and say and keeps a faithful record of our words
and actions, and that we must meet it all, we would fear to sin.[14]

75

A PRISON APPRENTICESHIP

His feet they hurt with fetters; he was laid in chains of iron: until the time that his word came to pass; the word of the Lord tried him. Ps. 105:18, 19, RV.

Joseph's faithful integrity led to the loss of his reputation and his liberty. This is the severest test that the virtuous and God-fearing are subjected to, that vice seems to prosper while virtue is trampled in the dust. . . . Joseph's religion kept his temper sweet and his sympathy with humanity warm and strong, notwithstanding all his trials. . . . No sooner does he enter upon prison life than he brings all the brightness of his Christian principles into active exercise: he begins to make himself useful to others. . . . He is cheerful, for he is a Christian gentleman. God was preparing him under this discipline for a situation of great responsibility, honor, and usefulness, and he was willing to learn; he took kindly to the lessons the Lord would teach him. He learned to bear the yoke in his youth. He learned to govern by first learning obedience himself.[15]

Joseph's real character shines out, even in the darkness of the dungeon. He held fast his faith and patience; his years of faithful service had been most cruelly repaid, yet this did not render him morose or distrustful. He had the peace that comes from conscious innocence, and he trusted his case with God. . . . He found a work to do, even in the prison. God was preparing him in the school of affliction for greater usefulness, and he did not refuse the needful discipline. In the prison, witnessing the results of oppression and tyranny and the effects of crime, he learned lessons of justice, sympathy, and mercy that prepared him to exercise power with wisdom and compassion. . . . It was the part he acted in the prison—the integrity of his daily life and his sympathy for those who were in trouble and distress—that opened the way for his future prosperity and honor. Every ray of light that we shed upon others is reflected upon ourselves. Every kind and sympathizing word spoken to the sorrowful, every act to relieve the oppressed, and every gift to the needy, if prompted by a right motive, will result in blessings to the giver.[16]

ALWAYS THE SAME

Seest thou a man diligent in his business? he shall stand before kings; he shall not stand before mean men. Prov. 22:29.

From the dungeon Joseph was exalted to be ruler over all the land of Egypt. It was a position of high honor, yet it was beset with difficulty and peril. One cannot stand upon a lofty height without danger. As the tempest leaves unharmed the lowly flower of the valley, while it uproots the stately tree upon the mountaintop, so those who have maintained their integrity in humble life may be dragged down to the pit by the temptations that assail worldly success and honor. But Joseph's character bore the test alike of adversity and prosperity. The same fidelity to God was manifest when he stood in the palace of the Pharaohs as when in a prisoner's cell. He was still a stranger in a heathen land, separated from his kindred, the worshipers of God: but he fully believed that the divine hand had directed his steps, and in constant reliance upon God he faithfully discharged the duties of his position. Through Joseph the attention of the king and great men of Egypt was directed to the true God: and though they adhered to their idolatry, they learned to respect the principles revealed in the life and character of the worshiper of Jehovah.

How was Joseph enabled to make such a record of firmness of character, uprightness, and wisdom? In his early years he had consulted duty rather than inclination: and the integrity, the simple trust, the noble nature, of the youth bore fruit in the deeds of the man. A pure and simple life had favored the vigorous development of both physical and intellectual powers. Communion with God through His works and the contemplation of the grand truths entrusted to the inheritors of faith had elevated and ennobled his spiritual nature, broadening and strengthening the mind as no other study could do. Faithful attention to duty in every station, from the lowliest to the most exalted, had been training every power for its highest service. He who lives in accordance with the Creator's will is securing to himself the truest and noblest development of character.[17]

ALL IN GOD'S PLAN

The fear of the Lord, that is wisdom; and to depart from evil is understanding. Job 28:28.

Joseph's checkered life was not an accident; it was ordered of Providence. But how was he enabled to make such a record of firmness of character, uprightness and wisdom? It was the result of careful training in his early years. He had consulted duty rather than inclination: and the purity and simple trust of the boy bore fruit in the deeds of the man. The most brilliant talents are of no value unless they are improved: industrious habits and force of character must be gained by cultivation. A high moral character and fine mental qualities are not the result of accident. God gives opportunities: success depends upon the use made of them. The openings of Providence must be quickly discerned and eagerly seized upon.[18]

Not to the people of Egypt alone, but to all the nations connected with that powerful kingdom, God manifested Himself through Joseph. He desired to make him a light bearer to all peoples, and He placed him next the throne of the world's greatest empire, that the heavenly illumination might extend far and near.[19]

There are few who realize the influence of the little things of life upon the development of character. Nothing with which we have to do is really small. The varied circumstances that we meet day by day are designed to test our faithfulness and to qualify us for greater trusts. By adherence to principle in the transactions of ordinary life, the mind becomes accustomed to hold the claims of duty above those of pleasure and inclination. Minds thus disciplined are not wavering between right and wrong, like the reed trembling in the wind; they are loyal to duty because they have trained themselves to habits of fidelity and truth. By faithfulness in that which is least they acquire strength to be faithful in greater matters. An upright character is of greater worth than the gold of Ophir. Without it none can rise to an honorable eminence. But character is not inherited. It cannot be bought. Moral excellence and fine mental qualities are not the result of accident. The most precious gifts are of no value unless they are improved.[20]

HE WAS LIKE CHRIST

The archers have sorely grieved him, and shot at him, and hated him: but his bow abode in strength. Gen. 49:23, 24.

The life of Joseph illustrates the life of Christ. It was envy that moved the brothers of Joseph to sell him as a slave; they hoped to prevent him from becoming greater than themselves. And when he was carried to Egypt, they flattered themselves that they were to be no more troubled with his dreams, that they had removed all possibility of their fulfillment. But their own course was overruled by God to bring about the very event that they designed to hinder. So the Jewish priests and elders were jealous of Christ, fearing that He would attract the attention of the people from them. They put Him to death, to prevent Him from becoming king, but they were thus bringing about this very result.

Joseph, through his bondage in Egypt, became a savior to his father's family; yet this fact did not lessen the guilt of his brothers. So the crucifixion of Christ by His enemies made Him the Redeemer of mankind, the Savior of the fallen race, and Ruler over the whole world: but the crime of His murderers was just as heinous as though God's providential hand had not controlled events for His own glory and the good of man.

As Joseph was sold to the heathen by his own brothers, so Christ was sold to His bitterest enemies by one of His disciples. Joseph was falsely accused and thrust into prison because of his virtue: so Christ was despised and rejected because His righteous, self-denying life was a rebuke to sin; and though guilty of no wrong, He was condemned upon the testimony of false witnesses. And Joseph's patience and meekness under injustice and oppression, his ready forgiveness and noble benevolence toward his unnatural brothers, represent the Savior's uncomplaining endurance of the malice and abuse of wicked men, and His forgiveness, not only of His murderers, but of all who have come to Him confessing their sins and seeking a pardon.[21]

He who receives Christ by living faith . . . has a living connection with God. . . . He carries with him the atmosphere of heaven, which is the grace of God, a treasure that the world cannot buy. He who is in living connection with God may be in humble stations, yet his moral worth is as precious as was that of Joseph.[22]

A SLAVE MOTHER

Train up a child in the way he should go: and when he is old he will not depart from it. Prov. 22:6.

Jochebed was a woman and a slave. Her lot in life was humble, her burden heavy. But through no other woman, save Mary of Nazareth, has the world received greater blessing. Knowing that her child [Moses] must soon pass beyond her care, to the guardianship of those who knew not God, she the more earnestly endeavored to link his soul with heaven.[23]

She endeavored to imbue his mind with the fear of God and the love of truth and justice, and earnestly prayed that he might be preserved from every corrupting influence. She showed him the folly and sin of idolatry, and early taught him to bow down and pray to the living God, who alone could hear him and help him in every emergency.

She kept the boy as long as she could, but was obliged to give him up when he was about twelve years old. From his humble cabin home he was taken to the royal palace, to the daughter of Pharaoh, "and he became her son." Yet even here he did not lose the impressions received in childhood. The lessons learned at his mother's side could not be forgotten. They were a shield from the pride, the infidelity, and the vice that flourished amid the splendor of the court.

How far-reaching in its results was the influence of that one Hebrew woman, and she an exile and a slave! The whole future life of Moses, the great mission which he fulfilled as the leader of Israel, testifies to the importance of the work of the Christian mother. There is no other work that can equal this. To a very great extent the mother holds in her own hands the destiny of her children. . . . She is sowing seed that will spring up and bear fruit, either for good or for evil. She has not to paint a form of beauty upon canvas or to chisel it from marble, but to impress upon a human soul the image of the divine. . . .

Let every mother feel that her moments are priceless; her work will be tested in the solemn day of accounts.[24]

THE RIGHT CHOICE

By faith Moses, when he was come to years, refused to be called the son of Pharaoh's daughter; choosing rather to suffer affliction with the people of God, than to enjoy the pleasures of sin for a season. Heb. 11:24, 25.

In the schools of Egypt, Moses received the highest civil and military training. Of great personal attractions, noble in form and stature, of cultivated mind and princely bearing, and renowned as a military leader, he became the nation's pride.[25]

All who occupied the throne of the Pharaohs must become members of the priestly caste; and Moses, as the heir apparent, was to be initiated into the mysteries of the national religion. . . . But while he was an ardent and untiring student, he could not be induced to participate in the worship of the gods. He was threatened with the loss of the crown, and warned that he would be disowned by the princess should he persist in his adherence to the Hebrew faith. But he was unshaken in his determination to render homage to none save the one God. . . .

Moses was fitted to take pre-eminence among the great of the earth, to shine in the courts of its most glorious kingdom, and to sway the scepter of its power. His intellectual greatness distinguishes him above the great men of all ages. As historian, poet, philosopher, general of armies, and legislator, he stands without a peer. Yet with the world before him, he had the moral strength to refuse the flattering prospects of wealth and greatness and fame. . . .

Moses had been instructed in regard to the final reward to be given to the humble and obedient servants of God, and worldly gain sank to its proper insignificance in comparison. The magnificent palace of Pharaoh and the monarch's throne were held out as an inducement to Moses; but he knew that the sinful pleasures that make men forget God were in its lordly courts. He looked beyond the gorgeous palace, beyond a monarch's crown, to the high honors that will be bestowed on the saints of the Most High in a kingdom untainted by sin. He saw by faith an imperishable crown that the King of heaven would place on the brow of the overcomer.[26]

NOT GOD'S WAY

And Moses was learned in all the wisdom of the Egyptians, and was mighty in words and in deeds. Acts 7:22.

Moses supposed that his education in the wisdom of Egypt had fully qualified him to lead Israel from bondage. Was he not learned in all the things necessary for a general of armies? Had he not had the greatest advantages of the best schools in the land? Yes: he felt that he was able to deliver them. He first set about his work by trying to gain the favor of his own people by redressing their wrongs. He killed an Egyptian who was imposing upon one of his brethren. In this he manifested the spirit of him who was a murderer from the beginning, and proved himself unfit to represent the God of mercy, love, and tenderness. He made a miserable failure of his first attempt. Like many another, he then immediately lost his confidence in God, and turned his back upon his appointed work: he fled from the wrath of Pharaoh. He concluded that because of his mistake . . . God would not permit him to have any part in the work of delivering His people from their cruel bondage. But the Lord permitted these things that He might be able to teach him the gentleness, goodness, long-suffering, which it is necessary for every laborer for the Master to possess. . . .

In the very height of his human glory the Lord permitted Moses to reveal the foolishness of man's wisdom, the weakness of human strength, that he might be led to understand his utter helplessness, and his inefficiency without being upheld by the Lord Jesus.[27]

In slaying the Egyptian, Moses had fallen into the same error so often committed by his fathers, of taking into their own hands the work that God has promised to do. It was not God's will to deliver His people by warfare, as Moses thought, but by His own mighty power, that the glory might be ascribed to Him alone. Yet even this rash act was overruled by God to accomplish His purposes. Moses was not prepared for his great work. He had yet to learn the same lesson of faith that Abraham and Jacob had been taught—not to rely upon human strength or wisdom, but upon the power of God for the fulfillment of His promises.[28]

GOD'S UNIVERSITY

For the wisdom of this world is foolishness with God. For it is written, He taketh the wise in their own craftiness. 1 Cor. 3:19.

In their efforts to qualify themselves to be colaborers with God, men frequently place themselves in such positions as will completely disqualify them for the molding and fashioning which the Lord desires to give them. Thus they are not found bearing, as did Moses, the divine similitude. By submitting to God's discipline, Moses became a sanctified channel through which the Lord could work. He did not hesitate to change *his way* for the Lord's way, even though it did lead in strange paths, in untried ways. . . .

It was not the teachings of the schools of Egypt that enabled Moses to triumph over all his enemies, but an ever-abiding faith, an unflinching faith, a faith that did not fail under the most trying circumstances. . . . Moses acted as seeing the Invisible.

God is not seeking for men of perfect education. . . . The Lord wants men to appreciate the privilege of being laborers together with God—men who will honor Him by rendering implicit obedience to His requirements regardless of previously inculcated theories. . . .

Many who are seeking efficiency for the exalted work of God by perfecting their education in the schools of men, will find that they have failed of learning the more important lessons which the Lord would teach them. By neglecting to submit themselves to the impressions of the Holy Spirit, by not living in obedience to all God's requirements, their spiritual efficiency has become weakened. . . . By absenting themselves from the school of Christ, they have forgotten the sound of the voice of the Teacher, and He cannot direct their course. Men may acquire all the knowledge possible to be imparted by the human teacher: but there is still greater wisdom required of them by God. Like Moses, they must learn meekness, lowliness of heart, and distrust of self. Our Savior Himself, bearing the test for humanity, acknowledged that of Himself He could do nothing. We must also learn that there is no strength in humanity alone. Man becomes efficient only by becoming a partaker of the divine nature.[29]

WORTH MORE

Esteeming the reproach of Christ greater riches than the treasures in Egypt: for he had respect unto the recompence of the reward. Heb. 11:26.

Moses had been a student. He was well educated in all the learning of the Egyptians, but this was not the only qualification which he needed to prepare him for his work. He was, in the providence of God, to learn patience, to temper his passions. In a school of self-denial and hardships he was to receive an education which would be of the utmost importance to him. These trials would prepare him to exercise a fatherly care over all who needed his help. No knowledge, no study, no eloquence, could be a substitute for this experience in trials to one who was to watch for souls as they that must give an account. In doing the work of a humble shepherd, in being forgetful of self and interested for the flock given to his charge, he was to become fitted for the most exalted work ever entrusted to mortals, that of being a shepherd of the sheep of the Lord's pasture.

Those who fear God in the world must be connected with Him. Christ is the most perfect educator the world ever knew. To receive wisdom and knowledge from Him was more valuable to Moses than all the learning of the Egyptians. . . .

The faith of Moses led him to look at the things which are unseen, which are eternal. He left the splendid attractions of court life because sin was there. He gave up present and seeming good that flattered only to ruin and destroy. The real attractions, the eternal, were of value to him. The sacrifices made by Moses were really no sacrifices. With him it was letting go a present, apparent, flattering good for sure, high, immortal good.

Moses endured the reproach of Christ, considering reproach greater riches than all the treasures of Egypt. He believed what God had said and was not influenced to swerve from his integrity by any of the world's reproaches. He walked the earth as God's free man. . . . He looked to the things unseen and faltered not. The recompense of reward was attractive to him, and it may be also to us. He was familiar with God.[30]

SEEING THE INVISIBLE

By faith he forsook Egypt, not fearing the wrath of the king: for he endured, as seeing him who is invisible. Heb. 11:27.

Moses had a deep sense of the personal presence of God. He was not only looking down through the ages for Christ to be made manifest in the flesh, but he saw Christ in a special manner accompanying the children of Israel in all their travels. God was real to him, ever present in his thoughts. When misunderstood, when called upon to face danger and to bear insult for Christ's sake, he endured without retaliation. Moses believed in God as one whom he needed and who would help him because of his need. God was to him a present help.

Much of the faith which we see is merely nominal: the real, trusting, persevering faith is rare. Moses realized in his own experience the promise that God will be a rewarder to those who diligently seek Him. He had respect unto the recompense of the reward. Here is another point in regard to faith which we wish to study: God will reward the man of faith and obedience. If this faith is brought into the life experience, it will enable everyone who fears and loves God to endure trials. Moses was full of confidence in God because he had appropriating faith. He needed help, and he prayed for it, grasped it by faith, and wove into his experience the belief that God cared for him. He believed that God ruled his life in particular. He saw and acknowledged God in every detail of his life and felt that he was under the eye of the All-seeing One, who weighs motives, who tries the heart. He looked to God and trusted in Him for strength to carry him uncorrupted through every form of temptation. . . . The presence of God was sufficient to carry him through the most trying situations in which a man could be placed.

Moses did not merely think of God: he saw Him. God was the constant vision before him: he never lost sight of His face. He saw Jesus as his Savior, and he believed that the Savior's merits would be imputed to him. This faith was to Moses no guesswork: it was a reality. This is the kind of faith we need, faith that will endure the test. Oh, how often we yield to temptation because we do not keep our eye upon Jesus![31]

LEARNING AND UNLEARNING

The Lord giveth wisdom: out of his mouth cometh knowledge and understanding. Prov. 2:6.

In the wilds of Midian, Moses spent forty years as a keeper of sheep. Apparently cut off forever from his life's mission, he was receiving the discipline essential for its fulfillment.[32]

Moses had been learning much that he must unlearn. The influences that had surrounded him in Egypt—the love of his foster mother, his own high position as the king's grandson, the dissipation on every hand, the refinement, the subtlety, and the mysticism of a false religion, the splendor of idolatrous worship, the solemn grandeur of architecture and sculpture—all had left deep impressions upon his developing mind and had molded, to some extent, his habits and character. Time, change of surroundings, and communion with God could remove these impressions. It would require on the part of Moses himself a struggle as for life to renounce error and accept truth, but God would be his helper when the conflict should be too severe for human strength. . . .

In order to receive God's help, man must realize his weakness and deficiency: he must apply his own mind to the great change to be wrought in himself. . . . Many never attain to the position that they might occupy, because they wait for God to do for them that which He has given them power to do for themselves. . . .

Shut in by the bulwarks of the mountains, Moses was alone with God. The magnificent temples of Egypt no longer impressed his mind with their superstition and falsehood. In the solemn grandeur of the everlasting hills he beheld the majesty of the Most High, and in contrast realized how powerless and insignificant were the gods of Egypt. Everywhere the Creator's name was written. Moses seemed to stand in His presence and to be overshadowed by His power. Here his pride and self-sufficiency were swept away. In the stern simplicity of his wilderness life, the results of the ease and luxury of Egypt disappeared. Moses became patient, reverent, and humble, "very meek, above all the men which were upon the face of the earth" (Num. 12:3), yet strong in faith in the mighty God of Jacob.[33]

GOD SENT HIM

Come now therefore, and I will send thee unto Pharaoh, that thou mayest bring forth my people the children of Israel out of Egypt. Ex. 3:10.

The time for Israel's deliverance had come. But God's purpose was to be accomplished in a manner to pour contempt on human pride. The deliverer was to go forth as a humble shepherd, with only a rod in his hand: but God would make that rod the symbol of His power. . . .

The divine command given to Moses found him self-distrustful, slow of speech, and timid. He was overwhelmed with a sense of his incapacity to be a mouthpiece for God to Israel. But having once accepted the work, he entered upon it with his whole heart, putting all his trust in the Lord. . . . God blessed his ready obedience, and he became eloquent, hopeful, self-possessed, and well fitted for the greatest work ever given to man. This is an example of what God does to strengthen the character of those who trust Him fully and give themselves unreservedly to His commands.

A man will gain power and efficiency as he accepts the responsibilities that God places upon him, and with his whole soul seeks to qualify himself to bear them aright. However humble his position or limited his ability, that man will attain true greatness who, trusting to divine strength, seeks to perform his work with fidelity. . . .

On the way from Midian, Moses received a startling and terrible warning of the Lord's displeasure. An angel appeared to him in a threatening manner, as if he would immediately destroy him. No explanation was given: but Moses remembered that he had . . . neglected to perform the rite of circumcision upon their youngest son. . . . In his mission to Pharaoh, Moses was to be placed in a position of great peril: his life could be preserved only through the protection of holy angels. But while living in neglect of a known duty, he would not be secure: for he could not be shielded by the angels of God.

In the time of trouble just before the coming of Christ, the righteous will be preserved through the ministration of heavenly angels: but there will be no security for the transgressor of God's law. Angels cannot then protect those who are disregarding one of the divine precepts.[34]

"WHO IS THE LORD?"

Be not deceived; God is not mocked: for whatsoever a man soweth, that shall he also reap. Gal. 6:7.

Pharaoh sowed obstinacy, and he reaped obstinacy. He himself put this seed into the soil. There was no more need for God by some new power to interfere with its growth than there is for Him to interfere with the growth of a grain of corn. All that is required is that a seed shall be left to germinate and spring up to bring forth fruit after its kind. The harvest reveals the kind of seed that has been sown.[35]

Pharaoh saw the mighty working of the Spirit of God: he saw the miracles which the Lord performed by His servant: but he refused obedience to God's command. The rebellious king had proudly inquired, "Who is the Lord, that I should obey his voice to let Israel go? . . . [Ex. 5:2]." And as the judgments of God fell more and more heavily upon him, he persisted in stubborn resistance. By rejecting light from heaven, he became hard and unimpressible. The providence of God was revealing His power, and these manifestations, unacknowledged, were the means of hardening Pharaoh's heart against greater light. Those who exalt their own ideas above the plainly specified will of God are saying, as did Pharaoh, "Who is the Lord, that I should obey His voice?" Every rejection of light hardens the heart and darkens the understanding: and thus men find it more and more difficult to distinguish between right and wrong, and they become bolder in resisting the will of God.[36]

He who has once yielded to temptation will yield more readily the second time. Every repetition of the sin lessens his power of resistance, blinds his eyes, and stifles conviction. Every seed of indulgence sown will bear fruit. God worked no miracle to prevent the harvest. . . . He who manifests an infidel hardihood, a stolid indifference to divine truth, is but reaping the harvest of that which he has himself sown. It is thus that multitudes come to listen with stoical indifference to the truths that once stirred their very souls. They sowed neglect and resistance to the truth, and such is the harvest which they reap.[37]

HARDENING OF THE HEART

But the Lord hardened Pharaoh's heart, so that he would not let the children of Israel go. Ex. 10:20.

How does the Lord harden the hearts of men? In the same way in which the heart of Pharaoh was hardened. God sent this king a message of warning and mercy, but he refused to acknowledge the God of heaven, and would not render obedience to His commands. He asked, "Who is the Lord, that I should obey his voice?"

The Lord gave him evidence of His power by working signs and miracles before him. The great I AM acquainted Pharaoh with His mighty works, showing him that He was the ruler of heaven and earth, but the king chose to defy the God of heaven. He would not consent to break his proud, stubborn heart even before the King of kings, that he might receive the light; for he was determined to have his own way, and work out his rebellion. He chose to do his own will, and set aside the command of God, and the very evidence given him that Jehovah was above all the gods of the nations, above all the wise men and magicians, only served to blind his mind and harden his heart.

Had Pharaoh accepted the evidence of God's power given in the first plague, he would have been spared all the judgments that followed. But his determined stubbornness called for still greater manifestations of the power of God, and plague followed plague, until at last he was called to look upon the dead face of his own firstborn, and those of his kindred; while the children of Israel, whom he had regarded as slaves, were unharmed by the plagues, untouched by the destroying angel. God made it evident upon whom rested His favor, who were His people.[38]

Every additional evidence of the power of God that the Egyptian monarch resisted carried him on to a stronger and more persistent defiance of God. . . . This case is a clear illustration of the sin against the Holy Ghost. "Whatsoever a man soweth, that shall he also reap." Gradually the Lord withdrew His Spirit. Removing His restraining power, He gave the king into the hands of the worst of all tyrants—self.[39]

FREE AT LAST!

And he brought forth his people with joy, and his chosen with gladness. Ps. 105:43.

With sandaled feet, and staff in hand, the people of Israel had stood, hushed, awed, yet expectant, awaiting the royal mandate that should bid them go forth. Before the morning broke, they were on their way. . . . That day completed the history revealed to Abraham in prophetic vision centuries before: "Thy seed shall be a stranger in a land that is not theirs, and shall serve them; and they shall afflict them four hundred years: and also that nation, whom they shall serve, will I judge: and afterward shall they come out with great substance" (Gen. 15:13, 14).[40]

In bringing forth Israel from Egypt, the Lord again manifested His power and His mercy. His wonderful works in their deliverance from bondage and His dealings with them in their travels through the wilderness were not for their benefit alone. These were to be as an object lesson to the surrounding nations. The Lord revealed Himself as a God above all human authority and greatness. The signs and wonders He wrought in behalf of His people showed His power over nature and over the greatest of those who worshiped nature.

God went through the proud land of Egypt as He will go through the earth in the last days. With fire and tempest, earthquake and death, the great I AM redeemed His people. He took them out of the land of bondage. He led them through the "great and terrible wilderness, wherein were fiery serpents, and scorpions, and drought" (Deut. 8:15). He brought them forth water out of "the rock of flint," and fed them with "the corn of heaven" (Ps. 78:24). "For," said Moses, "the Lord's portion is his people: Jacob is the lot of his inheritance. He found him in a desert land, and in the waste howling wilderness; he led him about, he instructed him, he kept him as the apple of his eye. As an eagle stirreth up her nest, fluttereth over her young, spreadeth abroad her wings, taketh them, beareth them on her wings: so the Lord alone did lead him, and there was no strange god with him" (Deut. 32:9-12). Thus He brought them unto Himself, that they might dwell as under the shadow of the Most High.[41]

CLOUD AND FIRE

He spread a cloud for a covering; and fire to give light in the night. Ps. 105:39.

"And the Lord went before them by day in a pillar of cloud, to lead them the way: and by night in a pillar of fire, to give them light." . . . The standard of their invisible Leader was ever with them. By day the cloud directed their journeyings or spread as a canopy above the host. It served as a protection from the burning heat, and by its coolness and moisture afforded grateful refreshment in the parched, thirsty desert. By night it became a pillar of fire, illuminating their encampment and constantly assuring them of the divine presence.

In one of the most beautiful and comforting passages of Isaiah's prophecy, reference is made to the pillar of cloud and of fire to represent God's care for His people in the great final struggle with the powers of evil: "The Lord will create upon every dwelling place of Mount Zion, and upon her assemblies, a cloud and smoke by day, and the shining of a flaming fire by night: for above all the glory shall be a covering. And there shall be a tabernacle for a shadow in the daytime from the heat, and for a place of refuge, and for a covert from storm and from rain" (Isa. 4:5, 6, margin).[42]

In the time of trial before us God's pledge of security will be placed upon those who have kept the word of His patience. Christ will say to His faithful ones: "Come, my people, enter thou into thy chambers, and shut thy doors about thee: hide thyself as it were for a little moment until the indignation be overpast" (Isa. 26:20). The Lion of Judah, so terrible to the rejectors of His grace, will be the Lamb of God to the obedient and faithful. The pillar of cloud which speaks wrath and terror to the transgressor of God's law is light and mercy and deliverance to those who have kept His commandments. The arm strong to smite the rebellious will be strong to deliver the loyal. Every faithful one will surely be gathered. "He shall send his angels with a great sound of a trumpet, and they shall gather together his elect from the four winds, from one end of heaven to the other" (Matt. 24:31).[43]

A SAFE PATH

And the Lord said unto Moses, Wherefore criest thou unto me? speak unto the children of Israel, that they go forward. Ex. 14:15.

God in His providence brought the Hebrews into the mountain fastnesses before the sea, that He might manifest His power in their deliverance and signally humble the pride of their oppressors. He might have saved them in any other way, but He chose this method in order to test their faith and strengthen their trust in Him. The people were weary and terrified, yet if they had held back when Moses bade them advance, God would never have opened the path for them. It was "by faith" that "they passed through the Red Sea as by dry land" (Heb. 11:29). In marching down to the very water, they showed that they believed the word of God as spoken by Moses. They did all that was in their power to do, and then the Mighty One of Israel divided the sea to make a path for their feet.

The great lesson here taught is for all time. Often the Christian life is beset by dangers, and duty seems hard to perform. The imagination pictures impending ruin before and bondage or death behind. Yet the voice of God speaks clearly, "Go forward." We should obey this command, even though our eyes cannot penetrate the darkness, and we feel the cold waves about our feet. The obstacles that hinder our progress will never disappear before a halting, doubting spirit. Those who defer obedience till every shadow of uncertainty disappears and there remains no risk of failure or defeat will never obey at all. Unbelief whispers, "Let us wait till the obstructions are removed, and we can see our way clearly": but faith courageously urges an advance, hoping all things, believing all things.

The cloud that was a wall of darkness to the Egyptians was to the Hebrews a great flood of light, illuminating the whole camp, and shedding brightness upon the path before them. So the dealings of Providence bring, to the unbelieving, darkness and despair, while to the trusting soul they are full of light and peace. The path where God leads the way may lie through the desert or the sea, but it is a safe path.[44]

THE SONG OF MOSES AND THE LAMB

The Lord is my strength and song, and he is become my salvation: this is my God, and I will praise him: my father's God, and I will exalt him. Ex. 15:2, RV.

From the most terrible peril one night had brought complete deliverance. That vast, helpless throng—bondmen unused to battle, women, children, and cattle, with the sea before them, and the mighty armies of Egypt pressing behind—had seen their path opened through the waters and their enemies overwhelmed in the moment of expected triumph. Jehovah alone had brought them deliverance, and to Him their hearts were turned in gratitude and faith. Their emotion found utterance in songs of praise. The Spirit of God rested upon Moses, and he led the people in a triumphant anthem of thanksgiving, the earliest and one of the most sublime that are known to man. . . .

That song does not belong to the Jewish people alone. It points forward to the destruction of all the foes of righteousness and the final victory of the Israel of God. The prophet of Patmos beholds the white-robed multitude that have "gotten the victory," standing on the "sea of glass mingled with fire," having "the harps of God. And they sing the song of Moses, the servant of God, and the song of the Lamb" (Rev. 15:2, 3). . . .

In freeing our souls from the bondage of sin, God has wrought for us a deliverance greater than that of the Hebrews at the Red Sea. Like the Hebrew host, we should praise the Lord with heart and soul and voice for His "wonderful works to the children of men." Those who dwell upon God's great mercies, and are not unmindful of His lesser gifts, will put on the girdle of gladness and make melody in their hearts to the Lord. The daily blessings that we receive from the hand of God, and above all else the death of Jesus to bring happiness and heaven within our reach, should be a theme for constant gratitude. . . .

All the inhabitants of heaven unite in praising God. Let us learn the song of the angels now, that we may sing it when we join their shining ranks.[45]

COMPLAINING AGAIN

And the whole congregation of the children of Israel murmured against Moses and Aaron in the wilderness. Ex. 16:2.

Many look back to the Israelites, and marvel at their unbelief and murmuring, feeling that they themselves would not have been so ungrateful: but when their faith is tested, even by little trials, they manifest no more faith or patience than did ancient Israel.[46]

God had promised to be their God, to take them to Himself as a people, and to lead them to a large and good land: but they were ready to faint at every obstacle encountered in the way to that land. . . . They forgot their bitter service in Egypt. They forgot the goodness and power of God displayed in their behalf in their deliverance from bondage. They forgot how their children had been spared when the destroying angel slew all the first-born of Egypt. They forgot the grand exhibition of divine power at the Red Sea. They forgot that while they had crossed safely in the path that had been opened for them, the armies of their enemies, attempting to follow them, had been overwhelmed by the waters of the sea. They saw and felt only their present inconveniences and trials: and instead of saying, "God has done great things for us; whereas we were slaves, He is making of us a great nation," they talked of the hardness of the way, and wondered when their weary pilgrimage would end.

The history of the wilderness life of Israel was chronicled for the benefit of the Israel of God to the close of time. The record of God's dealing with the wanderers of the desert in all their marchings to and fro, in their exposure to hunger, thirst, and weariness, and in the striking manifestations of His power for their relief, is fraught with warning and instruction for His people in all ages. The varied experience of the Hebrews was a school or preparation for their promised home in Canaan. God would have His people in these days review with a humble heart and teachable spirit the trials through which ancient Israel passed, that they may be instructed in their preparation for the heavenly Canaan.[47]

HANDS TOWARD HEAVEN

I will therefore that men pray every where, lifting up holy hands, without wrath and doubting. 1 Tim. 2:8.

Because of Israel's disobedience and departure from God, they were allowed to be brought into close places and to suffer adversity: their enemies were permitted to make war with them, to humble them and lead them to seek God in their trouble and distress. . . .

When Israel was assailed by the Amalekites, Moses gave Joshua directions to fight with their enemies.[48]

Moses and Aaron and Hur were stationed on a hill overlooking the battlefield. With arms outstretched toward heaven, and holding the rod of God in his right hand, Moses prayed for the success of the armies of Israel. As the battle progressed, it was observed that so long as his hands were reaching upward, Israel prevailed, but when they were lowered, the enemy was victorious. As Moses became weary, Aaron and Hur stayed up his hands until the going down of the sun, when the enemy was put to flight.

As Aaron and Hur supported the hands of Moses, they showed the people their duty to sustain him in his arduous work while he should receive the word from God to speak to them. And the act of Moses also was significant, showing that God held their destiny in His hands; while they made Him their trust, He would fight for them and subdue their enemies; but when they should let go their hold upon Him, and trust in their own power, they would be even weaker than those who had not the knowledge of God, and their foes would prevail against them.

As the Hebrews triumphed when Moses was reaching his hands toward heaven and interceding in their behalf, so the Israel of God prevail when they by faith take hold upon the strength of their mighty Helper. Yet divine strength is to be combined with human effort. Moses did not believe that God would overcome their foes while Israel remained inactive. While the great leader was pleading with the Lord, Joshua and his brave followers were putting forth their utmost efforts to repulse the enemies of Israel and of God.[49]

TWO HANDS FOR GOD

We then, as workers together with him, beseech you also that ye receive not the grace of God in vain. 2 Cor. 6:1.

The Lord gave an important lesson to His people in all ages when to Moses on the mount He gave instruction regarding the building of the tabernacle. In that work He required perfection in every detail. Moses was proficient in all the learning of the Egyptians: he had a knowledge of God, and God's purposes had been revealed to him in visions: but he did not know how to engrave and embroider.

Israel had been held all their days in the bondage of Egypt, and although there were ingenious men among them, they had not been instructed in the curious arts which were called for in the buildings of the tabernacle. They knew how to make bricks, but they did not understand how to work in gold or silver. How was the work to be done? . . .

Then God Himself explained how the work was to be accomplished. He signified by name the persons He desired to do a certain work. Bezaleel was to be the architect. This man belonged to the tribe of Judah—a tribe that God delighted to honor. . . .

"And I, behold, I have given with him Aholiab, the son of Ahisamach, of the tribe of Dan: and in the hearts of all that are wise-hearted I have put wisdom, that they may make all that I have commanded thee" (Ex. 31:1-6).[50]

Among the multitude were Egyptians, who had acted as overseers for such work, and thoroughly understood how it should be done. But the work was not dependent upon them. The Lord united with human agencies, giving them wisdom to work skillfully.[51]

Skill in the common arts is a gift from God. He provides both the gift and the wisdom to use the gift aright.[52]

In order that the earthly tabernacle might represent the heavenly, it must be perfect in all its parts, and it must be, in every smallest detail, like the pattern in the heavens. So it is with the characters of those who are finally accepted in the sight of heaven.[53]

Let the workmen in the service of God today pray to Him for wisdom and keen foresight, that they may do their work perfectly.[54]

A CRISIS IN ISRAEL

They made a calf in Horeb, and worshipped the molten image. Thus they changed their glory into the similitude of an ox that eateth grass. Ps. 106:19, 20.

In the absence of Moses, the judicial authority had been delegated to Aaron, and a vast crowd gathered about his tent, with the demand, "Make us gods, which shall go before us; for as for this Moses, . . . we wot not what is become of him." The cloud, they said, . . . now rested permanently upon the mount; it would no longer direct their travels. . . .

Such a crisis demanded a man of firmness, decision, and unflinching courage: one who held the honor of God above popular favor, personal safety, or life itself. But the present leader of Israel was not of this character. Aaron feebly remonstrated with the people, but his wavering and timidity at the critical moment only rendered them the more determined. . . . There were some who remained true to their covenant with God, but the greater part of the people joined in the apostasy. . . .

Aaron feared for his own safety: and instead of nobly standing up for the honor of God, he yielded to the demands of the multitude. . . . He made a molten calf, in imitation of the gods of Egypt. The people proclaimed, "These be thy gods, O Israel, which brought thee up out of the land of Egypt." And Aaron basely permitted this insult to Jehovah. He did more. Seeing with what satisfaction the golden god was received, he built an altar before it, and made proclamation, "Tomorrow is a feast to the Lord." The announcement was heralded by trumpeters from company to company throughout the camp. . . . Under the pretense of holding "a feast to the Lord," they gave themselves up to gluttony and licentious reveling.

How often, in our own day, is the love of pleasure disguised by a "form of godliness"! A religion that permits men, while observing the rites of worship, to devote themselves to selfish or sensual gratification is as pleasing to the multitudes now as in the days of Israel. And there are still pliant Aarons, who, while holding positions of authority in the church, will yield to the desires of the unconsecrated, and thus encourage them in sin.[1]

HE FAILED HIS BROTHER

And Moses said unto Aaron, What did this people unto thee, that thou hast brought so great a sin upon them? Ex. 32:21.

Aaron endeavored to shield himself by relating the clamors of the people. . . . But his excuses and prevarications were of no avail. . . .

The fact that Aaron had been blessed and honored so far above the people was what made his sin so heinous. It was Aaron, "the saint of the Lord" (Ps. 106:16), that had made the idol and announced the feast. It was he who had been appointed as spokesman for Moses, and concerning whom God Himself had testified, "I know that he can speak well" (Ex. 4:14), that had failed to check the idolaters in their heaven-daring purpose. He by whom God had wrought in bringing judgments both upon the Egyptians and upon their gods had heard unmoved the proclamation before the molten image, "These be thy gods, O Israel, which brought thee up out of the land of Egypt." It was he who had been with Moses on the mount, and had there beheld the glory of the Lord, who had seen that in the manifestation of that glory there was nothing of which an image could be made—it was he who had changed that glory into the similitude of an ox. He to whom God had committed the government of the people in the absence of Moses was found sanctioning their rebellion. "The Lord was very angry with Aaron to have destroyed him" (Deut. 9:20). But in answer to the earnest intercession of Moses, his life was spared: and in penitence and humiliation for his great sin, he was restored to the favor of God.

If Aaron had had courage to stand for the right, irrespective of consequences, he could have prevented that apostasy. If he had unswervingly maintained his own allegiance to God, if he had cited the people to the perils of Sinai, and had reminded them of their solemn covenant with God to obey His law, the evil would have been checked. But his compliance with the desires of the people and the calm assurance with which he proceeded to carry out their plans emboldened them to go to greater lengths in sin than had before entered their minds. . . .

Of all the sins that God will punish, none are more grievous in His sight than those that encourage others to do evil.[2]

FACE TO FACE

And the Lord spake unto Moses face to face, as a man speaketh unto his friend. Ex. 33:11.

After the transgression of Israel in making the golden calf, Moses again goes to plead with God in behalf of his people. . . . He has learned from experience that in order to have an influence with the people he must first have power with God. The Lord reads the sincerity and unselfish purpose of the heart of His servant and condescends to commune with this feeble mortal, face to face, as a man speaks with a friend. Moses casts himself and all his burdens fully upon God and freely pours out his soul before Him. The Lord does not reprove His servant, but stoops to listen to his supplications. . . .

The answer comes: "My presence shall go with thee, and I will give thee rest." But Moses does not feel that he can stop here. He has gained much, but he longs to come still nearer to God, to obtain a stronger assurance of His abiding presence. He has carried the burden of Israel: he has borne an overwhelming weight of responsibility: when the people sinned, he suffered keen remorse, as though he himself were guilty: and now there presses upon his soul a sense of the terrible results should God leave Israel to hardness and impenitence of heart. . . . Moses presses his petition with such earnestness and fervency that the answer comes: "I will do this thing also that thou hast spoken: for thou hast found grace in my sight, and I know thee by name."

Now, indeed, we would expect the prophet to cease pleading; but no, emboldened by his success, he ventures to come still nearer to God, with a holy familiarity which is almost beyond our comprehension. He now makes a request which no human being ever made before: "I beseech thee, show me thy glory." What a petition to come from finite, mortal man! But is he repulsed? Does God reprove him for presumption? No; we hear the gracious words: "I will make all my goodness pass before thee." . . .

In the history of Moses we may see what intimate communion with God it is man's privilege to enjoy.[3]

STRANGE FIRE

And Nadab and Abihu, the sons of Aaron, took either of them his censer, and put fire therein, and put incense thereon, and offered strange fire before the Lord, which he commanded them not. Lev. 10:1.

Next to Moses and Aaron, Nadab and Abihu had stood highest in Israel. They had been especially honored by the Lord, having been permitted with the seventy elders to behold His glory in the mount. But their transgression was not therefore to be excused or lightly regarded. All this rendered their sin more grievous. Because men have received great light, because they have, like the princes of Israel, ascended to the mount, and been privileged to have communion with God, and to dwell in the light of His glory, let them not flatter themselves that they can afterward sin with impunity, that because they have been thus honored, God will not be strict to punish their iniquity. This is a fatal deception. The great light and privileges bestowed require returns of virtue and holiness corresponding to the light given. Anything short of this, God cannot accept. Great blessings or privileges should never lull to security or carelessness. They should never give license to sin or cause the recipients to feel that God will not be exact with them. . . .

Nadab and Abihu had not in their youth been trained to habits of self-control. . . . Habits of self-indulgence, long cherished, obtained a hold upon them which even the responsibility of the most sacred office had not power to break. They had not been taught to respect the authority of their father, and they did not realize the necessity of exact obedience to the requirements of God. Aaron's mistaken indulgence of his sons prepared them to become the subjects of the divine judgments.

God designed to teach the people that they must approach Him with reverence and awe, and in His own appointed manner. He cannot accept partial obedience. It was not enough that in this solemn season of worship *nearly* everything was done as He had directed. . . . Let no one deceive himself with the belief that a part of God's commandments are nonessential, or that He will accept a substitute for that which He has required.[4]

TOO DRUNK TO CARE

Wine is a mocker, strong drink is raging: and whosoever is deceived thereby is not wise. Prov. 20:1.

Nadab and Abihu would never have committed that fatal sin had they not first become partially intoxicated by the free use of wine. They understood that the most careful and solemn preparation was necessary before presenting themselves in the sanctuary, where the divine Presence was manifested: but by intemperance they were disqualified for their holy office. Their minds became confused and their moral perceptions dulled so that they could not discern the difference between the sacred and the common. To Aaron and his surviving sons was given the warning: "Do not drink wine nor strong drink, . . . that ye may put difference between holy and unholy, and between unclean and clean. . . ." The use of spirituous liquors has the effect to weaken the body, confuse the mind, and debase the morals. It prevents men from realizing the sacredness of holy things or the binding force of God's requirements. All who occupied positions of sacred responsibility were to be men of strict temperance, that their minds might be clear to discriminate between right and wrong, that they might possess firmness of principle, and wisdom to administer justice and to show mercy.

The same obligation rests upon every follower of Christ. . . . To the church of Christ in all ages is addressed the solemn and fearful warning, "If any man defile the temple of God, him shall God destroy; for the temple of God is holy, which temple ye are" (1 Cor. 3:17).[5]

The case of Aaron's sons has been placed upon record for the benefit of God's people, and should teach those especially who are preparing for the second coming of Christ, that the indulgence of a depraved appetite destroys the fine feelings of the soul, and so affects the reasoning powers which God has given to man, that spiritual and holy things lose their sacredness. Disobedience looks pleasing, instead of exceeding sinful.[6]

MISPLACED LOVE

He sent Moses his servant; and Aaron whom he had chosen. Ps. 105:26.

Aaron was a man of amiable disposition, whom God selected to stand with Moses and speak for him. . . . God might have chosen Aaron as leader; but He who is acquainted with hearts, who understands character, knew that Aaron was yielding and lacked moral courage to stand in defense of the right under all circumstances, irrespective of consequences. Aaron's desire to have the good will of the people sometimes led him to commit great wrongs. . . . The same lack of firmness for the right in his family resulted in the death of two of his sons. . . . Nadab and Abihu failed to reverence the command of God to offer sacred fire upon their censers with the incense before Him. . . .

Here is seen the result of loose discipline. As these sons of Aaron had not been educated to respect and reverence the commands of their father, as they disregarded parental authority, they did not realize the necessity of explicitly following the requirements of God. . . . Contrary to God's express direction, they dishonored Him by offering common instead of sacred fire. God visited them with His wrath; fire went forth from His presence and destroyed them.

Aaron bore his severe affliction with patience and humble submission. Sorrow and keen agony wrung his soul. He was convicted of his neglect of duty. He was priest of the most high God, to make atonement for the sins of the people. He was priest of his household, yet he had been inclined to pass over the folly of his children. He had neglected his duty to train and educate them to obedience, self-denial, and reverence for parental authority. Through feelings of misplaced indulgence, he failed to mold their characters with high reverence for eternal things. Aaron did not see, any more than many Christian parents now see, that his misplaced love and the indulgence of his children in wrong was preparing them for the certain displeasure of God. . . . His gentle remonstrance, without a firm exercise of parental restraint, and his imprudent tenderness toward his sons were cruelty in the extreme.[7]

UNDERNOURISHED SOULS

They soon forgat his works; they waited not for his counsel: but lusted exceedingly in the wilderness, and tempted God in the desert. And he gave them their request; but sent leanness into their soul. Ps. 106:13-15.

Whenever their appetite was restricted, the Israelites were dissatisfied, and murmured and complained against Moses and Aaron, and against God.[8]

God gave the people that which was not for their highest good, because they persisted in desiring it: they would not be satisfied with those things that would prove a benefit to them. Their rebellious desires were gratified, but they were left to suffer the result. They feasted without restraint, and their excesses were speedily punished. . . . Large numbers were cut down by burning fevers, while the most guilty among them were smitten as soon as they tasted the food for which they had lusted.[9]

God might as easily have provided them with flesh as with manna, but a restriction was placed upon them for their good. It was His purpose to supply them with food better suited to their wants than the feverish diet to which many had become accustomed in Egypt. The perverted appetite was to be brought into a more healthy state, that they might enjoy the food originally provided for man—the fruits of the earth, which God gave to Adam and Eve in Eden. It was for this reason that the Israelites had been deprived, in a great measure, of animal food.

Satan tempted them to regard this restriction as unjust and cruel. He caused them to lust after forbidden things, because he saw that the unrestrained indulgence of appetite would tend to produce sensuality, and by this means the people could be more easily brought under his control. The author of disease and misery will assail men where he can have the greatest success. Through temptations addressed to the appetite he has, to a large extent, led men into sin from the time when he induced Eve to eat of the forbidden fruit. It was by this same means that he led Israel to murmur against God. Intemperance in eating and drinking, leading as it does to the indulgence of the lower passions, prepares the way for men to disregard all moral obligations. When assailed by temptation, they have little power of resistance.[10]

TWO AGAINST ONE

Wherefore then were ye not afraid to speak against my servant Moses? Num. 12:8.

In the affections of the people and the honor of Heaven she [Miriam] stood second only to Moses and Aaron. But the same evil that first brought discord in heaven sprang up in the heart of this woman of Israel, and she did not fail to find a sympathizer in her dissatisfaction. . . .

Had Aaron stood up firmly for the right, he might have checked the evil: but instead of showing Miriam the sinfulness of her conduct, he sympathized with her, listened to her words of complaint, and thus came to share her jealousy.[11]

In the appointment of the seventy elders Miriam and Aaron had not been consulted, and their jealousy was excited against Moses. . . . Miriam and Aaron had never known the weight of care and responsibility which had rested upon Moses; yet because they had been chosen to aid him they regarded themselves as sharing equally with him the burden of leadership, and they regarded the appointment of further assistants as uncalled for. . . .

"And they said, Hath the Lord indeed spoken only by Moses? hath he not spoken also by us?" Regarding themselves as equally favored by God, they felt that they were entitled to the same position and authority. . . .

God had chosen Moses, and had put His Spirit upon him: and Miriam and Aaron, by their murmurings, were guilty of disloyalty, not only to their appointed leader, but to God Himself. . . .

He who has placed upon men the heavy responsibility of leaders and teachers of His people will hold the people accountable for the manner in which they treat His servants. We are to honor those whom God has honored. The judgment visited upon Miriam should be a rebuke to all who yield to jealousy, and murmur against those upon whom God lays the burden of His work.[12]

THE MOST SATANIC TRAIT

Wrath is cruel, and anger is outrageous; but who is able to stand before envy? Prov. 27:4.

Their [Miriam's and Aaron's] accusations were borne by Moses in uncomplaining silence. It was the experience gained during the years of toil and waiting in Midian—the spirit of humility and long-suffering there developed—that prepared Moses to meet with patience the unbelief and murmuring of the people and the pride and envy of those who should have been his unswerving helpers. Moses "was very meek, above all the men which were upon the face of the earth," and this is why he was granted divine wisdom and guidance above all others. Says the Scripture, "The meek will he guide in judgment: and the meek will he teach his way" (Ps. 25:9). The meek are guided by the Lord, because they are teachable, willing to be instructed. . . .

"And Jehovah came down in the pillar of the cloud, and stood in the door of the tabernacle, and called Aaron and Miriam." . . . "And the anger of the Lord was kindled against them: and he departed." The cloud disappeared from the tabernacle in token of God's displeasure, and Miriam was smitten. She "became leprous, white as snow." . . . Now, their pride humbled in the dust, Aaron confessed their sin, and entreated that his sister might not be left to perish by that loathsome and deadly scourge. In answer to the prayers of Moses the leprosy was cleansed. Miriam was, however, shut out of the camp for seven days. . . .

This manifestation of the Lord's displeasure was designed to be a warning to all Israel, to check the growing spirit of discontent and insubordination. If Miriam's envy and dissatisfaction had not been signally rebuked, it would have resulted in great evil. Envy is one of the most satanic traits that can exist in the human heart, and it is one of the most baleful in its effects. . . . It was envy that first caused discord in heaven, and its indulgence has wrought untold evil among men. "Where envying and strife is, there is confusion and every evil work" (James 3:16).[13]

A CONTRADICTORY REPORT

And they brought up an evil report of the land which they had searched unto the children of Israel. Num. 13:32.

The Lord commanded Moses to send men to search the land of Canaan, which He would give unto the children of Israel. . . . After they had spoken of the fertility of the land, all but two spoke very discouragingly of their ability to possess it. . . . As the people listened to this report, they gave vent to their disappointment in bitter reproaches and wailing. They did not wait to reflect and reason that God, who had brought them out thus far, would certainly give them the land. . . .

Caleb urged his way to the front, and his clear, ringing voice was heard above all the clamor of the multitude. He opposed the cowardly views of his fellow spies, which had weakened the faith and courage of all Israel. He commanded the attention of the people, and they hushed their complaints for a moment to listen to him. . . . But as he spoke, the unfaithful spies interrupted him, crying: "We be not able to go up against the people; for they are stronger than we."

These men, starting upon a wrong course, set their hearts against God, against Moses and Aaron, and against Caleb and Joshua. Every step they advanced in this wrong direction made them firmer in their design to discourage every attempt to possess the land of Canaan. They distorted the truth in order to carry their baneful purpose. They represented the climate as being unhealthful and all the people of giant stature. . . .

This was not only an evil report, but a lying one also. It was contradictory: for if the land was unhealthy, and had eaten up the inhabitants, how was it that they had attained to such massive proportions? When men in responsible positions yield their hearts to unbelief, there are no bounds to the advance they will make in evil. . . . If only the two men had brought the evil report, and all the ten had encouraged them to possess the land in the name of the Lord, they would still have taken the advice of the two in preference to the ten, because of their wicked unbelief.[14]

WHY WAIT?

Let us go up at once, and possess it; for we are well able to overcome it. Num. 13:30.

It was Caleb's faith in God that gave him courage; that . . . enabled him to stand boldly and unflinchingly in defense of the right. From the same exalted source, the mighty General of the armies of heaven, every true soldier of the cross of Christ must receive strength and courage to overcome obstacles that often seem insurmountable. . . . Those who would do their duty must be ever ready to speak the words that God gives them, and not the words of doubt, discouragement, and despair. . . .

While the doubting ones talk of impossibilities, while they tremble at the thought of high walls and strong giants, let the faithful Calebs, who have "another spirit," come to the front. The truth of God, which bringeth salvation, will go forth to the people if ministers and professed believers will not hedge up its way, as did the unfaithful spies. . . .

Human agencies are to be employed in this work. Zeal and energy must be intensified; talents that are rusting from inaction must be pressed into service. The voice that would say, "Wait: do not allow yourself to have burdens imposed upon you," is the voice of the cowardly spies. We want Calebs now who will press to the front—chieftains in Israel who with courageous words will make a strong report in favor of immediate action. When the selfish, ease-loving, panic-stricken people, fearing tall giants and inaccessible walls, clamor for retreat, let the voice of the Calebs be heard, even though the cowardly ones stand with stones in their hands, ready to beat them down for their faithful testimony.[15]

It is when the unbelieving cast contempt upon the Word of God that the faithful Calebs are called for. It is then that they will stand firm at the post of duty, without parade, and without swerving because of reproach. The unbelieving spies stood ready to destroy Caleb. He saw the stones in the hands of those who had brought a false report, but this did not deter him: he had a message, and he would bear it. The same spirit will be manifested today by those who are true to God.[16]

REBELLION IN THE CAMP

These men are arrogant and presumptuous—they think nothing of scoffing at the glories of the unseen world. 2 Peter 2:10, Phillips.

It is hardly possible for men to offer greater insult to God than to despise and reject the instrumentalities He would use for their salvation. . . .

In the rebellion of Korah is seen the working out, upon a narrower stage, of the same spirit that led to the rebellion of Satan in heaven. It was pride and ambition that prompted Lucifer to complain of the government of God, and to seek the overthrow of the order which had been established in heaven. Since his fall it has been his object to infuse the same spirit of envy and discontent, the same ambition for position and honor, into the minds of men. He thus worked upon the minds of Korah, Dathan, and Abiram, to arouse the desire for self-exaltation and excite envy, distrust, and rebellion. Satan caused them to reject God as their leader, by rejecting the men of God's appointment. Yet while in their murmuring against Moses and Aaron they blasphemed God, they were so deluded as to think themselves righteous, and to regard those who had faithfully reproved their sins as actuated by Satan.

Do not the same evils still exist that lay at the foundation of Korah's ruin? Pride and ambition are widespread; and when these are cherished, they open the door to envy, and a striving for supremacy; the soul is alienated from God, and unconsciously drawn into the ranks of Satan. . . . While endeavoring to destroy the confidence of the people in the men of God's appointment, they really believe that they are engaged in a good work, verily doing God service. . . .

It is by sinful indulgence that men give Satan access to their minds, and they go from one stage of wickedness to another. The rejection of light darkens the mind and hardens the heart, so that it is easier for them to take the next step in sin and to reject still clearer light, until at last their habits of wrongdoing become fixed. Sin ceases to appear sinful to them.[17]

HE LOST HIS PATIENCE

But let patience have her perfect work, that ye may be perfect and entire, wanting nothing. James 1:4.

Notwithstanding the fact that Moses was the meekest man that lived upon the earth, on one occasion he drew the displeasure of God upon himself. . . . The undeserved reproaches of the people which fell upon him led him for a moment to forget that their murmuring was not against him, but against God; and instead of being grieved because the Spirit of God was insulted, he became irritated, offended, and in a self-willed, impatient manner struck the rock twice saying: "Hear now, ye rebels, must we fetch you water out of this rock?". . .

Moses revealed great weakness before the people. He showed a marked lack of self-control, a spirit similar to that possessed by the murmurers. He should have been an example of forbearance and patience before that multitude, who were ready to excuse their failures, disaffections, and unreasonable murmurings, on account of this exhibition of wrong on his part. The greatest sin consisted in assuming to take the place of God. The position of honor that Moses had heretofore occupied did not lessen his guilt, but greatly magnified it. Here was a man hitherto blameless, now fallen. Many in a similar position would reason that their sin would be overlooked because of their long life of unwavering fidelity. But no; it was a more serious matter for a man who had been honored of God to show weakness of character in the exhibition of passion than if he had occupied a less responsible position. Moses was a representative of Christ, but how sadly was the figure marred! Moses had sinned, and his past fidelity could not atone for the present sin. . . . Moses and Aaron must die without entering Canaan, subjected to the same punishment that fell upon those in a more lowly position. They bowed in submission, though with anguish of heart that was inexpressible; but their love for and confidence in God was unshaken. . . . But few realize the sinfulness of sin. . . . The cases of Moses and Aaron . . . show that it is not a safe thing to sin in word or thought or deed.[18]

NO EXCUSE FOR SINNING

They angered him at the waters of Meribah, and it went ill with Moses on their account; for they made his spirit bitter, and he spoke words that were rash. Ps. 106:32, 33, RSV.

Had Moses and Aaron been cherishing self-esteem or indulging a passionate spirit in the face of divine warning and reproof, their guilt would have been far greater. But they were not chargeable with willful or deliberate sin; they had been overcome by a sudden temptation, and their contrition was immediate and heartfelt. The Lord accepted their repentance, though because of the harm their sin might do among the people, He could not remit its punishment. . . .

God had forgiven the people greater transgressions, but He could not deal with sin in the leaders as in those who were led. He had honored Moses above every other man upon the earth. . . . The fact that Moses had enjoyed so great light and knowledge made his sin more grievous. Past faithfulness will not atone for one wrong act. The greater the light and privileges granted to man, the greater is his responsibility, the more aggravated his failure, and the heavier his punishment.

Moses was not guilty of a great crime, as men would view the matter. . . . But if God dealt so severely with this sin in His most faithful and honored servant, He will not excuse it in others. . . . All who profess godliness are under the most sacred obligation to guard the spirit, and to exercise self-control under the greatest provocation. The burdens placed upon Moses were very great; few men will ever be so severely tried as he was; yet this was not allowed to excuse his sin. God has made ample provision for His people; and if they rely upon His strength, they will never become the sport of circumstances. The strongest temptation cannot excuse sin. However great the pressure brought to bear upon the soul, transgression is our own act. It is not in the power of earth or hell to compel anyone to do evil. Satan attacks us at our weak points, but we need not be overcome. However severe or unexpected the assault, God has provided help for us, and in His strength we may conquer.[19]

FROM GRAVE TO GLORY

I besought the Lord at that time, saying, . . .
I pray thee, let me go over, and see the good land that is beyond Jordan, that goodly mountain, and Lebanon. But the Lord was wroth with me for your sakes, and would not hear me: and the Lord said unto me, Let it suffice thee; speak no more unto me of this matter. Deut. 3:23-26.

Never, till exemplified in the sacrifice of Christ, were the justice and the love of God more strikingly displayed than in His dealings with Moses. God shut Moses out of Canaan, to teach a lesson which should never be forgotten—that He requires exact obedience, and that men are to beware of taking to themselves the glory which is due to their Maker. He could not grant the prayer of Moses that he might share the inheritance of Israel, but He did not forget or forsake His servant. The God of heaven understood the suffering that Moses had endured; He had noted every act of faithful service through those long years of conflict and trial. On the top of Pisgah, God called Moses to an inheritance infinitely more glorious than the earthly Canaan.

Upon the mount of transfiguration Moses was present with Elijah, who had been translated. They were sent as bearers of light and glory from the Father to His Son. And thus the prayer of Moses, uttered so many centuries before, was at last fulfilled. He stood upon the "goodly mountain," within the heritage of his people. . . .

Moses was a type of Christ. . . . God saw fit to discipline Moses in the school of affliction and poverty before he could be prepared to lead the hosts of Israel to the earthly Canaan. The Israel of God, journeying to the heavenly Canaan, have a Captain who needed no human teaching to prepare Him for His mission as a divine leader; yet He was made perfect through sufferings; and "in that he himself hath suffered being tempted, he is able to succour them that are tempted" (Heb. 2:10, 18). Our Redeemer manifested no human weakness or imperfection; yet He died to obtain for us an entrance into the Promised Land.

"And Moses verily was faithful in all his house as a servant, but Christ as a son over his own house; whose house we are, if we hold fast the confidence and the rejoicing of the hope firm unto the end" (Heb. 3:5, 6).[20]

PROPHECY FOR PAY

They have abandoned the right road and wandered off to follow the old trail of Balaam, son of Beor, the man who had no objection to wickedness as long as he was paid for it. 2 Peter 2:15, Phillips.

Balaam was once a good man and a prophet of God; but he had apostatized, and had given himself up to covetousness; yet he still professed to be a servant of the Most High. He was not ignorant of God's work in behalf of Israel; and when the messengers announced their errand, he well knew that it was his duty to refuse the rewards of Balak and to dismiss the ambassadors. But he ventured to dally with temptation, and urged the messengers to tarry with him that night, declaring that he could give no decided answer till he had asked counsel of the Lord. Balaam knew that his curse could not harm Israel. God was on their side, and so long as they were true to Him no adverse power of earth or hell could prevail against them. But his pride was flattered by the words of the ambassadors, "He whom thou blessest is blessed, and he whom thou cursest is cursed." The bribe of costly gifts and prospective exaltation excited his covetousness. He greedily accepted the offered treasures, and then, while professing strict obedience to the will of God, he tried to comply with the desires of Balak. . . .

The sin of covetousness, which God declares to be idolatry, had made him a timeserver, and through this one fault Satan gained entire control of him. It was this that caused his ruin. The tempter is ever presenting worldly gain and honor to entice men from the service of God. He tells them it is their overconscientiousness that keeps them from prosperity. Thus many are induced to venture out of the path of strict integrity. One wrong step makes the next easier, and they become more and more presumptuous. They will do and dare most terrible things when once they have given themselves to the control of avarice and a desire of power. Many flatter themselves that they can depart from strict integrity for a time, . . . and that having gained their object, they can change their course when they please. Such are entangling themselves in the snare of Satan, and it is seldom that they escape.[21]

DUTY OR DESIRE

But ye have set at nought all my counsel, and would none of my reproof. Prov. 1:25.

In the night season the angel of God came to Balaam with the message, "Thou shalt not go with them; thou shalt not curse the people: for they are blessed.". . .

A second time Balaam was tested. In response to the solicitations of the ambassadors he professed great conscientiousness and integrity, assuring them that no amount of gold and silver could induce him to go contrary to the will of God. But he longed to comply with the king's request; and although the will of God had already been definitely made known to him, he urged the messengers to tarry, that he might further inquire of God; as though the Infinite One were a man, to be persuaded.

In the night season the Lord appeared to Balaam and said, "If the men come to call thee, rise up, and go with them; but yet the word which I shall say unto thee, that shalt thou do." Thus far the Lord would permit Balaam to follow his own will, because he was determined upon it. He did not seek to do the will of God, but chose his own course, and then endeavored to secure the sanction of the Lord.

There are thousands at the present day who are pursuing a similar course. They would have no difficulty in understanding their duty if it were in harmony with their inclinations. It is plainly set before them in the Bible or is clearly indicated by circumstances and reason. But because these evidences are contrary to their desires and inclinations they frequently set them aside and presume to go to God to learn their duty. With great apparent conscientiousness they pray long and earnestly for light. But God will not be trifled with. He often permits such persons to follow their own desires and to suffer the result. . . . When one clearly sees a duty, let him not presume to go to God with the prayer that he may be excused from performing it. He should rather, with a humble, submissive spirit, ask for divine strength and wisdom to meet its claims.[22]

TWO OF A KIND

*"Be on your guard against covetousness in any shape or form.
For a man's real life in no way depends upon the number of his
possessions." Luke 12:15, Phillips.*

The curse which Balaam had not been permitted to pronounce
against God's people, he finally succeeded in bringing upon them by
seducing them into sin.[23]

Balaam witnessed the success of his diabolical scheme. He saw
the curse of God visited upon His people, and thousands falling under
His judgments; but the divine justice that punished sin in Israel did
not permit the tempters to escape. In the war of Israel against the
Midianites, Balaam was slain. . . .

The fate of Balaam was similar to that of Judas, and their characters bear a marked resemblance to each other. Both these men
tried to unite the service of God and mammon, and met with signal
failure. Balaam acknowledged the true God, and professed to serve
Him; Judas believed in Jesus as the Messiah, and united with His followers. But Balaam hoped to make the service of Jehovah the step-
pingstone to the acquirement of riches and worldly honor; and
failing in this he stumbled and fell and was broken. Judas expected
by his connection with Christ to secure wealth and promotion in
that worldly kingdom which, as he believed, the Messiah was about
to set up. The failure of his hopes drove him to apostasy and ruin.
Both Balaam and Judas had received great light and enjoyed special
privileges, but a single cherished sin poisoned the entire character
and caused their destruction. . . .

One cherished sin will, little by little, debase the character, bringing all its nobler powers into subjection to the evil desire. The removal of one safeguard from the conscience, the indulgence of one
evil habit, one neglect of the high claims of duty, breaks down the defenses of the soul and opens the way for Satan to come in and lead us
astray. The only safe course is to let our prayers go forth daily from a
sincere heart, as did David, "Hold up my goings in thy paths, that my
footsteps slip not" (Ps. 17:5).[24]

SINS THAT SCAR

For the commandment is a lamp; and the law is light; and reproofs of instruction are the way of life: to keep thee from the evil woman, from the flattery of the tongue of a strange woman. Prov. 6:23, 24.

The crime that brought the judgments of God upon Israel was that of licentiousness. The forwardness of women to entrap souls did not end at Baal-peor. Notwithstanding the punishment that followed the sinners in Israel, the same crime was repeated many times. Satan was most active in seeking to make Israel's overthrow complete. Balak by the advice of Balaam laid the snare. Israel would have bravely met their enemies in battle, and resisted them, and come off conquerors; but when women invited their attention and sought their company and beguiled them by their charms, they did not resist temptations. They were invited to idolatrous feasts, and their indulgence in wine further beclouded their dazed minds. The power of self-control, their allegiance to God's law, was not preserved. Their senses were so beclouded with wine, and their unholy passions had such full sway, overpowering every barrier, that they invited temptation even to the attending of these idolatrous feasts. Those who had never flinched in battle, who were brave men, did not barricade their souls to resist temptation to indulge their basest passions. . . . They first defiled their conscience by lewdness, and then departed from God still farther by idolatry, thus showing contempt for the God of Israel.

Near the close of this earth's history Satan will work with all his powers in the same manner and with the same temptations wherewith he tempted ancient Israel just before their entering the land of promise. He will lay snares for those who claim to keep the commandments of God, and who are almost on the borders of the heavenly Canaan. He will use his powers to their utmost in order to entrap souls, and to take God's professed people upon their weakest points. . . .

It is now the duty of God's commandment-keeping people to watch and pray, to search the Scriptures diligently, to hide the word of God in the heart, lest they sin against Him in idolatrous thoughts and debasing practices, and thus the church of God become demoralized.[25]

THE ONLY WAY TO WIN

This book of the law shall not depart out of thy mouth; but thou shalt meditate therein day and night, that thou mayest observe to do according to all that is written therein: for then thou shalt make thy way prosperous, and then thou shalt have good success. Joshua 1:8.

If men will walk in the path that God has marked out for them, they will have a counselor whose wisdom is far above any human wisdom. Joshua was a wise general because God was his guide. The first sword that Joshua used was the sword of the Spirit, the Word of God. . . .

It was because the strongest influences were to be brought to bear against his principles of righteousness that the Lord in mercy charged him not to turn to the right hand or to the left. He was to follow a course of strictest integrity. . . . If there had been no peril before Joshua, God would not over and over again have charged him to be of good courage. But amid all his cares, Joshua had his God to guide him.

There is no greater deception than for man to suppose that in any difficulty he can find a better guide than God, a wiser counselor in any emergency, a stronger defense under any circumstance. . . .

The Lord has a great work to be done in our world. To every man He has given *His* work for man to do. But man is not to make man his guide, lest he be led astray; this is always unsafe. While Bible religion embodies the principles of activity in service, at the same time there is the necessity of asking for wisdom daily from the Source of all wisdom. What was Joshua's victory? Thou shalt meditate upon the Word of God day and night. The word of the Lord came to Joshua just before he passed over Jordan. . . . This was the secret of Joshua's victory. He made God his Guide.[26]

Those holding the positions of counselors should be unselfish men, men of faith, men of prayer, men that will not dare to rely upon their own human wisdom, but will seek earnestly for light and intelligence as to what is the best manner of conducting their business. Joshua, the commander of Israel, searched the books diligently in which Moses had faithfully chronicled the directions given by God—His requirements, reproofs, and restrictions—lest he should move unadvisedly.[27]

THE INVISIBLE ALLY

I will be with thee: I will not fail thee, nor forsake thee. Joshua 1:5.

Study carefully the experiences of Israel in their travels to Canaan. . . . We need to keep the heart and mind in training, by refreshing the memory with the lessons that the Lord taught His ancient people. Then to us, as He designed it should be to them, the teachings of His Word will ever be interesting and impressive.[28]

When Joshua went forth in the morning before the taking of Jericho, there appeared before him a warrior fully equipped for battle. And Joshua asked, "Art thou for us, or for our adversaries?" and he answered, "As Captain of the host of the Lord am I now come." If the eyes of Joshua had been opened as were the eyes of the servant of Elisha at Dothan, and he could have endured the sight, he would have seen the angels of the Lord encamped about the children of Israel; for the trained army of heaven had come to fight for the people of God, and the Captain of the Lord's host was there to command. When Jericho fell, no human hand touched the walls of the city, for the angels of the Lord overthrew the fortifications, and entered the fortress of the enemy. It was not Israel, but the Captain of the Lord's host, that took Jericho. But Israel had their part to act to show their faith in the Captain of their salvation.

Battles are to be fought every day. A great warfare is going on over every soul, between the prince of darkness and the Prince of life. . . . As God's agents you are to yield yourselves to Him, that He may plan and direct and fight the battle for you, with your cooperation. The Prince of life is at the head of His work. He is to be with you in your daily battle with self, that you may be true to principle; that passion, when warring for the mastery, may be subdued by the grace of Christ; that you come off more than conqueror through Him that hath loved us. Jesus has been over the ground. He knows the power of every temptation. He knows just how to meet every emergency, and how to guide you through every path of danger. Then why not trust Him?[29]

ONLY GOD COULD DO IT

All the people shall shout with a great shout; and the wall of the city shall fall down flat. Joshua 6:5.

At the taking of Jericho the mighty General of armies planned the battle in such simplicity that no human being could take the glory to himself. No human hand must cast down the walls of the city, lest man should take to himself the glory of victory. So today no human being is to take to himself glory for the work he accomplishes. The Lord alone is to be magnified. Oh, that men would see the necessity for looking to God for their orders! . . .

The Lord marshaled His armies about the doomed city; no human hand was raised against it; the hosts of heaven overthrew its walls, that God's name alone might have the glory. It was that proud city whose mighty bulwarks had struck terror to the unbelieving spies. Now in the capture of Jericho, God declared to the Hebrews that their fathers might have possessed the city forty years before, had they but trusted in Him.[30]

Men's weakness shall find supernatural strength and help in every stern conflict to do the deeds of Omnipotence, and perseverance in faith and perfect trust in God will ensure success. While the past confederacy of evil is arrayed against them He bids them to be brave and strong and fight valiantly for they have a heaven to win, and they have more than an angel in their ranks, the mighty General of armies leads on the armies of heaven. As on the occasion of the taking of Jericho, not one of the armies of Israel could boast of exercising their finite strength to overthrow the walls of the city, but the Captain of the Lord's host planned that battle in the greatest simplicity, that the Lord alone should receive the glory and man should not be exalted. God has promised us all power; for the promise is unto you and your children, and to all that are afar off, even as many as the Lord our God shall call.[31]

There must be continual faith and trust in the Captain of our salvation. We must obey His orders. The walls of Jericho came down as a result of obeying orders.[32]

ONE MAN'S SIN

Keep your life free from love of money, and be content with what you have. Heb. 13:5, RSV.

Achan had fostered covetousness and deception in his heart, until his perceptions of sin had become blunted, and he fell an easy prey to temptation. Those who venture to indulge in a known sin will be more readily overcome the second time. The first transgression opens the door to the tempter, and he gradually breaks down all resistance and takes full possession of the citadel of the soul. Achan had listened to oft-repeated warnings against the sin of covetousness. The law of God, pointed and positive, had forbidden stealing and all deception, but he continued to cherish sin. As he was not detected and openly rebuked, he grew bolder; warnings had less and less effect upon him, until his soul was bound in chains of darkness.[33]

Shame, defeat, and death were brought upon Israel by one man's sin. That protection which had covered their heads in the time of battle was withdrawn. Various sins that are cherished and practiced by professed Christians bring the frown of God upon the church. . . .

The influence most to be feared by the church is not that of open opposers, infidels, and blasphemers, but of inconsistent professors of Christ. These are the ones who keep back the blessing of the God of Israel and bring weakness upon the church, a reproach that is not easily wiped away. . . .

Christianity is not to be merely paraded on the Sabbath and displayed in the sanctuary; it is for every day in the week and for every place. Its claims must be recognized and obeyed in the workshop, at home, and in business transactions with brethren and with the world. . . .

It is better to die than to sin; better to want than to defraud; better to hunger than to lie. Let all who are tempted meet Satan with the words: "Blessed is every one that feareth the Lord; that walketh in his ways. For thou shalt eat the labour of thine hands: happy shalt thou be, and it shall be well with thee" (Ps. 128:1, 2).[34]

NO HIDING FROM GOD

Neither will I be with you any more, except ye destroy the accursed from among you. Joshua 7:12.

The sin of one man caused Israel to be beaten before the enemy. Something more than prayer was required. They were to get up and cleanse the camp of Israel.[35]

Have you considered why it was that all who were connected with Achan were also subjects of the punishment of God? It was because they had not been trained and educated according to the directions given them in the great standard of the law of God. Achan's parents had educated their son in such a way that he felt free to disobey the Word of the Lord; the principles inculcated in his life led him to deal with his children in such a way that they also were corrupted. . . . The punishment . . . reveals the fact that all were involved in the transgression.[36]

The history of Achan teaches the solemn lesson that for one man's sin the displeasure of God will rest upon a people or a nation till the transgression is searched out and punished. Sin is corrupting in its nature. One man infected with its deadly leprosy may communicate the taint to thousands. Those who occupy responsible positions as guardians of the people are false to their trust if they do not faithfully search out and reprove sin. . . .

The love of God will never lead to the belittling of sin; it will never cover or excuse an unconfessed wrong. . . . It has to do with all our acts and thoughts and feelings. It follows us, and reaches every secret spring of action. By indulgence in sin, men are led to lightly regard the law of God. Many conceal their transgressions from their fellow men, and flatter themselves that God will not be strict to mark iniquity. But His law is the great standard of right, and with it every act of life must be compared in that day when God shall bring every work into judgment, with every secret thing, whether it be good or evil. Purity of heart will lead to purity of life. All excuses for sin are vain. Who can plead for the sinner when God testifies against him?[37]

TOO LATE!

He that covereth his sins shall not prosper: but whoso confesseth and forsaketh them shall have mercy. Prov. 28:13.

Achan acknowledged his guilt, but when it was too late for the confession to benefit himself. He had seen the armies of Israel return from Ai defeated and disheartened; yet he did not come forward and confess his sin. He had seen Joshua and the elders of Israel bowed to the earth in grief too great for words. Had he then made confession, he would have given some proof of true penitence; but he still kept silence. He had listened to the proclamation that a great crime had been committed, and had even heard its character definitely stated. But his lips were sealed. Then came the solemn investigation. How his soul thrilled with terror as he saw his tribe pointed out, then his family and his household! But still he uttered no confession, until the finger of God was placed upon him. Then, when his sin could no longer be concealed, he admitted the truth. How often are similar confessions made. There is a vast difference between admitting facts after they have been proved and confessing sins known only to ourselves and to God. Achan would not have confessed had he not hoped by so doing to avert the consequences of his crime. But his confession only served to show that his punishment was just. There was no genuine repentance for sin, no contrition, no change of purpose, no abhorrence of evil.

So confessions will be made by the guilty when they stand before the bar of God, after every case has been decided for life or death. . . . When the records of heaven shall be opened, the Judge will not in words declare to man his guilt, but will cast one penetrating, convicting glance, and every deed, every transaction of life, will be vividly impressed upon the memory of the wrongdoer. The person will not . . . need to be hunted out . . . but his own lips will confess his shame. The sins hidden from the knowledge of men will then be proclaimed to the whole world.[38]

If you have sins to confess, lose no time. These moments are golden. "If we confess our sins, he is faithful and just to forgive us our sins, and to cleanse us from all unrighteousness" (1 John 1:9).[39]

THE PRICE OF A LIE

Lying lips are abomination to the Lord: but they that deal truly are his delight. Prov. 12:22.

From Shechem the Israelites returned to their encampment at Gilgal. Here they were soon after visited by a strange deputation, who desired to enter into treaty with them. The ambassadors represented that they had come from a distant country, and this seemed to be confirmed by their appearance. Their clothing was old and worn, their sandals were patched, their provisions moldy, and the skins that served them for wine bottles were rent and bound up, as if hastily repaired on the journey. . . .

These representations prevailed. . . . "And Joshua made peace with them, and made a league with them, to let them live: and the princes of the congregation sware unto them." Thus the treaty was entered into. . . .

But it would have fared better with the Gibeonites had they dealt honestly with Israel. While their submission to Jehovah secured the preservation of their lives, their deception brought them only disgrace and servitude. God had made provision that all who would renounce heathenism, and connect themselves with Israel, should share the blessings of the covenant. They were included under the term, "the stranger that sojourneth among you," and with few exceptions this class were to enjoy equal favors and privileges with Israel. The Lord's direction was—"If a stranger sojourn with thee in your land, ye shall not vex him. But the stranger that dwelleth with you shall be unto you as one born among you, and thou shalt love him as thyself" (Lev. 19:33, 34). . . .

Such was the footing on which the Gibeonites might have been received, but for the deception to which they had resorted. It was no light humiliation to those citizens of a "royal city," "all the men whereof were mighty," to be made hewers of wood and drawers of water throughout their generations. But they had adopted the garb of poverty for the purpose of deception, and it was fastened upon them as a badge of perpetual servitude. Thus through all their generations their servile condition would testify to God's hatred of falsehood.[40]

"GIVE ME THIS MOUNTAIN"

*I am as strong this day as I was in the day that Moses sent me.
. . . Now therefore give me this mountain. Joshua 14:11, 12.*

Before the distribution of the land had been entered upon, Caleb, accompanied by the heads of his tribe, came forward with a special claim. Except Joshua, Caleb was now the oldest man in Israel. Caleb and Joshua were the only ones among the spies who had brought a good report of the Land of Promise, encouraging the people to go up and possess it in the name of the Lord. Caleb now reminded Joshua of the promise then made, as the reward of his faithfulness: "The land whereon thy feet have trodden shall be thine inheritance, and thy children's forever, because thou hast wholly followed the Lord." He therefore presented a request that Hebron be given him for a possession. . . . His claim was immediately granted. To none could the conquest of this giant stronghold be more safely entrusted. . . .

Caleb's faith now was just what it was when his testimony had contradicted the evil report of the spies. He had believed God's promise that He would put His people in possession of Canaan, and in this he had followed the Lord fully. He had endured with his people the long wandering in the wilderness, thus sharing the disappointments and burdens of the guilty; yet he made no complaint of this, but exalted the mercy of God that had preserved him in the wilderness when his brethren were cut off. . . . The brave old warrior was desirous of giving to the people an example that would honor God, and encourage the tribes fully to subdue the land which their fathers had deemed unconquerable. Caleb obtained the inheritance upon which his heart had been set for forty years, and, trusting in God to be with him, he "drove thence the three sons of Anak.". . .

The cowards and rebels had perished in the wilderness, but the righteous spies ate of the grapes of Eshcol. To each was given according to his faith. The unbelieving had seen their fears fulfilled. Notwithstanding God's promise, they had declared that it was impossible to inherit Canaan, and they did not possess it. But those who trusted in God, looking not so much to the difficulties to be encountered as to the strength of their Almighty Helper, entered the goodly land.[41]

IRON CHARIOTS

And the children of Joseph spake unto Joshua, saying, Why hast thou given me but one lot and one portion to inherit? Joshua 17:14.

Another claim concerning the division of the land revealed a spirit widely different from that of Caleb. It was presented by the children of Joseph, the tribe of Ephraim with the half tribe of Manasseh. In consideration of their superior numbers, these tribes demanded a double portion of territory. The lot designated for them was the richest in the land, including the fertile plain of Sharon; but many of the principal towns in the valley were still in possession of the Canaanites, and the tribes shrank from the toil and danger of conquering their possessions, and desired an additional portion in territory already subdued. The tribe of Ephraim was one of the largest in Israel, as well as the one to which Joshua himself belonged, and its members naturally regarded themselves as entitled to special consideration. "Why hast thou given me but one lot and one portion to inherit," they said, "seeing I am a great people?" But no departure from strict justice could be won from the inflexible leader.

His answer was, "If thou be a great people, then get thee up to the wood country, and cut down for thyself there in the land of the Perizzites and of the giants, if Mount Ephraim be too narrow for thee."

Their reply showed the real cause of complaint. They lacked faith and courage to drive out the Canaanites. "The hill is not enough for us," they said; "and all the Canaanites that dwell in the land of the valley have chariots of iron."

The power of the God of Israel had been pledged to His people, and had the Ephraimites possessed the courage and faith of Caleb, no enemy could have stood before them. Their evident desire to shun hardship and danger was firmly met by Joshua. "Thou art a great people, and hast great power," he said; "thou shalt drive out the Canaanites, though they have iron chariots, and though they be strong." Thus their own arguments were turned against them. Being a great people, as they claimed, they were fully able to make their own way, as did their brethren. With the help of God they need not fear the chariots of iron.[42]

"AS FOR ME . . ."

Choose you this day whom ye will serve. Joshua 24:15.

As Joshua felt the infirmities of age stealing upon him, and realized that his work must soon close, he was filled with anxiety for the future of his people. It was with more than a father's interest that he addressed them, as they gathered once more about their aged chief. . . .

By Joshua's direction the ark had been brought from Shiloh. The occasion was one of great solemnity, and this symbol of God's presence would deepen the impression he wished to make upon the people. After presenting the goodness of God toward Israel, he called upon them, in the name of Jehovah, to choose whom they would serve. The worship of idols was still to some extent secretly practiced, and Joshua endeavored now to bring them to a decision that should banish this sin from Israel. . . . Joshua desired to lead them to serve God, not by compulsion, but willingly. . . .

"As for me and my house," said Joshua, "we will serve Jehovah." The same holy zeal that inspired the leader's heart was communicated to the people. His appeals called forth the unhesitating response, "God forbid that we should forsake Jehovah, to serve other gods." . . . Joshua endeavored to lead his hearers to weigh well their words, and refrain from vows which they would be unprepared to fulfill. With deep earnestness they repeated the declaration: "Nay; but we will serve the Lord." Solemnly consenting to the witness against themselves that they had chosen Jehovah, they once more reiterated their pledge of loyalty: "The Lord our God will we serve, and his voice will we obey. . . ." Having written an account of this solemn transaction, he placed it, with the book of the law, in the side of the ark. . . .

Joshua's work for Israel was done. He had "wholly followed the Lord"; and in the book of God he is written, "The servant of Jehovah." The noblest testimony to his character as a public leader is the history of the generation that had enjoyed his labors: "Israel served the Lord all the days of Joshua, and all the days of the elders that overlived Joshua."[43]

HAVEN'T I SENT YOU?

*And the Lord looked upon him, and said, Go in this thy might
. . . : have not I sent thee? Judges 6:14.*

To Gideon came the divine call to deliver his people. He was engaged at the time in threshing wheat. A small quantity of grain had
been concealed, and not daring to beat it out on the ordinary threshing floor, he had resorted to a spot near the winepress; for the season
of ripe grapes being still far off, little notice was now taken of the
vineyards. As Gideon labored in secrecy and silence, he sadly pondered upon the condition of Israel and considered how the oppres-
sor's yoke might be broken from off his people.

Suddenly the "Angel of the Lord" appeared and addressed him
with the words, "Jehovah is with thee, thou mighty man of valor."

"O my Lord," was his answer, "if the Lord be with us, why then
is all this befallen us? and where be all his miracles which our
fathers told us of, saying, Did not the Lord bring us up from Egypt?
but now the Lord hath forsaken us, and delivered us into the hands
of the Midianites."

The Messenger of heaven replied, "Go in this thy might, and
thou shalt save Israel from the hand of the Midianites: have not I
sent thee?"[44]

Gideon deeply felt his own insufficiency for the great work
before him. . . . The Lord does not always choose for His work men
of the greatest talents, but He selects those whom He can best use.
Individuals who might do good service for God may for a time be left
in obscurity, apparently unnoticed and unemployed by their Master.
But if they faithfully perform the duties of their humble position,
cherishing a willingness to labor and to sacrifice for Him, He will in
His own time intrust them with greater responsibilities.

Before honor is humility. The Lord can use most effectually those
who are most sensible of their own unworthiness and inefficiency.
He will teach them to exercise the courage of faith. He will make
them strong by uniting their weakness to His might, wise by connecting their ignorance with His wisdom.[45]

TOO MANY SOLDIERS

And the Lord said unto Gideon, The people that are with thee are too many for me to give the Midianites into their hands, lest Israel vaunt themselves against me, saying, Mine own hand hath saved me. Judges 7:2.

It had been made a law in Israel that before they went to battle the following proclamation should be made throughout the army: "What man is there that hath built a new house, and hath not dedicated it? let him go and return to his house, lest he die in the battle, and another man dedicate it. And what man is he that hath planted a vineyard, and hath not yet eaten of it? let him also go and return unto his house, lest he die in the battle, and another man eat of it. And what man is there that hath betrothed a wife, and hath not taken her? let him go and return unto his house, lest he die in the battle, and another man take her." And the officers were to speak further to the people, saying, "What man is there that is fearful and fainthearted? let him go and return unto his house, lest his brethren's heart faint as well as his heart" (Deut. 20:5-8).

Because his numbers were so few compared with those of the enemy, Gideon had refrained from making the usual proclamation. He was filled with astonishment at the declaration that his army was too large. But the Lord saw the pride and unbelief existing in the hearts of His people. Aroused by the stirring appeals of Gideon, they had readily enlisted; but many were filled with fear when they saw the multitudes of the Midianites. Yet, had Israel triumphed, those very ones would have taken the glory to themselves instead of ascribing the victory to God.

Gideon obeyed the Lord's direction, and with a heavy heart he saw twenty-two thousand, or more than two thirds of his entire force, depart for their homes.[1]

The Lord is willing to do great things for us. We shall not gain the victory through numbers, but through the full surrender of the soul to Jesus. We are to go forward in His strength, trusting in the mighty God of Israel. There is a lesson for us in the story of Gideon's army. . . . The Lord is just as willing to work through human efforts now, and to accomplish great things through weak instrumentalities.[2]

STILL TOO MANY

And the Lord said unto Gideon, The people are yet too many;
bring them down unto the water, and I will try them for thee there:
and it shall be, that of whom I say unto thee, This shall go with
thee, the same shall go with thee; and of whomsoever I say unto
thee, This shall not go with thee, the same shall not go. Judges 7:4.

The people were led down to the waterside, expecting to make
an immediate advance upon the enemy. A few hastily took a little
water in the hand and sucked it up as they went on; but nearly all
bowed upon their knees, and leisurely drank from the surface of the
stream. Those who took of the water in their hands were but three
hundred out of ten thousand; yet these were selected; all the rest
were permitted to return to their homes.

By the simplest means character is often tested. Those who in
time of peril were intent upon supplying their own wants were not
the men to be trusted in an emergency. The Lord has no place in His
work for the indolent and self-indulgent. The men of His choice were
the few who would not permit their own wants to delay them in the
discharge of duty. The three hundred chosen men not only possessed
courage and self-control, but they were men of faith. They had not defiled themselves with idolatry. God could direct them, and through
them He could work deliverance for Israel. Success does not depend
upon numbers. God can deliver by few as well as by many. He is honored not so much by the great numbers as by the character of those
who serve Him.[3]

All who would be soldiers of the cross of Christ, must gird on the
armor and prepare for conflict. They should not be intimidated by
threats, or terrified by dangers. They must be cautious in peril, yet
firm and brave in facing the foe and doing battle for God. The consecration of Christ's follower must be complete. Father, mother, wife,
children, houses, lands, everything, must be held secondary to the
work and cause of God. He must be willing to bear patiently, cheerfully, joyfully, whatever in God's providence he may be called to suffer. His final reward will be to share with Christ the throne of
immortal glory.[4]

BETRAYED INTO ERROR

And Gideon made an ephod . . . which thing became a snare unto Gideon, and to his house. Judges 8:27.

The people of Israel, in their gratitude at deliverance from the Midianites, proposed to Gideon that he should become their king, and that the throne should be confirmed to his descendants. This proposition was in direct violation of the principles of the theocracy. . . . Gideon recognized this fact; his answer shows how true and noble were his motives. "I will not rule over you," he declared; "neither shall my son rule over you: the Lord shall rule over you."

But Gideon was betrayed into another error, which brought disaster upon his house and upon all Israel. The season of inactivity that succeeds a great struggle is often fraught with greater danger than is the period of conflict. To this danger Gideon was now exposed. A spirit of unrest was upon him. Hitherto he had been content to fulfill the directions given him from God; but now, instead of waiting for divine guidance, he began to plan for himself. When the armies of the Lord have gained a signal victory, Satan will redouble his efforts to overthrow the work of God. . . .

Because he had been commanded to offer sacrifice upon the rock where the Angel appeared to him, Gideon concluded that he had been appointed to officiate as a priest. Without waiting for the divine sanction, he determined to provide a suitable place, and to institute a system of worship similar to that carried on at the tabernacle. With the strong popular feeling in his favor he found no difficulty in carrying out his plan.[5]

Those who are placed in the highest positions may lead astray, especially if they feel that there is no danger. The wisest err; the strongest grow weary. . . . It is a solemn thought that the removal of one safeguard from the conscience, the failure to fulfill one good resolution, the formation of one wrong habit, may result not only in our own ruin, but in the ruin of those who have put confidence in us. Our only safety is to follow where the steps of the Master lead the way, to trust for protection implicitly to Him who says, "Follow me."[6]

BEFORE THE BABY COMES

Teach us what we shall do unto the child that shall be born. Judges 13:8.

God Himself appeared to the wife of Manoah and told her that she should have a son, and that he should be a great man and should deliver Israel. Then He gave her special instructions regarding her diet. . . . Let us regard this as instruction given to every mother in our world. If you want your children to have well-balanced minds, you must be temperate yourselves. Keep your own heart and affections sound and healthful, that you may impart to your offspring a healthful mind and body.[7]

Every mother may understand her duty. She may know that the character of her children will depend vastly more upon her habits before their birth and her personal efforts after their birth, than upon external advantages or disadvantages. . . . The mother who is a fit teacher for her children must, before their birth, form habits of self-denial and self-control; for she transmits to them her own qualities, her own strong or weak traits of character.[8]

Unwise advisers will urge upon the mother the necessity of gratifying every wish and impulse, but such teaching is false and mischievous. The mother is by the command of God Himself placed under the most solemn obligation to exercise self-control. And fathers as well as mothers are involved in this responsibility. Both parents transmit their own characteristics, mental and physical, their dispositions and appetites, to their children.[9]

Many make the subject of temperance a matter of jest. They claim that the Lord does not concern Himself with such minor matters as our eating and drinking. But if the Lord had no care for these things, He would not have revealed Himself to the wife of Manoah, giving her definite instructions, and twice enjoining upon her to beware lest she disregard them.[10]

The effect of prenatal influences is by many parents looked upon as a matter of little moment; but heaven does not so regard it. . . . In the words spoken to the Hebrew mother, God speaks to all mothers in every age.[11]

COMPROMISE

Be ye not unequally yoked together with unbelievers: for what fellowship hath righteousness with unrighteousness? 2 Cor. 6:14.

The town of Zorah being near the country of the Philistines, Samson came to mingle with them on friendly terms. Thus in his youth intimacies sprang up, the influence of which darkened his whole life. A young woman dwelling in the Philistine town of Timnath engaged Samson's affections, and he determined to make her his wife. To his God-fearing parents, who endeavored to dissuade him from his purpose, his only answer was, "She pleaseth me well." The parents at last yielded to his wishes, and the marriage took place.

Just as he was entering upon manhood, the time when he must execute his divine mission—the time above all others when he should have been true to God—Samson connected himself with the enemies of Israel. He did not ask whether he could better glorify God when united with the object of his choice, or whether he was placing himself in a position where he could not fulfill the purpose to be accomplished by his life. To all who seek first to honor Him, God has promised wisdom; but there is no promise to those who are bent upon self-pleasing. . . .

Christianity ought to have a controlling influence upon the marriage relation, but it is too often the case that the motives which lead to this union are not in keeping with Christian principles. Satan is constantly seeking to strengthen his power over the people of God by inducing them to enter into alliance with his subjects; and in order to accomplish this he endeavors to arouse unsanctified passions in the heart. . . .

At his marriage feast Samson was brought into familiar association with those who hated the God of Israel. Whoever voluntarily enters into such relations will feel it necessary to conform, to some degree, to the habits and customs of his companions. The time thus spent is worse than wasted. Thoughts are entertained and words are spoken that tend to break down the strongholds of principle, and to weaken the citadel of the soul.[12]

MIGHTY WEAKLING

He shall begin to deliver Israel out of the hand of the Philistines. Judges 13:5.

God's promise that through Samson He would "begin to deliver Israel out of the hand of the Philistines" was fulfilled; but how dark and terrible the record of that life which might have been a praise to God and a glory to the nation! Had Samson been true to his divine calling, the purpose of God could have been accomplished in his honor and exaltation. But he yielded to temptation and proved untrue to his trust, and his mission was fulfilled in defeat, bondage, and death.

Physically, Samson was the strongest man upon the earth; but in self-control, integrity, and firmness, he was one of the weakest of men. Many mistake strong passions for a strong character, but the truth is that he who is mastered by his passions is a weak man. The real greatness of the man is measured by the power of the feelings that he controls, not by those that control him.

God's providential care had been over Samson, that he might be prepared to accomplish the work which he was called to do. At the very outset of life he was surrounded with favorable conditions for physical strength, intellectual vigor, and moral purity. But under the influence of wicked associates he let go that hold upon God which is man's only safeguard, and he was swept away by the tide of evil. Those who in the way of duty are brought into trial may be sure that God will preserve them; but if men willfully place themselves under the power of temptation, they will fall, sooner or later.

The very ones whom God purposes to use as His instruments for a special work, Satan employs his utmost power to lead astray. He attacks us at our weak points, working through defects in the character to gain control of the whole man; and he knows that if these defects are cherished, he will succeed. But none need be overcome. Man is not left alone to conquer the power of evil by his own feeble efforts. Help is at hand and will be given to every soul who really desires it.[13]

WHAT'S THE SECRET?

And Delilah said to Samson, Tell me, I pray thee, wherein thy great strength lieth. Judges 16:6.

The Israelites made Samson judge, and he ruled Israel for twenty years. But one wrong step prepares the way for another. . . . He continued to seek those sensuous pleasures that were luring him to ruin. "He loved a woman in the valley of Sorek," not far from his own birthplace. Her name was Delilah, "the consumer." . . . The Philistines kept a vigilant watch over the movements of their enemy, and when he degraded himself by this new attachment, they determined, through Delilah, to accomplish his ruin.

A deputation consisting of one leading man from each of the Philistine provinces was sent to the vale of Sorek. They dared not attempt to seize him while in possession of his great strength, but it was their purpose to learn, if possible, the secret of his power. They therefore bribed Delilah to discover and reveal it.

As the betrayer plied Samson with her questions, he deceived her by declaring that the weakness of other men would come upon him if certain processes were tried. When she put the matter to the test, the cheat was discovered. Then she accused him of falsehood, saying, "How canst thou say, I love thee, when thine heart is not with me?" . . . Three times Samson had the clearest evidence that the Philistines had leagued with his charmer to destroy him; but when her purpose failed, she treated the matter as a jest, and he blindly banished fear.[14]

In the society of this enchantress, the judge of Israel squandered precious hours that should have been sacredly devoted to the welfare of his people. But the blinding passions which make even the strongest weak had gained control of reason and of conscience. . . .

Samson's infatuation seems almost incredible. At first he was not so wholly enthralled as to reveal the secret; but he had deliberately walked into the net of the betrayer of souls, and its meshes were drawing close about him at every step.[15]

THIS IS THE SECRET

And he wist not that the Lord was departed from him. Judges 16:20.

Day by day Delilah urged him, until "his soul was vexed unto death"; yet a subtle power kept him by her side. Overcome at last, Samson made known the secret: "There hath not come a razor upon mine head; for I have been a Nazarite unto God from my mother's womb: if I be shaven, then my strength will go from me, and I shall become weak, and be like any other man." A messenger was immediately dispatched to the lords of the Philistines, urging them to come to her without delay. While the warrior slept, the heavy masses of his hair were severed from his head. Then, as she had done three times before, she called, "The Philistines be upon thee, Samson!" Suddenly awaking, he thought to exert his strength as before, and destroy them; but his powerless arms refused to do his bidding, and he knew that "Jehovah was departed from him." When he had been shaven, Delilah began to annoy him and cause him pain, thus making a trial of his strength; for the Philistines dared not approach him till fully convinced that his power was gone. Then they seized him and, having put out both his eyes, they took him to Gaza. Here he was bound with fetters in their prison house and confined to hard labor.

What a change to him who had been the judge and champion of Israel!—now weak, blind, imprisoned, degraded to the most menial service! Little by little he had violated the conditions of his sacred calling. God had borne long with him; but when he had so yielded himself to the power of sin as to betray his secret, the Lord departed from him. There was no virtue in his long hair merely, but it was a token of his loyalty to God; and when the symbol was sacrificed in the indulgence of passion, the blessings of which it was a token were also forfeited.[16]

Had Samson's head been shaven without fault on his part, his strength would have remained. But his course had shown contempt for the favor and authority of God as much as if he had in disdain himself severed his locks from his head. Therefore God left him to endure the results of his own folly.[17]

A SURE CROP

My son, if sinners entice thee, consent thou not. Prov. 1:10.

Samson in his peril had the same source of strength as had Joseph. He could choose the right or the wrong as he pleased. But instead of taking hold of the strength of God, he permitted the wild passions of his nature to have full sway. The reasoning powers were perverted, the morals corrupted. God had called Samson to a position of great responsibility, honor, and usefulness; but he must first learn to govern by first learning to obey the laws of God. Joseph was a free moral agent. Good and evil were before him. He could choose the path of purity, holiness, and honor, or the path of immorality and degradation. He chose the right way, and God approved. Samson, under similar temptations, which he had brought upon himself, gave loose rein to passion. The path which he entered upon he found to end in shame, disaster, and death. What a contrast to the history of Joseph![18]

The Lord has in His Word plainly instructed His people not to unite themselves with those who have not His love and fear before them. Such companions will seldom be satisfied with the love and respect which are justly theirs. They will constantly seek to gain from the God-fearing wife or husband some favor which shall involve a disregard of the divine requirements. To a godly man, and to the church with which he is connected, a worldly wife or a worldly friend is as a spy in the camp, who will watch every opportunity to betray the servant of Christ, and expose him to the enemy's attacks.[19]

The history of Samson conveys a lesson for those whose characters are yet unformed, who have not yet entered upon the stage of active life. The youth who enter our schools and colleges will find there every class of mind. If they desire sport and folly, if they seek to shun the good and unite with the evil, they have the opportunity. Sin and righteousness are before them, and they are to choose for themselves. But let them remember that "Whatsoever a man soweth, that shall he also reap."[20]

GOD REMEMBERED

And Samson called unto the Lord, and said, O Lord God, Remember me. Judges 16:28.

In suffering and humiliation, a sport for the Philistines, Samson learned more of his own weakness than he had ever known before; and his afflictions led him to repentance. As his hair grew, his power gradually returned; but his enemies, regarding him as a fettered and helpless prisoner, felt no apprehensions.

The Philistines ascribed their victory to their gods; and, exulting, they defied the God of Israel. A feast was appointed in honor of Dagon, the fish god, "the protector of the sea." From town and country throughout the Philistine plain the people and their lords assembled. Throngs of worshipers filled the vast temple and crowded the galleries about the roof. It was a scene of festivity and rejoicing. There was the pomp of the sacrificial service, followed by music and feasting. Then, as the crowning trophy of Dagon's power, Samson was brought in. Shouts of exultation greeted his appearance. People and rulers mocked his misery and adored the god who had overthrown "the destroyer of their country." After a time, as if weary, Samson asked permission to rest against the two central pillars which supported the temple roof. Then he silently uttered the prayer, "O Lord God, remember me, I pray thee, and strengthen me, I pray thee, only this once, O God, that I may be at once avenged of the Philistines." With these words he encircled the pillars with his mighty arms; and crying, "Let me die with the Philistines!" he bowed himself, and the roof fell, destroying at one crash all that vast multitude. "So the dead which he slew at his death were more than they which he slew in his life."

The idol and its worshipers, priest and peasant, warrior and noble, were buried together beneath the ruins of Dagon's temple. And among them was the giant form of him whom God had chosen to be the deliverer of His people.[21]

The contest, instead of being between Samson and the Philistines, was now between Jehovah and Dagon, and thus the Lord was moved to assert His almighty power and His supreme authority.[22]

136

SHE KEPT HER PROMISE

I will give him unto the Lord all the days of his life. 1 Sam. 1:11.

Elkanah, a Levite of Mount Ephraim, was a man of wealth and influence, and one who loved and feared the Lord. His wife, Hannah, was a woman of fervent piety. Gentle and unassuming, her character was marked with deep earnestness and a lofty faith.

The blessing so earnestly sought by every Hebrew was denied this godly pair; their home was not gladdened by the voice of childhood; and the desire to perpetuate his name led the husband—as it had led many others—to contract a second marriage. But this step, prompted by a lack of faith in God, did not bring happiness. Sons and daughters were added to the household; but the joy and beauty of God's sacred institution had been marred and the peace of the family was broken. Peninnah, the new wife, was jealous and narrow-minded, and she bore herself with pride and insolence. To Hannah, hope seemed crushed and life a weary burden; yet she met the trial with uncomplaining meekness. . . .

The burden which she could share with no earthly friend she cast upon God. Earnestly she pleaded that He would take away her reproach and grant her the precious gift of a son to nurture and train for Him. And she made a solemn vow that if her request were granted, she would dedicate her child to God, even from its birth. . . .

Hannah's prayer was granted; she received the gift for which she had so earnestly entreated. As she looked upon the child, she called him Samuel—asked of God." [23]

As soon as the little one was old enough to be separated from its mother, she fulfilled her solemn vow. She loved her child with all the devotion of a mother's heart; day by day her affections entwined about him more closely as she watched his expanding powers, and listened to the childish prattle; he was her only son, the especial gift of heaven; but she had received him as a treasure consecrated to God, and she would not withhold from the Giver His own. Faith strengthened the mother's heart, and she yielded not to the pleadings of natural affection. [24]

GOD'S PROPERTY

I have lent him to the Lord. 1 Sam. 1:28.

From Shiloh, Hannah quietly returned to her home at Ramah, leaving the child Samuel to be trained for service in the house of God, under the instruction of the high priest. From the earliest dawn of intellect she had taught her son to love and reverence God and to regard himself as the Lord's. By every familiar object surrounding him she had sought to lead his thoughts up to the Creator. When separated from her child, the faithful mother's solicitude did not cease. Every day he was the subject of her prayers. Every year she made, with her own hands, a robe of service for him; and as she went up with her husband to worship at Shiloh, she gave the child this reminder of her love. Every fiber of the little garment had been woven with a prayer that he might be pure, noble, and true. She did not ask for her son worldly greatness, but she earnestly pleaded that he might attain that greatness which Heaven values—that he might honor God and bless his fellow men.

What a reward was Hannah's! and what an encouragement to faithfulness is her example! There are opportunities of incstimable worth, interests infinitely precious, committed to every mother. The humble round of duties which women have come to regard as a wearisome task should be looked upon as a grand and noble work. It is the mother's privilege to bless the world by her influence, and in doing this she will bring joy to her own heart. She may make straight paths for the feet of her children, through sunshine and shadow, to the glorious heights above. But it is only when she seeks, in her own life, to follow the teachings of Christ that the mother can hope to form the character of her children after the divine pattern. The world teems with corrupting influences. Fashion and custom exert a strong power over the young. If the mother fails in her duty to instruct, guide, and restrain, her children will naturally accept the evil, and turn from the good. Let every mother go often to her Savior with the prayer, "Teach us, how shall we order the child, and what shall we do unto him?" Let her heed the instruction which God has given in His word, and wisdom will be given her as she shall have need.[25]

LIKE PARENT, LIKE CHILD

My son, keep your father's commandment, and forsake not your mother's teaching. Prov. 6:20, RSV.

What the parents are, that, to a great extent, the children will be. The physical conditions of the parents, their dispositions and appetites, their mental and moral tendencies, are, to a greater or less degree, reproduced in their children.

The nobler the aims, the higher the mental and spiritual endowments, and the better developed the physical powers of the parents, the better will be the life equipment they give their children. In cultivating that which is best in themselves, parents are exerting an influence to mold society and to uplift future generations.

Fathers and mothers need to understand their responsibility. The world is full of snares for the feet of the young. . . . They cannot discern the hidden dangers or the fearful ending of the path that seems to them the way of happiness. . . .

Even before the birth of the child, the preparation should begin that will enable it to fight successfully the battle against evil.

Especially does responsibility rest upon the mother. She, by whose lifeblood the child is nourished and its physical frame built up, imparts to it also mental and spiritual influences that tend to the shaping of mind and character. . . .

It was Hannah, the woman of prayer and self-sacrifice and heavenly inspiration, who gave birth to Samuel, the heaven-instructed child, the incorruptible judge, the founder of Israel's sacred schools.[26]

Would that every mother could realize how great are her duties and her responsibilities, and how great will be the reward of faithfulness. The mother's daily influence upon her children is preparing them for everlasting life or eternal death. She exercises in her home a power more decisive than the minister in the desk, or even the king upon his throne.[27]

A DANGEROUS EXAMPLE

They hearkened not unto the voice of their father. 1 Sam. 2:25.

Eli was priest and judge in Israel. He held the highest and most responsible positions among the people of God. As a man divinely chosen for the sacred duties of the priesthood, and set over the land as the highest judicial authority, he was looked up to as an example, and he wielded a great influence over the tribes of Israel. But although he had been appointed to govern the people, he did not rule his own household. . . . Loving peace and ease, he did not exercise his authority to correct the evil habits and passions of his children. Rather than contend with them or punish them, he would submit to their will and give them their own way. Instead of regarding the education of his sons as one of the most important of his responsibilities, he treated the matter as of little consequence. The priest and judge of Israel had not been left in darkness as to the duty of restraining and governing the children that God had given to his care. But Eli shrank from this duty, because it involved crossing the will of his sons, and would make it necessary to punish and deny them. . . .

The curse of transgression was apparent in the corruption and evil that marked the course of his sons. They had no proper appreciation of the character of God or of the sacredness of His law. His service was to them a common thing. From childhood they had been accustomed to the sanctuary and its service; but instead of becoming more reverent, they had lost all sense of its holiness and significance. The father had not corrected their want of reverence for his authority, had not checked their disrespect for the solemn services of the sanctuary; and when they reached manhood, they were full of the deadly fruits of skepticism and rebellion. . . .

There is no greater curse upon households than to allow the youth to have their own way. When parents regard every wish of their children and indulge them in what they know is not for their good, the children soon lose all respect for their parents, all regard for the authority of God or man, and are led captive at the will of Satan.[28]

NO RESTRAINT

I will judge his house for ever for the iniquity which he knoweth; because his sons made themselves vile, and he restrained them not. 1 Sam. 3:13.

Eli was a good man, pure in morals; but he was too indulgent. He incurred the displeasure of God because he did not strengthen the weak points in his character. He did not want to hurt the feelings of anyone and had not the moral courage to rebuke and reprove sin. . . .

He loved purity and righteousness; but he had not sufficient moral force to suppress the evil. He loved peace and harmony, and became more and more insensible to impurity and crime. . . .

Eli was gentle, loving, and kind, and had a true interest in the service of God and the prosperity of His cause. He was a man who had power in prayer. He never rose up in rebellion against the words of God. But he was wanting; he did not have firmness of character to reprove sin and execute justice against the sinner so that God could depend upon him to keep Israel pure. He did not add to his faith the courage and power to say No at the right time and in the right place.[29]

Eli was acquainted with the divine will. He knew what characters God could accept, and what He would condemn. Yet he suffered his children to grow up with unbridled passions, perverted appetites, and corrupt morals.

Eli had instructed his children in the law of God, and had given them a good example in his own life; but this was not his whole duty. God required him, both as a father and as a priest, to restrain them from following their own perverse will. This he had failed to do.[30]

Those who have too little courage to reprove wrong, or who through indolence or lack of interest make no earnest effort to purify the family or the church of God, are held accountable for the evil that may result from their neglect of duty. We are just as responsible for evils that we might have checked in others by exercise of parental or pastoral authority as if the acts had been our own.[31]

141

DELAYED JUDGMENT

In that day I will perform against Eli all things which I have spoken concerning his house: when I begin, I will also make an end. 1 Sam. 3:12.

Eli had greatly erred in permitting his sons to minister in holy office. By excusing their course, on one pretext and another, he became blinded to their sins; but at last they reached a pass where he could no longer hide his eyes from the crimes of his sons. The people complained of their violent deeds, and the high priest was grieved and distressed. He dared remain silent no longer. But his sons had been brought up to think of no one but themselves, and now they cared for no one else. They saw the grief of their father, but their hard hearts were not touched. They heard his mild admonitions, but they were not impressed, nor would they change their evil course though warned of the consequences of their sin. Had Eli dealt justly with his wicked sons, they would have been rejected from the priestly office and punished with death.[32]

Year after year the Lord delayed His threatened judgments. Much might have been done in those years to redeem the failures of the past, but the aged priest took no effective measures to correct the evils that were polluting the sanctuary of the Lord and leading thousands in Israel to ruin. The forbearance of God caused Hophni and Phinehas to harden their hearts and to become still bolder in transgression. The messages of warning and reproof to his house were made known by Eli to the whole nation. By this means he hoped to counteract, in some measure, the evil influence of his past neglect. But the warnings were disregarded by the people, as they had been by the priests.[33]

God condemns the negligence that dallies with sin and crime, and the insensibility that is slow to detect its baleful presence in the families of professed Christians. He holds parents accountable in a great degree for the faults and follies of their offspring. God visited with His curse not only the sons of Eli, but Eli himself, and this fearful example should be a warning to the parents of this time.[34]

142

A FAINTHEARTED FATHER

The iniquity of Eli's house shall not be purged with sacrifice nor offering for ever. 1 Sam. 3:14.

Eli did not manage his household according to God's rules for family government. He followed his own judgment. . . . Many are now making a similar mistake. They think they know a better way of training their children than that which God has given in His word. They foster wrong tendencies in them, urging as an excuse, "They are too young to be punished. Wait till they become older, and can be reasoned with." Thus wrong habits are left to strengthen until they become second nature. The children grow up without restraint, with traits of character that are a lifelong curse to them and are liable to be reproduced in others.[35]

In contrast with the story of Abraham's faithfulness, and the words of commendation spoken of him, is the record of Eli, who kept his sons in office while they were committing great iniquity. Here is a lesson for all parents. . . . Evil, without restraint, was tolerated by Eli. The result was sin that would not be atoned for, by sacrifice or by offerings, forevermore.[36]

While some err upon the side of undue severity, Eli went to the opposite extreme. . . . Their faults were overlooked in their childhood, and excused in their days of youth. The commands of the parents were disregarded, and the father did not enforce obedience.

The children saw that they could hold the lines of control, and they improved the opportunity. As the sons advanced in years, they lost all respect for their fainthearted father. They went on in sin without restraint. He remonstrated with them, but his words fell unheeded. Gross sins and revolting crimes were daily committed by them, until the Lord Himself visited with judgment the transgressors of His law. . . .

The Lord Himself decreed that for the sins of Eli's sons no atonement should be made by sacrifice or offering forever. How great, how lamentable, was their fall—men upon whom rested sacred responsibilities, proscribed, outlawed from mercy, by a just and holy God![37]

NO GENERATION GAP

*And the child Samuel ministered unto the Lord before Eli.
1 Sam. 3:1.*

Young as he was when brought to minister in the tabernacle,
Samuel had even then duties to perform in the service of God, according to his capacity. These were at first very humble, and not
always pleasant; but they were performed to the best of his ability,
and with a willing heart. . . .

If children were taught to regard the humble round of everyday
duties as the course marked out for them by the Lord, as a school in
which they were to be trained to render faithful and efficient service,
how much more pleasant and honorable would their work appear.
To perform every duty as unto the Lord throws a charm around the
humblest employment and links the workers on earth with the holy
beings who do God's will in heaven.[38]

The life of Samuel from early childhood had been a life of piety
and devotion. He had been placed under the care of Eli in his youth,
and the loveliness of his character drew forth the warm affection of
the aged priest. He was kind, generous, diligent, obedient, and respectful. The contrast between the course of the youth Samuel and
that of the priest's own sons was very marked, and Eli found rest and
comfort and blessing in the presence of his charge. It was a singular
thing that between Eli, the chief magistrate of the nation, and the simple child so warm a friendship should exist. Samuel was helpful and
affectionate, and no father ever loved his child more tenderly than did
Eli this youth. As the infirmities of age came upon Eli, he felt more
keenly the disheartening, reckless, profligate course of his own sons,
and he turned to Samuel for comfort and support.

How touching to see youth and old age relying one upon the
other, the youth looking up to the aged for counsel and wisdom, the
aged looking to the youth for help and sympathy. This is as it should
be. God would have the young possess such qualifications of character that they shall find delight in the friendship of the old, that they
may be united in the endearing bonds of affection to those who are
approaching the borders of the grave.[39]

REVIVAL

We have sinned against the Lord. . . . Cry unto the Lord our God for us. 1 Sam. 7:6, 8.

Samuel visited the cities and villages throughout the land, seeking to turn the hearts of the people to the God of their fathers; and his efforts were not without good results. After suffering the oppression of their enemies for twenty years, the Israelites "mourned after the Lord." Samuel counseled them, "If ye do return unto the Lord with all your hearts, then put away the strange gods and Ashtaroth from among you, and prepare your hearts unto the Lord, and serve him only." Here we see that practical piety, heart religion, was taught in the days of Samuel as taught by Christ when He was upon the earth. Without the grace of Christ the outward forms of religion were valueless to ancient Israel. They are the same to modern Israel.

There is need today of such a revival of true heart religion as was experienced by ancient Israel. Repentance is the first step that must be taken by all who would return to God. No one can do this work for another. We must individually humble our souls before God and put away our idols. When we have done all that we can do, the Lord will manifest to us His salvation. . . .

A large assembly was gathered at Mizpeh. Here a solemn fast was held. With deep humiliation the people confessed their sins; and as an evidence of their determination to obey the instructions they had heard, they invested Samuel with the authority of judge. . . .

While Samuel was in the act of presenting a lamb as a burnt offering, the Philistines drew near for battle. . . . A terrible storm burst upon the advancing host, and the earth was strewn with the dead bodies of mighty warriors. The Israelites had stood in silent awe, trembling with hope and fear. When they beheld the slaughter of their enemies, they knew that God had accepted their repentance. . . .

For nations as well as for individuals, the path of obedience to God is the path of safety and happiness, while that of transgression leads only to disaster and defeat.[40]

LIKE EVERYONE ELSE

Nay; but we will have a king over us; that we also may be like all the nations. 1 Sam. 8:19, 20.

The Hebrews demanded a king of Samuel, like the nations around them. By preferring a despotic monarch to the wise and mild government of God Himself, by the jurisdiction of His prophets, they showed a great want of faith in God, and confidence in His providence to raise them up rulers to lead and govern them. The children of Israel being peculiarly the people of God, their form of government was essentially different from all the nations around them. God had given them statutes and laws, and had chosen their rulers for them, and these leaders the people were to obey in the Lord. In all cases of difficulty and great perplexity, God was to be inquired of. Their demand for a king was a rebellious departure from God, their special leader. He knew that a king would not be best for His chosen people. . . . If they had a king, whose heart was lifted up and not right with God, he would lead them away from Him, and cause them to rebel against Him. The Lord knew that no one could occupy the position of king, and receive the honors usually given to a king, without becoming exalted, and their ways seem right in their own eyes, while at the same time they were sinning against God.[41]

God had separated the Israelites from every other people, to make them His own peculiar treasure. But they, disregarding this high honor, eagerly desired to imitate the example of the heathen! And still the longing to conform to worldly practices and customs exists among the professed people of God. As they depart from the Lord they become ambitious for the gains and honors of the world. Christians are constantly seeking to imitate the practices of those who worship the god of this world. Many urge that by uniting with worldlings and conforming to their customs they might exert a stronger influence over the ungodly. But all who pursue this course thereby separate from the Source of their strength. Becoming the friends of the world, they are the enemies of God.[42]

NO APOLOGIES NEEDED

And he said unto them, The Lord is witness against you, and his anointed is witness this day, that ye have not found ought in my hand. 1 Sam. 12:5.

The dissatisfied longing for worldly power and display is as difficult to cure now as in the days of Samuel. Christians seek to build as worldlings build, to dress as worldlings dress—to imitate the customs and practices of those who worship only the god of this world. The instructions of God's Word, the counsels and reproofs of His servants, and even warnings sent directly from His throne, seem powerless to subdue this unworthy ambition. When the heart is estranged from God, almost any pretext is sufficient to justify a disregard of His authority. . . .

The most useful men are seldom appreciated. Those who have labored most actively and unselfishly for their fellow man, and who have been instrumental in achieving the greatest results, are often repaid with ingratitude and neglect. When such men find themselves set aside, their counsels slighted and despised, they may feel that they are suffering great injustice. But let them learn from the example of Samuel not to justify or vindicate themselves, unless the Spirit of God unmistakably prompts to such a course.[43]

The honor accorded him who is concluding his work is of far more worth than the applause and congratulations which those receive who are just entering upon their duties, and who have yet to be tested.[44]

How many retiring from a position of responsibility as a judge can say in regard to their purity, Which of you convinceth me of sin? Who can prove that I have turned aside from my righteousness to accept bribes? I have never stained my record as a man who does judgment and justice. Who today can say what Samuel said when he was taking leave of the people of Israel, because they were determined to have a king? . . . Brave, noble judge! But it is a sorrowful thing that a man of the strictest integrity should have to humble himself to make his own defense.[45]

THE PEOPLE'S CHOICE

Behold the king whom ye have chosen, and whom ye have desired. 1 Sam. 12:13.

In Saul, God had given to Israel a king after their own heart. . . . Comely in person, of noble stature and princely bearing, his appearance accorded with their conceptions of royal dignity; and his personal valor and his ability in the conduct of armies were the qualities which they regarded as best calculated to secure respect and honor from other nations. They felt little solicitude that their king should possess those higher qualities which alone could fit him to rule with justice and equity. They did not ask for one who had true nobility of character, who possessed the love and fear of God. They had not sought counsel from God as to the qualities a ruler should possess, in order to preserve their distinctive, holy character as His chosen people. They were not seeking God's way, but their own way. Therefore God gave them such a king as they desired—one whose character was a reflection of their own. Their hearts were not in submission to God, and their king also was unsubdued by divine grace. Under the rule of this king they would obtain the experience necessary in order that they might see their error, and return to their allegiance to God.

Yet the Lord, having placed on Saul the responsibility of the kingdom, did not leave him to himself. He caused the Holy Spirit to rest upon Saul to reveal to him his own weakness and his need of divine grace; and had Saul relied upon God, God would have been with him. So long as his will was controlled by the will of God, so long as he yielded to the discipline of His Spirit, God could crown his efforts with success. But when Saul chose to act independently of God, the Lord could no longer be his guide, and was forced to set him aside. Then He called to the throne "a man after his own heart" (1 Sam. 13:14)—not one who was faultless in character, but who, instead of trusting to himself, would rely upon God, and be guided by His Spirit; who, when he sinned, would submit to reproof and correction.[46]

THE POTENTIAL IS THERE

There was not among the children of Israel a goodlier person than he. 1 Sam. 9:2.

The personal qualities of the future monarch were such as to gratify that pride of heart which prompted the desire for a king. . . . Of noble and dignified bearing, in the prime of life, comely and tall, he appeared like one born to command. Yet with these external attractions, Saul was destitute of those higher qualities that constitute true wisdom. He had not in youth learned to control his rash, impetuous passions; he had never felt the renewing power of divine grace.[47]

The Lord would not leave Saul to be placed in a position of trust without divine enlightenment. He was to have a new calling, and the Spirit of the Lord came upon him. The effect was that he was changed into a new man. The Lord gave Saul a new spirit, other thoughts, other aims and desires than he had previously had. This enlightenment, with the spiritual knowledge of God, placing him on vantage ground, was to bind his will to the will of Jehovah. . . .

Saul had a mind and influence capable of governing a kingdom, if his powers had been submitted to the control of God, but the very endowments that qualified him for doing good could be used by Satan, when surrendered to his power, and would enable him to exert widespread influence for evil. He could be more sternly vindictive, more injurious and determined in prosecuting his unholy designs, than could others, because of the superior powers of mind and heart that had been given him of God.[48]

Should he trust to his own strength and judgment, Saul would move impulsively, and would commit grave errors. But if he would remain humble, seeking constantly to be guided by divine wisdom, and advancing as the providence of God opened the way, he would be enabled to discharge the duties of his high position with success and honor. Under the influence of divine grace, every good quality would be gaining strength, while evil traits would as steadily lose their power. This is the work which the Lord proposes to do for all who consecrate themselves to Him.[49]

RUNNING AHEAD OF GOD

And he tarried seven days, according to the set time that Samuel had appointed: but Samuel came not to Gilgal; and the people were scattered from him. 1 Sam. 13:8.

It was not until the second year of Saul's reign that an attempt was made to subdue the Philistines. The first blow was struck by Jonathan, the king's son, who attacked and overcame their garrison at Geba. The Philistines, exasperated by this defeat, made ready for a speedy attack upon Israel. Saul now caused war to be proclaimed. . . .

Before the time appointed by the prophet had fully expired, he became impatient at the delay and allowed himself to be discouraged by the trying circumstances that surrounded him. . . .

The time for the proving of Saul had come. He was now to show whether or not he would depend on God and patiently wait according to His command, thus revealing himself as one whom God could trust in trying places as the ruler of His people, or whether he would be vacillating and unworthy of the sacred responsibility that had devolved upon him.[50]

In detaining Samuel, it was the purpose of God that the heart of Saul should be revealed, that others might know what he would do in an emergency. It was a trying position in which to be placed, but Saul did not obey orders. He felt that it would make no difference who approached God, or in what way; and, full of energy and self-complacency, he put himself forward into the sacred office.

The Lord has His appointed agencies; and if these are not discerned and respected by those who are connected with His work, if men feel free to disregard God's requirements, they must not be kept in positions of trust. They would not listen to counsel, nor to the commands of God through His appointed agencies. Like Saul, they would rush into a work that was never appointed them, and the mistakes they would make in following their human judgment would place the Israel of God where their Leader could not reveal Himself to them.[51]

FOUND WANTING

And it came to pass, that as soon as he had made an end of offering the burnt offering, behold, Samuel came; and Saul went out to meet him, that he might salute him. 1 Sam. 13:10.

God had directed that only those consecrated to the office should present sacrifices before Him. But Saul commanded, "Bring hither a burnt offering"; and, equipped as he was with armor and weapons of war, he approached the altar and offered sacrifice before God. . . . If Saul had fulfilled the conditions upon which divine help was promised, the Lord would have wrought a marvelous deliverance for Israel, with the few who were loyal to the king. But Saul was so well satisfied with himself and his work that he went out to meet the prophet as one who should be commended rather than disapproved.[52]

Saul endeavored to vindicate his own course, and blamed the prophet, instead of condemning himself. There are today many who pursue a similar course. Like Saul they are blinded to their errors. When the Lord seeks to correct them, they receive reproof as insult, and find fault with the one who brings the divine message.

Had Saul been willing to see and confess his error, this bitter experience would have proved a safeguard for the future. He would afterward have avoided the mistakes which called forth divine reproof. But feeling that he was unjustly condemned, he would, of course, be likely again to commit the same sin.

The Lord would have His people, under all circumstances, manifest implicit trust in Him. Although we cannot always understand the workings of His providence, we should wait with patience and humility until He sees fit to enlighten us.[53]

Saul's transgression proved him unworthy to be intrusted with sacred responsibilities. . . . Had he patiently endured the divine test, the crown would have been confirmed to him and to his house. In fact, Samuel had come to Gilgal for this very purpose. But Saul had been weighed in the balance, and found wanting. He must be removed to make way for one who would sacredly regard the divine honor and authority.[54]

151

A TIME FOR COURAGE

And Jonathan said to the young man that bare his armour, Come, and let us go over unto the garrison of these uncircumcised: it may be that the Lord will work for us: for there is no restraint to the Lord to save by many or by few. 1 Sam. 14:6.

Because of Saul's sin in his presumptuous offering, the Lord would not give him the honor of vanquishing the Philistines. Jonathan, the king's son, a man who feared the Lord, was chosen as the instrument to deliver Israel. Moved by a divine impulse, he proposed to his armor-bearer that they should make a secret attack upon the enemy's camp. . . .

Together they withdrew from the camp, secretly, lest their purpose should be opposed. With earnest prayer to the Guide of their fathers, they agreed upon a sign by which they might determine how to proceed. . . . Approaching the Philistine fortress, they were revealed to the view of their enemies, who said, tauntingly, "Behold, the Hebrews come forth out of the holes where they had hid themselves," then challenged them, "Come up to us, and we will show you a thing," meaning that they would punish the two Israelites for their daring. This challenge was the token that Jonathan and his companion had agreed to accept as evidence that the Lord would prosper their undertaking. Passing now from the sight of the Philistines, and choosing a secret and difficult path, the warriors made their way to the summit of a cliff that had been deemed inaccessible, and was not very strongly guarded. Thus they penetrated the enemy's camp and slew the sentinels, who, overcome with surprise and fear, offered no resistance.

Angels of heaven shielded Jonathan and his attendant, angels fought by their side, and the Philistines fell before them.[55]

These two men gave evidence that they were moving under the influence and command of a more than human general. To outward appearance, their venture was rash, and contrary to all military rules. But the action of Jonathan was not done in human rashness. He depended not on what he and his armor-bearer themselves could do; he was the instrument that God used in behalf of His people Israel.[56]

THE REAL KING

Cursed be the man that eateth any food until evening, that I may be avenged on mine enemies. 1 Sam. 14:24.

The command to refrain from food was prompted by selfish ambition, and it showed the king to be indifferent to the needs of his people when these conflicted with his desire for self-exaltation. To confirm his prohibition by a solemn oath showed Saul to be both rash and profane. The very words of the curse give evidence that Saul's zeal was for himself, and not for the honor of God. He declared his object to be, not "that the Lord may be avenged on *His* enemies," but "that *I* may be avenged on *mine* enemies.". . .

During the day's battle Jonathan, who had not heard of the king's command, unwittingly offended by eating a little honey as he passed through a wood. Saul learned of this at evening. He had declared that the violation of his edict should be punished with death; and though Jonathan had not been guilty of a willful sin, though God had miraculously preserved his life and had wrought deliverance through him, the king declared that the sentence must be executed. To spare the life of his son would have been an acknowledgment on the part of Saul that he had sinned in making so rash a vow. This would have been humiliating to his pride. "God do so, and more also," was his terrible sentence: "thou shalt surely die, Jonathan.". . .

At Gilgal, but a short time before, Saul had presumed to officiate as priest, contrary to the command of God. When reproved by Samuel, he had stubbornly justified himself. Now, when his own command was disobeyed—though the command was unreasonable and had been violated through ignorance—the king and father sentenced his son to death.

The people refused to allow the sentence to be executed. Braving the anger of the king, they declared, "Shall Jonathan die, who hath wrought this great salvation in Israel? God forbid: as the Lord liveth, there shall not one hair of his head fall to the ground; for he hath wrought with God this day." The proud monarch dared not disregard this unanimous verdict, and the life of Jonathan was preserved.[57]

IT WORKS TWO WAYS

With what judgment ye judge, ye shall be judged: and with what measure ye mete, it shall be measured to you again. Matt. 7:2.

Saul could not but feel that his son was preferred before him, both by the people and by the Lord. Jonathan's deliverance was a severe reproof to the king's rashness. He felt a presentiment that his curses would return upon his own head. He did not longer continue the war with the Philistines, but returned to his home, moody and dissatisfied.

Those who are most ready to excuse or justify themselves in sin are often most severe in judging and condemning others. Many, like Saul, bring upon themselves the displeasure of God, but they reject counsel and despise reproof. Even when convinced that the Lord is not with them, they refuse to see in themselves the cause of their trouble. They cherish a proud, boastful spirit, while they indulge in cruel judgment or severe rebuke of others who are better than they. . . .

Often those who are seeking to exalt themselves are brought into positions where their true character is revealed. So it was in the case of Saul. His own course convinced the people that kingly honor and authority were dearer to him than justice, mercy, or benevolence. Thus the people were led to see their error in rejecting the government that God had given them. They had exchanged the pious prophet, whose prayers had brought down blessings, for a king who in his blind zeal had prayed for a curse upon them.

Had not the men of Israel interposed to save the life of Jonathan, their deliverer would have perished by the king's decree. With what misgivings must that people afterward have followed Saul's guidance! How bitter the thought that he had been placed upon the throne by their own act! The Lord bears long with the waywardness of men, and to all He grants opportunity to see and forsake their sins; but while He may seem to prosper those who disregard His will and despise His warnings, He will, in His own time, surely make manifest their folly.[58]

TESTED AGAIN

Now go and smite Amalek, and utterly destroy all that they have, and spare them not. 1 Sam. 15:3.

The Lord sent His servant with another message to Saul. By obedience he might still prove his fidelity to God and his worthiness to walk before Israel. Samuel came to the king and delivered the word of the Lord. . . .

The Amalekites had been the first to make war upon Israel in the wilderness; and for this sin, together with their defiance of God and their debasing idolatry, the Lord, through Moses, had pronounced sentence upon them. . . . For four hundred years the execution of this sentence had been deferred; but the Amalekites had not turned from their sins. The Lord knew that this wicked people would, if it were possible, blot out His people and His worship from the earth. Now the time had come for the sentence, so long delayed, to be executed.

The forbearance that God has exercised toward the wicked emboldens men in transgression; but their punishment will be none the less certain and terrible for being long delayed. . . . While He does not delight in vengeance, He will execute judgment upon the transgressors of His law. He is forced to do this, to preserve the inhabitants of the earth from utter depravity and ruin. In order to save some He must cut off those who become hardened in sin. . . . And the very fact of His reluctance to execute justice testifies to the enormity of the sins that call forth His judgments and to the severity of the retribution awaiting the transgressor.

But while inflicting judgment, God remembered mercy. The Amalekites were to be destroyed, but the Kenites, who dwelt among them, were spared. This people, though not wholly free from idolatry, were worshipers of God and were friendly to Israel. Of this tribe was the brother-in-law of Moses, Hobab, who had accompanied the Israelites in their travels through the wilderness, and by his knowledge of the country had rendered them valuable assistance.[59]

NOT TO BE TRUSTED

But Saul and the people spared Agag, and the best of the sheep, and of the oxen, and of the fatlings, and the lambs, and all that was good, and would not utterly destroy them. 1 Sam. 15:9.

Since the defeat of the Philistines at Michmash, Saul had made war against Moab, Ammon, and Edom, and against the Amalekites and the Philistines; and wherever he turned his arms, he gained fresh victories. On receiving the commission against the Amalekites, he at once proclaimed war. To his own authority was added that of the prophet, and at the call to battle the men of Israel flocked to his standard. The expedition was not to be entered upon for the purpose of self-aggrandizement; the Israelites were not to receive either the honor of the conquest or the spoils of their enemies. They were to engage in the war solely as an act of obedience to God, for the purpose of executing His judgment upon the Amalekites. God intended that all nations should behold the doom of that people that had defied His sovereignty, and should mark that they were destroyed by the very people whom they had despised. . . .

This victory over the Amalekites was the most brilliant victory that Saul had ever gained, and it served to rekindle the pride of heart that was his greatest peril. The divine edict devoting the enemies of God to utter destruction was but partially fulfilled. Ambitious to heighten the honor of his triumphal return by the presence of a royal captive, Saul ventured to imitate the customs of the nations around him and spared Agag, the fierce and warlike king of the Amalekites. The people reserved for themselves the finest of the flocks, herds, and beasts of burden, excusing their sin on the ground that the cattle were reserved to be offered as sacrifices to the Lord. It was their purpose, however, to use these merely as a substitute, to save their own cattle.

Saul had now been subjected to the final test. His presumptuous disregard of the will of God, showing his determination to rule as an independent monarch, proved that he could not be trusted with royal power as the vicegerent of the Lord.[60]

I HEAR THE SHEEP

It repenteth me that I have set up Saul to be king: for he is turned back from following me, and hath not performed my commandments. 1 Sam. 15:11.

While Saul and his army were marching home in the flush of victory, there was deep anguish in the home of Samuel the prophet. He had received a message from the Lord denouncing the course of the king. . . . The prophet was deeply grieved over the course of the rebellious king, and he wept and prayed all night for a reversing of the terrible sentence.

God's repentance is not like man's repentance. "The Strength of Israel will not lie nor repent: for he is not a man, that he should repent." Man's repentance implies a change of mind. God's repentance implies a change of circumstances and relations. Man may change his relation to God by complying with the conditions upon which he may be brought into the divine favor, or he may, by his own action, place himself outside the favoring condition; but the Lord is the same "yesterday, and to day, and for ever" (Heb. 13:8). Saul's disobedience changed his relation to God; but the conditions of acceptance with God were unaltered—God's requirements were still the same, for with Him there "is no variableness, neither shadow of turning" (James 1:17).

With an aching heart the prophet set forth the next morning to meet the erring king. Samuel cherished a hope that, upon reflection, Saul might become conscious of his sin, and by repentance and humiliation be again restored to the divine favor. But when the first step is taken in the path of transgression the way becomes easy. Saul, debased by his disobedience, came to meet Samuel with a lie upon his lips. He exclaimed, "Blessed be thou of the Lord: I have performed the commandment of the Lord." The sounds that fell on the prophet's ears disproved the statement of the disobedient king.[61]

Saul denied his sin even while the lowing of the oxen and the bleating of the sheep were publishing his guilt.[62]

NOT REALLY SORRY

Because thou hast rejected the word of the Lord, he hath also rejected thee from being king. 1 Sam. 15:23.

Terrified by the denunciation of the prophet, Saul acknowledged his guilt, which he had before stubbornly denied; but he still persisted in casting blame upon the people, declaring that he had sinned through fear of them.

It was not sorrow for sin, but fear of its penalty, that actuated the king of Israel. . . . It was his chief anxiety to maintain his authority and retain the allegiance of the people. . . . As Samuel turned to depart, the king, in an agony of fear, laid hold of his mantle to hold him back, but it rent in his hands. Upon this, the prophet declared, "The Lord hath rent the kingdom of Israel from thee this day, and hath given it to a neighbor of thine, that is better than thou.". . .

Saul presumed upon his exaltation, and dishonored God by unbelief and disobedience. Though when first called to the throne he was humble and self-distrustful, success made him self-confident. . . . The sacrificial offerings were in themselves of no value in the sight of God. They were designed to express on the part of the offerer penitence for sin and faith in Christ and to pledge future obedience to the law of God. But without penitence, faith, and an obedient heart, the offerings were worthless. When, in direct violation of God's command, Saul proposed to present a sacrifice of that which God had devoted to destruction, open contempt was shown for the divine authority. The service would have been an insult to Heaven.

Yet with the sin of Saul and its result before us, how many are pursuing a similar course. While they refuse to believe and obey some requirement of the Lord, they persevere in offering up to God their formal services of religion. There is no response of the Spirit of God to such service. No matter how zealous men may be in their observance of religious ceremonies, the Lord cannot accept them if they persist in willful violation of one of His commands.[1]

SANITY ALMOST GONE

And Samuel said unto Saul, I will not return with thee: for thou hast rejected the word of the Lord, and the Lord hath rejected thee from being king over Israel. 1 Sam. 15:26.

When Saul saw that Samuel came no more to instruct him, he knew that the Lord had rejected him for his wicked course, and his character seemed ever after to be marked with extremes. His servants . . . at times dared not approach him, for he seemed like an insane man, violent and abusive. He often seemed filled with remorse. He was melancholy, and often afraid where there was no danger. . . . He was always full of anxiety, and when in his gloomy moods he wished not to be disturbed, and at times would suffer none to approach him. . . . He would repeat prophetically sayings against himself with distracted energy, even in the presence of his lords and of the people.

Those who witnessed these strange exhibitions in Saul recommended to him music, as calculated to have a soothing influence upon his mind when thus distracted. In the providence of God, David was brought to his notice as a skillful musician. . . .

David's skillful playing upon the harp soothed the troubled spirit of Saul. As he listened to the enchanting strains of music, it had an influence to dispel the gloom which settled upon him, and to bring his excited mind into a more rational, happy state.[2]

Saul was shorn of his strength, because he failed to make obedience to God's commandments the rule of his life. It is a fearful thing for a man to set his will against the will of God, as revealed in His specified requirements. All the honor that a man could receive on the throne of a kingdom would be a poor compensation for the loss of the favor of God through an act of disloyalty to heaven. Disobedience to the commandments of God can only bring disaster and dishonor at last. God has given to every man his work, just as truly as He appointed to Saul the government of Israel; and the practical and important lesson to us is to accomplish our appointed work in such a manner that we may meet our life records with joy, and not with grief.[3]

GOD'S CHOICE, NOT MAN'S

And the Lord said unto Samuel, . . . fill thine horn with oil, and go, I will send thee to Jesse the Bethlehemite: for I have provided me a king among his sons. 1 Sam. 16:1.

When the sacrifice was ended, and before partaking of the offering feast, Samuel began his prophetic inspection of the noble-appearing sons of Jesse. Eliab was the eldest, and more nearly resembled Saul for stature and beauty than the others. His comely features and finely developed form attracted the attention of the prophet. As Samuel looked upon his princely bearing, he thought, "This is indeed the man whom God has chosen as successor to Saul." . . . But Jehovah did not look upon the outward appearance. Eliab did not fear the Lord. Had he been called to the throne, he would have been a proud, exacting ruler. . . .

No outward beauty can recommend the soul to God. The wisdom and excellence revealed in the character and deportment express the true beauty of the man; and it is the inner worth, the excellency of the heart, that determines our acceptance with the Lord of hosts. How deeply should we feel this truth in the judgment of ourselves and others. We may learn from the mistake of Samuel how vain is the estimation that rests on beauty of face or nobility of stature.[4]

The elder brothers, from whom Samuel would have chosen, did not possess the qualifications that God saw to be essential in a ruler of His people. Proud, self-centered, self-confident, they were set aside for the one whom they lightly regarded, one who had preserved the simplicity and sincerity of his youth, and who, while little in his own sight, could be trained by God for the responsibilities of the kingdom. So today, in many a child whom the parents would pass by, God sees capabilities far above those revealed by others who are thought to possess great promise. And as regards life's possibilities, who is capable of deciding what is great and what is small? How many a worker in the lowly places of life, by setting on foot agencies for the blessing of the world, has achieved results that kings might envy![5]

PREPARING TO LEAD

When there came a lion, or a bear, and took a lamb out of the flock, I went out after him, and smote him, and delivered it out of his mouth: and when he arose against me, I caught him by his beard, and smote him, and slew him. 1 Sam. 17:34, 35, RV.

David was growing in favor with God and man. He had been instructed in the way of the Lord, and he now set his heart more fully to do the will of God than ever before. He had new themes for thought. He had been in the court of the king and had seen the responsibilities of royalty. He had discovered some of the temptations that beset the soul of Saul and had penetrated some of the mysteries in the character and dealings of Israel's first king. He had seen the glory of royalty shadowed with a dark cloud of sorrow, and he knew that the household of Saul, in their private life, were far from happy. All these things served to bring troubled thoughts to him who had been anointed to be king over Israel. But while he was absorbed in deep meditation, and harassed by thoughts of anxiety, he turned to his harp, and called forth strains that elevated his mind to the Author of every good, and the dark clouds that seemed to shadow the horizon of the future were dispelled.

God was teaching David lessons of trust. As Moses was trained for his work, so the Lord was fitting the son of Jesse to become the guide of His chosen people. In his watchcare for his flocks, he was gaining an appreciation of the care that the Great Shepherd has for the sheep of His pasture.

The lonely hills and the wild ravines where David wandered with his flocks were the lurking place of beasts of prey. Not infrequently the lion from the thickets by the Jordan, or the bear from his lair among the hills, came, fierce with hunger, to attack the flocks. According to the custom of his time, David was armed only with his sling and shepherd's staff; yet he early gave proof of his strength and courage in protecting his charge. . . .

His experience in these matters proved the heart of David and developed in him courage and fortitude and faith.[6]

HUMAN BOASTING

And the Philistine said, I defy the armies of Israel this day; give me a man, that we may fight together. 1 Sam. 17:10.

When war was declared by Israel against the Philistines, three of the sons of Jesse joined the army under Saul; but David remained at home. After a time, however, he went to visit the camp of Saul. By his father's direction he was to carry a message and a gift to his elder brothers and to learn if they were still in safety and health. . . . As David drew near to the army, he heard the sound of commotion, as if an engagement was about to begin. . . .

Goliath, the champion of the Philistines, came forth, and with insulting language defied Israel and challenged them to provide a man from their ranks who would meet him in single combat. . . .

For forty days the host of Israel had trembled before the haughty challenge of the Philistine giant. Their hearts failed within them as they looked upon his massive form, in height measuring six cubits and a span. Upon his head was a helmet of brass, he was clothed with a coat of mail that weighed five thousand shekels, and he had greaves of brass upon his legs. The coat was made of plates of brass that overlaid one another, like the scales of a fish, and they were so closely joined that no dart or arrow could possibly penetrate the armor. At his back the giant bore a huge javelin, or lance, also of brass. "The staff of his spear was like a weaver's beam; and his spear's head weighed six hundred shekels of iron; and one bearing a shield went before him."[7]

Israel did not defy Goliath, but Goliath made his proud boasts against God and His people. The defying, the boasting, and the railing must come from the opposers of truth, who act the Goliath. But none of this spirit should be seen in those whom God has sent forth to proclaim the last message of warning to a doomed world.

Goliath trusted in his armor. He terrified the armies of Israel by his defiant, savage boastings, while he made a most imposing display of his armor, which was his strength.[8]

FIVE SMOOTH STONES

David said. . . , The Lord that delivered me out of the paw of the lion, and out of the paw of the bear, he will deliver me out of the hand of this Philistine. And Saul said unto David, Go, and the Lord be with thee. 1 Sam. 17:37.

When David saw that all Israel were filled with fear, and learned that the Philistine's defiance was hurled at them day after day, without arousing a champion to silence the boaster, his spirit was stirred within him. He was fired with zeal to preserve the honor of the living God and the credit of His people.[9]

David, in his humility and zeal for God and his people, proposed to meet this boaster. Saul consented and had his own kingly armor placed upon David. But he would not consent to wear it. He laid off the king's armor, for he had not proved it. He had proved God and, in trusting in Him, had gained special victories. To put on Saul's armor would give the impression that he was a warrior, when he was only little David who tended the sheep. He did not mean that any credit be given to the armor of Saul, for his trust was in the Lord God of Israel.[10]

Choosing five smooth stones out of the brook, he put them in his bag, and, with his sling in his hand, drew near to the Philistine. The giant strode boldly forward, expecting to meet the mightiest of the warriors of Israel. His armor-bearer walked before him, and he looked as if nothing could withstand him. As he came nearer to David he saw but a stripling, called a boy because of his youth. David's countenance was ruddy with health, and his well-knit form, unprotected by armor, was displayed to advantage; yet between its youthful outline and the massive proportions of the Philistine, there was a marked contrast.

Goliath was filled with amazement and anger. "Am I a dog," he exclaimed, "that thou comest to me with staves?" Then he poured upon David the most terrible curses by all the gods of his knowledge. He cried in derision, "Come to me, and I will give thy flesh unto the fowls of the air, and to the beasts of the field."[11]

A SURE OUTCOME

Then said David to the Philistine, . . . I come to thee in the name of the Lord of hosts, the God of the armies of Israel, whom thou hast defied. 1 Sam. 17:45.

Goliath railed upon David and cursed him by his gods. He felt that it was an insult upon his dignity to have a mere stripling, without so much as an armor, come to meet him. . . . David did not become irritated because he was looked upon as so inferior, neither did he tremble at his terrible threats, but replied: "Thou comest to me with a sword, and with a spear, and with a shield: but I come to thee in the name of the Lord of hosts, the God of the armies of Israel, whom thou hast defied." [12]

This speech, given in a clear, musical voice, rang out on the air, and was distinctly heard by the listening thousands marshaled for war. The anger of Goliath was roused to the very highest heat. In his rage he pushed up the helmet that protected his forehead and rushed forward to wreak vengeance upon his opponent. The son of Jesse was preparing for his foe. "And it came to pass, when the Philistine arose, and came and drew nigh to meet David, that David hasted, and ran toward the army to meet the Philistine. And David put his hand in his bag, and took thence a stone, and slang it, and smote the Philistine in the forehead, that the stone sunk into his forehead; and he fell upon his face to the earth."

Amazement spread along the lines of the two armies. They had been confident that David would be slain; but when the stone went whizzing through the air, straight to the mark, they saw the mighty warrior tremble, and reach forth his hands, as if he were struck with sudden blindness. The giant reeled, and staggered, and like a smitten oak, fell to the ground. David did not wait an instant. He sprang upon the prostrate form of the Philistine, and with both hands laid hold of Goliath's heavy sword. A moment before, the giant had boasted that with it he would sever the youth's head from his shoulders and give his body to the fowls of the air. Now it was lifted in the air, and then the head of the boaster rolled from his trunk, and a shout of exultation went up from the camp of Israel. [13]

NO ONE SORRY

All of you have conspired against me . . . and there is none of you that is sorry for me. 1 Sam. 22:8.

The spirit of evil was upon Saul. He felt that his doom had been sealed by the solemn message of his rejection from the throne of Israel. His departure from the plain requirements of God was bringing its sure results. He did not turn, and repent, and humble his heart before God, but opened it to receive every suggestion of the enemy. He listened to every false witness, eagerly receiving anything that was detrimental to the character of David, hoping that he might find an excuse for manifesting his increasing envy and hatred of him who had been anointed to the throne of Israel.

Every rumor was credited, no matter how inconsistent and irreconcilable it was with the former character and custom of David.

Every evidence that the protecting care of God was over David seemed to imbitter and deepen his one engrossing and determined purpose. The failure to accomplish his own designs appeared in marked contrast to the success of the fugitive in eluding his search, but it only made the determination of the king the more unrelenting and firm. He was not careful to conceal his designs toward David, nor scrupulous as to what means should be employed in accomplishing his purpose.

It was not the man David, who had done him no harm, against whom the king was contending. He was in controversy with the King of heaven; for when Satan is permitted to control the mind that will not be ruled by Jehovah, he will lead it according to his will, until the man who is thus in his power becomes an efficient agent to carry out his designs. So bitter is the enmity of the great originator of sin against the purposes of God, so terrible is his power for evil, that when men disconnect from God, Satan influences them, and their minds are brought more and more into subjection, until they cast off the fear of God, and the respect of men, and become bold and avowed enemies of God and of His people. . . . God hates all sin, and when man persistently refuses all the counsel of heaven, he is left to the deceptions of the enemy.[14]

MUSIC IN A CAVE

My soul is among lions; and I lie even among them that are set on fire. Ps. 57:4.

Oh, how precious is the sweet influence of the Spirit of God as it comes to depressed or despairing souls, encouraging the faint-hearted, strengthening the feeble, and imparting courage and help to the tried servants of the Lord! Oh, what a God is ours, who deals gently with the erring and manifests His patience and tenderness in adversity, and when we are overwhelmed with some great sorrow!

Every failure on the part of the children of God is due to their lack of faith. When shadows encompass the soul, when we want light and guidance, we must look up: there is light beyond the darkness. David ought not to have distrusted God for one moment. He had cause for trusting in Him; he was the Lord's anointed, and in the midst of danger he had been protected by the angels of God; he had been armed with courage to do wonderful things; and if he had but removed his mind from the distressing situation in which he was placed and had thought of God's power and majesty, he would have been at peace even in the midst of the shadows of death. . . .

Among the mountains of Judah, David sought refuge from the pursuit of Saul. He made good his escape to the cave of Adullam, a place that, with a small force, could be held against a large army. "And when his brethren and all his father's house heard it, they went down thither to him.". . .

In the cave of Adullam the family were united in sympathy and affection. The son of Jesse could make melody with voice and harp as he sang, "Behold, how good and how pleasant it is for brethren to dwell together in unity!" (Ps. 133:1). He had tasted the bitterness of distrust on the part of his own brothers; and the harmony that had taken the place of discord brought joy to the exile's heart. It was here that David composed the fifty-seventh psalm.[15]

RESULT OF INSANITY

And the king said, Thou shalt surely die, Ahimelech, thou, and all thy father's house. 1 Sam. 22:16.

Men cannot depart from the counsel of God and still retain that calmness and wisdom which will enable them to act with justice and discretion. There is no insanity so dreadful, so hopeless, as that of following human wisdom, unguided by the wisdom of God.

Saul had been preparing to ensnare and capture David in the cave of Adullam, and when it was discovered that David had left this place of refuge, the king was greatly enraged. The flight of David was a mystery to Saul. He could account for it only by the belief that there had been traitors in his camp, who had informed the son of Jesse of his proximity and design.

He affirmed to his counselors that a conspiracy had been formed against him, and with the offer of rich gifts and positions of honor he bribed them to reveal who among his people had befriended David. Doeg the Edomite turned informer. Moved by ambition and avarice, and by hatred of the priest, who had reproved his sins, Doeg reported David's visit to Ahimelech, representing the matter in such a light as to kindle Saul's anger against the man of God. The words of that mischievous tongue, set on fire of hell, stirred up the worst passions in Saul's heart. Maddened with rage, he declared that the whole family of the priest should perish. And the terrible decree was executed. Not only Ahimelech, but the members of his father's house . . . were slain at the king's command, by the murderous hand of Doeg. . . .

This is what Saul could do under the control of Satan. When God had said that the iniquity of the Amalekites was full, and had commanded him to destroy them utterly, he thought himself too compassionate to execute the divine sentence, and he spared that which was devoted to destruction; but now, without a command from God, under the guidance of Satan, he could slay the priests of the Lord and bring ruin upon the inhabitants of Nob. Such is the perversity of the human heart that has refused the guidance of God.[16]

A MISMATCHED PAIR

Favour is deceitful, and beauty is vain: but a woman that feareth the Lord, she shall be praised. Prov. 31:30.

In the character of Abigail, the wife of Nabal, we have an illustration of womanhood after the order of Christ; while her husband illustrates what a man may become who yields himself to the control of Satan.[17]

When David was a fugitive from the face of Saul, he had camped near the possessions of Nabal, and had protected the flocks and the shepherds of this man. . . . In a time of need, David sent messengers to Nabal with a courteous message, asking for food for himself and his men, and Nabal answered with insolence, returning evil for good, and refusing to share his abundance with his neighbors. No message could have been more respectful than that which David sent to this man, but Nabal accused David and his men falsely in order to justify himself in his selfishness, and represented David and his followers as runaway slaves. When the messenger returned with this insolent taunt, David's indignation was aroused, and he determined to have speedy revenge. One of the young men in the employ of Nabal, fearing that evil results would follow Nabal's insolence, came and stated the case to Nabal's wife, knowing that she had a different spirit from her husband, and was a woman of great discretion. . . .

Abigail saw that something must be done to avert the result of Nabal's fault, and that she must take the responsibility of acting immediately without the counsel of her husband. She knew that it would be useless to speak to him, for he would only receive her proposition with abuse and contempt. He would remind her that he was the lord of his household, that she was his wife, and therefore in subjection to him, and must do as he should dictate. . . .

Without his consent, she gathered together such stores as she thought best to conciliate the wrath of David; for she knew he was determined to avenge himself for the insult he had received. . . . Abigail's course in this matter was one that God approved, and the circumstance revealed in her a noble spirit and character.[18]

GENTLE REBUKE

I pray thee, forgive the trespass of thine handmaid: for the Lord will certainly make my lord a sure house; because my lord lighteth the battles of the Lord, and evil hath not been found in thee all thy days. 1 Sam. 25:28.

Abigail met David with respect, showing him honor and deference, and pleaded her case eloquently and successfully. While not excusing her husband's insolence, she still pleaded for his life. She also revealed the fact that she was not only a discreet woman, but a godly woman, acquainted with the works and ways of God in David. She stated her firm faith in the fact that David was the anointed of the Lord.[19]

Abigail presented by implication the course that David ought to pursue. He should fight the battles of the Lord. He was not to seek revenge for personal wrongs, even though persecuted as a traitor. . . . These words could have come only from the lips of one who had partaken of the wisdom from above. The piety of Abigail, like the fragrance of a flower, breathed out all unconsciously in face and word and action. The Spirit of the Son of God was abiding in her soul. Her speech, seasoned with grace, and full of kindness and peace, shed a heavenly influence. Better impulses came to David, and he trembled as he thought what might have been the consequences of his rash purpose. . . .

A consecrated Christian life is ever shedding light and comfort and peace. It is characterized by purity, tact, simplicity, and usefulness. It is controlled by that unselfish love that sanctifies the influence. It is full of Christ, and leaves a track of light wherever its possessor may go.

Abigail was a wise reprover and counselor. David's passion died away under the power of her influence and reasoning. . . .

With a humble heart he received the rebuke. . . . He gave thanks and blessings because she advised him righteously. There are many who, when they are reproved, think it praiseworthy if they receive the rebuke without becoming impatient; but how few take reproof with gratitude of heart and bless those who seek to save them from pursuing an evil course.[20]

169

DIVINE VENGEANCE

Dearly beloved, avenge not yourselves, but rather give place unto wrath: for it is written, Vengeance is mine; I will repay, saith the Lord. Rom. 12:19.

Although Nabal had refused the needy company of David and his men, yet that very night he made an extravagant feast for himself and his riotous friends, and indulged in eating and drinking till he sank in drunken stupor.[21]

Nabal thought nothing of spending an extravagant amount of his wealth to indulge and glorify himself; but it seemed too painful a sacrifice for him to make to bestow compensation which he never would have missed upon those who had been like a wall to his flocks and herds. Nabal was like the rich man in the parable. He had only one thought—to use God's merciful gifts to gratify his selfish animal appetites. He had no thought of gratitude to the Giver. He was not rich toward God; for eternal treasure had no attraction for him. Present luxury, present gain, was the one absorbing thought of his life. This was his god.[22]

Nabal was a coward at heart; and when he realized how near his folly had brought him to a sudden death, he seemed smitten with paralysis. Fearful that David would still pursue his purpose of revenge, he was filled with horror, and sank down in a condition of helpless insensibility. After ten days he died. The life that God had given him had been only a curse to the world. In the midst of his rejoicing and making merry, God had said to him, as He said to the rich man of the parable, "This night thy soul shall be required of thee" (Luke 12:20).[23]

When David heard the tidings of the death of Nabal, he gave thanks that God had taken vengeance into His own hands. He had been restrained from evil, and the Lord had returned the wickedness of the wicked upon his own head. In this dealing of God with Nabal and David, men may be encouraged to put their cases into the hands of God; for in His own good time He will set matters right.[24]

NO ANSWER FROM GOD

The Lord answered him not, neither by dreams, nor by Urim, nor by prophets. 1 Sam. 28:6.

The Lord never turned away a soul that came to Him in sincerity and humility. Why did he turn Saul away unanswered? The king had by his own act forfeited the benefits of all the methods of inquiring of God. He had rejected the counsel of Samuel the prophet; he had exiled David, the chosen of God; he had slain the priests of the Lord. . . . He had sinned away the Spirit of grace, and could he be answered by dreams and revelations from the Lord? Saul did not turn to God with humility and repentance. It was not pardon for sin and reconciliation with God that he sought, but deliverance from his foes. By his own stubbornness and rebellion he had cut himself off from God. There could be no return but by the way of penitence and contrition; but the proud monarch, in his anguish and despair, determined to seek help from another source. . . . It was told the king that a woman who had a familiar spirit was living in concealment at Endor. . . . Disguising himself, Saul went forth by night with but two attendants, to seek the retreat of the sorceress. . . .

What bondage so terrible as that of him who is given over to the control of the worst of tyrants—himself! Trust in God and obedience to His will were the only conditions upon which Saul could be king of Israel. Had he complied with these conditions throughout his reign, his kingdom would have been secure; God would have been his guide, the Omnipotent his shield. God had borne long with Saul; and although his rebellion and obstinacy had well-nigh silenced the divine voice in the soul, there was still opportunity for repentance. But when in his peril he turned from God to obtain light from a confederate of Satan, he had cut the last tie that bound him to his Maker. . . .

By consulting that spirit of darkness Saul had destroyed himself. Oppressed by the horror of despair, it would be impossible for him to inspire his army with courage. Separated from the Source of strength, he could not lead the minds of Israel to look to God as their helper. Thus the prediction of evil would work its own accomplishment.[25]

THAT'S NOT SAMUEL

For the living know that they shall die: but the dead know not any thing, neither have they any more a reward; for the memory of them is forgotten. Eccl. 9:5.

When Saul inquired for Samuel, the Lord did not cause Samuel to appear to Saul. He saw nothing. Satan was not allowed to disturb the rest of Samuel in the grave, and bring him up in reality to the witch of Endor. God does not give Satan power to resurrect the dead. But Satan's angels assume the form of dead friends, and speak and act like them, that through professed dead friends he can the better carry on his work of deception. Satan knew Samuel well, and he knew how to represent him before the witch of Endor, and to utter correctly the fate of Saul and his sons.

Satan will come in a very plausible manner to such as he can deceive, and will insinuate himself into their favor, and lead them almost imperceptibly from God. He wins them under his control, cautiously at first, until their perceptibilities become blunted. Then he will make bolder suggestions, until he can lead them to commit almost any degree of crime. When he has led them fully into his snare, he is then willing that they should see where they are, and he exults in their confusion, as in the case of Saul. He had suffered Satan to lead him a willing captive, and now Satan spreads before Saul a correct description of his fate. By giving Saul a correct statement of his end, through the woman of Endor, Satan opens a way for Israel to be instructed by his satanic cunning, that they may, in their rebellion against God, learn of him, and by thus doing, sever the last link which would hold them to God.

Saul knew that in this last act, of consulting the witch of Endor, he cut the last shred which held him to God. He knew that if he had not before willfully separated himself from God, this act sealed that separation, and made it final. He had made an agreement with death, and a covenant with hell. The cup of his iniquity was full.[26]

GOD'S SECRETS

It is not for you to know the times or the seasons, which the Father hath put in his own power. Acts 1:7.

The witch of Endor had made agreement with Satan to follow his directions in all things; and he would perform wonders and miracles for her, and would reveal to her the most secret things, if she would yield herself unreservedly to be controlled by his satanic majesty. This she had done.[27]

By the prediction of Saul's doom, given through the woman of Endor, Satan planned to ensnare the people of Israel. He hoped that they would be inspired with confidence in the sorceress, and would be led to consult her. Thus they would turn from God as their counselor and would place themselves under the guidance of Satan. The lure by which spiritualism attracts the multitudes is its pretended power to draw aside the veil from the future and reveal to men what God has hidden. God has in His word opened before us the great events of the future—all that it is essential for us to know—and He has given us a safe guide for our feet amid all its perils; but it is Satan's purpose to destroy men's confidence in God, to make them dissatisfied with their condition in life, and to lead them to seek a knowledge of what God has wisely veiled from them, and to despise what He has revealed in His Holy Word.

There are many who become restless when they cannot know the definite outcome of affairs. They cannot endure uncertainty, and in their impatience they refuse to wait to see the salvation of God. Apprehended evils drive them nearly distracted. They give way to their rebellious feelings, and run hither and thither in passionate grief, seeking intelligence concerning that which has not been revealed. If they would but trust in God, and watch unto prayer, they would find divine consolation. Their spirit would be calmed by communion with God. The weary and the heavy-laden would find rest unto their souls if they would only go to Jesus; but when they neglect the means that God has ordained for their comfort, and resort to other sources, hoping to learn what God has withheld, they commit the error of Saul, and thereby gain only a knowledge of evil.[28]

173

A SUICIDE

The righteousness of the perfect shall direct his way: but the wicked shall fall by his own wickedness. Prov. 11:5.

On the plain of Shunem and the slopes of Mount Gilboa the armies of Israel and the hosts of the Philistines closed in mortal combat. Though the fearful scene in the cave of Endor had driven all hope from his heart, Saul fought with desperate valor for his throne and his kingdom. But it was in vain. "The men of Israel fled from before the Philistines, and fell down slain in Mount Gilboa." Three brave sons of the king died at his side. The archers pressed upon Saul. He had seen his soldiers falling around him and his princely sons cut down by the sword. Himself wounded, he could neither fight nor fly. Escape was impossible, and determined not to be taken alive by the Philistines, he bade his armor-bearer, "Draw thy sword, and thrust me through therewith." When the man refused to lift his hand against the Lord's anointed, Saul took his own life by falling upon his sword. Thus the first king of Israel perished, with the guilt of self-murder upon his soul.[29]

By following the dictates of Satan, Saul was himself hastening the very result which, with unsanctified ability, he was endeavoring to avert.

The counsel of the Lord had been disregarded again and again by the rebellious king, and the Lord had given him up to the folly of his own wisdom. The influences of the Spirit of God would have restrained him from the course of evil which he had chosen, that eventually worked out his ruin. God hates all sin, and when man persistently refuses all the counsel of heaven, he is left to the deceptions of the enemy, to be drawn away of his own lusts, and enticed.[30]

The first king of Israel proved a failure, because he set his will above the will of God. Through the prophet Samuel the Lord instructed Saul that as king of Israel his course of action must be one of strictest integrity. Then God would bless his government with prosperity. But Saul refused to make obedience to God his first consideration, and the principles of heaven the government of his conduct. He died in dishonor and despair.[31]

A FRIEND MOURNS

How are the mighty fallen, and the weapons of war perished!
2 Sam. 1:27.

Twice David had had Saul in his power; but when urged to slay him, he had refused to lift his hand against him who had been consecrated by the command of God to rule over Israel. . . .

David's grief at the death of Saul was sincere and deep, evincing the generosity of a noble nature. He did not exult in the fall of his enemy. The obstacle that had barred his access to the throne of Israel was removed, but at this he did not rejoice. Death had obliterated the remembrance of Saul's distrust and cruelty, and now nothing in his history was thought of but that which was noble and kingly. The name of Saul was linked with that of Jonathan, whose friendship had been so true and so unselfish.[32]

Jonathan, by birth heir to the throne, yet knowing himself set aside by the divine decree; to his rival the most tender and faithful of friends, shielding David's life at the peril of his own; steadfast at his father's side through the dark days of his declining power, and at his side falling at the last—the name of Jonathan is treasured in heaven, and it stands on earth a witness to the existence and the power of unselfish love.[33]

The song in which David gave utterance to the feelings of his heart became a treasure to his nation, and to the people of God in all subsequent ages: . . .

"How are the mighty fallen in the midst of the battle!
Jonathan is slain upon thy high places.
I am distressed for thee, my brother Jonathan:
Very pleasant hast thou been unto me:
Thy love to me was wonderful,
Passing the love of women.
How are the mighty fallen,
And the weapons of war perished!"[34]

HIS LAST MISTAKE

Uzzah put forth his hand to the ark of God, and took hold of it; for the oxen shook it. And the anger of the Lord was kindled against Uzzah, and God smote him there for his error. 2 Sam. 6:6, 7.

The fate of Uzzah was a divine judgment upon the violation of a most explicit command. Through Moses the Lord had given special instruction concerning the transportation of the ark. None but the priests, the descendants of Aaron, were to touch it, or even to look upon it uncovered. . . .

The priests were to cover the ark, and then the Kohathites must lift it by the staves, which were placed in rings upon each side of the ark and were never removed. To the Gershonites and Merarites, who had in charge the curtains and boards and pillars of the tabernacle, Moses gave carts and oxen for the transportation of that which was committed to them. "But unto the sons of Kohath he gave none: because the service of the sanctuary belonging unto them was that they should bear *upon their shoulders*" (Num. 7:9). Thus in the bringing of the ark from Kirjathjearim there had been a direct and inexcusable disregard of the Lord's directions. . . .

The Philistines, who had not a knowledge of God's law, had placed the ark upon a cart when they returned it to Israel, and the Lord accepted the effort which they made. But the Israelites had in their hands a plain statement of the will of God in all these matters, and their neglect of these instructions was dishonoring to God. Upon Uzzah rested the greater guilt of presumption. Transgression of God's law had lessened his sense of its sacredness, and with unconfessed sins upon him he had, in face of the divine prohibition, presumed to touch the symbol of God's presence. God can accept no partial obedience, no lax way of treating His commandments. By the judgment upon Uzzah He designed to impress upon all Israel the importance of giving strict heed to His requirements. Thus the death of that one man, by leading the people to repentance, might prevent the necessity of inflicting judgments upon thousands.[35]

SATAN'S STEALTHY WORK

For our fight is not against any physical enemy: it is against organizations and powers that are spiritual. We are up against the unseen power that controls this dark world, and spiritual agents from the very headquarters of evil. Eph. 6:12, Phillips.

The Bible has little to say in praise of men. Little space is given to recounting the virtues of even the best men who have ever lived. This silence is not without purpose; it is not without a lesson. All the good qualities that men possess are the gift of God; their good deeds are performed by the grace of God through Christ. Since they owe all to God, the glory of whatever they are or do belongs to Him alone; they are but instruments in His hands. More than this—as all the lessons of Bible history teach—it is a perilous thing to praise or exalt men; for if one comes to lose sight of his entire dependence on God, and to trust to his own strength, he is sure to fall. . . .

It is impossible for us in our own strength to maintain the conflict; and whatever diverts the mind from God, whatever leads to self-exaltation or to self-dependence, is surely preparing the way for our overthrow. The tenor of the Bible is to inculcate distrust of human power and to encourage trust in divine power.

It was the spirit of self-confidence and self-exaltation that prepared the way for David's fall. Flattery and the subtle allurements of power and luxury were not without effect upon him. Intercourse with surrounding nations also exerted an influence for evil. According to the customs prevailing among Eastern rulers, crimes not to be tolerated in subjects were uncondemned in the king; the monarch was not under obligation to exercise the same self-restraint as the subject. All this tended to lessen David's sense of the exceeding sinfulness of sin. And instead of relying in humility upon the power of Jehovah, he began to trust to his own wisdom and might.

As soon as Satan can separate the soul from God, the only Source of strength, he will seek to arouse the unholy desires of man's carnal nature. The work of the enemy is not abrupt; it is not, at the outset, sudden and startling; it is a secret undermining of the strongholds of principle.[36]

ONE SIN LEADS TO ANOTHER

The thing that David had done displeased the Lord. 2 Sam. 11:27.

When in ease and self-security he let go his hold upon God, David yielded to Satan and brought upon his soul the stain of guilt. He, the Heaven-appointed leader of the nation, chosen by God to execute His law, himself trampled upon its precepts. He who should have been a terror to evildoers, by his own act strengthened their hands.

Amid the perils of his earlier life David in conscious integrity could trust his case with God. The Lord's hand had guided him safely past the unnumbered snares that had been laid for his feet. But now, guilty and unrepentant, he did not ask help and guidance from Heaven, but sought to extricate himself from the dangers in which sin had involved him. Bathsheba, whose fatal beauty had proved a snare to the king, was the wife of Uriah the Hittite, one of David's bravest and most faithful officers. None could foresee what would be the result should the crime become known. . . .

Every effort which David made to conceal his guilt proved unavailing. . . . In his desperation he was hurried on to add murder to adultery. He who had compassed the destruction of Saul was seeking to lead David also to ruin. Though the temptations were different, they were alike in leading to transgression of God's law. . . .

Uriah was made the bearer of his own death warrant. A letter sent by his hand to Joab from the king commanded, "Set ye Uriah in the forefront of the hottest battle, and retire ye from him, that he may be smitten, and die." Joab, already stained with the guilt of one wanton murder, did not hesitate to obey the king's instructions, and Uriah fell by the sword of the children of Ammon. . . .

He whose tender conscience and high sense of honor would not permit him, even when in peril of his life, to put forth his hand against the Lord's anointed had so fallen that he could wrong and murder one of his most faithful and most valiant soldiers, and hope to enjoy undisturbed the reward of his sin. Alas! how had the fine gold become dim! how had the most fine gold changed![37]

A KING REBUKED

And Nathan said to David, Thou art the man. 2 Sam. 12:7.

As time passed on, David's sin toward Bathsheba became known, and suspicion was excited that he had planned the death of Uriah. The Lord was dishonored. He had favored and exalted David, and David's sin misrepresented the character of God and cast reproach upon His name. It tended to lower the standard of godliness in Israel, to lessen in many minds the abhorrence of sin; while those who did not love and fear God were by it emboldened in transgression.

Nathan the prophet was bidden to bear a message of reproof to David. It was a message terrible in its severity. To few sovereigns could such a reproof be given but at the price of certain death to the reprover. Nathan delivered the divine sentence unflinchingly, yet with such heaven-born wisdom as to engage the sympathies of the king, to arouse his conscience, and to call from his lips the sentence of death upon himself. . . .

The guilty may attempt, as David had done, to conceal their crime from men; they may seek to bury the evil deed forever from human sight or knowledge; but "all things are naked and opened unto the eyes of him with whom we have to do" (Heb. 4:13).[38]

The prophet Nathan's parable of the ewe lamb, given to King David, may be studied by all. . . . While he was following his course of self-indulgence and commandment breaking, the parable of a rich man who took from a poor man his one ewe lamb was presented before him. But the king was so completely wrapped in his garments of sin that he did not see that he was the sinner. He fell into the trap, and . . . passed his sentence upon another man, as he supposed, condemning him to death. . . .

This experience was most painful to David, but it was most beneficial. But for the mirror which Nathan held up before him, in which he so clearly recognized his own likeness, he would have gone on unconvicted of his heinous sin, and would have been ruined. The conviction of his guilt was the saving of his soul. He saw himself in another light, as the Lord saw him, and as long as he lived he repented of his sin.[39]

SIN'S WAY IS HARD

By this deed thou hast given great occasion to the enemies of the Lord to blaspheme. 2 Sam. 12:14.

Through successive generations infidels have pointed to the character of David, bearing this dark stain, and have exclaimed in triumph and derision, "This is the man after God's own heart!" Thus a reproach has been brought upon religion, God and His word have been blasphemed, souls have been hardened in unbelief, and many, under a cloak of piety, have become bold in sin.

But the history of David furnishes no countenance to sin. It was when he was walking in the counsel of God that he was called a man after God's own heart. When he sinned, this ceased to be true of him until by repentance he had returned to the Lord. . . .

Though David repented of his sin, and was forgiven and accepted by the Lord, he reaped the baleful harvest of the seed he himself had sown. . . . His authority in his own household, his claim to respect and obedience from his sons, was weakened. A sense of his guilt kept him silent when he should have condemned sin; it made his arm feeble to execute justice in his house. . . .

Those who, by pointing to the example of David, try to lessen the guilt of their own sins should learn from the Bible record that the way of transgression is hard. Though like David they should turn from their evil course, the results of sin, even in this life, will be found bitter and hard to bear.[40]

A man incurs guilt by injuring a fellow-being, but his chief guilt is the sin that he has committed against the Lord, and the evil influence of his example upon others. The sincere child of God does not make light of any of His requirements.[41]

God intended the history of David's fall to serve as a warning that even those whom He has greatly blessed and favored are not to feel secure and neglect watchfulness and prayer. And thus it has proved to those who in humility have sought to learn the lesson that God designed to teach.[42]

SUPERFICIAL BEAUTY

But thou, O Lord, art a shield for me; my glory, and the lifter up of mine head. Ps. 3:3.

With the memory ever before him of his own transgression of the law of God, David seemed morally paralyzed; he was weak and irresolute, when before his sin he had been courageous and decided. His influence with the people had been weakened. And all this favored the designs of his unnatural son. . . .

While the king was more and more inclined to desire retirement and solitude, Absalom sedulously courted the popular favor. . . . Day by day this man of noble mien might be seen at the gate of the city, where a crowd of suppliants waited to present their wrongs for redress. Absalom mingled with them and listened to their grievances, expressing sympathy with their sufferings and regret at the inefficiency of the government.[43]

By his remarkable beauty, winning manners, and pretended kindness, he cunningly stole the hearts of the people. He did not possess benevolence at heart, but was ambitious and, as his course shows, would resort to intrigue and crime to obtain the kingdom. He would have returned his father's love and kindness by taking his life. He was proclaimed king by his followers in Hebron, and led them out to pursue his father.[44]

In humility and sorrow David passed out of the gate of Jerusalem— driven from his throne, from his palace, from the ark of God, by the insurrection of his cherished son. The people followed in long, sad procession, like a funeral train.[45]

Many who see not as God seeth, but view matters from man's standpoint, might reason that with David there might have been excuse for repining and that the sincerity of his repentance years before might have excepted him from present judgment. . . . David utters no complaint. The most eloquent psalm he ever sang was when he was climbing Mount Olivet, weeping and barefooted, yet humbled in spirit, unselfish and generous, submissive and resigned.[46]

GREATNESS IN HUMILIATION

When I sit in darkness, the Lord shall be a light unto me. I will bear the indignation of the Lord, because I have sinned against him, until he plead my cause, and execute judgment for me. Micah 7:8, 9.

Conscience was uttering bitter and humiliating truths to David. While his faithful subjects wondered at his sudden reverse of fortune, it was no mystery to the king. He had often had forebodings of an hour like this. He had wondered that God had so long borne with his sins, and had delayed the merited retribution. And now in his hurried and sorrowful flight, his feet bare, his royal robes changed for sackcloth, the lamentations of his followers awaking the echoes of the hills, he thought of his loved capital—of the place which had been the scene of his sin—and as he remembered the goodness and long-suffering of God, he was not altogether without hope. . . .

Many a wrongdoer has excused his own sin by pointing to David's fall, but how few there are who manifest David's penitence and humility. How few would bear reproof and retribution with the patience and fortitude that he manifested. He had confessed his sin, and for years had sought to do his duty as a faithful servant of God; he had labored for the upbuilding of his kingdom, and under his rule it had attained to strength and prosperity never reached before. He had gathered rich stores of material for the building of the house of God, and now was all the labor of his life to be swept away? Must the results of years of consecrated toil, the work of genius and devotion and statesmanship, pass into the hands of his reckless and traitorous son, who regarded not the honor of God nor the prosperity of Israel? How natural it would have seemed for David to murmur against God in this great affliction!

But he saw in his own sin the cause of his trouble. . . . And the Lord did not forsake David. This chapter in his experience, when, under cruelest wrong and insult, he shows himself to be humble, unselfish, generous, and submissive, is one of the noblest in his whole experience. Never was the ruler of Israel more truly great in the sight of heaven than at this hour of his deepest outward humiliation.[47]

A FOOLISH WISE MAN

The Lord had appointed to defeat the good counsel of Ahithophel, to the intent that the Lord might bring evil upon Absalom. 2 Sam. 17:14.

Ahithophel urged upon Absalom the necessity of immediate action against David. . . . This plan was approved by the king's counselors. Had it been followed, David would surely have been slain, unless the Lord had directly interposed to save him. But a wisdom higher than that of the renowned Ahithophel was directing events. . . .

Hushai had not been called to the council, and he would not intrude himself unasked, lest suspicion should be drawn upon him as a spy; but after the assembly had dispersed, Absalom, who had a high regard for the judgment of his father's counselor, submitted to him the plan of Ahithophel. Hushai saw that if the proposed plan were followed, David would be lost. And he said, "The counsel that Ahithophel hath given is not good at this time." . . . He suggested a plan attractive to a vain and selfish nature, fond of the show of power. . . . "And Absalom and all the men of Israel said, The counsel of Hushai the Archite is better than the counsel of Ahithophel." But there was one who was not deceived—one who clearly foresaw the result of this fatal mistake of Absalom's.

Ahithophel knew that the cause of the rebels was lost. And he knew that whatever might be the fate of the prince, there was no hope for the counselor who had instigated his greatest crimes. Ahithophel had encouraged Absalom in rebellion; he had counseled him to the most abominable wickedness, to the dishonor of his father; he had advised the slaying of David and had planned its accomplishment; he had cut off the last possibility of his own reconciliation with the king; and now another was preferred before him, even by Absalom.

Jealous, angry, and desperate, Ahithophel "gat him home to his house, to his city, and put his household in order, and hanged himself, and died." Such was the result of the wisdom of one, who, with all his high endowments, did not make God his counselor.[48]

A MONUMENT OF STONES

And they took Absalom, and cast him into a great pit in the wood, and laid a very great heap of stones upon him. 2 Sam. 18:17.

David and all his company—warriors and statesmen, old men and youth, the women and the little children—in the darkness of night crossed the deep and swift-flowing river. . . . Hushai's counsel had achieved its object, gaining for David opportunity for escape; but the rash and impetuous prince could not be long restrained, and he soon set out in pursuit of his father. . . .

The place of battle was a wood near the Jordan, in which the great numbers of Absalom's army were only a disadvantage to him. Among the thickets and marshes of the forest these undisciplined troops became confused and unmanageable. . . . Absalom, seeing that the day was lost, had turned to flee, when his head was caught between the branches of a widespreading tree, and his mule going out from under him, he was left helplessly suspended, a prey to his enemies. In this condition he was found by a soldier, who, for fear of displeasing the king, spared Absalom, but reported to Joab what he had seen. Joab was restrained by no scruples. He had befriended Absalom, having twice secured his reconciliation with David, and the trust had been shamelessly betrayed. But for the advantages gained by Absalom through Joab's intercession, this rebellion, with all its horrors, could never have occurred. Now it was in Joab's power at one blow to destroy the instigator of all this evil. "And he took three darts in his hand, and thrust them through the heart of Absalom. . . ."

Thus perished the instigators of rebellion in Israel. Ahithophel had died by his own hand. The princely Absalom, whose glorious beauty had been the pride of Israel, had been cut down in the vigor of his youth, his dead body thrust into a pit, and covered with a heap of stones, in token of everlasting reproach. During his lifetime Absalom had reared for himself a costly monument in the king's dale, but the only memorial which marked his grave was that heap of stones in the wilderness.[49]

MORE THAN MONEY

Then the people rejoiced, for that they offered willingly, because with perfect heart they offered willingly to the Lord. 1 Chron. 29:9.

From the very opening of David's reign one of his most cherished plans had been that of erecting a temple to the Lord. Though he had not been permitted to execute this design, he had manifested no less zeal and earnestness in its behalf. He had provided an abundance of the most costly material—gold, silver, onyx stones, and stones of divers colors; marble, and the most precious woods. And now these valuable treasures that he had collected must be committed to others; for other hands must build the house for the ark, the symbol of God's presence.

Seeing that his end was near, the king summoned the princes of Israel, with representative men from all parts of the kingdom, to receive this legacy in trust. He desired to commit to them his dying charge and secure their concurrence and support in the great work to be accomplished. . . .

"Who then," he asked of the assembled multitude that had brought their liberal gifts—"who then is willing to consecrate his *service* this day unto the Lord?" There was a ready response from the assembly. . . .

With deepest interest the king had gathered the rich material for building and beautifying the temple. He had composed the glorious anthems that in afteryears should echo through its courts. Now his heart was made glad in God, as the chief of the fathers and the princes of Israel so nobly responded to his appeal, and offered themselves to the important work before them. . . .

All that man receives of God's bounty still belongs to God. Whatever God has bestowed in the valuable and beautiful things of earth is placed in the hands of men to test them—to sound the depths of their love for Him and their appreciation of His favors. Whether it be the treasures of wealth or of intellect, they are to be laid, a willing offering, at the feet of Jesus; the giver saying, meanwhile, with David, "All things come of thee, and of thine own have we given thee."[50]

GROWING OLD GRACEFULLY

Cast me not off in the time of old age; forsake me not when my strength faileth. Ps. 71:9.

David entreated the Lord not to forsake him in old age. And why did he thus pray? He saw that most of the aged around him were unhappy, because of the unfortunate traits of their character being increased with their age. If they had been naturally close and covetous, they were most disagreeably so in mature years. If they had been jealous, fretful, and impatient, they were especially so when aged.[51]

David was distressed as he saw that kings and nobles who seemed to have the fear of God before them while in the strength of manhood became jealous of their best friends and relatives when aged. They were in continual fear that it was selfish motives which led their friends to manifest an interest for them. They would listen to the hints and the deceptive advice of strangers in regard to those in whom they should confide. Their unrestrained jealousy sometimes burned into a flame because all did not agree with their failing judgment. Their covetousness was dreadful. They often thought that their own children and relatives were wishing them to die in order to take their place and possess their wealth, and receive the homage which had been bestowed upon them. And some were so controlled by their jealous, covetous feelings as to destroy their own children.

David marked that although the lives of some while in the strength of manhood had been righteous, as old age came upon them they seemed to lose their self-control. Satan stepped in and guided their minds, making them restless and dissatisfied. . . .

David was deeply moved; he was distressed as he looked forward to the time when he should be aged. He feared that God would leave him and that he would be as unhappy as other aged persons whose course he had noticed, and would be left to the reproach of the enemies of the Lord. With this burden upon him he earnestly prays: "Cast me not off in the time of old age; forsake me not when my strength faileth."[52]

LAST WORDS

Now these be the last words of David. 2 Sam. 23:1.

David's "last words," as recorded, are a song—a song of trust, of loftiest principle, and undying faith:

> "David the son of Jesse saith,
> And the man who was raised on high saith,
> The anointed of the God of Jacob,
> And the sweet psalmist of Israel:
> The Spirit of Jehovah spake by me:. . .
> One that ruleth over men righteously,
> That ruleth in the fear of God,
> He shall be as the light of the morning, when the
>   sun riseth,
> A morning without clouds,
> When the tender grass springeth out of the earth,
> Through clear shining after rain.
> Verily my house is not so with God,
> Yet he hath made me an everlasting covenant,
> Ordered in all things, and sure:
> For it is all my salvation, and all my desire"
>   (2 Sam. 23:1-5, RV).

Great had been David's fall, but deep was his repentance, ardent was his love, and strong his faith. He had been forgiven much, and therefore he loved much (Luke 7:48).

The psalms of David pass through the whole range of experience, from the depths of conscious guilt and self-condemnation to the loftiest faith and the most exalted communing with God. His life record declares that sin can bring only shame and woe, but that God's love and mercy can reach to the deepest depths, that faith will lift up the repenting soul to share the adoption of the sons of God. Of all the assurances which His word contains, it is one of the strongest testimonies to the faithfulness, the justice, and the covenant mercy of God. . . . Glorious are the promises made to David and his house, promises that look forward to the eternal ages, and find their complete fulfillment in Christ.[53]

A CONTRACT WITH GOD

And Solomon the son of David was strengthened in his kingdom, and the Lord his God was with him, and magnified him exceedingly. 2 Chron. 1:1.

Not in the surpassing wisdom, the fabulous riches, the far-reaching power and fame that were his lay the real glory of Solomon's early reign; but in the honor that he brought to the name of the God of Israel through a wise use of the gifts of Heaven.[1]

Noble in youth, noble in manhood, the beloved of his God, Solomon entered on a reign that gave high promise of prosperity and honor. Nations marveled at the knowledge and insight of the man to whom God had given wisdom. But the pride of prosperity brought separation from God. From the joy of divine communion Solomon turned to find satisfaction in the pleasures of sense.[2]

Satan well knew the results that would attend obedience, and during the earlier years of Solomon's reign—years glorious because of the wisdom, the beneficence, and the uprightness of the king—he sought to bring in influences that would insidiously undermine Solomon's loyalty to principle, and cause him to separate from God.[3]

Did the Lord make a mistake in placing Solomon in a position of so great responsibility? Nay. God prepared him to bear these responsibilities, and promised him grace and strength on condition of obedience. . . .

The Lord sets men in responsible places, not to act out their own wills, but His will. So long as they cherish His pure principles of government, He will bless and strengthen them, recognizing them as His instrumentalities. God never forsakes the one who is true to principle.[4]

The Lord told Solomon that if he would walk in His way, His blessing would go with him, and wisdom would be given him. But Solomon failed to keep his contract with God. He followed the promptings of his own heart, and the Lord left him to his own impulses.

Today each one has a part to act—duties to perform and responsibilities to carry. No one can act his part acceptably without wisdom from on high.[5]

AS A LITTLE CHILD

I am but a little child. . . . Give therefore thy servant an understanding heart to judge thy people. 1 Kings 3:7-9.

The language used by Solomon while praying to God before the ancient altar at Gibeon reveals his humility and his strong desire to honor God. He realized that without divine aid he was as helpless as a little child to fulfill the responsibilities resting on him. He knew that he lacked discernment, and it was a sense of his great need that led him to seek God for wisdom. In his heart there was no selfish aspiration for a knowledge that would exalt him above others. He desired to discharge faithfully the duties devolving upon him, and he chose the gift that would be the means of causing his reign to bring glory to God. Solomon was never so rich or so wise or so truly great as when he confessed, "I am but a little child: I know not how to go out or come in."

Those who today occupy positions of trust should seek to learn the lesson taught by Solomon's prayer. The higher the position a man occupies, the greater the responsibility that he has to bear, the wider will be the influence that he exerts and the greater his need of dependence on God. Ever should he remember that with the call to work comes the call to walk circumspectly before his fellow men. He is to stand before God in the attitude of a learner. Position does not give holiness of character. It is by honoring God and obeying His commands that a man is made truly great.[6]

Our petitions to God should not proceed from hearts that are filled with selfish aspirations. God exhorts us to choose those gifts that will redound to His glory. He would have us choose the heavenly instead of the earthly. He throws open before us the possibilities and advantages of a heavenly commerce. He gives encouragement to our loftiest aims, security to our choicest treasure. When the worldly possession is swept away, the believer will rejoice in his heavenly treasure, the riches that cannot be lost in any earthly disaster.[7]

WISDOM FOR THE ASKING

If any of you lack wisdom, let him ask of God, that giveth to all men liberally, and upbraideth not; and it shall be given him. James 1:5.

The God whom we serve is no respecter of persons. He who gave to Solomon the spirit of wise discernment is willing to impart the same blessing to His children today. . . . When a burden bearer desires wisdom more than he desires wealth, power, or fame, he will not be disappointed. Such a one will learn from the Great Teacher not only what to do, but how to do it in a way that will meet with the divine approval.

So long as he remains consecrated, the man whom God has endowed with discernment and ability will not manifest an eagerness for high position, neither will he seek to rule or control. Of necessity men must bear responsibilities; but instead of striving for the supremacy, he who is a true leader will pray for an understanding heart, to discern between good and evil.

The path of men who are placed as leaders is not an easy one. But they are to see in every difficulty a call to prayer. Never are they to fail of consulting the great Source of all wisdom. Strengthened and enlightened by the Master Worker, they will be enabled to stand firm against unholy influences and to discern right from wrong, good from evil. They will approve that which God approves, and will strive earnestly against the introduction of wrong principles into His cause. The wisdom that Solomon desired above riches, honor, or long life, God gave him. His petition for a quick mind, a large heart, and a tender spirit was granted.[8]

It would be well for us carefully to study Solomon's prayer, and to consider every point on which depended his receiving the rich blessings that the Lord was ready to give him.[9]

God commended Solomon's prayer. And He will today hear and commend the prayers of those who in faith and humility cry to Him for aid. He will certainly answer the fervent prayer for a preparation for service. In answer He will say, Here I am. What wilt thou that I shall do for thee? . . . He who led Solomon's mind as he made this prayer will today teach His servants how to pray for what they need.[10]

WISEST AMONG MEN

And he spake of trees, from the cedar tree that is in Lebanon even unto the hyssop that springeth out of the wall: he spake also of beasts, and of fowl, and of creeping things, and of fishes. 1 Kings 4:33.

As the years went by and Solomon's fame increased, he sought to honor God by adding to his mental and spiritual strength, and by continuing to impart to others the blessings he received. None understood better than he that it was through the favor of Jehovah that he had come into possession of power and wisdom and understanding, and that these gifts were bestowed that he might give to the world a knowledge of the King of kings.

Solomon took an especial interest in natural history, but his researches were not confined to any one branch of learning. Through a diligent study of all created things, both animate and inanimate, he gained a clear conception of the Creator. In the forces of nature, in the mineral and the animal world, and in every tree and shrub and flower, he saw a revelation of God's wisdom; and as he sought to learn more and more, his knowledge of God and his love for Him constantly increased.

Solomon's divinely inspired wisdom found expression in songs of praise and in many proverbs. . . . In the proverbs of Solomon are outlined principles of holy living and high endeavor, principles that are heaven-born and that lead to godliness, principles that should govern every act of life. It was the wide dissemination of these principles, and the recognition of God as the One to whom all praise and honor belong, that made Solomon's early reign a time of moral uplift as well as of material prosperity. . . .

O that in later years Solomon had heeded these wonderful words of wisdom! O that he who had declared, "The lips of the wise disperse knowledge" (Prov. 15:7), and who had himself taught the kings of the earth to render to the King of kings the praise they desired to give to an earthly ruler, had never with a "froward mouth," in "pride and arrogancy," taken to himself the glory due to God alone![11]

191

WHAT AN EPITAPH!

Wherefore come out from among them, and be ye separate, saith the Lord. 2 Cor. 6:17.

Many who started out in life with as fair and promising a morning, in their limited sphere, as Solomon had in his exalted station, through one false and irrevocable step in the marriage relation, lose their souls, and draw others down to ruin with them. As Solomon's wives turned his heart away from God to idolatry, so do frivolous companions, who have no depth of principle, turn away the hearts of those who were once noble and true, to vanity, corrupting pleasures, and downright vice.[12]

Solomon flattered himself that his wisdom and the power of his example would lead his wives from idolatry to the worship of the true God, and also that the alliances thus formed would draw the nations round about into close touch with Israel. Vain hope! Solomon's mistake in regarding himself as strong enough to resist the influence of heathen associates was fatal. And fatal, too, the deception that led him to hope that notwithstanding a disregard of God's law on his part, others might be led to revere and obey its sacred precepts.[13]

Let the sad memory of Solomon's apostasy warn every soul to shun the same precipice. . . . The greatest king that ever wielded a scepter, of whom it had been said that he was the beloved of God, through misplaced affection became contaminated and was miserably forsaken of his God. The mightiest ruler of the earth had failed to rule his own passions. Solomon may have been saved "as by fire," yet his repentance could not efface those high places, nor demolish those stones, which remained as evidences of his crimes. He dishonored God, choosing rather to be controlled by lust than to be a partaker of the divine nature. What a legacy Solomon's life has committed to those who would use his example to cover their own base actions. We must either transmit a heritage of good or evil. Shall our lives and our example be a blessing or a curse? Shall people look at our graves and say, He ruined me, or, He saved me?[14]

SOLD OUT

No man can serve two masters: for either he will hate the one, and love the other; or else he will hold to the one, and despise the other. Ye cannot serve God and mammon. Matt. 6:24.

So gradual was Solomon's apostasy that before he was aware of it, he had wandered far from God. Almost imperceptibly he began to trust less and less in divine guidance and blessing, and to put confidence in his own strength. . . .

Engrossed in an overmastering desire to surpass other nations in outward display, the king overlooked the need of acquiring beauty and perfection of character. In seeking to glorify himself before the world, he sold his honor and integrity. . . .

The conscientious, considerate spirit that had marked his dealings with the people during the early part of his reign was now changed. From the wisest and most merciful of rulers, he degenerated into a tyrant. Once the compassionate, God-fearing guardian of the people, he became oppressive and despotic.[15]

Men who have the use of money are to learn a lesson from the history of Solomon. Those who have a competence are in continual danger of thinking that money and position will ensure them respect, and they need not be so particular. But self-exaltation is but a bubble. By misusing the talents given him, Solomon apostatized from God. When God gives men prosperity, they are to beware of following the imaginations of their own hearts, lest they endanger the simplicity of their faith and deteriorate in religious experience.[16]

The lesson for us to learn from the history of this perverted life is the necessity of continual dependence upon the counsels of God; to carefully watch the tendency of our course, and to reform every habit calculated to draw us from God. It teaches us that great caution, watchfulness, and prayer are needed to keep undefiled the simplicity and purity of our faith. If we would rise to the highest moral excellence, and attain to the perfection of religious character, what discrimination should be used in the formation of friendships, and the choice of a companion for life![17]

TRUE RICHES

The blessing of the Lord, it maketh rich, and he addeth no sorrow with it. Prov. 10:22.

Many envied the popularity and abundant glory of Solomon, thinking that of all men he must be the most happy. But amid all that glory of artificial display the man envied is the one to be most pitied. His countenance is dark with despair. All the splendor about him is but to him mockery of the distress and anguish of his thoughts as he reviews his misspent life in seeking for happiness through indulgence and selfish gratification of every desire.[18]

In the midst of prosperity lurks danger. Throughout the ages, riches and honor have ever been attended with peril to humility and spirituality. It is not the empty cup that we have difficulty in carrying; it is the cup full to the brim that must be carefully balanced. Affliction and adversity may cause sorrow, but it is prosperity that is most dangerous to spiritual life. Unless the human subject is in constant submission to the will of God, unless he is sanctified by the truth, prosperity will surely arouse the natural inclination to presumption.

In the valley of humiliation, where men depend on God to teach them and to guide their every step, there is comparative safety. But the men who stand, as it were, on a lofty pinnacle, and who, because of their position, are supposed to possess great wisdom—these are in gravest peril. Unless such men make God their dependence, they will surely fall.

Whenever pride and ambition are indulged, the life is marred, for pride, feeling no need, closes the heart against the infinite blessings of Heaven. He who makes self-glorification his aim will find himself destitute of the grace of God, through whose efficiency the truest riches and the most satisfying joys are won. But he who gives all and does all for Christ will know the fulfillment of the promise, "The blessing of the Lord, it maketh rich, and He addeth no sorrow with it."[19]

All the sins and excesses of Solomon can be traced to his great mistake in ceasing to rely upon God for wisdom, and to walk in humility before Him.[20]

AT THE CROSSROADS

And there came of all people to hear the wisdom of Solomon, from all kings of the earth, which had heard of his wisdom. 1 Kings 4:34.

In the days of Solomon the kingdom of Israel extended from Hamath on the north to Egypt on the south, and from the Mediterranean Sea to the river Euphrates. Through this territory ran many natural highways of the world's commerce, and caravans from distant lands were constantly passing to and fro. Thus there was given to Solomon and his people opportunity to reveal to men of all nations the character of the King of kings, and to teach them to reverence and obey Him. . . .

Placed at the head of a nation that had been set as a beacon light to the surrounding nations, Solomon should have used his God-given wisdom and power of influence in organizing and directing a great movement for the enlightenment of those who were ignorant of God and His truth. Thus multitudes would have been won to allegiance to the divine precepts, Israel would have been shielded from the evils practiced by the heathen, and the Lord of glory would have been greatly honored. But Solomon lost sight of this high purpose. He failed of improving his splendid opportunities for enlightening those who were continually passing through his territory or tarrying at the principal cities.

The missionary spirit that God had implanted in the heart of Solomon and in the hearts of all true Israelites was supplanted by a spirit of commercialism. The opportunities afforded by contact with many nations were used for personal aggrandizement. . . .

In this our day the opportunities for coming into contact with men and women of all classes and many nationalities are much greater than in the days of Israel. The thoroughfares of travel have multiplied a thousandfold. Like Christ, the messengers of the Most High today should take their position in these great thoroughfares, where they can meet the passing multitudes from all parts of the world. Like Him, hiding self in God, they are to sow the gospel seed, presenting before others the precious truths of Holy Scripture that will take deep root in mind and heart, and spring up unto life eternal.[21]

A LATE AWAKENING

Then I looked on all the works that my hands had wrought, and on the labour that I had laboured to do: and, behold, all was vanity and vexation of spirit, and there was no profit under the sun. Eccl. 2:11.

By his own bitter experience, Solomon learned the emptiness of a life that seeks in earthly things its highest good. He erected altars to heathen gods, only to learn how vain is their promise of rest to the spirit. Gloomy and soul-harassing thoughts troubled him night and day. For him there was no longer any joy of life or peace of mind, and the future was dark with despair.

Yet the Lord forsook him not. By messages of reproof and by severe judgments, He sought to arouse the king to a realization of the sinfulness of his course. . . . At last the Lord, through a prophet, delivered to Solomon the startling message: . . . "I will surely rend the kingdom from thee, and will give it to thy servant. Notwithstanding in thy days I will not do it for David thy father's sake: but I will rend it out of the hand of thy son."

Awakened as from a dream by this sentence of judgment pronounced against him and his house, Solomon with quickened conscience began to see his folly in its true light. Chastened in spirit, with mind and body enfeebled, he turned wearied and thirsting from earth's broken cisterns, to drink once more at the fountain of life. . . . He could never hope to escape the blasting results of sin; he could never free his mind from all remembrance of the self-indulgent course he had been pursuing; but he would endeavor earnestly to dissuade others from following after folly. . . .

The true penitent does not put his past sins from his remembrance. He does not, as soon as he has obtained peace, grow unconcerned in regard to the mistakes he has made. He thinks of those who have been led into evil by his course, and tries in every possible way to lead them back into the true path. The clearer the light that he has entered into, the stronger is his desire to set the feet of others in the right way.[22]

THE VOICE OF EXPERIENCE

Rejoice, O young man, in thy youth; and let thy heart cheer thee in the days of thy youth, and walk in the ways of thine heart, and in the sight of thine eyes: but know thou, that for all these things God will bring thee into judgment. Eccl. 11:9.

The lesson to be learned from the life of Solomon has a special moral bearing upon the life of the aged, of those who are no longer climbing the mountain but are descending and facing the western sun. We expect to see defects in the characters of youth who are not controlled by love and faith in Jesus Christ. We see youth wavering between right and wrong, vacillating between fixed principle and the almost overpowering current of evil that is bearing them off their feet to ruin. But of those of mature age we expect better things. We look for the character to be established, for principles to be rooted, and for them to be beyond the danger of pollution. But the case of Solomon is before us as a beacon of warning. When thou, aged pilgrim who hast fought the battles of life, thinkest that thou standest take heed lest thou fall. How, in Solomon's case, was weak, vacillating character, naturally bold, firm, and determined, shaken like a reed in the wind under the tempter's power! How was an old gnarled cedar of Lebanon, a sturdy oak of Bashan, bent before the blast of temptation! What a lesson for all who desire to save their souls to watch unto prayer continually! What a warning to keep the grace of Christ ever in their heart, to battle with inward corruptions and outward temptations![23]

Let none venture into sin as he did, in the hope that they too may recover themselves. Sin can be indulged only at the peril of infinite loss. But none who have fallen need give themselves up to despair. Aged men, once honored of God, may have defiled their souls, sacrificing virtue on the altar of lust; but there is still hope for them if they repent, forsake sin, and turn to God.

The misapplication of noble talents in Solomon's case should be a warning to all. Goodness alone is true greatness.[24]

UNSANCTIFIED SKILL

And Huram finished the work that he was to make for king Solomon for the house of God. 2 Chron. 4:11.

Chosen men were specially endowed by God with skill and wisdom for the construction of the wilderness tabernacle (Ex. 35:30-35). . . . The descendants of these men inherited to a large degree the skill conferred upon their forefathers. . . . For a time these men remained humble and unselfish; but gradually, almost imperceptibly, they lost their hold upon God and His truth. They began to ask for higher wages because of their superior skill. In some instances their request was granted, but more often those asking higher wages found employment in the surrounding nations. . . . It was to these apostates that Solomon looked for a master workman to superintend the construction of the temple on Mount Moriah. . . .

This master workman, Huram, was a descendant, on his mother's side, of Aholiab, to whom, hundreds of years before, God had given special wisdom for the construction of the tabernacle. Thus at the head of Solomon's company of workmen there was placed an unsanctified man, who demanded large wages because of his unusual skill. . . . The baleful influences set in operation by the employment of this man of a grasping spirit permeated all branches of the Lord's service, and extended throughout Solomon's kingdom. . . . Extravagance and corruption were to be seen on every hand. The poor were oppressed by the rich; the spirit of self-sacrifice in God's service was well-nigh lost.

Herein lies a most important lesson for God's people today—a lesson that many are slow to learn. . . . Those who claim to be followers of the Master Worker, and who engage in His service as colaborers with God, are to bring into their work the exactitude and skill, the tact and wisdom, that the God of perfection required in the building of the earthly tabernacle. And now, as in that time and as in the days of Christ's earthly ministry, devotion to God and a spirit of sacrifice should be regarded as the first requisites of acceptable service.[25]

PRAISE WHERE IT BELONGS

Blessed be the Lord thy God, which delighted in thee, to set thee on the throne of Israel: because the Lord loved Israel for ever, therefore made he thee king, to do judgment and justice. 1 Kings 10:9.

A Greater than Solomon was the designer of the temple; the wisdom and glory of God stood there revealed. Those who were unacquainted with this fact naturally admired and praised Solomon as the architect and builder; but the king disclaimed any honor for its conception or erection.

Thus it was when the Queen of Sheba came to visit Solomon. Hearing of his wisdom and of the magnificent temple he had built, she determined "to prove him with hard questions" and to see for herself his famous works. Attended by a retinue of servants, and with camels bearing "spices, and gold in abundance, and precious stones," she made the long journey to Jerusalem. "And when she was come to Solomon, she communed with him of all that was in her heart." She talked with him of the mysteries of nature; and Solomon taught her of the God of nature, the great Creator, who dwells in the highest heaven and rules over all. "Solomon told her all her questions: there was not anything hid from the king, which he told her not."

"When the Queen of Sheba had seen all Solomon's wisdom, and the house that he had built, . . . there was no more spirit in her." "It was a true report," she acknowledged, "which I heard in mine own land of thine acts, and of thy wisdom: howbeit I believed not their words, until I came, and mine eyes had seen it:" "and, behold, the half was not told me: thy wisdom and prosperity exceedeth the fame which I heard.". . .

By the time of the close of her visit the queen had been so fully taught by Solomon as to the source of his wisdom and prosperity that she was constrained, not to extol the human agent, but to exclaim, "Blessed be the Lord thy God, which delighted in thee, to set thee on the throne of Israel: because the Lord loved Israel forever, therefore made He thee king, to do judgment and justice." This is the impression that God designed should be made upon all peoples.[26]

DISGRACEFUL MONUMENTS

There is an evil which I have seen under the sun, as an error which proceedeth from the ruler: folly is set in great dignity. Eccl. 10:5, 6.

In the days of King Josiah a strange appearance could be seen opposite the temple of God. Crowning the eminence of the Mount of Olives, peering above the groves of myrtle and olive trees, were unseemly, gigantic idols. Josiah gave commandment that these idols should be destroyed. This was done, and the broken fragments rolled down the channel of the Kidron. The shrines were left a mass of ruins.

But the question was asked by many a devout worshiper, How came that architecture on the opposite side of the Jehoshaphat ravine, thus impiously confronting the temple of God? The truthful answer must be made: The builder was Solomon, the greatest king that ever wielded a sceptre. These idols bore testimony that he who had been honored and applauded as the wisest among kings, became a humiliating wreck. . . .

His once noble character, bold and true for God and righteousness, became deteriorated. His profligate expenditure for selfish indulgence made him the instrument of Satan's devices. His conscience became hardened. His conduct as a judge changed from equity and righteousness to tyranny and oppression. . . . Solomon tried to incorporate light with darkness, Christ with Belial, purity with impurity. But in the place of converting the heathen to the truth, pagan sentiments incorporated themselves with his religion. He became an apostate.[27]

The marks of Solomon's apostasy lived ages after him. In the days of Christ, the worshipers in the temple could look, just opposite them, upon the Mount of Offense, and be reminded that the builder of their rich and glorious temple, the most renowned of all kings, had separated himself from God, and reared altars to heathen idols; that the mightiest ruler on earth had failed in ruling his own spirit. Solomon went down to death a repentant man; but his repentance and tears could not efface from the Mount of Offense the signs of his miserable departure from God. Ruined walls and broken pillars bore silent witness for a thousand years to the apostasy of the greatest king that ever sat upon an earthly throne.[28]

"ALL ISRAEL WITH HIM"

It came to pass, when Rehoboam had established the kingdom, and had strengthened himself, he forsook the law of the Lord, and all Israel with him. 2 Chron. 12:1.

The extravagance of Solomon's reign during his apostasy had led him to tax the people heavily and to require of them much menial service. . . . Had Rehoboam and his inexperienced counselors understood the divine will concerning Israel, they would have listened to the request of the people for decided reforms in the administration of the government. But in the hour of opportunity that came to them during the meeting in Shechem, they failed to reason from cause to effect. . . .

The pen of inspiration has traced the sad record of Solomon's successor as one who failed to exert a strong influence for loyalty to Jehovah. Naturally headstrong, confident, self-willed, and inclined to idolatry, nevertheless, had he placed his trust wholly in God, he would have developed strength of character, steadfast faith, and submission to the divine requirements. But as time passed, the king put his trust in the power of position and in the strongholds he had fortified. Little by little he gave way to inherited weaknesses, until he threw his influence wholly on the side of idolatry. . . .

How sad, how filled with significance, the words, "And all Israel with him"! The people whom God had chosen to stand as a light to the surrounding nations were turning from their Source of strength and seeking to become like the nations about them. As with Solomon, so with Rehoboam—the influence of wrong example led many astray. And as with them, so to a greater or less degree is it today with everyone who gives himself up to work evil—the influence of wrongdoing is not confined to the doer. No man liveth unto himself. None perish alone in their iniquity. Every life is a light that brightens and cheers the pathway of others, or a dark and desolating influence that tends toward despair and ruin. We lead others either upward to happiness and immortal life, or downward to sorrow and eternal death. And if by our deeds we strengthen or force into activity the evil powers of those around us, we share their sin.[29]

A PARALYZED ARM

And his hand, which he put forth against him, dried up, so that he could not pull it in again to him. 1 Kings 13:4.

Jeroboam was filled with a spirit of defiance against God and attempted to restrain the one who had delivered the message. In wrath "he put forth his hand from the altar" and cried out, "Lay hold on him." His impetuous act met with swift rebuke. The hand outstretched against the messenger of Jehovah suddenly became powerless and withered, and could not be withdrawn.

Terror-stricken, the king appealed to the prophet to intercede with God in his behalf. . . . "And the man of God besought the Lord, and the king's hand was restored him again, and became as it was before."

Vain had been Jeroboam's effort to invest with solemnity the dedication of a strange altar, respect for which would have led to disrespect for the worship of Jehovah in the temple at Jerusalem. By the message of the prophet, the king of Israel should have been led to repent and to renounce his wicked purposes, which were turning the people away from the true worship of God. But he hardened his heart and determined to follow a way of his own choosing. . . .

The Lord seeks to save, not to destroy. He delights in the rescue of sinners. "As I live, saith the Lord God, I have no pleasure in the death of the wicked" (Eze. 33:11). By warnings and entreaties He calls the wayward to cease from their evil-doing and to turn to Him and live. He gives His chosen messengers a holy boldness, that those who hear may fear and be brought to repentance. How firmly the man of God rebuked the king! And this firmness was essential; in no other way could the existing evils have been rebuked. The Lord gave His servant boldness, that an abiding impression might be made on those who heard. The messengers of the Lord are never to fear the face of man, but are to stand unflinchingly for the right. So long as they put their trust in God, they need not fear; for He who gives them their commission gives them also the assurance of His protecting care.[30]

ASA TRUSTED GOD

And Asa cried unto the Lord his God, and said, Lord, it is nothing with thee to help, whether with many, or with them that have no power: help us, O Lord our God; for we rest on thee, and in thy name we go against this multitude. O Lord, thou art our God; let not man prevail against thee. 2 Chron. 14:11.

The faith of Asa was put to a severe test when "Zerah the Ethiopian with an host of a thousand thousand, and three hundred chariots," invaded his kingdom. In this crisis Asa did not put his trust in the "fenced cities in Judah" that he had built, with "walls, and towers, gates, and bars," nor in the "mighty men of valor" in his carefully trained army. The king's trust was in Jehovah of hosts. . . . Setting his forces in battle array, he sought the help of God.

The opposing armies now stood face to face. It was a time of test and trial to those who served the Lord. Had every sin been confessed? Had the men of Judah full confidence in God's power to deliver? Such thoughts as these were in the minds of the leaders. From every human viewpoint the vast host from Egypt would sweep everything before it. But in time of peace Asa had not been giving himself to amusement and pleasure; he had been preparing for any emergency. He had an army trained for conflict; he had endeavored to lead his people to make their peace with God. And now, although his forces were fewer in number than the enemy, his faith in the One whom he had made his trust did not weaken.

Having sought the Lord in the days of prosperity, the king could now rely upon Him in the day of adversity. His petitions showed that he was not a stranger to God's wonderful power. . . .

The prayer of Asa is one that every Christian believer may fittingly offer. . . . In life's conflict we must meet evil agencies that have arrayed themselves against the right. Our hope is not in man, but in the living God. With full assurance of faith we may expect that He will unite His omnipotence with the efforts of human instrumentalities, for the glory of His name. Clad with the armor of His righteousness, we may gain the victory over every foe.[31]

JEZEBEL'S BLIGHTING INFLUENCE

But there was none like unto Ahab, which did sell himself to work wickedness in the sight of the Lord, whom Jezebel his wife stirred up. 1 Kings 21:25.

Ahab was weak in moral power. His union by marriage with an idolatrous woman of decided character and positive temperament resulted disastrously both to himself and to the nation. Unprincipled, and with no high standard of rightdoing, his character was easily molded by the determined spirit of Jezebel. . . .

Under the blighting influence of Ahab's rule, Israel wandered far from the living God and corrupted their ways before Him. . . . The dark shadow of apostasy covered the whole land. Images of Baalim and Ashtoreth were everywhere to be seen. Idolatrous temples and consecrated groves, wherein were worshiped the works of men's hands, were multiplied. The air was polluted with the smoke of the sacrifices offered to false gods. Hill and vale resounded with the drunken cries of a heathen priesthood who sacrificed to the sun, moon, and stars.

Through the influence of Jezebel and her impious priests, the people were taught that the idol gods that had been set up were deities, ruling by their mystic power the elements of earth, fire, and water. All the bounties of heaven—the running brooks, the streams of living water, the gentle dew, the showers of rain which refreshed the earth and caused the fields to bring forth abundantly—were ascribed to the favor of Baal and Ashtoreth, instead of to the Giver of every good and perfect gift. The people forgot that the hills and valleys, the streams and fountains, were in the hand of the living God, that He controlled the sun, the clouds of heaven, and all the powers of nature. . . .

In their blind folly they chose to reject God and His worship.[32]

How few realize the power of an unconsecrated woman. . . . God would have been with Ahab if he had walked in the counsel of heaven. But Ahab did not do this. He married a woman given to idolatry. Jezebel had more power over the king than God had. She led him into idolatry, and with him the people.[33]

A VOICE IN THE WILDERNESS

And Elijah the Tishbite, . . . said unto Ahab, As the Lord God of Israel liveth, before whom I stand, there shall not be dew nor rain these years, but according to my word. 1 Kings 17:1.

Among the mountains of Gilead, east of the Jordan, there dwelt in the days of Ahab a man of faith and prayer whose fearless ministry was destined to check the rapid spread of apostasy in Israel. Far removed from any city of renown, and occupying no high station in life, Elijah the Tishbite nevertheless entered upon his mission confident in God's purpose to prepare the way before him and to give him abundant success. The word of faith and power was upon his lips, and his whole life was devoted to the work of reform. His was the voice of one crying in the wilderness to rebuke sin and press back the tide of evil. And while he came to the people as a reprover of sin, his message offered the balm of Gilead to the sin-sick souls of all who desired to be healed. . . .

To Elijah was entrusted the mission of delivering to Ahab Heaven's message of judgment. He did not seek to be the Lord's messenger; the word of the Lord came to him. And jealous for the honor of God's cause, he did not hesitate to obey the divine summons, though to obey seemed to invite swift destruction at the hand of the wicked king. . . .

It was only by the exercise of strong faith in the unfailing power of God's word that Elijah delivered his message. Had he not possessed implicit confidence in the One whom he served, he would never have appeared before Ahab. On his way to Samaria, Elijah had passed by ever-flowing streams, hills covered with verdure, and stately forests that seemed beyond the reach of drought. Everything on which the eye rested was clothed with beauty. The prophet might have wondered how the streams that had never ceased their flow could become dry, or how those hills and valleys could be burned with drought. But he gave no place to unbelief. He fully believed that God would humble apostate Israel, and that through judgments they would be brought to repentance. The fiat of Heaven had gone forth; God's word could not fail; and at the peril of his life Elijah fearlessly fulfilled his commission.[34]

SHARING HER MORSEL

And Elijah said unto her, Fear not; go and do as thou hast said: but make me thereof a little cake first, and bring it unto me, and after make for thee and for thy son. For thus saith the Lord God of Israel, The barrel of meal shall not waste, neither shall the cruse of oil fail, until the day that the Lord sendeth rain upon the earth. 1 Kings 17:13, 14.

This woman was not an Israelite. She had never had the privileges and blessings that the chosen people of God had enjoyed; but she was a believer in the true God and had walked in all the light that was shining on her pathway. And now, when there was no safety for Elijah in the land of Israel, God sent him to this woman to find an asylum in her home. . . .

In this poverty-stricken home the famine pressed sore, and the pitifully meager fare seemed about to fail. The coming of Elijah on the very day when the widow feared that she must give up the struggle to sustain life tested to the utmost her faith in the power of the living God to provide for her necessities. But even in her dire extremity she bore witness to her faith by a compliance with the request of the stranger who was asking her to share her last morsel with him. . . .

No greater test of faith than this could have been required. The widow had hitherto treated all strangers with kindness and liberality. Now, regardless of the suffering that might result to herself and child, and trusting in the God of Israel to supply her every need, she met this supreme test of hospitality. . . .

The widow of Zarephath shared her morsel with Elijah, and in return her life and that of her son were preserved. And to all who, in time of trial and want, give sympathy and assistance to others more needy, God has promised great blessing.[35]

That God who cared for Elijah in the time of famine will not pass by one of His self-sacrificing children. He who has numbered the hairs of their head will care for them, and in the days of famine they will be satisfied. While the wicked are perishing all around them for want of bread, their bread and water will be sure.[36]

"MORE BLESSED TO GIVE"

But my God shall supply all your need according to his riches in glory by Christ Jesus. Phil. 4:19.

Read the story of the widow of Sarepta. To this woman in a heathen land God sent His servant in time of famine to ask for food. . . . Wonderful was the hospitality shown to God's prophet by this Phoenician woman, and wonderfully were her faith and generosity rewarded. . . .

God has not changed. His power is no less now than in the days of Elijah. . . . To His faithful servants today as well as to His first disciples Christ's words apply: "He that receiveth you receiveth me, and he that receiveth me receiveth him that sent me" (Matt. 10:40). No act of kindness shown in His name will fail to be recognized and rewarded. And in the same tender recognition Christ includes even the feeblest and lowliest of the family of God. "Whosoever shall give to drink," He says, "unto one of these little ones"—those who are as children in their faith and their knowledge of Christ—"a cup of cold water only in the name of a disciple, verily I say unto you, he shall in no wise lose his reward" (Matt. 10:42).

Poverty need not shut us out from showing hospitality. We are to impart what we have. There are those who struggle for a livelihood and who have great difficulty in making their income meet their necessities; but they love Jesus in the person of His saints and are ready to show hospitality to believers and unbelievers, trying to make their visits profitable. At the family board and the family altar the guests are made welcome. The season of prayer makes its impression on those who receive entertainment, and even one visit may mean the saving of a soul from death. For this work the Lord makes a reckoning, saying: "I will repay.". . .

"Man doth not live by bread only," and as we impart to others our temporal food, so we are to impart hope and courage and Christlike love. . . . And the assurance is ours: "God is able to make all grace abound toward you; that ye, always having all sufficiency in all things, may abound to every good work" (2 Cor. 9:8).[37]

ELIJAH BEFORE AHAB

And he answered, I have not troubled Israel; but thou, and thy father's house, in that ye have forsaken the commandments of the Lord, and thou hast followed Baalim. 1 Kings 18:18.

Through the long years of drought and famine, Elijah prayed earnestly that the hearts of Israel might be turned from idolatry to allegiance to God. Patiently the prophet waited, while the hand of the Lord rested heavily on the stricken land. . . .

At last, "after many days," the word of the Lord came to Elijah, "Go, show thyself unto Ahab; and I will send rain upon the earth.". . .

The king and the prophet stand face to face. Though Ahab is filled with passionate hatred, yet in the presence of Elijah he seems unmanned, powerless. In his first faltering words, "Art thou he that troubleth Israel?" he unconsciously reveals the inmost feelings of his heart. Ahab knew that it was by the word of God that the heavens had become as brass, yet he sought to cast upon the prophet the blame for the heavy judgments resting on the land. . . .

Standing in conscious innocence before Ahab, Elijah makes no attempt to excuse himself or to flatter the king. Nor does he seek to evade the king's wrath by the good news that the drought is almost over. He has no apology to offer. Indignant, and jealous for the honor of God, he casts back the imputation of Ahab, fearlessly declaring to the king that it is *his* sins, and the sins of *his* fathers, that have brought upon Israel this terrible calamity. . . .

Today there is need of the voice of stern rebuke; for grievous sins have separated the people from God. . . . The smooth sermons so often preached make no lasting impression; the trumpet does not give a certain sound. Men are not cut to the heart by the plain, sharp truths of God's word. . . .

God calls for men like Elijah, Nathan, and John the Baptist—men who will bear His message with faithfulness, regardless of the consequences; men who will speak the truth bravely, though it call for the sacrifice of all they have.[38]

GOD'S HEROES

How long halt ye between two opinions? if the Lord be God, follow him: but if Baal, then follow him. 1 Kings 18:21.

Elijah, amid the general apostasy, did not seek to hide the fact that he served the God of heaven. Baal's prophets numbered four hundred and fifty, his priests, four hundred, and his worshipers were thousands; yet Elijah did not try to make it appear that he was on the popular side. He grandly stood alone. . . . With clear, trumpetlike tones Elijah addressed the vast multitude: "How long halt ye between two opinions? . . ." . . . Where are the Elijahs of today?[39]

God would have His honor exalted before men as supreme, and His counsels confirmed in the eyes of the people. The witness of the prophet Elijah on Mount Carmel gives the example of one who stood wholly for God and His work in the earth. . . . "Let it be known this day that thou art God in Israel," he prays, "and that I am thy servant, and that I have done all these things at thy word. Hear me, O Lord," he pleads, "hear me.". . .

His zeal for God's glory and his deep love for the house of Israel present lessons for the instruction of all who stand today as representatives of God's work in the earth.[40]

Nothing is gained by cowardice or by fearing to let it be known that we are God's commandment-keeping people. Hiding our light, as if ashamed of our faith, will result only in disaster. God will leave us to our own weakness. May the Lord forbid that we should refuse to let our light shine forth in any place to which He may call us. If we venture to go forth of ourselves, following our own ideas, our own plans, and leave Jesus behind, we need not expect to gain fortitude, courage, or spiritual strength. God has had moral heroes, and He has them now—those who are not ashamed of being His peculiar people. Their wills and plans are all subordinate to the law of God. The love of Jesus has led them not to count their lives dear unto themselves. Their work has been to catch the light from the word of God and to let it shine forth in clear, steady rays to the world. "Fidelity to God" is their motto.[41]

IDOLATRY THEN AND NOW

Thou shalt have no other gods before me. Ex. 20:3.

Though in a different form, idolatry exists in the Christian world today as verily as it existed among ancient Israel in the days of Elijah. The god of many professedly wise men, of philosophers, poets, politicians, journalists—the god of polished fashionable circles, of many colleges and universities, even of some theological institutions—is little better than Baal, the sun-god of Phoenicia.

No error accepted by the Christian world strikes more boldly against the authority of Heaven, . . . none is more pernicious in its results than the modern doctrine, so rapidly gaining ground, that God's law is no longer binding upon men.[42]

The Bible is within the reach of all, but there are few who really accept it as the guide of life. Infidelity prevails to an alarming extent, not in the world merely, but in the church. Many have come to deny doctrines which are the very pillars of the Christian faith. The great facts of creation as presented by the inspired writers, the fall of man, the atonement, and the perpetuity of the law of God, are practically rejected, either wholly or in part, by a large share of the professedly Christian world. Thousands who pride themselves upon their wisdom and independence regard it as an evidence of weakness to place implicit confidence in the Bible; they think it a proof of superior talent and learning to cavil at the Scriptures and to spiritualize and explain away their most important truths. Many ministers are teaching their people, and many professors and teachers are instructing their students, that the law of God has been changed or abrogated; and those who regard its requirements as still valid, to be literally obeyed, are thought to be deserving only of ridicule or contempt.[43]

The last great conflict between truth and error is but the final struggle of the long-standing controversy concerning the law of God. Upon this battle we are now entering.[44]

WAITING UPON GOD

And Elijah said unto Ahab, Get thee up, eat and drink; for there is a sound of abundance of rain. 1 Kings 18:41.

It was not because of any outward evidence that the showers were about to fall, that Elijah could so confidently bid Ahab prepare for rain. The prophet saw no clouds in the heavens; he heard no thunder. He simply spoke the word that the Spirit of the Lord had moved him to speak in response to his own strong faith. . . . Having done all that was in his power to do, he knew that Heaven would freely bestow the blessings foretold. The same God who had sent the drought had promised an abundance of rain as the reward of rightdoing; and now Elijah waited for the promised outpouring. In an attitude of humility, "his face between his knees," he interceded with God in behalf of penitent Israel. . . .

Six times the servant returned with the word that there was no sign of rain in the brassy heavens. Undaunted, Elijah sent him forth once more; and this time the servant returned with the word, "Behold, there ariseth a little cloud out of the sea, like a man's hand."

This was enough. Elijah did not wait for the heavens to gather blackness. In that small cloud he beheld by faith an abundance of rain; and he acted in harmony with his faith. . . . As he prayed, his faith reached out and grasped the promises of Heaven, and he persevered in prayer until his petitions were answered. He did not wait for the full evidence that God had heard him, but was willing to venture all on the slightest token of divine favor. And yet what he was enabled to do under God, all may do in their sphere of activity in God's service. . . .

Faith such as this is needed in the world today—faith that will lay hold on the promises of God's word and refuse to let go until Heaven hears. . . .

With the persevering faith of Jacob, with the unyielding persistence of Elijah, we may present our petitions to the Father, claiming all that He has promised. The honor of His throne is staked for the fulfillment of His word.[45]

EMPTIED OF SELF

Elias was a man subject to like passions as we are, and he prayed earnestly that it might not rain: and it rained not on the earth by the space of three years and six months. And he prayed again, and the heaven gave rain, and the earth brought forth her fruit. James 5:17, 18.

Important lessons are presented to us in the experience of Elijah. When upon Mount Carmel he offered the prayer for rain, his faith was tested, but he persevered in making known his request unto God. . . . Had he given up in discouragement at the sixth time, his prayer would not have been answered, but he persevered till the answer came. We have a God whose ear is not closed to our petitions; and if we prove His word, He will honor our faith. He wants us to have all our interests interwoven with His interests, and then He can safely bless us; for we shall not then take glory to self when the blessing is ours, but shall render all the praise to God. God does not always answer our prayers the first time we call upon Him; for should He do this, we might take it for granted that we had a right to all the blessings and favors He bestowed upon us. Instead of searching our hearts to see if any evil was entertained by us, any sin indulged, we should become careless, and fail to realize our dependence upon Him, and our need of His help.

Elijah humbled himself until he was in a condition where he would not take the glory to himself. This is the condition upon which the Lord hears prayer, for then we shall give the praise to Him. The custom of offering praise to men is one that results in great evil. One praises another, and thus men are led to feel that glory and honor belong to them. When you exalt man, you lay a snare for his soul, and do just as Satan would have you. . . . God alone is worthy to be glorified.[46]

As he [Elijah] searched his heart, he seemed to be less and less, both in his own estimation and in the sight of God. It seemed to him that he was nothing, and that God was everything; and when he reached the point of renouncing self, while he clung to the Savior as his only strength and righteousness, the answer came.[47]

OVERWHELMED BY DISCOURAGEMENT

And he requested for himself that he might die; and said, It is enough; now, O Lord, take away my life; for I am not better than my fathers. 1 Kings 19:4.

It would seem that after showing courage so undaunted, after triumphing so completely over king and priests and people, Elijah could never afterward have given way to despondency nor been awed into timidity. But he who had been blessed with so many evidences of God's loving care was not above the frailties of mankind, and in this dark hour his faith and courage forsook him. . . . Had he remained where he was, had he made God his refuge and strength, standing steadfast for the truth, he would have been shielded from harm. The Lord would have given him another signal victory by sending His judgments on Jezebel. . . .

Into the experience of all there come times of keen disappointment and utter discouragement—days when sorrow is the portion, and it is hard to believe that God is still the kind benefactor of His earthborn children; days when troubles harass the soul, till death seems preferable to life. It is then that many lose their hold on God. . . . Could we at such times discern with spiritual insight the meaning of God's providences we should see angels seeking to save us from ourselves, striving to plant our feet upon a foundation more firm than the everlasting hills, and new faith, new life, would spring into being. . . .

For the disheartened there is a sure remedy—faith, prayer, work. Faith and activity will impart assurance and satisfaction that will increase day by day. . . . In the darkest days, when appearances seem most forbidding, fear not. Have faith in God. He knows your need. He has all power. His infinite love and compassion never weary. . . . And He will bestow upon His faithful servants the measure of efficiency that their need demands. . . .

Did God forsake Elijah in his hour of trial? Oh, no! He loved His servant no less when Elijah felt himself forsaken of God and man than when, in answer to his prayer, fire flashed from heaven and illuminated the mountaintop.[48]

WHAT DOEST THOU HERE?

And he came thither unto a cave, and lodged there; and, behold, the word of the Lord came to him, and he said unto him, What doest thou here, Elijah? 1 Kings 19:9.

Elijah's retreat on Mount Horeb, though hidden from man, was known to God; and the weary and discouraged prophet was not left to struggle alone with the powers of darkness that were pressing upon him. . . .

God met His tried servant with the inquiry, "What doest thou here, Elijah?" I sent you to the brook Cherish and afterward to the widow of Sarepta. I commissioned you to return to Israel and to stand before the idolatrous priests on Carmel, and I girded you with strength to guide the chariot of the king to the gate of Jezreel. But who sent you on this hasty flight into the wilderness? What errand have you here? . . .

Much depends on the unceasing activity of those who are true and loyal, and for this reason Satan puts forth every possible effort to thwart the divine purpose to be wrought out through the obedient. He causes some to lose sight of their high and holy mission, and to become satisfied with the pleasures of this life. . . . Others he causes to flee in discouragement from duty, because of opposition or persecution. . . . To every child of God whose voice the enemy of souls has succeeded in silencing, the question is addressed, "What doest thou here?" I commissioned you to go into all the world and preach the gospel, to prepare a people for the day of God. Why are you here? . . .

Of families, as of individuals, the question is asked, "What doest thou here?" In many churches there are families well instructed in the truths of God's word, who might widen the sphere of their influence by moving to places in need of the ministry they are capable of giving. God calls for Christian families to go into the dark places of the earth and work wisely and perseveringly for those who are enshrouded in spiritual gloom. . . . For the sake of worldly advantage, for the sake of acquiring scientific knowledge, men are willing to venture into pestilential regions and to endure hardship and privation. Where are those who are willing to do as much for the sake of telling others of the Savior?[49]

ELIJAHS NEEDED TODAY

Yet I have left me seven thousand in Israel, all the knees which have not bowed unto Baal, and every mouth which hath not kissed him. 1 Kings 19:18.

Elijah had thought that he alone in Israel was a worshiper of the true God. But He who reads the hearts of all revealed to the prophet that there were many others who, through the long years of apostasy, had remained true to Him. . . .

From Elijah's experience during those days of discouragement and apparent defeat there are many lessons to be drawn, lessons invaluable to the servants of God in this age, marked as it is by general departure from right. The apostasy prevailing today is similar to that which in the prophet's day overspread Israel. In the exaltation of the human above the divine, in the praise of popular leaders, in the worship of mammon, and in the placing of the teachings of science above the truths of revelation, multitudes today are following after Baal. Doubt and unbelief are exercising their baleful influence over mind and heart, and many are substituting for the oracles of God the theories of men. It is publicly taught that we have reached a time when human reason should be exalted above the teachings of the Word. The law of God, the divine standard of righteousness, is declared to be of no effect. The enemy of all truth is working with deceptive power to cause men and women to place human institutions where God should be, and to forget that which was ordained for the happiness and salvation of mankind.

Yet this apostasy, widespread as it has come to be, is not universal. Not all in the world are lawless and sinful; not all have taken sides with the enemy. God has many . . . who are hoping against hope that Jesus will come soon to end the reign of sin and death. . . . These need the personal help of those who have learned to know God and the power of His word. . . . As those who have an understanding of Bible truth try to seek out the men and women who are longing for light, angels of God will attend them. . . . Many will cease to pay homage to man-made institutions and will take their stand fearlessly on the side of God and His laws.[50]

215

IN MOMENTS OF WEAKNESS

And he said, I have been very jealous for the Lord God of hosts:
because the children of Israel have forsaken thy covenant, thrown
down thine altars, and slain thy prophets with the sword; and I, even
I only, am left; and they seek my life, to take it away. 1 Kings 19:14.

If, under trying circumstances, men of spiritual power, pressed
beyond measure, become discouraged and desponding, if at times
they see nothing desirable in life, that they should choose it, this is
nothing strange or new. Let all such remember that one of the mightiest of the prophets fled for his life before the rage of an infuriated
woman. . . . Those who, while spending their life energies in self-
sacrificing labor, are tempted to give way to despondency and distrust, may gather courage from the experience of Elijah. . . .

It is at the time of greatest weakness that Satan assails the soul
with the fiercest temptations. . . . He who had maintained his trust in
Jehovah during the years of drought and famine, he who had stood
undaunted before Ahab, he who throughout that trying day on
Carmel had stood before the whole nation of Israel the sole witness
to the true God, in a moment of weariness allowed the fear of death
to overcome his faith in God. . . .

When we are encompassed with doubt, perplexed by circumstances, or afflicted by poverty or distress, Satan seeks to shake our
confidence in Jehovah. . . . But God understands, and He still pities
and loves. He reads the motives and the purposes of the heart. To
wait patiently, to trust when everything looks dark, is the lesson that
the leaders in God's work need to learn. Heaven will not fail them in
their day of adversity. Nothing is apparently more helpless, yet really
more invincible, than the soul that feels its nothingness and relies
wholly on God.

Not alone for men in positions of large responsibility is the lesson
of Elijah's experience in learning anew how to trust God in the hour
of trial. He who was Elijah's strength is strong to uphold every struggling child of His, no matter how weak. Of everyone He expects loyalty, and to everyone He grants power according to the need.[51]

THE BATTLE IS THE LORD'S

O our God, wilt thou not judge them? for we have no might against this great company that cometh against us; neither know we what to do: but our eyes are upon thee. 2 Chron. 20:12.

Toward the close of Jehoshaphat's reign the kingdom of Judah was invaded by an army before whose approach the inhabitants of the land had reason to tremble. . . . Jehoshaphat was a man of courage and valor. For years he had been strengthening his armies and his fortified cities. He was well prepared to meet almost any foe; yet in this crisis he put not his trust in the arm of flesh. Not by disciplined armies and fenced cities, but by a living faith in the God of Israel, could he hope to gain the victory over these heathen who boasted of their power to humble Judah in the eyes of the nations.

"Jehoshaphat feared, and set himself to seek the Lord, and proclaimed a fast throughout all Judah. And Judah gathered themselves together, to ask help of the Lord: even out of all the cities of Judah they came to seek the Lord." Standing in the temple court before his people, Jehoshaphat poured out his soul in prayer, pleading God's promises, with confession of Israel's helplessness. . . .

With confidence Jehoshaphat could say to the Lord, "Our eyes are upon Thee." For years he had taught the people to trust in the One who in past ages had so often interposed to save His chosen ones from utter destruction; and now, when the kingdom was in peril, Jehoshaphat did not stand alone; "all Judah stood before the Lord, with their little ones, their wives, and their children." Unitedly they fasted and prayed; unitedly they besought the Lord to put their enemies to confusion, that the name of Jehovah might be glorified. . . .

God was the strength of Judah in this crisis, and He is the strength of His people today. We are not to trust in princes, or to set men in the place of God. We are to remember that human beings are fallible and erring, and that He who has all power is our strong tower of defense. In every emergency we are to feel that the battle is His. His resources are limitless, and apparent impossibilities will make the victory all the greater.[52]

THE BATTLE SONG

And when he had consulted with the people, he appointed singers unto the Lord, and that should praise the beauty of holiness, as they went out before the army, and to say, Praise the Lord; for his mercy endureth for ever. 2 Chron. 20:21.

It was a singular way of going to battle against the enemy's army—praising the Lord with singing, and exalting the God of Israel. This was their battle song. They possessed the beauty of holiness. If more praising of God were engaged in now, hope and courage and faith would steadily increase. And would not this strengthen the hands of the valiant soldiers who today are standing in defense of truth? [53]

They praised God for the victory, and four days thereafter the army returned to Jerusalem, laden with the spoils of their enemies, singing praise for the victory won. [54]

When we have a deeper appreciation of the mercy and loving-kindness of God, we shall praise Him, instead of complaining. We shall talk of the loving watchcare of the Lord, of the tender compassion of the Good Shepherd. The language of the heart will not be selfish murmuring and repining. Praise, like a clear, flowing stream, will come from God's truly believing ones. . . .

Why not awake the voice of spiritual song in the days of our pilgrimage? . . . We need to study God's Word, to meditate and pray. Then we shall have spiritual eyesight to discern the inner courts of the celestial temple. We shall catch the notes of thanksgiving sung by the heavenly choir around the throne. When Zion shall arise and shine, her light will be most penetrating, and songs of praise and thanksgiving will be heard in the assembly of the saints. Little disappointments and difficulties will be lost sight of.

The Lord is our helper. . . . No one ever trusted God in vain. He never disappoints those who put their dependence on Him. If we would only do the work that the Lord would have us do, walking in the footsteps of Jesus, our hearts would become sacred harps, every chord of which would send forth praise and thanksgiving to the One sent by God to take away the sin of the world. [55]

SORCERY, ANCIENT AND MODERN

And he said unto him, Thus saith the Lord, Forasmuch as thou hast sent messengers to enquire of Baalzebub the god of Ekron, is it not because there is no God in Israel to enquire of his word? therefore thou shalt not come down off that bed on which thou art gone up, but shalt surely die. 2 Kings 1:16.

During his father's reign, Ahaziah had witnessed the wondrous works of the Most High. He had seen the terrible evidences that God had given apostate Israel of the way in which He regards those who set aside the binding claims of His law. Ahaziah had acted as if these awful realities were but idle tales. Instead of humbling his heart before the Lord, he had followed after Baal, and at last he had ventured upon this, his most daring act of impiety. . . .

Today the mysteries of heathen worship are replaced by the secret associations and séances, the obscurities and wonders, of spiritistic mediums. The disclosures of these mediums are eagerly received by thousands who refuse to accept light from God's word or through His Spirit. . . .

The apostles of nearly all forms of spiritism claim to have power to heal. . . . And there are not a few, even in this Christian age, who go to these healers, instead of trusting in the power of the living God and the skill of well-qualified physicians. . . .

The king of Israel, turning from God to ask help of the worst enemy of his people, proclaimed to the heathen that he had more confidence in their idols than in the God of heaven. In the same manner do men and women dishonor Him when they turn from the Source of strength and wisdom to ask help or counsel from the powers of darkness. . . .

Those who give themselves up to the sorcery of Satan may boast of great benefit received; but does this prove their course to be wise or safe? What if life should be prolonged? What if temporal gain should be secured? Will it pay in the end to have disregarded the will of God? All such apparent gain will prove at last an irrecoverable loss. We cannot with impunity break down a single barrier which God has erected to guard His people from Satan's power.[1]

THE WORK LYING NEAREST

He that is faithful in that which is least is faithful also in much.
Luke 16:10.

God had bidden Elijah anoint another to be prophet in his stead.
"Elisha the son of Shaphat . . . shalt thou anoint to be prophet in thy
room," He had said; and in obedience to the command, Elijah went to
find Elisha. . . .

Elisha's father was a wealthy farmer, a man whose household were
among the number that in a time of almost universal apostasy had not
bowed the knee to Baal. Theirs was a home where God was honored
and where allegiance to the faith of ancient Israel was the rule of daily
life. In such surroundings the early years of Elisha were passed. In the
quietude of country life, under the teaching of God and nature and the
discipline of useful work, he received the training in habits of simplicity and of obedience to his parents and to God that helped to fit him
for the high position he was afterward to occupy.

The prophetic call came to Elisha while, with his father's servants, he was plowing in the field. He had taken up the work that lay
nearest. He possessed both the capabilities of a leader among men
and the meekness of one who is ready to serve. Of a quiet and gentle
spirit, he was nevertheless energetic and steadfast. Integrity, fidelity,
and the love and fear of God were his, and in the humble round of
daily toil he gained strength of purpose and nobleness of character,
constantly increasing in grace and knowledge. While co-operating
with his father in the home-life duties, he was learning to co-operate
with God.

By faithfulness in little things, Elisha was preparing for weightier
trusts. Day by day, through practical experience, he gained a fitness
for a broader, higher work. . . . None can know what may be God's
purpose in His discipline; but all may be certain that faithfulness in little things is the evidence of fitness for greater responsibilities. Every
act of life is a revelation of character, and he only who in small duties
proves himself "a workman that needeth not to be ashamed" can be
honored by God with higher service.[2]

WHY ELISHA?

*He that loveth father or mother more than me is not worthy of
me: and he that loveth son or daughter more than me is not worthy
of me. And he that taketh not his cross, and followeth after me is
not worthy of me. Matt. 10:37, 38.*

As Elijah, divinely directed in seeking a successor, passed the field
in which Elisha was plowing, he cast upon the young man's shoulders
the mantle of consecration. . . . To him it was the signal that God had
called him to be the successor of Elijah. . . . Elisha must count the
cost—decide for himself to accept or reject the call. If his desires
clung to his home and its advantages, he was at liberty to remain
there. But Elisha understood the meaning of the call. . . . Not for any
worldly advantage would he forego the opportunity of becoming
God's messenger, or sacrifice the privilege of association with His servant. . . . Without hesitation he left a home where he was beloved, to
attend the prophet in his uncertain life.[3]

Because they are not connected with some directly religious
work, many feel that their lives are useless, that they are doing nothing for the advancement of God's kingdom. . . . Because they can
serve only in little things, they think themselves justified in doing
nothing. In this they err. A man may be in the active service of God
while engaged in the ordinary, everyday duties—while felling trees,
clearing the ground, or following the plow. The mother who trains
her children for Christ is as truly working for God as is the minister
in the pulpit.

Many long for special talent with which to do a wonderful work,
while the duties lying close at hand, the performance of which would
make the life fragrant, are lost sight of. . . . Success depends not so
much on talent as on energy and willingness. It is not the possession
of splendid talents that enables us to render acceptable service, but
the conscientious performance of daily duties, the contented spirit,
the unaffected, sincere interest in the welfare of others. In the humblest lot true excellence may be found. The commonest tasks,
wrought with loving faithfulness, are beautiful in God's sight.[4]

ALL ON THE ALTAR

No man, having put his hand to the plough, and looking back, is fit for the kingdom of God. Luke 9:62.

We are not all asked to serve as Elisha served, nor are we all bidden to sell everything we have; but God asks us to give His service the first place in our lives, to allow no day to pass without doing something to advance His work in the earth. He does not expect from all the same kind of service. One may be called to ministry in a foreign land; another may be asked to give of his means for the support of gospel work. God accepts the offering of each. It is the consecration of the life and all its interests, that is necessary. Those who make this consecration will hear and obey the call of Heaven. . . .

It was no great work that was at first required of Elisha; commonplace duties still constituted his discipline. He is spoken of as pouring water on the hands of Elijah, his master. He was willing to do anything that the Lord directed, and at every step he learned lessons of humility and service. . . . Elisha's life after uniting with Elijah was not without temptations. Trials he had in abundance; but in every emergency he relied on God. He was tempted to think of the home that he had left, but to this temptation he gave no heed. Having put his hand to the plow, he was resolved not to turn back, and through test and trial he proved true to this trust. . . .

As Elisha accompanied the prophet . . . his faith and resolution were once more tested. At Gilgal, and again at Bethel and Jericho, he was invited by the prophet to turn back. . . . But . . . he would not be diverted from his purpose. . . . "And . . . Elijah said unto Elisha, Ask what I shall do for thee, before I be taken away from thee."

Elisha asked not for worldly honor, or for a high place among the great men of earth. That which he craved was a large measure of the Spirit that God had bestowed so freely upon the one about to be honored with translation. He knew that nothing but the Spirit which had rested upon Elijah could fit him to fill the place in Israel to which God had called him; and so he asked, "I pray thee, let a double portion of thy Spirit be upon me."[5]

ELIJAH'S SUCCESSOR

Behold, I shew you a mystery; We shall not all sleep, but we shall all be changed, in a moment, in the twinkling of an eye, at the last trump: for the trumpet shall sound, and the dead shall be raised incorruptible, and we shall be changed. 1 Cor. 15:51, 52.

In the desert, in loneliness and discouragement, Elijah had said that he had had enough of life and had prayed that he might die. But the Lord in His mercy had not taken him at his word. There was yet a great work for Elijah to do; and when his work was done, he was not to perish in discouragement and solitude. Not for him the descent into the tomb, but the ascent with God's angels to the presence of His glory.

"And Elisha saw it, and he cried, My father, my father, the chariot of Israel, and the horsemen thereof. And he saw him no more: and he took hold of his own clothes, and rent them in two pieces. He took up also the mantle of Elijah that fell from him, and went back, and stood by the bank of Jordan; and he took the mantle of Elijah that fell from him, and smote the waters, and said, Where is the Lord God of Elijah? and when he also had smitten the waters, they parted hither and thither: and Elisha went over. And when the sons of the prophets which were to view at Jericho saw him, they said, The Spirit of Elijah doth rest on Elisha. And they came to meet him, and bowed themselves to the ground before him."

When the Lord in His providence sees fit to remove from His work those to whom He has given wisdom, He helps and strengthens their successors, if they will look to Him for aid and will walk in His ways. They may be even wiser than their predecessors; for they may profit by their experience and learn wisdom from their mistakes.[6]

Elijah, the man of power, had been God's instrument for the overthrow of gigantic evils. . . . As successor to Elijah was needed one who by careful, patient instruction could guide Israel in safe paths. For this work Elisha's early training under God's direction had prepared him. . . .

Every act of life is a revelation of character, and he only who in small duties proves himself "a workman that needeth not to be ashamed" will be honored by God with weightier trusts.[7]

POLLUTION AND PURIFICATION

And he went forth unto the spring of the waters, and cast the salt in there, and said, Thus saith the Lord, I have healed these waters; there shall not be from thence any more death or barren land. 2 Kings 2:21.

In casting salt into the bitter spring, Elisha taught the same spiritual lesson imparted centuries later by the Savior to His disciples when He declared, "Ye are the salt of the earth." The salt mingling with the polluted spring purified its waters and brought life and blessing where before had been blighting and death. When God compares His children to salt, He would teach them that His purpose in making them the subjects of His grace is that they may become agents in saving others. . . .

Salt must be mingled with the substance to which it is added; it must penetrate, infuse it, that it may be preserved. So it is through personal contact and association that men are reached by the saving power of the gospel. They are not saved as masses, but as individuals. Personal influence is a power. It is to work with the influence of Christ, . . . and to stay the progress of the world's corruption. . . . It is to uplift, to sweeten the lives and characters of others by the power of a pure example united with earnest faith and love. . . .

The polluted stream represents the soul that is separate from God. . . . Through sin, the whole human organism is deranged, the mind is perverted, the imagination corrupted; the faculties of the soul are degraded. There is an absence of pure religion, of heart holiness. The converting power of God has not wrought in transforming the character. . . .

The heart that receives the word of God is not as a pool that evaporates. . . . It is like a river constantly flowing and, as it advances, becoming deeper and wider, until its life-giving waters are spread over all the earth. . . . So it is with the true child of God. The religion of Christ reveals itself as a vitalizing, pervading principle, a living, working, spiritual energy. When the heart is opened to the heavenly influence of truth and love, these principles will flow forth again like streams in the desert, causing fruitfulness to appear where now are barrenness and dearth.[8]

RUDENESS REBUKED

Thou shalt rise up before the hoary head, and honour the face of the old man, and fear thy God: I am the Lord. Lev. 19:32.

Elisha was a man of mild and kindly spirit; but that he could also be stern is shown by his course when, on the way to Bethel, he was mocked by ungodly youth who had come out of the city. These youth had heard of Elijah's ascension, and they made this solemn event the subject of their jeers, saying to Elisha, "Go up, thou bald head; go up, thou bald head." At the sound of their mocking words the prophet turned back, and under the inspiration of the Almighty he pronounced a curse upon them. The awful judgment that followed was of God. "There came forth two she-bears out of the wood, and tare forty and two" of them (2 Kings 2:23, 24).

Had Elisha allowed the mockery to pass unnoticed, he would have continued to be ridiculed and reviled by the rabble, and his mission to instruct and save in a time of grave national peril might have been defeated. This one instance of terrible severity was sufficient to command respect throughout his life. For fifty years he went in and out of the gate of Bethel, and to and fro in the land, from city to city, passing through crowds of idle, rude, dissolute youth; but none mocked him or made light of his qualifications as the prophet of the Most High. . . .

Reverence, in which the youth who mocked Elisha were so lacking, is a grace that should be carefully cherished. Every child should be taught to show true reverence for God. Never should His name be spoken lightly or thoughtlessly. Angels, as they speak it, veil their faces. With what reverence should we, who are fallen and sinful, take it upon our lips!. . .

Courtesy, also, is one of the graces of the Spirit and should be cultivated by all. It has power to soften natures which without it would grow hard and rough. Those who profess to be followers of Christ, and are at the same time rough, unkind, and uncourteous, have not learned of Jesus. Their sincerity may not be doubted, their uprightness may not be questioned; but sincerity and uprightness will not atone for a lack of kindness and courtesy.[9]

TABLE IN THE WILDERNESS

Behold, the eye of the Lord is upon them that fear him, upon them that hope in his mercy; to deliver their soul from death, and to keep them alive in famine. Ps. 33:18, 19.

Like the Savior of mankind, of whom he was a type, Elisha in his ministry among men combined the work of healing with that of teaching. Faithfully, untiringly, throughout his long and effective labors, Elisha endeavored to foster and advance the important educational work carried on by the schools of the prophets. . . . It was on the occasion of one of his visits to the school established at Gilgal that he healed the poisoned pottage. . . .

At Gilgal, also, while the dearth was still in the land, Elisha fed one hundred men with the present brought to him by "a man from Baalshalisha," "bread of the first fruits, twenty loaves of barley, and full ears of corn in the husk thereof.". . .

What condescension it was on the part of Christ, through His messenger, to work this miracle to satisfy hunger! Again and again since that time, though not always in so marked and perceptible a manner, has the Lord Jesus worked to supply human need. . . .

It is the grace of God on the small portion that makes it all-sufficient. God's hand can multiply it a hundredfold. From His resources He can spread a table in the wilderness. By the touch of His hand He can increase the scanty provision and make it sufficient for all. It was His power that increased the loaves and corn in the hands of the sons of the prophets. . . .

When the Lord gives a work to be done, let not men stop to inquire into the reasonableness of the command or the probable result of their efforts to obey. The supply in their hands may seem to fall short of the need to be filled; but in the hands of the Lord it will prove more than sufficient. The servitor "set it before them, and they did eat, and left thereof, according to the word of the Lord.". . . .

The gift brought to Him with thanksgiving and with prayer for His blessing, He will multiply as He multiplied the food given to the sons of the prophets and to the weary multitude.[10]

"EVEN A CHILD"

And the Syrians had gone out by companies, and had brought away captive out of the land of Israel a little maid; and she waited on Naaman's wife. 2 Kings 5:2.

A slave, far from her home, this little maid was nevertheless one of God's witnesses, unconsciously fulfilling the purpose for which God had chosen Israel as His people. As she ministered in that heathen home, her sympathies were aroused in behalf of her master; and, remembering the wonderful miracles of healing wrought through Elisha, she said to her mistress, "Would God my lord were with the prophet that is in Samaria! for he would recover him of his leprosy." She knew that the power of Heaven was with Elisha, and she believed that by this power Naaman could be healed.

The conduct of the captive maid, the way that she bore herself in that heathen home, is a strong witness to the power of early home training. There is no higher trust than that committed to fathers and mothers in the care and training of their children. Parents have to do with the very foundations of habit and character. By their example and teaching, the future of their children is largely decided.

Happy are the parents whose lives are a true reflection of the divine, so that the promises and commands of God awaken in the child gratitude and reverence; the parents . . . who by teaching the child to love and trust and obey them are teaching him to love and trust and obey his Father in heaven. Parents who impart to the child such a gift have endowed him with a treasure more precious than the wealth of all the ages, a treasure as enduring as eternity.

We know not in what line our children may be called to serve. They may spend their lives within the circle of the home; they may engage in life's common vocations, or go as teachers of the gospel to heathen lands; but all are alike called to be missionaries for God, ministers of mercy to the world.[11]

He who sent . . . the little Israelitish maiden to the help of Naaman, the Syrian captain, sends men and women and youth today as His representatives to those in need of divine help and guidance.[12]

GOD'S WAYS

For my thoughts are not your thoughts, neither are your ways my ways, saith the Lord. For as the heavens are higher than the earth, so are my ways higher than your ways, and my thoughts than your thoughts. Isa. 55:8, 9.

Naaman the Syrian consulted the prophet of God as to how he could be cured of a loathsome disease, the leprosy. He was bidden to go and bathe in Jordan seven times. Why did he not immediately follow the directions of Elisha, the prophet of God? . . . In his mortification and disappointment he became passionate, and in a rage refused to follow the humble course marked out by the prophet of God. "I thought," said he, "he will surely come out to me, and stand, and call on the name of the Lord his God, and strike his hand over the place, and recover the leper. Are not Ababa and Pharpar, rivers of Damascus, better than all the waters of Israel? may I not wash in them, and be clean? So he turned and went away in a rage." His servant said: "My father, if the prophet had bid thee do some *great thing,* wouldest thou not have done it? how much rather then, when he saith to thee, Wash [merely], and be clean?" Yes, this great man considered it beneath his dignity to go to the humble river Jordan, and wash. The rivers he mentioned and desired were beautified by surrounding trees and groves, and idols were placed in these groves. Many flocked to these rivers to worship their idol gods; therefore it would have cost him no humility. But it was following the specified directions of the prophet which would humble his proud and lofty spirit. Willing obedience would bring the desired result. He washed, and was made whole.[13]

Our plans are not always God's plans. . . . In His loving care and interest for us, often He who understands us better than we understand ourselves refuses to permit us selfishly to seek the gratification of our own ambition. . . . Many things He asks us to yield to Him, but in doing this we are but giving up that which hinders us in the heavenward way. . . .

In the future life the mysteries that here have annoyed and disappointed us will be made plain. We shall see that our seemingly unanswered prayers and disappointed hopes have been among our greatest blessings.[14]

NO FIERY CHARIOT

Blessed are the dead which die in the Lord from henceforth: Yea, saith the Spirit, that they may rest from their labours; and their works do follow them. Rev. 14:13.

It was not given Elisha to follow his master in a fiery chariot. Upon him the Lord permitted to come a lingering illness. During the long hours of human weakness and suffering his faith laid fast hold on the promises of God, and he beheld ever about him heavenly messengers of comfort and peace. As on the heights of Dothan he had seen the encircling hosts of heaven, the fiery chariots of Israel and the horsemen thereof, so now he was conscious of the presence of sympathizing angels, and he was sustained. Throughout his life he had exercised strong faith, and as he had advanced in a knowledge of God's providences and of His merciful kindness, faith had ripened into an abiding trust in his God, and when death called him he was ready to rest from his labors. . . .

Elisha could say in all confidence, "God will redeem my soul from the power of the grave: for he shall receive me." And with rejoicing he could testify, "I know that my Redeemer liveth, and that he shall stand at the latter day upon the earth." "As for me, I will behold thy face in righteousness: I shall be satisfied, when I awake, with thy likeness." [15]

Christ claims all those as His who have believed in His name. The vitalizing power of the Spirit of Christ dwelling in the mortal body binds every believing soul to Jesus Christ. Those who believe in Jesus are sacred to His heart; for their life is hid with Christ in God. . . .

What a glorious morning will the resurrection morning be! What a wonderful scene will open when Christ shall come to be admired of them that believe! All who were partakers with Christ in His humiliation and sufferings will be partakers with Him in His glory. By the resurrection of Christ from the dead every believing saint who falls asleep in Jesus will come forth from his prison house in triumph. The resurrected saint will proclaim, "O death, where is thy sting? O grave, where is thy victory?" (1 Cor. 15:55). [16]

RELUCTANT PROPHET

Arise, go to Nineveh, that great city, and cry against it; for their wickedness is come up before me. Jonah 1:2.

Nineveh, wicked though it had become, was not wholly given over to evil. He who "beholdeth all the sons of men" (Ps. 33:13) . . . perceived in that city many who were reaching out after something better and higher. . . . God revealed Himself to them in an unmistakable manner, to lead them, if possible, to repentance.

The instrument chosen for this work was the prophet Jonah. . . . Had the prophet obeyed unquestioningly, he would have been spared many bitter experiences, and would have been blessed abundantly. Yet in the hour of Jonah's despair the Lord did not desert him. Through a series of trials and strange providences, the prophet's confidence in God and in His infinite power to save was to be revived. . . .

Once more the servant of God was commissioned to warn Nineveh. . . . As Jonah entered the city, he began at once to "cry against" it the message, "Yet forty days, and Nineveh shall be overthrown." From street to street he went, sounding the note of warning.

The message was not in vain. The cry that rang through the streets of the godless city was passed from lip to lip until all the inhabitants had heard the startling announcement. The Spirit of God pressed the message home to every heart and caused multitudes to tremble because of their sins and to repent in deep humiliation. . . . Their doom was averted, the God of Israel was exalted and honored throughout the heathen world, and His law was revered. Not until many years later was Nineveh to fall a prey to the surrounding nations through forgetfulness of God and through boastful pride. . . .

The lesson is for God's messengers today, when the cities of the nations are as verily in need of a knowledge of the attributes and purposes of the true God as were the Ninevites of old. . . . The only city that will endure is the city whose builder and maker is God. . . . The Lord Jesus is calling upon men to strive with sanctified ambition to secure the immortal inheritance.[17]

THERE IS A LIMIT

Behold, the Lord cometh out of his place to punish the inhabitants of the earth for their iniquity: the earth also shall disclose her blood, and shall no more cover her slain. Isa. 26:21.

Our God is a God of mercy. With long-sufferance and tender compassion He deals with the transgressors of His law. . . . But there is a point beyond which divine patience is exhausted, and the judgments of God are sure to follow. The Lord bears long with men, and with cities, mercifully giving warnings to save them from divine wrath; but a time will come when pleadings for mercy will no longer be heard. . . .

The time is at hand when there will be sorrow in the world that no human balm can heal. The Spirit of God is being withdrawn. Disasters by sea and by land follow one another in quick succession. How frequently we hear of earthquakes and tornadoes, of destruction by fire and flood, with great loss of life and property! Apparently these calamities are capricious outbreaks of disorganized, unregulated forces of nature, wholly beyond the control of man; but in them all, God's purpose may be read. They are among the agencies by which He seeks to arouse men and women to a sense of their danger.

God's messengers in the great cities are not to become discouraged over the wickedness, the injustice, the depravity, which they are called upon to face while endeavoring to proclaim the glad tidings of salvation. . . . In every city, filled though it may be with violence and crime, there are many who with proper teaching may learn to become followers of Jesus. . . . God's message for the inhabitants of earth today is, "Be ye also ready: for in such an hour as ye think not the Son of man cometh" (Matt. 24:44). . . . We are standing on the threshold of the crisis of the ages. . . .

The storm of God's wrath is gathering; and those only will stand who respond to the invitations of mercy, as did the inhabitants of Nineveh under the preaching of Jonah, and become sanctified through obedience to the laws of the divine Ruler. The righteous alone shall be hid with Christ in God till the desolation be overpast.[18]

"SEND ME"

*Also I heard the voice of the Lord, saying, Whom shall I send,
and who will go for us? Then said I, Here am I; send me. Isa. 6:8.*

It was under circumstances of difficulty and discouragement that
Isaiah, while yet a young man, was called to the prophetic mission.
Disaster was threatening his country. By their transgression of God's
law the people of Judah had forfeited His protection, and the Assyrian
forces were about to come against the kingdom of Judah. But the danger from their enemies was not the greatest trouble. It was the perversity of the people that brought upon the Lord's servant the deepest
depression. By their apostasy and rebellion they were inviting the
judgments of God. The youthful prophet had been called to bear to
them a message of warning, and he knew that he would meet with obstinate resistance. . . . His task seemed to him almost hopeless. . . .

Such thoughts as these were crowding upon his mind as he stood
under the portico of the holy temple. Suddenly the gate and the inner
veil of the temple seemed to be uplifted or withdrawn, and he was
permitted to gaze within, upon the holy of holies, where even the
prophet's feet might not enter. There rose up before him a vision of
Jehovah sitting upon a throne high and lifted up, while His train filled
the temple. On each side of the throne hovered the seraphim, two
wings bearing them up, two veiling their faces in adoration, and two
covering their feet. . . .

Never before had Isaiah realized so fully the greatness of Jehovah
or His perfect holiness; and he felt that in his human frailty and unworthiness he must perish in that divine presence. "Woe is me!" he
cried; "for I am undone; because I am a man of unclean lips, and I
dwell in the midst of a people of unclean lips: for mine eyes have seen
the King, the Lord of hosts." But a seraph came to him to fit him for
his great mission. A living coal from the altar was laid upon his lips
with the words: "Lo, this hath touched thy lips; and thine iniquity is
taken away, and thy sin purged." And when the voice of God was
heard saying, "Whom shall I send, and who will go for us?" Isaiah
with holy confidence responded, "Here am I; send me." . . . The
prophet was nerved for the work before him.[19]

232

HUMILITY—TRUE OR FALSE?

And one cried unto another, and said, Holy, holy, holy, is the Lord of hosts: the whole earth is full of his glory. Isa. 6:3.

These holy beings sang forth the praise and glory of God with lips unpolluted with sin. The contrast between the feeble praise which he [Isaiah] had been accustomed to bestow upon the Creator and the fervid praises of the seraphim astonished and humiliated the prophet. . . .

While he listened to the song of the angels, . . . the glory, the infinite power, and the unsurpassed majesty of the Lord passed before his vision, and was impressed upon his soul. In the light of this matchless radiance that made manifest all he could bear in the revelation of the divine character, his own inward defilement stood out before him with startling clearness. His very words seemed vile to him.

Thus when the servant of God is permitted to behold the glory of the God of heaven, as He is unveiled to humanity, and realizes to a slight degree the purity of the Holy One of Israel, he will make startling confessions of the pollution of his soul, rather than proud boasts of his holiness. In deep humiliation Isaiah exclaimed, "Woe is me! for I am undone; because I am a man of unclean lips. . . ." This is not that voluntary humility and servile self-reproach that so many seem to consider it a virtue to display. This vague mockery of humility is prompted by hearts full of pride and self-esteem. There are many who demerit themselves in words, who would be disappointed if this course did not call forth expressions of praise and appreciation from others. But the conviction of the prophet was genuine.[20]

The seraphim before the throne are so filled with reverential awe in beholding the glory of God that they do not for an instant look upon themselves with self-complacency, or in admiration of themselves or one another. Their praise and glory are for the Lord of Hosts. . . . They are fully satisfied to glorify God; and in His presence, beneath His smile of approbation, they wish for nothing more. In bearing His image, in doing His service and worshiping Him, their highest ambition is fully reached.[21]

THE LIVING COAL

Then flew one of the seraphims unto me, having a live coal in his hand, which he had taken with the tongs from off the altar: and he laid it upon my mouth, and said, Lo, this hath touched thy lips; and thine iniquity is taken away, and thy sin purged. Isa. 6:6, 7.

Isaiah had denounced the sin of others; but now he sees himself exposed to the same condemnation he had pronounced upon them. He had been satisfied with a cold, lifeless ceremony in his worship of God. He had not known this until the vision was given him of the Lord. How little now appeared his wisdom and talents as he looked upon the sacredness and majesty of the sanctuary. How unworthy he was! how unfitted for sacred service! . . .

The vision given to Isaiah represents the condition of God's people in the last days. They are privileged to see by faith the work that is going forward in the heavenly sanctuary. "And the temple of God was opened in heaven, and there was seen in his temple the ark of his testament." As they look by faith into the holy of holies, and see the work of Christ in the heavenly sanctuary, they perceive that they are a people of unclean lips—a people whose lips have often spoken vanity, and whose talents have not been sanctified and employed to the glory of God. Well may they despair as they contrast their own weakness and unworthiness with the purity and loveliness of the glorious character of Christ. But if they, like Isaiah, will receive the impression the Lord designs shall be made upon the heart, if they will humble their souls before God, there is hope for them. The bow of promise is above the throne, and the work done for Isaiah will be performed in them. God will respond to the petitions coming from the contrite heart.[22]

We want the living coal from off the altar placed upon our lips. We want to hear the word spoken, "Thine iniquity is taken away, and thy sin purged."[23]

The live coal is symbolical of purification. If it touches the lips, no impure word will fall from them.[24]

WHITE LIKE SNOW

For thus saith the high and lofty One that inhabiteth eternity, whose name is Holy; I dwell in the high and holy place, with him also that is of a contrite and humble spirit, to revive the spirit of the humble, and to revive the heart of the contrite ones. Isa. 57:15.

In the vision that came to Isaiah in the temple court, he was given a clear view of the character of the God of Israel. "The high and lofty One that inhabiteth eternity, whose name is Holy," had appeared before him in great majesty; yet the prophet was made to understand the compassionate nature of his Lord. . . .

In beholding his God, the prophet . . . had not only been given a view of his own unworthiness; there had come to his humbled heart the assurance of forgiveness, full and free; and he had arisen a changed man. He had seen his Lord. He had caught a glimpse of the loveliness of the divine character. He could testify of the transformation wrought through beholding Infinite Love. Henceforth he was inspired with longing desire to see erring Israel set free from the burden and penalty of sin. "Why should ye be stricken any more?" the prophet inquired. "Come now, and let us reason together, saith the Lord: though your sins be as scarlet, they shall be as white as snow; though they be red like crimson, they shall be as wool." . . . The God whom they had been claiming to serve, but whose character they had misunderstood, was set before them as the great Healer of spiritual disease. . . .

The heart of Infinite Love yearns after those who feel powerless to free themselves from the snares of Satan; and He graciously offers to strengthen them to live for Him. "Fear thou not," He bids them; "for I am with thee: be not dismayed; for I am thy God: I will strengthen thee; yea, I will help thee; yea, I will uphold thee with the right hand of My righteousness." . . .

Have you, reader, chosen your own way? Have you wandered far from God? Have you sought to feast upon the fruits of transgression, only to find them turn to ashes upon your lips? . . . Return to your Father's house. He invites you, saying, "Return unto me; for I have redeemed thee." "Come unto me: hear, and your soul shall live." [25]

FOR EVERYONE

Princes shall come out of Egypt; Ethiopia shall soon stretch out her hands unto God. Ps. 68:31.

Throughout his ministry Isaiah bore a plain testimony concerning God's purpose for the heathen. Other prophets had made mention of the divine plan, but their language was not always understood. To Isaiah it was given to make very plain to Judah the truth that among the Israel of God were to be numbered many who were not descendants of Abraham after the flesh. This teaching was not in harmony with the theology of his age, yet he fearlessly proclaimed the messages given him of God and brought hope to many a longing heart reaching out after the spiritual blessings promised to the seed of Abraham. . . .

Often the Israelites seemed unable or unwilling to understand God's purpose for the heathen. Yet it was this very purpose that had made them a separate people and had established them as an independent nation among the nations of the earth. Abraham, their father, to whom the covenant promise was first given, had been called to go forth from his kindred, to the regions beyond, that he might be a light bearer to the heathen. Although the promise to him included a posterity as numerous as the sand by the sea, yet it was for no selfish purpose that he was to become the founder of a great nation. . . . "I will bless thee," Jehovah declared, "and make thy name great; . . . in thee shall all families of the earth be blessed.". . .

No distinction on account of nationality, race, or caste is recognized by God. . . . Christ came to demolish every wall of partition, to throw open every compartment of the temple courts, that every soul may have free access to God. His love is so broad, so deep, so full, that it penetrates everywhere. It lifts out of Satan's influence those who have been deluded by his deceptions, and places them within reach of the throne of God, the throne encircled by the rainbow of promise. In Christ there is neither Jew nor Greek, bond nor free.[26]

JEREMIAH, GOD'S MOUTHPIECE

It is good that a man should both hope and quietly wait for the salvation of the Lord. Lam. 3:26.

Among those who had hoped for a permanent spiritual revival as the result of the reformation under Josiah was Jeremiah, called of God to the prophetic office while still a youth. . . .

In the youthful Jeremiah, God saw one who would be true to his trust and who would stand for the right against great opposition. . . . "Say not, I am a child," the Lord bade His chosen messenger; "for thou shalt go to all that I shall send thee, and whatsoever I command thee thou shalt speak. Be not afraid of their faces: for I am with thee to deliver thee." . . .

For forty years Jeremiah was to stand before the nation as a witness for truth and righteousness. In a time of unparalleled apostasy he was to exemplify in life and character the worship of the only true God. During the terrible sieges of Jerusalem he was to be the mouthpiece of Jehovah.[27]

Naturally of a timid and shrinking disposition, Jeremiah longed for the peace and quiet of a life of retirement, where he need not witness the continued impenitence of his beloved nation. His heart was wrung with anguish over the ruin wrought by sin. . . .

The experiences through which Jeremiah passed in the days of his youth and also in the later years of his ministry, taught him the lesson that "the way of man is not in himself: it is not in man that walketh to direct his steps." He learned to pray, "O Lord, correct me, but with judgment; not in thine anger, lest thou bring me to nothing" (Jer. 10:23, 24).

When called to drink of the cup of tribulation and sorrow, and when tempted in his misery to say, "My strength and my hope is perished from the Lord," he recalled the providences of God in his behalf and triumphantly exclaimed, "It is of the Lord's mercies that we are not consumed, because his compassions fail not. . . . The Lord is my portion, saith my soul; therefore will I hope in him."[28]

THE RECHABITES

And Jeremiah said unto the house of the Rechabites, . . . Because ye have obeyed the commandment of Jonadab your father, and kept all his precepts. . . . therefore thus saith the Lord of hosts, the God of Israel; Jonadab the son of Rechab shall not want a man to stand before me for ever. Jer. 35:18, 19.

God commanded Jeremiah to gather the Rechabites into the house of the Lord, into one of the chambers, and set wine before them and invite them to drink. Jeremiah did as the Lord commanded him. "But they said, We will drink no wine: for Jonadab the son of Rechab our father commanded us, saying, Ye shall drink no wine, neither ye, nor your sons forever."

"Then came the word of the Lord unto Jeremiah, saying, . . . Go and tell the men of Judah and the inhabitants of Jerusalem, Will ye not receive instruction to hearken to my words? saith the Lord. The words of Jonadab the son of Rechab, that he commanded his sons not to drink wine, are performed; for unto this day they drink none, but obey their father's commandment." Here God contrasts the obedience of the Rechabites with the disobedience and rebellion of His people, who will not receive His words of reproof and warning. . . . The Rechabites were commended for their ready and willing obedience, while God's people refused to be reproved by their prophets.[29]

If the requirements of a good and wise father, who took the best and most effectual means to secure his posterity against the evils of intemperance, were worthy of strict obedience, surely God's authority should be held in as much greater reverence as He is holier than man. Our Creator and our Commander, infinite in power, terrible in judgment, seeks by every means to bring men to see and repent of their sins. By the mouth of His servants He predicts the dangers of disobedience; He sounds the note of warning and faithfully reproves sin. His people are kept in prosperity only by His mercy, through the vigilant watchcare of chosen instrumentalities. He cannot uphold and guard a people who reject His counsel and despise His reproofs. For a time He may withhold His retributive judgments; yet He cannot always stay His hand.[30]

JEHOVAH'S HONOR VINDICATED

With him is an arm of flesh; but with us is the Lord our God to help us, and to fight our battles. And the people rested themselves upon the words of Hezekiah, king of Judah. 2 Chron. 32:8.

Hezekiah, in the earlier years of his reign, had continued to pay tribute to Assyria, in harmony with the agreement entered into by Ahaz. Meanwhile the king had taken "counsel with his princes and his mighty men," and had done everything possible for the defense of his kingdom. . . .

The long-expected crisis finally came. The forces of Assyria, advancing from triumph to triumph, appeared in Judea. . . . Judah's only hope was now in God. All possible help from Egypt had been cut off, and no other nations were near to lend a friendly hand. . . . Sennacherib wrote "letters to rail on the Lord God of Israel, and to speak against Him, saying, As the gods of the nations of other lands have not delivered their people out of mine hand, so shall not the God of Hezekiah deliver His people out of mine hand.". . .

When the king of Judah received the taunting letter, he took it into the temple and "spread it before the Lord" and prayed with strong faith for help from heaven, that the nations of earth might know that the God of the Hebrews still lived and reigned. The honor of Jehovah was at stake; He alone could bring deliverance. . . .

Hezekiah was not left without hope. Isaiah sent to him, saying, "Thus saith the Lord God of Israel, That which thou hast prayed to Me against Sennacherib king of Assyria I have heard." . . . That very night deliverance came. "The angel of the Lord went out, and smote in the camp of the Assyrians an hundred fourscore and five thousand." . . .

The God of the Hebrews had prevailed over the proud Assyrian. The honor of Jehovah was vindicated in the eyes of the surrounding nations. In Jerusalem the hearts of the people were filled with holy joy. Their earnest entreaties for deliverance had been mingled with confession of sin and with many tears. In their great need they had trusted wholly in the power of God to save, and He had not failed them.[31]

DIVINE HEALING

I beseech thee, O Lord, remember now how I have walked before thee in truth and with a perfect heart, and have done that which is good in thy sight. And Hezekiah wept sore. 2 Kings 20:3.

In the midst of his prosperous reign King Hezekiah was suddenly stricken with a fatal malady. "Sick unto death," his case was beyond the power of man to help. And the last vestige of hope seemed removed when the prophet Isaiah appeared before him with the message, "Thus saith the Lord, Set thine house in order: for thou shalt die, and not live."

The outlook seemed utterly dark; yet the king could still pray to the One who had hitherto been his "refuge and strength, a very present help in trouble" (Ps. 46:1). And so "he turned his face to the wall, and prayed unto the Lord.". . .

He whose "compassions fail not" heard the prayer of His servant. "It came to pass, afore Isaiah was gone out into the middle court, that the word of the Lord came to him, saying, Turn again, and tell Hezekiah the captain of my people, Thus saith the Lord, the God of David thy father, I have heard thy prayer, I have seen thy tears: behold, I will heal thee. . . ." Gladly the prophet returned with the words of assurance and hope. Directing that a lump of figs be laid upon the diseased part, Isaiah delivered to the king the message of God's mercy and protecting care.[32]

Those who seek healing by prayer should not neglect to make use of the remedial agencies within their reach. It is not a denial of faith to use such remedies as God has provided to alleviate pain and to aid nature in her work of restoration. . . . God has put it in our power to obtain a knowledge of the laws of life. This knowledge has been placed within our reach for use. We should employ every facility for the restoration of health, taking every advantage possible, working in harmony with natural laws. When we have prayed for the recovery of the sick, we can work with all the more energy, thanking God that we have the privilege of co-operating with Him, and asking His blessing on the means which He Himself has provided.[33]

WHAT DO THEY SEE?

Then said he, What have they seen in thine house? And Hezekiah answered, All that is in mine house have they seen: there is nothing among my treasures that I have not shewed them. Isa. 39:4.

The visit of the ambassadors to Hezekiah was a test of his gratitude and devotion. . . . Had Hezekiah improved the opportunity given him to bear witness to the power, the goodness, the compassion, of the God of Israel, the report of the ambassadors would have been as light piercing darkness. But he magnified himself above the Lord of hosts. He "rendered not again according to the benefit done unto him; for his heart was lifted up." . . .

The story of Hezekiah's failure to prove true to his trust . . . is fraught with an important lesson for all. Far more than we do, we need to speak of the precious chapters in our experience, of the mercy and loving-kindness of God, of the matchless depths of the Savior's love. When mind and heart are filled with the love of God, it will not be difficult to impart that which enters into the spiritual life. Great thoughts, noble aspirations, clear perceptions of truth, unselfish purposes, yearnings for piety and holiness, will find expression in words that reveal the character of the heart treasure.

Those with whom we associate day by day need our help, our guidance. They may be in such a condition of mind that a word spoken in season will be as a nail in a sure place. Tomorrow some of these souls may be where we can never reach them again. What is our influence over these fellow travelers?[34]

What have your friends and acquaintances seen in your house? Are you, instead of revealing the treasures of the grace of Christ, displaying those things that will perish with the using? Or do you, to those with whom you are brought in contact, communicate some new thought of Christ's character and work? . . . O that those for whom God has done marvelous things would show forth His praises, and tell of His mighty works. But how often those for whom God works are like Hezekiah—forgetful of the Giver of all their blessings.[35]

FAITH AND GOD'S PROMISES

Behold, his soul which is lifted up is not upright in him: but the just shall live by his faith. Hab. 2:4.

At the time Josiah began to rule, and for many years before, the truehearted in Judah were questioning whether God's promises to ancient Israel could ever be fulfilled. . . .

These anxious questionings were voiced by the prophet Habakkuk. Viewing the situation of the faithful in his day, he expressed the burden of his heart in the inquiry: "O Lord, how long shall I cry, and thou wilt not hear!" . . . And then, his faith reaching out beyond the forbidding prospect of the immediate future, and laying fast hold on the precious promises that reveal God's love for His trusting children, the prophet added, "We shall not die." With this declaration of faith he rested his case, and that of every believing Israelite, in the hands of a compassionate God. . . .

The faith that strengthened Habakkuk and all the holy and the just in those days of deep trial was the same faith that sustains God's people today. In the darkest hours, under circumstances the most forbidding, the Christian believer may keep his soul stayed upon the source of all light and power. Day by day, through faith in God, his hope and courage may be renewed. "The just shall live by his faith.". . .

We must cherish and cultivate the faith of which prophets and apostles have testified—the faith that lays hold on the promises of God and waits for deliverance in His appointed time and way. The sure word of prophecy will meet its final fulfillment in the glorious advent of our Lord and Savior Jesus Christ, as King of kings and Lord of lords. . . . With the prophet who endeavored to encourage Judah in a time of unparalleled apostasy, let us confidently declare, "The Lord is in his holy temple: let all the earth keep silence before him." Let us ever hold in remembrance the cheering message, "The vision is yet for an appointed time, but at the end it shall speak, and not lie: though it tarry, wait for it; because it will surely come."[36]

TOO DRUNK TO THINK

When the heart of the king was merry with wine, he commanded . . . to bring Vashti the queen before the king with the crown royal, to shew the people and the princes her beauty: for she was fair to look on. Esther 1:10, 11.

When this command came from the king, Vashti did not carry out his orders, because she knew that wine had been freely used, and that Ahasuerus was under the influence of the intoxicating liquor. For her husband's sake as well as her own, she decided not to leave her position at the head of the women of the court.[37]

It was when the king was not himself, when his reason was dethroned by wine-drinking that he sent for the queen, that those present at his feast, men besotted by wine, might gaze on her beauty. She acted in harmony with a pure conscience.

Vashti refused to obey the king's command, thinking that when he came to himself, he would commend her course of action. But the king had unwise advisers. They argued it would be a power given to woman that would be to her injury.[38]

However high their office, men are amenable to God. The great power exercised by kings often leads to extremes in exaltation of self. And the worthless vows made to enact laws which disregard the higher laws of God lead to great injustice.

Occasions of indulgence such as are pictured in the first chapter of Esther do not glorify God. But the Lord accomplishes His will through men who are nevertheless misleading others. If God did not stretch forth His restraining hand, strange presentations would be seen. But God impresses human minds to accomplish His purpose, even though the one used continues to follow wrong practices. And the Lord works out His plans through men who do not acknowledge His lessons of wisdom. In His hand is the heart of every earthly ruler, to turn whithersoever He will, as He turneth the waters of the river.[39]

FOR SUCH A TIME AS THIS

And who knoweth whether thou art come to the kingdom for such a time as this? Esther 4:14.

A certain day was appointed on which the Jews were to be destroyed and their property confiscated. Little did the king realize the far-reaching results that would have accompanied the complete carrying out of this decree. Satan himself, the hidden instigator of the scheme, was trying to rid the earth of those who preserved the knowledge of the true God. . . . The decree of the Medes and Persians could not be revoked; apparently there was no hope; all the Israelites were doomed to destruction.

But the plots of the enemy were defeated by a Power that reigns among the children of men. In the providence of God, Esther, a Jewess who feared the Most High, had been made queen of the Medo-Persian kingdom. Mordecai was a near relative of hers. In their extremity, they decided to appeal to Xerxes in behalf of their people. Esther was to venture into his presence as an intercessor. "Who knoweth," said Mordecai, "whether thou art come to the kingdom for such a time as this?"

The crisis that Esther faced demanded quick, earnest action; but both she and Mordecai realized that unless God should work mightily in their behalf, their own efforts would be unavailing. So Esther took time for communion with God, the source of her strength. "Go," she directed Mordecai, "gather together all the Jews that are present in Shushan, and fast ye for me . . . : I also and my maidens will fast likewise; and so will I go in unto the king, which is not according to the law: and if I perish, I perish." [40]

To every household and every school, to every parent, teacher, and child upon whom has shone the light of the gospel, comes at this crisis the question put to Esther the queen at that momentous crisis in Israel's history. "Who knoweth whether *thou* art come to the kingdom for such a time as this?" [41]

MEN'S DECREES VERSUS GOD'S

And the dragon was wroth with the woman, and went to make war with the remnant of her seed, which keep the commandments of God, and have the testimony of Jesus Christ. Rev. 12:17.

Through Esther the queen the Lord accomplished a mighty deliverance for His people. At a time when it seemed that no power could save them, Esther and the women associated with her, by fasting and prayer and prompt action, met the issue, and brought salvation to their people.[42]

The trying experiences that came to God's people in the days of Esther were not peculiar to that age alone. . . . The same spirit that in ages past led men to persecute the true church will in the future lead to the pursuance of a similar course toward those who maintain their loyalty to God. . . . The decree that will finally go forth against the remnant people of God will be very similar to that issued by Ahasuerus against the Jews. Today the enemies of the true church see in the little company keeping the Sabbath commandment a Mordecai at the gate. The reverence of God's people for His law is a constant rebuke to those who have cast off the fear of the Lord and are trampling on His Sabbath. . . .

Men of position and reputation will join with the lawless and the vile to take counsel against the people of God. Wealth, genius, education, will combine to cover them with contempt. Persecuting rulers, ministers, and church members will conspire against them.

With voice and pen, by boasts, threats, and ridicule, they will seek to overthrow their faith. By false representations and angry appeals, men will stir up the passions of the people. Not having a "Thus saith the Scriptures" to bring against the advocates of the Bible Sabbath, they will resort to oppressive enactments to supply the lack. To secure popularity and patronage, legislators will yield to the demand for Sunday laws. But those who fear God cannot accept an institution that violates a precept of the Decalogue. On this battlefield will be fought the last great conflict in the controversy between truth and error. And we are not left in doubt as to the issue. Today, as in the days of Esther and Mordecai, the Lord will vindicate His truth and His people.[43]

FOUR BOYS IN BABYLON

As for these four children, God gave them knowledge and skill in all learning and wisdom. Dan. 1:17.

Daniel and his companions enjoyed the benefits of correct training and education in early life, but these advantages alone would not have made them what they were. The time came when they must act for themselves—when their future depended upon their own course. Then they decided to be true to the lessons given them in childhood.[44]

What a lifework was that of these noble Hebrews! As they bade farewell to their childhood home, how little did they dream of their high destiny! Faithful and steadfast, they yielded themselves to the divine guiding, so that through them God could fulfill His purpose.[45]

Daniel and his companions in Babylon were, in their youth, apparently more favored of fortune than was Joseph in the earlier years of his life in Egypt; yet they were subjected to tests of character scarcely less severe. From the comparative simplicity of their Judean home these youth of royal line were transported to the most magnificent of cities, to the court of its greatest monarch, and were singled out to be trained for the king's special service. Strong were the temptations surrounding them in that corrupt and luxurious court. . . . The direction that their food should be supplied from the royal table was an expression both of the king's favor and of his solicitude for their welfare. But a portion having been offered to idols, the food from the king's table was consecrated to idolatry; and in partaking of the king's bounty these youth would be regarded as uniting in his homage to false gods.[46]

The history of Daniel and his youthful companions has been recorded on the pages of the inspired word for the benefit of the youth of all succeeding ages. Through the record of their fidelity to the principles of temperance, God is speaking today to young men and young women, bidding them gather up the precious rays of light He has given on the subject of Christian temperance, and place themselves in right relation to the laws of health.[47]

THE SOURCE OF WISDOM

Only the Lord give thee wisdom and understanding, and give thee charge concerning Israel, that thou mayest keep the law of the Lord thy God. 1 Chron. 22:12.

In acquiring the wisdom of the Babylonians, Daniel and his companions were far more successful than their fellow students; but their learning did not come by chance. . . . They placed themselves in connection with the Source of all wisdom, making the knowledge of God the foundation of their education. In faith they prayed for wisdom, and they lived their prayers. They placed themselves where God could bless them. They avoided that which would weaken their powers, and improved every opportunity to become intelligent in all lines of learning. They followed the rules of life that could not fail to give them strength of intellect. They sought to acquire knowledge for one purpose—that they might honor God. . . . In order to stand as representatives of true religion amid the false religions of heathenism they must have clearness of intellect and must perfect a Christian character. And God Himself was their teacher. Constantly praying, conscientiously studying, keeping in touch with the Unseen, they walked with God as did Enoch.

True success in any line of work is not the result of chance or accident or destiny. It is the outworking of God's providences, the reward of faith and discretion, of virtue and perseverance. Fine mental qualities and a high moral tone are not the result of accident. God gives opportunities; success depends upon the use made of them. . . .

His grace is given to work in us to will and to do, but never as a substitute for our effort. As the Lord cooperated with Daniel and his fellows, so He will cooperate with all who strive to do His will. And by the impartation of His Spirit He will strengthen every true purpose, every noble resolution. Those who walk in the path of obedience will encounter many hindrances. Strong, subtle influences may bind them to the world; but the Lord is able to render futile every agency that works for the defeat of His chosen ones; in His strength they may overcome every temptation, conquer every difficulty.[48]

NO COMPROMISE

Them that honour me, I will honour. 1 Sam. 2:30.

In the experience of Daniel and his companions we have an instance of the triumph of principle over temptation to indulge the appetite. It shows us that through religious principle young men may triumph over the lusts of the flesh, and remain true to God's requirements, even though it costs them a great sacrifice.

What if Daniel and his companions had made a compromise with those heathen officers, and had yielded to the pressure of the occasion, by eating and drinking as was customary with the Babylonians? That single instance of departure from principle would have weakened their sense of right and their abhorrence of wrong. Indulgence of appetite would have invoked the sacrifice of physical vigor, clearness of intellect, and spiritual power. One wrong step would probably have led to others, until, their connection with Heaven being severed, they would have been swept away by temptation. . . .

While Daniel clung to his God with unwavering trust, the spirit of prophetic power came upon him. While he was instructed of man in the duties of court life, he was taught of God to read the mysteries of future ages, and to present to coming generations, through figures and similitudes, the wonderful things that would come to pass in the last days.[49]

God designed that man should be constantly improving, daily reaching a higher point in the scale of excellence. He will help us, if we seek to help ourselves. Our hope of happiness in two worlds depends upon our improvement in one. At every point we should be guarded against the first approach to intemperance.

Dear youth, God calls upon you to do a work which through His grace you can do. . . . Show a purity of tastes, appetite, and habits that bears comparison with Daniel's. God will reward you with calm nerves, a clear brain, an unimpaired judgment, keen perceptions. The youth of today whose principles are firm and unwavering will be blessed with health of body, mind, and soul.[50]

WITNESSING

But I keep under my body, and bring it into subjection: lest that by any means, when I have preached to others, I myself should be a castaway. 1 Cor. 9:27.

As God called Daniel to witness for Him in Babylon, so He calls us to be His witnesses in the world today. In the smallest as well as the largest affairs of life, He desires us to reveal to men the principles of His kingdom. Many are waiting for some great work to be brought to them, while daily they lose opportunities for revealing faithfulness to God. Daily they fail of discharging with wholeheartedness the little duties of life. . . .

In the life of the true Christian there are no nonessentials; in the sight of Omnipotence every duty is important. The Lord measures with exactness every possibility for service. The unused capabilities are just as much brought into account as those that are used. We shall be judged by what we ought to have done, but did not accomplish because we did not use our powers to glorify God.

A noble character is not the result of accident; it is not due to special favors or endowments of Providence. It is the result of self-discipline, of subjection of the lower to the higher nature, of the surrender of self to the service of God and man. . . .

The body is a most important medium through which the mind and the soul are developed for the upbuilding of character. Hence it is that the adversary of souls directs his temptations to the enfeebling and degrading of the physical powers. . . .

The body is to be brought into subjection to the higher powers of the being. The passions are to be controlled by the will, which is itself to be under the control of God. The kingly power of reason, sanctified by divine grace, is to bear sway in the life. Intellectual power, physical stamina, and the length of life depend upon immutable laws. Through obedience to these laws, man may stand conqueror of himself, conqueror of his own inclinations, conqueror of . . . "the rulers of the darkness of this world," and of "spiritual wickedness in high places." [51]

UNDER GOD'S CONTROL

Daniel answered and said, Blessed be the name of God for ever and ever: for wisdom and might are his: and he changeth the times and the seasons: he removeth kings, and setteth up kings: he giveth wisdom unto the wise, and knowledge to them that know understanding. Dan. 2:20, 21.

Behold the Jewish captive, calm and self-possessed, in the presence of the monarch of the world's most powerful empire. In his first words he disclaimed honor for himself and exalted God as the source of all wisdom. To the anxious inquiry of the king, "Art thou able to make known unto me the dream which I have seen, and the interpretation thereof?" he replied: "The secret which the king hath demanded cannot the wise men, the astrologers, the magicians, the soothsayers, show unto the king; but there is a God in heaven that revealeth secrets, and maketh known to the king Nebuchadnezzar what shall be in the latter days.". . .

In the annals of human history, the growth of nations, the rise and fall of empires, appear as if dependent on the will and prowess of man; the shaping of events seems, to a great degree, to be determined by his power, ambition, or caprice. But in the word of God the curtain is drawn aside, and we behold, above, behind, and through all the play and counterplay of human interest and power and passions, the agencies of the All-merciful One, silently, patiently working out the counsels of His own will. . . .

In the history of nations the student of God's word may behold the literal fulfillment of divine prophecy. Babylon, shattered and broken at last, passed away because in prosperity its rulers had regarded themselves as independent of God, and had ascribed the glory of their kingdom to human achievement. . . . The kingdoms that followed were even more base and corrupt; and these sank lower and still lower in the scale of moral worth.

The power exercised by every ruler on the earth is Heaven-imparted; and upon his use of the power thus bestowed, his success depends. . . . To recognize the outworking of these principles in the manifestation of His power who "removeth kings, and setteth up kings"—this is to understand the philosophy of history.[1]

BABYLON'S LEADING CITIZEN

There is a God in heaven that revealeth secrets, and maketh known to the king Nebuchadnezzar what shall be in the latter days. Dan. 2:28.

Daniel sought the Lord when the decree went forth to slay all the wise men of the kingdom of Babylon because they could not relate or interpret a dream which had gone from the king's mind. Nebuchadnezzar demanded not only the interpretation of the dream, but the relation of the dream itself. . . . They declared that the request of the king was . . . beyond that which had ever been required of any man. The king became furious, and acted like all men who have great power and uncontrollable passions. He decided that every one of them should be put to death, and as Daniel and his fellows were numbered with the wise men, they also were to share this fate.[2]

Daniel was imbued with the spirit of Jesus Christ, and he pleaded that the wise men of Babylon should not be destroyed. The followers of Christ do not possess the attributes of Satan, which make it a pleasure to grieve and afflict the creatures of God. They have the spirit of their Master who said, "I am come to seek and to save that which was lost. I came not to call the righteous but sinners to repentance." Had Daniel possessed the same quality of religious zeal which is so quickly inflamed today in the churches, and men are led by it to afflict and oppress and destroy those who do not serve God after their prescribed plan, he would have said to Arioch, "These men who claim to be wise men are deceiving the king. They have not the knowledge they claim to have, and should be destroyed. They dishonor the God of heaven, they serve idols, and their lives in no way do honor to God; let them die; but bring me in before the king and I will show unto the king the interpretation."

The transforming grace of God was made manifest in His servant, and he pleaded most earnestly for the lives of the very men who afterwards, in a secret, underhanded manner, made plans by which they thought to put an end to the life of Daniel. These men became jealous of Daniel because he found favor with kings and nobles, and was honored as the greatest man in Babylon.[3]

251

FOUR IN THE FURNACE

Our God whom we serve is able to deliver us from the burning fiery furnace, and he will deliver us out of thine hand, O king. Dan. 3:17.

The Lord did not forget His own. As His witnesses were cast into the furnace, the Savior revealed Himself to them in person, and together they walked in the midst of the fire. In the presence of the Lord of heat and cold, the flames lost their power to consume.

From his royal seat the king looked on, expecting to see the men who had defied him utterly destroyed. But his feelings of triumph suddenly changed. The nobles standing near saw his face grow pale as he started from the throne and looked intently into the glowing flames. In alarm the king, turning to his lords, asked, "Did not we cast three men bound into the midst of the fire? . . . Lo, I see four men loose, walking in the midst of the fire, and they have no hurt; and the form of the fourth is like the Son of God."

How did that heathen king know what the Son of God was like? The Hebrew captives filling positions of trust in Babylon had in life and character represented before him the truth. When asked for a reason of their faith, they had given it without hesitation. Plainly and simply they had presented the principles of righteousness, thus teaching those around them of the God whom they worshiped. They had told of Christ, the Redeemer to come; and in the form of the fourth in the midst of the fire the king recognized the Son of God. . . .

He who walked with the Hebrew worthies in the fiery furnace will be with His followers wherever they are. His abiding presence will comfort and sustain. In the midst of the time of trouble—trouble such as has not been since there was a nation—His chosen ones will stand unmoved. Satan with all the hosts of evil cannot destroy the weakest of God's saints. Angels that excel in strength will protect them, and in their behalf Jehovah will reveal Himself as a "God of gods," able to save to the uttermost those who have put their trust in Him.[4]

NEBUCHADNEZZAR HUMILIATED

And all the inhabitants of the earth are reputed as nothing: and he doeth according to his will in the army of heaven, and among the inhabitants of the earth: and none can stay his hand, or say unto him, What doest thou? Dan. 4:35.

The last dream which God gave to Nebuchadnezzar, and the experience of the king in connection with it, contain lessons of vital importance to all those who are connected with the work of God. The king was troubled with his dream; for it was evidently a prediction of adversity, and none of his wise men would attempt to interpret it. The faithful Daniel stood before the king, not to flatter, not to misinterpret in order to secure favor. A solemn duty rested upon him to tell the king of Babylon the truth. . . .

Nebuchadnezzar did not heed the heaven-sent message. One year after he had been thus warned, as he walked in his palace, he said within himself, "Is not this great Babylon, that I have built . . . ?" The God of heaven read the heart of the king, and heard its whisperings of self-congratulation. . . . "There fell a voice from heaven, saying, . . . The kingdom is departed from thee. And they shall drive thee from men, and thy dwelling shall be with the beasts of the field: they shall make thee to eat grass as oxen, and seven times shall pass over thee, until thou know that the Most High ruleth in the kingdom of men, and giveth it to whomsoever he will. The same hour was the thing fulfilled upon Nebuchadnezzar."[5]

For seven years Nebuchadnezzar was an astonishment to all his subjects; for seven years he was humbled before all the world. Then his reason was restored and, looking up in humility to the God of heaven, he recognized the divine hand in his chastisement. In a public proclamation he acknowledged his guilt and the great mercy of God in his restoration. . . .

God's purpose that the greatest kingdom in the world should show forth His praise was now fulfilled. This public proclamation, in which Nebuchadnezzar acknowledged the mercy and goodness and authority of God, was the last act of his life recorded in sacred history.[6]

DANIEL, GOD'S AMBASSADOR

Then the presidents and princes sought to find occasion against Daniel concerning the kingdom; but they could find none occasion nor fault; forasmuch as he was faithful, neither was there any error or fault found in him. Dan. 6:4.

Daniel, the prime minister of the greatest of earthly kingdoms, was at the same time a prophet of God, receiving the light of heavenly inspiration. A man of like passions as ourselves, the pen of inspiration describes him as without fault. His business transactions, when subjected to the closest scrutiny of his enemies, were found to be without one flaw. He was an example of what every businessman may become when his heart is converted and consecrated, and when his motives are right in the sight of God. . . .

Unwavering in his allegiance to God, unyielding in his mastery of self, Daniel, by his noble dignity and unswerving integrity, while yet a young man, won the "favor and tender love" of the heathen officer in whose charge he had been placed. . . . He rose speedily to the position of prime minister of the kingdom of Babylon. Through the reign of successive monarchs, the downfall of the nation, and the establishment of another world empire, such were his wisdom and statesmanship, so perfect his tact, his courtesy, his genuine goodness of heart, his fidelity to principle, that even his enemies were forced to the confession that "they could find none occasion nor fault; forasmuch as he was faithful."

Honored by men with the responsibilities of state and with the secrets of kingdoms bearing universal sway, Daniel was honored by God as His ambassador, and was given many revelations of the mysteries of ages to come. His wonderful prophecies, as recorded by him in chapters 7 to 12 of the book bearing his name, were not fully understood even by the prophet himself; but before his life labors closed, he was given the blessed assurance that "at the end of the days"—in the closing period of this world's history—he would again be permitted to stand in his lot and place. . . .

We may, like Daniel and his fellows, live for that which is true and noble and enduring. And learning in this life the principles of the kingdom of our Lord and Savior, . . . we may be prepared at His coming to enter with Him into its possession.[7]

254

GOD SENT HIS ANGEL

Then the king commanded, and they brought Daniel, and cast him into the den of lions. Now the king spake and said unto Daniel, Thy God whom thou servest continually, he will deliver thee. Dan. 6:16.

Daniel was high in command. The accusing host of evil angels stirred up the presidents and princes to envy and jealousy. . . . These agents of Satan sought to make his faithfulness to God the cause of his destruction. . . .

The king was ignorant of the subtle mischief purposed against Daniel. With full knowledge of the king's decree, Daniel still bows before his God, "his windows being open." He considers supplication to God of so great importance that he would rather sacrifice his life than relinquish it.[8]

God did not prevent Daniel's enemies from casting him into the lions' den; He permitted evil angels and wicked men thus far to accomplish their purpose; but it was that He might make the deliverance of His servant more marked, and the defeat of the enemies of truth and righteousness more complete. . . . Through the courage of this one man who chose to follow right rather than policy, Satan was to be defeated, and the name of God was to be exalted and honored.

Early the next morning King Darius hastened to the den and "cried with a lamentable voice," "O Daniel, servant of the living God, is thy God, whom thou servest continually, able to deliver thee from the lions?"

The voice of the prophet replied: "O king, live forever. My God hath sent his angel, and hath shut the lions' mouths, that they have not hurt me." . . .

Daniel in the lions' den was the same Daniel who stood before the king as chief among the ministers of state and as a prophet of the Most High. A man whose heart is stayed upon God will be the same in the hour of his greatest trial as he is in prosperity, when the light and favor of God and of man beam upon him. . . . The power that is near to deliver from physical harm or distress is also near to save from the greater evil, making it possible for the servant of God to maintain his integrity under all circumstances, and to triumph through divine grace.[9]

BURDEN-SHARING

And I set my face unto the Lord God, to seek by prayer and supplications, with fasting, and sackcloth, and ashes: and I prayed unto the Lord my God, and made my confession. Dan. 9:3, 4.

Burdened in behalf of Israel, Daniel studied anew the prophecies of Jeremiah. They were very plain—so plain that he understood by these testimonies recorded in books "the number of the years, whereof the word of the Lord came to Jeremiah the prophet, that He would accomplish seventy years in the desolations of Jerusalem."

With faith founded on the sure word of prophecy, Daniel pleaded with the Lord for the speedy fulfillment of these promises. He pleaded for the honor of God to be preserved. In his petition he identified himself fully with those who had fallen short of the divine purpose, confessing their sins as his own.[10]

What a prayer was that which came forth from the lips of Daniel! What humbling of soul it reveals! The warmth of heavenly fire was recognized in the words that were going upward to God. Heaven responded to that prayer by sending its messenger to Daniel. In this our day, prayers offered in like manner will prevail with God. "The effectual fervent prayer of a righteous man availeth much." As in ancient times, when prayer was offered, fire descended from heaven, and consumed the sacrifice upon the altar, so in answer to our prayers, the heavenly fire will come into our souls. The light and power of the Holy Spirit will be ours. . . .

Have not we as great need to call upon God as had Daniel? I address those who believe that we are living in the very last period of this earth's history. I entreat you to take upon your own souls a burden for our churches, our schools, and our institutions. That God who heard Daniel's prayer will hear ours when we come to Him in contrition. Our necessities are as urgent, our difficulties are as great, and we need to have the same intensity of purpose, and in faith roll our burden upon the great Burden-bearer. There is need for hearts to be as deeply moved in our time as in the time when Daniel prayed.[11]

GOD'S HAND ON THE MACHINERY

That saith of Cyrus, He is my shepherd, and shall perform all my pleasure: even saying to Jerusalem, Thou shalt be built; and to the temple, Thy foundation shall be laid. Isa. 44:28.

The Lord has resources. His hand is on the machinery. When the time came for His temple to be rebuilt, He moved upon Cyrus as His agent to discern the prophecies concerning Himself, and to grant the Jewish people their liberty.[12]

The deliverance of Daniel from the den of lions had been used of God to create a favorable impression upon the mind of Cyrus the Great. . . .

As the king saw the words foretelling, more than a hundred years before his birth, the manner in which Babylon should be taken; as he read the message addressed to him by the Ruler of the universe, . . . his heart was profoundly moved, and he determined to fulfill his divinely appointed mission. He would let the Judean captives go free; he would help them restore the temple of Jehovah. In a written proclamation published "throughout all his kingdom," Cyrus made known his desire to provide for the return of the Hebrews and for the rebuilding of their temple. . . .

Tidings of this decree reached the farthermost provinces of the king's realm, and everywhere among the children of the dispersion there was great rejoicing. Many, like Daniel, had been studying the prophecies, and had been asking God for His promised intervention in behalf of Zion. . . .

Upon Zerubbabel . . . Cyrus placed the responsibility of acting as governor of the company returning to Judea; and with him was associated Joshua the high priest. The long journey across the desert wastes was accomplished in safety, and the happy company . . . at once undertook the work of re-establishing that which had been broken down and destroyed.[13]

The Lord God omnipotent reigneth. All kings, all nations, are His, under His rule and government. His resources are infinite. The wise man declares, "The king's heart is in the hand of the Lord, as the rivers of water: he turneth it whithersoever he will." Those upon whose actions hang the destinies of nations are watched over with a vigilance that knows no relaxation by Him who "giveth salvation unto kings."[14]

OBSTACLES A TEST OF FAITH

For who hath despised the day of small things? Zech. 4:10.

In rebuilding the house of the Lord, Zerubbabel had labored in the face of manifold difficulties. From the beginning, adversaries had "weakened the hands of the people of Judah, and troubled them in building," "and made them to cease by force and power." But the Lord had interposed in behalf of the builders, and now He spoke through His prophet to Zerubbabel, saying, "Who art thou, O great mountain? before Zerubbabel thou shalt become a plain.". . .

Throughout the history of God's people great mountains of difficulty, apparently insurmountable, have loomed up before those who were trying to carry out the purposes of Heaven. Such obstacles are permitted by the Lord as a test of faith. When we are hedged about on every side, this is the time above all others to trust in God and in the power of His Spirit. The exercise of a living faith means an increase of spiritual strength and the development of an unfaltering trust. It is thus that the soul becomes a conquering power. Before the demand of faith, the obstacles placed by Satan across the pathway of the Christian will disappear; for the powers of heaven will come to his aid. "Nothing shall be impossible unto you."

The way of the world is to begin with pomp and boasting. God's way is to make the day of small things the beginning of the glorious triumph of truth and righteousness. Sometimes He trains His workers by bringing to them disappointment and apparent failure. It is His purpose that they shall learn to master difficulties.

Often men are tempted to falter before the perplexities and obstacles that confront them. But if they will hold the beginning of their confidence steadfast unto the end, God will make the way clear. . . . Before the intrepid spirit and unwavering faith of a Zerubbabel, great mountains of difficulty will become a plain; and he whose hands have laid the foundation, even "his hands shall also finish it." [15]

EZRA, STUDENT AND TEACHER

Ezra . . . prepared his heart to seek the law of the Lord, and to do it. Ezra 7:10.

Born of the sons of Aaron, Ezra had been given a priestly training; and in addition to this he had acquired a familiarity with the writings of the magicians, the astrologers, and the wise men of the Medo-Persian realm. But he was not satisfied with his spiritual condition. He longed to be in full harmony with God; he longed for wisdom to carry out the divine will. . . . This led him to apply himself diligently to a study of the history of God's people, as recorded in the writings of prophets and kings. He searched the historical and poetical books of the Bible to learn why the Lord had permitted Jerusalem to be destroyed and His people carried captive into a heathen land. . . .

He studied the instruction given at Mount Sinai and through the long period of wilderness wandering. As he learned more and still more concerning God's dealings with His children, and comprehended the sacredness of the law given at Sinai, Ezra's heart was stirred. He experienced a new and thorough conversion and determined to master the records of sacred history, that he might use this knowledge to bring blessing and light to his people.

Ezra endeavored to gain a heart preparation for the work he believed was before him. He sought God earnestly, that he might be a wise teacher in Israel. As he learned to yield mind and will to divine control, there were brought into his life the principles of true sanctification, which, in later years, had a molding influence, not only upon the youth who sought his instruction, but upon all others associated with him. . . .

Ezra became a mouthpiece for God, educating those about him in the principles that govern heaven. . . . Whether near the court of the king of Medo-Persia or at Jerusalem, his principal work was that of a teacher. As he communicated to others the truths he learned, his capacity for labor increased. He became a man of piety and zeal. He was the Lord's witness to the world of the power of Bible truth to ennoble the daily life.[16]

KNOWLEDGE REQUIRES ACTION

Ezra . . . was a ready scribe in the law of Moses, which the Lord God of Israel had given. Ezra 7:6.

More than two thousand years have passed since Ezra "prepared his heart to seek the law of the Lord, and to do it, yet the lapse of time has not lessened the influence of his pious example. Through the centuries the record of his life of consecration has inspired many with the determination "to seek the law of the Lord, and to do it."

Ezra's motives were high and holy; in all that he did he was actuated by a deep love for souls. The compassion and tenderness that he revealed toward those who had sinned, either willfully or through ignorance, should be an object lesson to all who seek to bring about reforms. . . .

There is no such thing as weakening or strengthening the law of Jehovah. As it has been, so it is. It always has been, and always will be, holy, just, and good, complete in itself. It cannot be repealed or changed. To "honor" or "dishonor" it is but the speech of men. . . .

Christians should be preparing for what is soon to break upon the world as an overwhelming surprise, and this preparation they should make by diligently studying the word of God and striving to conform their lives to its precepts. The tremendous issues of eternity demand of us something besides an imaginary religion, a religion of words and forms, where truth is kept in the outer court. . . .

If the saints of the Old Testament bore so bright a testimony of loyalty, should not those upon whom is shining the accumulated light of centuries bear a still more signal witness to the power of truth?[17]

Shall we let the example of Ezra teach us the use we should make of our knowledge of the Scriptures? The life of this servant of God should be an inspiration to us to serve the Lord with heart and mind and strength. We each have an appointed work to do, and this can be accomplished only by consecrated effort. We need first to set ourselves to know the requirements of God, and then to practise them. Then we can sow seeds of truth that will bear fruit unto eternal life.[18]

GOD THEIR PROTECTOR

For I was ashamed to require of the king a band of soldiers and horsemen to help us against the enemy in the way: because we had spoken unto the king, saying, The hand of our God is upon all them for good that seek him; but his power and his wrath is against all them that forsake him. Ezra 8:22.

Ezra's faith that God would do a mighty work for His people, led him to tell Artaxerxes of his desire to return to Jerusalem to revive an interest in the study of God's word and to assist his brethren in restoring the holy city. As Ezra declared his perfect trust in the God of Israel as one abundantly able to protect and care for His people, the king was deeply impressed. . . . He made him a special representative of the Medo-Persian kingdom, and conferred on him extensive powers for the carrying out of the purposes that were in his heart. . . .

Thus again the children of the dispersion were given opportunity to return to the land with the possession of which were linked the promises to the house of Israel. . . .

Before them was a journey that would occupy several months. The men were taking with them their wives and children, and their substance, besides large treasure for the temple and its service. Ezra was aware that enemies lay in wait by the way, ready to plunder and destroy him and his company; yet he had asked from the king no armed force for protection. . . .

In this matter, Ezra and his companions saw an opportunity to magnify the name of God before the heathen. Faith in the power of the living God would be strengthened if the Israelites themselves should now reveal implicit faith in their divine Leader. They therefore determined to put their trust wholly in Him. They would ask for no guard of soldiers. They would give the heathen no occasion to ascribe to the strength of man the glory that belongs to God alone. They could not afford to arouse in the minds of their heathen friends one doubt as to the sincerity of their dependence on God as His people. . . . Only by keeping the law of the Lord before them, and striving to obey it, would they be protected. . . . "So we fasted and besought our God for this: and He was entreated of us." [19]

A HOLY PURPOSE

O Lord, I beseech thee, let now thine ear be attentive to the prayer of thy servant, . . . and prosper, I pray thee, thy servant this day, and grant him mercy in the sight of this man. Neh. 1:11.

Nehemiah, one of the Hebrew exiles, occupied a position of influence and honor in the Persian court. As cupbearer to the king he was admitted freely to the royal presence. . . . Through this man . . . God purposed to bring blessing to His people in the land of their fathers. . . .

The Hebrew patriot learned that days of trial had come to Jerusalem, the chosen city. The returned exiles were suffering affliction and reproach. . . . The work of restoration was hindered, the temple services were disturbed, and the people kept in constant alarm by the fact that the walls of the city were still largely in ruins. . . .

Nehemiah had often poured out his soul in behalf of his people. But now as he prayed a holy purpose formed in his mind. He resolved that if he could obtain the consent of the king, and the necessary aid in procuring implements and material, he would himself undertake the task of rebuilding the walls of Jerusalem. . . .

Four months Nehemiah waited for a favorable opportunity to present his request to the king. . . . He had a sacred trust to fulfill, in which he required help from the king; and he realized that much depended upon his presenting the matter in such a way as to win his approval and enlist his aid. "I prayed," he said, "to the God of heaven." In that brief prayer, Nehemiah pressed into the presence of the King of kings and won to his side a power that can turn hearts as the rivers of waters are turned.

To pray as Nehemiah prayed in his hour of need is a resource at the command of the Christian under circumstances when other forms of prayer may be impossible. . . . In times of sudden difficulty or peril the heart may send up its cry for help to One who has pledged Himself to come to the aid of His faithful, believing ones whenever they call upon Him. In every circumstance, under every condition, the soul weighed down with grief and care, or fiercely assailed by temptation, may find assurance, support, and succor in the unfailing love and power of a covenant-keeping God.[20]

A MAN OF ACTION

It pleased the king to send me; and I set him a time. Neh. 2:6.

While Nehemiah implored the help of God, he did not fold his own hands, feeling that he had no more care or responsibility in the bringing about of his purpose to restore Jerusalem. With admirable prudence and forethought he proceeded to make all the arrangements necessary to insure the success of the enterprise. . . .

The example of this holy man should be a lesson to all the people of God, that they are not only to pray in faith, but to work with diligence and fidelity. How many difficulties we encounter, how often we hinder the working of Providence in our behalf, because prudence, forethought, and painstaking are regarded as having little to do with religion! This is a grave mistake. It is our duty to cultivate and to exercise every power that will render us more efficient workers for God. Careful consideration and well-matured plans are as essential to the success of sacred enterprises today as in the time of Nehemiah. . . . Men of prayer should be men of action. Those who are ready and willing will find ways and means of working. Nehemiah did not depend upon uncertainties. The means which he lacked he solicited from those who were able to bestow.

The Lord still moves upon the hearts of kings and rulers in behalf of His people. Those who are laboring for Him are to avail themselves of the help that He prompts men to give for the advancement of His cause. . . . These men may have no sympathy with God's work, no faith in Christ, no acquaintance with His word; but their gifts are not on this account to be refused. . . .

As long as we are in this world, as long as the Spirit of God strives with the children of men, so long are we to receive favors as well as to impart them. We are to give to the world the light of truth, as revealed in the Scriptures; and we are to receive from the world that which God moves upon them to give in behalf of His cause. . . . O that Christians might realize more and still more fully that it is their privilege and their duty, while cherishing right principles, to take advantage of every Heaven-sent opportunity for advancing God's kingdom in this world![21]

LET US BUILD

Then I told them of the hand of my God which was good upon me . . . and they said, Let us rise up and build. So they strengthened their hands for this good work. Neh. 2:18.

With sorrow-stricken heart, the visitor from afar gazed upon the ruined defenses of his loved Jerusalem. And is it not thus that angels of heaven survey the condition of the church of Christ? Like the dwellers at Jerusalem, we become accustomed to existing evils, and often are content while making no effort to remedy them. But how are these evils regarded by beings divinely illuminated? Do not they, like Nehemiah, look with sorrow-burdened heart upon ruined walls, and gates burned with fire?[22]

Nehemiah bore a royal commission requiring the inhabitants to co-operate with him in rebuilding the walls of the city, but he did not depend upon the exercise of authority. He sought rather to gain the confidence and sympathy of the people, knowing that a union of hearts as well as of hands was essential in the great work before him.[23]

There is need of Nehemiahs in the church today—not men who can pray and preach only, but men whose prayers and sermons are braced with firm and eager purpose. . . . The success attending Nehemiah's efforts shows what prayer, faith, and wise, energetic action will accomplish. . . . The spirit manifested by the leader will be, to a great extent, reflected by the people. If the leaders professing to believe the solemn, important truths that are to test the world at this time manifest no ardent zeal to prepare a people to stand in the day of God, we must expect the church to be careless, indolent, and pleasure-loving.[24]

Nehemiah was a reformer, a great man raised up for an important time. As he came in contact with evil and every kind of opposition, fresh courage and zeal were aroused. His energy and determination inspired the people of Jerusalem; and strength and courage took the place of feebleness and discouragement. His holy purpose, his high hope, his cheerful consecration to the work, were contagious. The people caught the enthusiasm of their leader, and in his sphere each man became a Nehemiah, and helped to make stronger the hand and heart of his neighbor.[25]

UNINVOLVED

And next unto them the Tekoites repaired; but their nobles put not their necks to the work of their Lord. Neh. 3:5.

Among the first to catch Nehemiah's spirit of zeal and earnestness were the priests. Because of their influential position, these men could do much to advance or hinder the work; and their ready cooperation at the very outset, contributed not a little to its success. The majority of the princes and rulers of Israel came up nobly to their duty, and these faithful men have honorable mention in the book of God. There were a few, the Tekoite nobles, who "put not their necks to the work of their Lord." The memory of these slothful servants is branded with shame and has been handed down as a warning to all future generations.

In every religious movement there are some who, while they cannot deny that the cause is God's, still hold themselves aloof, refusing to make any effort to help. It were well for such ones to remember the record kept on high—that book in which there are no omissions, no mistakes, and out of which they will be judged. There every neglected opportunity to do service for God is recorded; and there, too, every deed of faith and love is held in everlasting remembrance.

Against the inspiring influence of Nehemiah's presence the example of the Tekoite nobles had little weight. The people in general were animated by patriotism and zeal. Men of ability and influence organized the various classes of citizens into companies, each leader making himself responsible for the erection of a certain part of the wall. And of some it is written that they builded "everyone over against his house."

Nor did Nehemiah's energy abate, now that the work was actually begun. With tireless vigilance he superintended the building, directing the workmen, noting the hindrances, and providing for emergencies. . . . In his many activities Nehemiah did not forget the source of his strength. His heart was constantly uplifted to God, the great Overseer of all. "The God of heaven," he exclaimed, "He will prosper us"; and the words, echoed and re-echoed, thrilled the hearts of all the workers on the wall.[26]

UNHOLY ALLIANCE

Our God shall fight for us. Neh. 4:20.

The restoration of the defenses of Jerusalem did not go forward unhindered. Satan was working to stir up opposition, and bring discouragement. . . . But taunts and ridicule, opposition and threats, seemed only to inspire Nehemiah with firmer determination and to arouse him to greater watchfulness. He recognized the dangers that must be met in this warfare with their enemies, but his courage was undaunted. "We made our prayer unto our God," he declares, "and set a watch against them day and night.". . .

Beside Nehemiah stood a trumpeter, and on different parts of the wall were stationed priests bearing the sacred trumpets. The people were scattered in their labors; but on the approach of danger at any point, a signal was given for them to repair thither without delay. "So we labored in the work," Nehemiah says, "and half of them held the spears from the rising of the morning till the stars appeared." . . . Nehemiah and his companions did not shrink from hardship or trying service. Neither by day nor night, not even during the short time given to sleep, did they put off their clothing, or lay aside their armor.

The opposition and discouragement that the builders in Nehemiah's day met from open enemies and pretended friends is typical of the experience that those today will have who work for God. Christians are tried, not only by the anger, contempt, and cruelty of enemies, but by the indolence, inconsistency, lukewarmness, and treachery of avowed friends and helpers. . . .

Satan takes advantage of every unconsecrated element for the accomplishment of his purposes. Among those who profess to be the supporters of God's cause there are those who unite with His enemies and thus lay His cause open to the attacks of His bitterest foes. Even some who desire the work of God to prosper will yet weaken the hands of His servants by hearing, reporting, and half believing the slanders, boasts, and menaces of His adversaries. . . . The response of faith today will be the response made by Nehemiah, "Our God shall fight for us"; for God is in the work, and no man can prevent its ultimate success.[27]

REMEMBER THE POOR

If there be among you a poor man of one of thy brethren within any of thy gates in thy land which the Lord thy God giveth thee, . . . thou shalt open thine hand wide unto him, and shalt surely lend him sufficient for his need. Deut. 15:7, 8.

At times following the return of the exiles from Babylon, the wealthy Jews had gone directly contrary to these commands. When the poor were obliged to borrow to pay tribute to the king, the wealthy had lent them money, but had exacted a high rate of interest. By taking mortgages on the lands of the poor, they had gradually reduced the unfortunate debtors to the deepest poverty. Many had been forced to sell their sons and daughters into servitude; and there seemed no hope of improving their condition, no way to redeem either their children or their lands, no prospect before them but ever-increasing distress, with perpetual want and bondage. Yet they were of the same nation, children of the same covenant, as their more favored brethren. . . .

As Nehemiah heard of this cruel oppression, his soul was filled with indignation. . . . He saw that if he succeeded in breaking up the oppressive custom of exaction he must take a decided stand for justice. With characteristic energy and determination he went to work to bring relief to his brethren.

The fact that the oppressors were men of wealth, whose support was greatly needed in the work of restoring the city, did not for a moment influence Nehemiah. He sharply rebuked the nobles and rulers, and when he had gathered a great assembly of the people he set before them the requirements of God touching the case. . . .

This record teaches an important lesson. "The love of money is the root of all evil" (1 Tim. 6:10). In this generation the desire for gain is the absorbing passion. . . . We were all debtors to divine justice, but we had nothing with which to pay the debt. Then the Son of God, who pitied us, paid the price of our redemption. He became poor that through His poverty we might be rich. By deeds of liberality toward His poor we may prove the sincerity of our gratitude for the mercy extended to us.[28]

"I CANNOT COME DOWN"

I am doing a great work, so that I cannot come down: why should the work cease, whilst I leave it, and come down to you? Neh. 6:3.

Nehemiah was chosen by God because he was willing to cooperate with the Lord as a restorer. . . . When he saw wrong principles being acted upon, he did not stand by as an onlooker, and by his silence give consent. He did not leave the people to conclude that he was standing on the wrong side. He took a firm, unyielding stand for the right.[29]

Every device that the prince of darkness can suggest will be employed to induce God's servants to form a confederacy with the agents of Satan. . . . Like Nehemiah, they should steadfastly reply, "I am doing a great work, so that I cannot come down." God's workers may safely keep on with their work, letting their efforts refute the falsehoods that malice may coin for their injury. Like the builders on the walls of Jerusalem they must refuse to be diverted from their work by threats or mockery. . . .

As the time of the end draws near, Satan's temptations will be brought to bear with greater power upon God's workers. He will employ human agents to mock and revile those who "build the wall." But should the builders come down to meet the attacks of their foes, this would but retard the work. They should endeavor to defeat the purposes of their adversaries, but they should not allow anything to call them from their work. Truth is stronger than error, and right will prevail over wrong. . . . In Nehemiah's firm devotion to the work of God, and his equally firm reliance on God, lay the reason of the failure of his enemies to draw him into their power. The soul that is indolent falls an easy prey to temptation; but in the life that has a noble aim, an absorbing purpose, evil finds little foothold. . . .

God has provided divine assistance for all the emergencies to which our human resources are unequal. He gives the Holy Spirit to help in every strait, to strengthen our hope and assurance, to illuminate our minds and purify our hearts. He provides opportunities and opens channels of working. If His people are watching the indications of His providence, and are ready to co-operate with Him, they will see mighty results.[30]

BUILD—REPAIR—RESTORE

They that shall be of thee shall build the old waste places: thou shalt raise up the foundations of many generations; and thou shalt be called, The repairer of the breach, The restorer of paths to dwell in. Isa. 58:12.

In the work of reform to be carried forward today, there is need of men who, like Ezra and Nehemiah, will not palliate or excuse sin, nor shrink from vindicating the honor of God. Those upon whom rests the burden of this work will not hold their peace when wrong is done, neither will they cover evil with a cloak of false charity. They will remember that God is no respecter of persons, and that severity to a few may prove mercy to many. They will remember also that in the one who rebukes evil the spirit of Christ should ever be revealed.

In their work, Ezra and Nehemiah humbled themselves before God, confessing their sins and the sins of their people, and entreating pardon as if they themselves were the offenders. . . . Nehemiah was not a priest; he was not a prophet; he made no pretension to high title. He was a reformer raised up for an important time. It was his aim to set his people right with God. Inspired with a great purpose, he bent every energy of his being to its accomplishment. . . . As he came into contact with evil and opposition to right he took so determined a stand that the people were roused to labor with fresh zeal and courage. . . .

The work of restoration and reform carried on by the returned exiles, under the leadership of Zerubbabel, Ezra, and Nehemiah, presents a picture of a work of spiritual restoration that is to be wrought in the closing days of this earth's history. . . . God's remnant people, standing before the world as reformers, are to show that the law of God is the foundation of all enduring reform and that the Sabbath of the fourth commandment is to stand as a memorial of creation, a constant reminder of the power of God. In clear, distinct lines they are to present the necessity of obedience to all the precepts of the Decalogue. Constrained by the love of Christ, they are to cooperate with Him in building up the waste places. They are to be repairers of the breach, restorers of paths to dwell in.[31]

ONE OF GOD'S GREAT MEN

He will be one of God's great men; he will touch neither wine nor strong drink and he will be filled with the Holy Spirit from the moment of his birth. Luke 1:15, Phillips.

On heaven's record of noble men the Savior declared that there stood not one greater than John the Baptist. The work committed to him was one demanding not only physical energy and endurance, but the highest qualities of mind and soul. So important was right physical training as a preparation for this work that the highest angel in heaven was sent with a message of instruction to the parents of the child.[32]

They were to faithfully co-operate with God in forming such a character in John as would fit him to perform the part God had assigned him. . . . John was the son of their old age, he was a child of miracle, and the parents might have reasoned that he had a special work to do for the Lord and the Lord would take care of him. But the parents did not thus reason; they moved to a retired place in the country, where their son would not be exposed to the temptations of city life, or induced to depart from the counsel and instruction which they as parents would give him.[33]

In the wilderness, John could the more readily deny himself and bring his appetite under control, and dress in accordance to natural simplicity. And there was nothing in the wilderness that would take his mind from meditation and prayer. Satan had access to John, even after he had closed every avenue in his power through which he would enter. But his habits of life were so pure and natural that he could discern the foe, and had strength of spirit and decision of character to resist him.

The book of nature was open before John with its inexhaustible store of varied instruction. He sought the favor of God, and the Holy Spirit rested upon him, and kindled in his heart a glowing zeal to do the great work of calling the people to repentance, and to a higher and holier life. John was fitting himself, by the privations and hardships of his secluded life, to so control all his physical and mental powers that he could stand among the people as unmoved by surrounding circumstances as the rocks and mountains of the wilderness that had surrounded him for thirty years.[34]

IN THE SPIRIT OF ELIJAH

He will go out before God in the spirit and power of Elijah—to reconcile fathers and children, and bring back the disobedient to the wisdom of good men—and he will make a people fully ready for their Lord. Luke 1:17, Phillips.

God had called the son of Zacharias to a great work, the greatest ever committed to men. . . . John was to go forth as Jehovah's messenger, to bring to men the light of God. He must give a new direction to their thoughts. He must impress them with the holiness of God's requirements, and their need of His perfect righteousness. Such a messenger must be holy. He must be a temple for the indwelling Spirit of God. In order to fulfill his mission, he must have a sound physical constitution, and mental and spiritual strength. Therefore it would be necessary for him to control the appetites and passions. He must be able so to control all his powers that he could stand among men as unmoved by surrounding circumstances as the rocks and mountains of the wilderness.

In the time of John the Baptist, greed for riches, and the love of luxury and display had become widespread. Sensuous pleasures, feasting and drinking, were causing physical disease and degeneracy, benumbing the spiritual perceptions, and lessening the sensibility to sin. John was to stand as a reformer. By his abstemious life and plain dress he was to rebuke the excesses of his time. Hence the directions given to the parents of John—a lesson of temperance by an angel from the throne of heaven. . . .

In preparing the way for Christ's first advent, he was a representative of those who are to prepare a people for our Lord's second coming. The world is given to self-indulgence. Errors and fables abound. Satan's snares for destroying are multiplied. All who would perfect holiness in the fear of God must learn the lessons of temperance and self-control, The appetites and passions must be held in subjection to the higher powers of the mind. This self-discipline is essential to that mental strength and spiritual insight which will enable us to understand and to practice the sacred truths of God's word. For this reason temperance finds its place in the work of preparation for Christ's second coming.[35]

A STRAIGHT MESSAGE

Prepare to meet thy God, O Israel. Amos 4:12, last part.

John the Baptist in his desert life was taught of God. He studied the revelations of God in nature. Under the guiding of the divine Spirit, he studied the scrolls of the prophets. By day and by night, Christ was his study, his meditation, until mind and heart and soul were filled with the glorious vision. He looked upon the King in His beauty, and self was lost sight of. He beheld the majesty of holiness, and knew himself to be inefficient and unworthy. It was God's message that he was to declare. It was in God's power and His righteousness that he was to stand. He was ready to go forth as Heaven's messenger, unawed by the human, because he had looked upon the Divine. . . .

With no elaborate arguments or fine-spun theories did John declare his message. Startling and stern, yet full of hope, his voice was heard from the wilderness, "Repent ye: for the kingdom of heaven is at hand." . . . Unlearned peasants and fishermen from the surrounding country; the Roman soldiers from the barracks of Herod; chieftains with their swords at their sides, ready to put down anything that might savor of rebellion; the avaricious tax-gatherers from their toll-booths; and from the Sanhedrim the phylactered priests—all listened as if spellbound; and all . . . went away . . . cut to the heart with a sense of their sins. . . .

In this age, just prior to the second coming of Christ in the clouds of heaven, such a work as that of John is to be done. God calls for men who will prepare a people to stand in the great day of the Lord. . . . As a people who believe in Christ's soon coming, we have a message to bear—"prepare to meet thy God." Our message must be as direct as was the message of John. He rebuked kings for their iniquity. Notwithstanding that his life was imperiled, he did not hesitate to declare God's word. And our work in this age must be done as faithfully.

In order to give such a message as John gave, we must have a spiritual experience like his. The same work must be wrought in us. We must behold God, and in beholding Him, lose sight of self.[36]

A LIVING SACRIFICE

With eyes wide open to the mercies of God, I beg you, my brothers, as an act of intelligent worship, to give him your bodies, as a living sacrifice, consecrated to him and acceptable by him. Rom. 12:1, Phillips.

The Lord has been calling the attention of His people to health reform. This is one of the great branches of the work of preparation for the coming of the Son of man. John the Baptist went forth in the spirit and power of Elijah to prepare the way of the Lord. . . .

John separated himself from friends and from the luxuries of life. The simplicity of his dress, a garment woven of camel's hair, was a standing rebuke to the extravagance and display of the Jewish priests, and of the people generally. His diet, purely vegetable, of locusts and wild honey was a rebuke to the indulgence of appetite and the gluttony that everywhere prevailed. . . . Those who are to prepare the way for the second coming of Christ are represented by faithful Elijah, as John came in the spirit of Elijah to prepare the way for Christ's first advent. The great subject of reform is to be agitated. . . . Temperance in all things is to be connected with the message, to turn the people of God from their idolatry, their gluttony, and their extravagance in dress and other things.

The self-denial, humility, and temperance required of the righteous, whom God especially leads and blesses, is to be presented to the people in contrast to the extravagant, health-destroying habits of those who live in this degenerate age. . . . There is nowhere to be found so great a cause of physical and moral degeneracy as a neglect of this important subject. Those who indulge appetite and passion, and close their eyes to the light for fear they will see sinful indulgences which they are unwilling to forsake, are guilty before God. Whoever turns from the light in one instance hardens his heart to disregard the light upon other matters. Whoever violates moral obligations in the matter of eating and dressing prepares the way to violate the claims of God in regard to eternal interests. Our bodies are not our own. God has claims upon us to take care of the habitation He has given us, that we may present our bodies to Him a living sacrifice, holy and acceptable.[37]

READY TO STEP ASIDE

Behold the Lamb of God, which taketh away the sin of the world. John 1:29.

For a time the Baptist's influence over the nation had been greater than that of its rulers, priests, or princes. If he had announced himself as the Messiah, and raised a revolt against Rome, priests and people would have flocked to his standard. Every consideration that appeals to the ambition of the world's conquerors Satan had stood ready to urge upon John the Baptist. But with the evidence before him of his power, he had steadfastly refused the splendid bribe. The attention which was fixed upon him he had directed to Another. Now he saw the tide of popularity turning away from himself to the Savior. Day by day the crowds about him lessened. . . .

The disciples of John came to him . . . saying, "Rabbi, he that was with thee beyond Jordan, to whom thou bearest witness, behold, the same baptizeth, and all men come to him." Through these words, Satan brought temptation upon John. Though John's mission seemed about to close, it was still possible for him to hinder the work of Christ. If he had sympathized with himself, and expressed grief or disappointment at being superseded, he would have sown the seeds of dissension, would have encouraged envy and jealousy, and would seriously have impeded the progress of the gospel.

John had by nature the faults and weaknesses common to humanity, but the touch of divine love had transformed him. He dwelt in an atmosphere uncontaminated with selfishness and ambition, and far above the miasma of jealousy. . . . It was his joy to witness the success of the Savior's work. . . .

Looking in faith to the Redeemer, John had risen to the height of self-abnegation. He sought not to attract men to himself, but to lift their thoughts higher and still higher, until they should rest upon the Lamb of God. He himself had been only a voice, a cry in the wilderness. Now with joy he accepted silence and obscurity that the eyes of all might be turned to the Light of life. Those who are true to their calling as messengers for God will not seek honor for themselves. Love for self will be swallowed up in love for Christ.[38]

274

"I MUST DECREASE"

That is why my happiness is now complete. He must grow greater and greater and I less and less. John 3:29, 30, Phillips.

In every stage of this earth's history God has had His agencies to carry forward His work. . . . John the Baptist had a special work, for which he was born and to which he was appointed—the work of preparing the way of the Lord.[39]

When, after Christ's ministry began, the disciples of John came to him with the complaint that all men were following the new Teacher, John showed how clearly he understood his relation to the Messiah, and how gladly he welcomed the One for whom he had prepared the way.[40]

John had been called to lead out as a reformer. Because of this, his disciples were in danger of fixing their attention upon him . . . and losing sight of the fact that he was only an instrument through which God had wrought. But the work of John was not sufficient to lay the foundation of the Christian church. When he had fulfilled his mission, another work was to be done, which his testimony could not accomplish. His disciples did not understand this. When they saw Christ coming in to take the work, they were jealous and dissatisfied.

The same dangers still exist. God calls a man to do a certain work; and when he has carried it as far as he is qualified to take it, the Lord brings in others, to carry it still farther. But, like John's disciples, many feel that the success of the work depends on the first laborer. Attention is fixed upon the human instead of the divine, jealousy comes in, and the work of God is marred. The one thus unduly honored is tempted to cherish self-confidence. He does not realize his dependence on God. The people are taught to rely on man for guidance, . . . and are led away from God.

The work of God is not to bear the image and superscription of man. From time to time the Lord will bring in different agencies, through whom His purpose can best be accomplished. Happy are they who are willing for self to be humbled, saying with John the Baptist, "He must increase, but I must decrease."[41]

WHAT MADE HIM GREAT?

Verily I say unto you, Among them that are born of women there hath not risen a greater than John the Baptist: notwithstanding he that is least in the kingdom of heaven is greater than he. Matt. 11:11.

What was it that made John the Baptist great? He closed his mind to the mass of tradition presented by the teachers of the Jewish nation, and opened it to the wisdom which comes from above.[42]

John the Baptist was not fitted for his high calling as the forerunner of Christ by association with the great men of the nation in the schools of Jerusalem. He went out into the wilderness, where the customs and doctrines of men could not mold his mind, and where he could hold unobstructed communion with God.[43]

John the Baptist was a man filled with the Holy Ghost from his birth, and if there was anyone who could remain unaffected by the corrupting influences of the age in which he lived, it was surely he. Yet he did not venture to trust his strength; he separated himself from his friends and relatives, that his natural affections might not prove a snare to him. He would not place himself unnecessarily in the way of temptation nor where the luxuries or even the conveniences of life would lead him to indulge in ease or to gratify his appetite, and thus lessen his physical and mental strength. . . .

He subjected himself to privation and solitude in the wilderness, where he could preserve the sacred sense of the majesty of God by studying His great book of nature. . . . It was an atmosphere calculated to perfect moral culture and to keep the fear of the Lord continually before him. John, the forerunner of Christ, did not expose himself to evil conversation and the corrupting influences of the world. He feared the effect upon his conscience, that sin might not appear to him so exceedingly sinful. He chose rather to have his home in the wilderness, where his senses would not be perverted by his surroundings. Should we not learn something from this example of one whom Christ honored and of whom He said: "Among them that are born of women there hath not risen a greater than John the Baptist"?[44]

IN PRISON FOR CHRIST'S SAKE

For unto you it is given in the behalf of Christ, not only to believe on him, but also to suffer for his sake. Phil. 1:29.

John the Baptist had been first in heralding Christ's kingdom, and he was also first in suffering. . . . He was now shut in by the walls of a dungeon cell. . . . As week after week passed, bringing no change, despondency and doubt crept over him. His disciples did not forsake him. . . . But they questioned why, if this new teacher was the Messiah, He did nothing to effect John's release. . . .

Like the Savior's disciples, John the Baptist did not understand the nature of Christ's kingdom. He expected Jesus to take the throne of David; and as time passed, and the Savior made no claim to kingly authority, John became perplexed and troubled. . . . There were hours when the whisperings of demons tortured his spirit, and the shadow of a terrible fear crept over him. Could it be that the long-hoped-for Deliverer had not yet appeared? . . .

But the Baptist did not surrender his faith in Christ. . . . He determined to send a message of inquiry to Jesus. This he entrusted to two of his disciples. . . . The disciples came to Jesus with their message, "Art thou he that should come, or do we look for another?" . . . The Savior did not at once answer the disciples' question. As they stood wondering at His silence, the sick and afflicted were coming to Him to be healed. . . . While He healed their diseases, He taught the people. . . .

Thus the day wore away, the disciples of John seeing and hearing all. At last Jesus called them to Him, and bade them go and tell John what they had witnessed. . . . The evidence of His divinity was seen in its adaptation to the needs of suffering humanity. . . .

The disciples bore the message, and it was enough. . . . The works of Christ not only declared Him to be the Messiah, but showed in what manner His kingdom was to be established. . . . Understanding more clearly now the nature of Christ's mission, he [John] yielded himself to God for life or for death, as should best serve the interests of the cause he loved.[45]

THE HIGHEST HONOR

And fear not them which kill the body, but are not able to kill the soul: but rather fear him which is able to destroy both soul and body in hell. Matt. 10:28.

To many minds a deep mystery surrounds the fate of John the Baptist. They question why he should have been left to languish and die in prison. The mystery of this dark providence our human vision cannot penetrate; but it can never shake our confidence in God when we remember that John was but a sharer in the sufferings of Christ. . . .

Jesus did not interpose to deliver His servant. He knew that John would bear the test. Gladly would the Savior have come to John, to brighten the dungeon gloom with His own presence. But He was not to place Himself in the hands of enemies and imperil His own mission. Gladly would He have delivered His faithful servant. But for the sake of thousands who in after years must pass from prison to death, John was to drink the cup of martyrdom. As the followers of Jesus should languish in lonely cells, or perish by the sword, the rack, or the fagot, . . . what a stay to their hearts would be the thought that John the Baptist, to whose faithfulness Christ Himself had borne witness, had passed through a similar experience!

Satan was permitted to cut short the earthly life of God's messenger; but that life which "is hid with Christ in God," the destroyer could not reach (Col. 3:3). He exulted that he had brought sorrow upon Christ, but he had failed of conquering John. Death itself only placed him forever beyond the power of temptation. . . .

God never leads His children otherwise than they would choose to be led, if they could see the end from the beginning, and discern the glory of the purpose which they are fulfilling as coworkers with Him. Not Enoch, who was translated to heaven, not Elijah, who ascended in a chariot of fire, was greater or more honored than John the Baptist, who perished alone in the dungeon. "Unto you it is given in the behalf of Christ, not only to believe on him, but also to suffer for his sake" (Phil. 1:29). And of all the gifts that Heaven can bestow upon men, fellowship with Christ in His sufferings is the most weighty trust and the highest honor.[46]

A TRUE WITNESS

John did no miracle: but all things that John spake of this man were true. And many believed on him there. John 10:41, 42.

In the announcement to Zacharias before the birth of John, the angel had declared, "He shall be great in the sight of the Lord" (Luke 1:15). In the estimation of Heaven, what is it that constitutes greatness? Not that which the world accounts greatness; not wealth, or rank, or noble descent, or intellectual gifts, in themselves considered. . . . It is moral worth that God values. Love and purity are the attributes He prizes most. John was great in the sight of the Lord, when, before the messengers from the Sanhedrin, before the people, and before his own disciples, he refrained from seeking honor for himself, but pointed all to Jesus as the Promised One. His unselfish joy in the ministry of Christ presents the highest type of nobility ever revealed in man. . . .

Aside from the joy that John found in his mission, his life had been one of sorrow. His voice had been seldom heard except in the wilderness. His was a lonely lot. And he was not permitted to see the result of his own labors. It was not his privilege to be with Christ and witness the manifestation of divine power attending the greater light. It was not for him to see the blind restored to sight, the sick healed, and the dead raised to life. He did not behold the light that shone through every word of Christ, shedding glory upon the promises of prophecy. The least disciple who saw Christ's mighty works and heard His words was in this sense more highly privileged than John the Baptist, and therefore is said to have been greater than he.[47]

It was not given to John to call down fire from heaven, or to raise the dead, as Elijah did, nor to wield Moses' rod of power in the name of God. He was sent to herald the Savior's advent, and to call upon the people to prepare for His coming. So faithfully did he fulfill his mission that as the people recalled what he had taught them of Jesus, they could say, "All things that John spake of this Man were true." Such witness to Christ every disciple of the Master is called upon to bear.[48]

"COME AND SEE"

Philip findeth Nathanael, and saith unto him, We have found him, of whom Moses in the law, and the prophets, did write, Jesus of Nazareth, the son of Joseph. John 1:45.

Philip called Nathanael. . . . If Nathanael had trusted to the rabbis for guidance, he would never have found Jesus. It was by seeing and judging for himself that he became a disciple. So in the case of many today whom prejudice withholds from good. How different would be the result if they would "come and see"! . . .

Like Nathanael, we need to study God's word for ourselves, and pray for the enlightenment of the Holy Spirit. He who saw Nathanael under the fig tree will see us in the secret place of prayer. Angels from the world of light are near to those who in humility seek for divine guidance.

With the calling of John and Andrew and Simon, of Philip and Nathanael, began the foundation of the Christian church. John directed two of his disciples to Christ. Then one of these, Andrew, found his brother, and called him to the Savior. Philip was then called, and he went in search of Nathanael. These examples should teach us the importance of personal effort, of making direct appeals to our kindred, friends, and neighbors. . . .

There are many who need the ministration of loving Christian hearts. Many have gone down to ruin who might have been saved if their neighbors, common men and women, had put forth personal effort for them. Many are waiting to be personally addressed. In the very family, the neighborhood, the town, where we live, there is work for us to do as missionaries for Christ. If we are Christians, this work will be our delight. No sooner is one converted than there is born within him a desire to make known to others what a precious friend he has found in Jesus. The saving and sanctifying truth cannot be shut up in his heart. . . .

Now that Jesus has ascended to heaven, His disciples are His representatives among men, and one of the most effective ways of winning souls to Him is in exemplifying His character in our daily life. . . . A consistent life, characterized by the meekness of Christ, is a power in the world.[1]

UNDER THE FIG TREE

When Jesus saw Nathanael coming, he said, "Here is an Israelite worthy of the name: there is nothing false in him." John 1:47, NEB.

Nathanael heard John as he pointed to the Savior and said, "Behold the Lamb of God, which taketh away the sin of the world" (John 1:29)! Nathanael looked at Jesus, but he was disappointed in the appearance of the world's Redeemer. Could He who bore the marks of toil and poverty be the Messiah? Jesus was a worker; He had toiled with humble workingmen, and Nathanael went away. But he did not form his opinion decidedly as to what the character of Jesus was. He knelt down under a fig tree, inquiring of God if indeed this man was the Messiah. While he was there, Philip came and said, "We have found him, of whom Moses in the law, and the prophets, did write, Jesus of Nazareth, the son of Joseph." But the word "Nazareth" again aroused his unbelief, and he said, "Can there any good thing come out of Nazareth?" He was full of prejudice, but Philip did not seek to combat his prejudice; he simply said, "Come and see.". . .

Would it not be well for us to go under the fig tree to plead with God as to what is truth? Would not the eye of God be upon us as it was upon Nathanael? Nathanael believed on the Lord, and exclaimed, "Rabbi, thou art the Son of God; thou art the King of Israel." [2]

His unbelief was swept away, and faith, firm, strong, and abiding, took possession of his soul. Jesus commended the trusting faith of Nathanael.

There are many in the same condition as was Nathanael. They are prejudiced and unbelieving because they have never come in contact with the special truths for these last days or with the people who hold them, and it will require but attendance upon a meeting full of the Spirit of Christ to sweep away their unbelief. No matter what we have to meet, what opposition, what effort to turn souls away from the truth of heavenly origin, we must give publicity to our faith, that honest souls may see and hear and be convinced for themselves. Our work is to say, as did Philip: "Come and see." We hold no doctrine that we wish to hide. [3]

APPRENTICED TO CHRIST

And Jesus said unto them, Come ye after me, and I will make you to become fishers of men. And straightway they forsook their nets, and followed him. Mark 1:17, 18.

They were humble and unlearned men, those fishers of Galilee; but Christ, the light of the world, was abundantly able to qualify them for the position for which He had chosen them. The Savior did not despise education; for when controlled by the love of God, and devoted to His service, intellectual culture is a blessing. But He passed by the wise men of His time, because they were so self-confident that they could not sympathize with suffering humanity, and become colaborers with the man of Nazareth. In their bigotry they scorned to be taught by Christ. The Lord Jesus seeks the co-operation of those who will become unobstructed channels for the communion of His grace. . . .

Jesus chose unlearned fishermen because they had not been schooled in the traditions and erroneous customs of their time. They were men of native ability, and they were humble and teachable— men whom He could educate for His work. In the common walks of life there is many a man patiently treading the round of daily toil, unconscious that he possesses powers which, if called into action, would raise him to an equality with the world's most honored men. The touch of a skillful hand is needed to arouse those dormant faculties. It was such men that Jesus called to be His colaborers; and He gave them the advantage of association with Himself. Never had the world's great men such a teacher. When the disciples came forth from the Savior's training, they were no longer ignorant and uncultured. They had become like Him in mind and character, and men took knowledge of them that they had been with Jesus.[4]

He who called the fishermen of Galilee is still calling men to His service. And He is just as willing to manifest His power through us as through the first disciples. However imperfect and sinful we may be, the Lord holds out to us the offer of partnership with Himself, of apprenticeship to Christ. He invites us to come under the divine instruction, that, uniting with Christ, we may work the works of God.[5]

"FOLLOW ME"

And after these things he went forth, and saw a publican, named Levi, sitting at the receipt of custom: and he said unto him, Follow me. And he left all, rose up, and followed him. Luke 5:27, 28.

Of the Roman officials in Palestine, none were more hated than the publicans. The fact that the taxes were imposed by a foreign power was a continual irritation to the Jews, being a reminder that their independence had departed. And the taxgatherers were . . . extortioners on their own account, enriching themselves at the expense of the people. A Jew who accepted this office at the hands of the Romans was looked upon as betraying the honor of his nation. He was despised as an apostate, and was classed with the vilest of society.

To this class belonged Levi-Matthew, who, after the four disciples at Gennesaret, was the next to be called to Christ's service. The Pharisees had judged Matthew according to his employment, but Jesus saw in this man a heart open for the reception of truth. Matthew had listened to the Savior's teaching. As the convicting Spirit of God revealed his sinfulness, he longed to seek help from Christ; but he was accustomed to the exclusiveness of the rabbis, and had not thought that this Great Teacher would notice him.

Sitting at his toll booth one day, the publican saw Jesus approaching. Great was his astonishment to hear the words addressed to himself, "Follow me." Matthew "left all, rose up, and followed him." There was no hesitation, no questioning, no thought of the lucrative business to be exchanged for poverty and hardship. It was enough for him that he was to be with Jesus, that he might listen to IIis words, and unite with Him in His work. . . .

To Matthew in his wealth, and to Andrew and Peter in their poverty, the same test was brought; the same consecration was made by each. At the moment of success, when the nets were filled with fish, and the impulses of the old life were strongest, Jesus asked the disciples at the sea to leave all for the work of the gospel. So every soul is tested as to whether the desire for temporal good or for fellowship with Christ is strongest.[6]

PUBLICANS NOT EXCLUDED

For I desired mercy, and not sacrifice; and the knowledge of God more than burnt offerings. Hosea 6:6.

The calling of Matthew to be one of Christ's disciples excited great indignation. For a religious teacher to choose a publican as one of his immediate attendants was an offense against the religious, social, and national customs.[7]

In his grateful humility, Matthew desired to show his appreciation of the honor bestowed upon him; and, calling together those who had been his associates in business, in pleasure, and in sin, he made a great feast for the Savior. If Jesus would call him, who was so sinful and unworthy, He would surely accept his former companions, who were, thought Matthew, far more deserving than himself. Matthew had a great longing that they should share the benefits of the mercies and grace of Christ. He desired them to know that Christ did not . . . despise and hate the publicans and sinners. He wanted them to know Christ as the blessed Savior. . . .

Jesus never refused an invitation to such a feast. The object ever before Him was to sow in the hearts of His hearers the seeds of truth—through His winning conversation to draw hearts to Himself. In His every act Christ had a purpose, and the lesson which He gave on this occasion was timely and appropriate. By this act He declared that even publicans and sinners were not excluded from His presence. . . .

The Pharisees beheld Christ sitting and eating with publicans and sinners. . . . These self-righteous men, who felt no need of help, could not appreciate the work of Christ. They placed themselves where they could not accept the salvation which He came to bring. They would not come unto Him that they might have life. The poor publicans and sinners felt their need of help, and they accepted the instruction and aid which they knew Christ was able to give them.[8]

To Matthew himself the example of Jesus at the feast was a constant lesson. The despised publican became one of the most devoted evangelists, in his own ministry following closely in his Master's steps.[9]

JUDAS, SELF-SEEKING DISCIPLE

But there are some of you that believe not. For Jesus knew from the beginning who they were that believed not, and who should betray him. John 6:64.

While Jesus was preparing the disciples for their ordination, one who had not been summoned urged his presence among them. It was Judas Iscariot, a man who professed to be a follower of Christ. . . . Judas believed Jesus to be the Messiah; and by joining the apostles, he hoped to secure a high position in the new kingdom. . . .

The disciples were anxious that Judas should become one of their number. He was of commanding appearance, a man of keen discernment and executive ability, and they commended him to Jesus as one who would greatly assist Him in His work. . . . The after history of Judas would show them the danger of allowing any worldly consideration to have weight in deciding the fitness of men for the work of God. . . .

Yet when Judas joined the disciples, he was not insensible to the beauty of the character of Christ. He felt the influence of that divine power which was drawing souls to the Savior. . . . The Savior read the heart of Judas; He knew the depths of iniquity to which, unless delivered by the grace of God, Judas would sink. In connecting this man with Himself, He placed him where he might, day by day, be brought in contact with the outflowing of His own unselfish love. If he would open his heart to Christ, divine grace would banish the demon of selfishness, and even Judas might become a subject of the kingdom of God.

God takes men as they are . . . and trains them for His service, if they will be disciplined and learn of Him. They are not chosen because they are perfect, but notwithstanding their imperfections, that through the knowledge and practice of the truth, through the grace of Christ, they may become transformed into His image.

Judas had the same opportunities as had the other disciples. He listened to the same precious lessons. But the practice of the truth, which Christ required, was at variance with the desires and purposes of Judas, and he would not yield his ideas in order to receive wisdom from Heaven.[10]

WITHOUT EXCUSE

For the love of money is the root of all evil: which while some coveted after, they have erred from the faith, and pierced themselves through with many sorrows. 1 Tim. 6:10.

How tenderly the Savior dealt with him who was to be His betrayer! In His teaching, Jesus dwelt upon principles of benevolence that struck at the very root of covetousness. He presented before Judas the heinous character of greed, and many a time the disciple realized that his character had been portrayed, and his sin pointed out; but he would not confess and forsake his unrighteousness. He was self-sufficient, and instead of resisting temptation, he continued to follow his fraudulent practices. . . . Jesus dealt him no sharp rebuke for his covetousness, but with divine patience bore with this erring man, even while giving him evidence that He read his heart as an open book. He presented before him the highest incentives for right doing; and in rejecting the light of Heaven, Judas would be without excuse.[11]

Satan is playing the game of life for every soul. He knows that practical sympathy is a test of the purity and unselfishness of the heart, and he will make every possible effort to close our hearts to the needs of others. . . . He will bring in many things to prevent the expression of love and sympathy. It is thus that he ruined Judas. Judas was constantly planning to benefit self. In this he represents a large class of professed Christians of today. Therefore we need to study his case. We are as near to Christ as he was. Yet if, as with Judas, association with Christ does not make us one with Him, if it does not cultivate within our hearts a sincere sympathy for those for whom Christ gave His life, we are in the same danger as was Judas. . . .

We need to guard against the first deviation from righteousness; for one transgression, one neglect to manifest the spirit of Christ, opens the way for another and still another, until the mind is overmastered by the principles of the enemy. If cultivated, the spirit of selfishness becomes a devouring passion which nothing but the power of Christ can subdue.[12]

SOWER OF STRIFE

*Whosoever will be great among you, let him be your minister;
and whosoever will be chief among you, let him be your servant.
Matt. 20:26, 27.*

With Judas an element of antagonism was introduced among the
disciples. . . . That which ruled him was the hope of selfish benefit
in the worldly kingdom which he expected Christ to establish.
Though recognizing the divine power of the love of Christ, Judas did
not yield to its supremacy. He continued to cherish his own judgment and opinions, his disposition to criticize and condemn. Christ's
motives and movements, often so far above his comprehension, excited doubt and disapproval, and his own questionings and ambi-
tions were insinuated to the disciples. Many of their contentions for
supremacy, much of their dissatisfaction with Christ's methods, orig-
inated with Judas.[13]

He introduced controversies and misleading sentiments, repeating the arguments urged by the scribes and Pharisees against the
claims of Christ. . . . He would introduce texts of Scripture that had
no connection with the truths Christ was presenting. These texts,
separated from their connection, perplexed the disciples. . . . Yet all
this was done by Judas in such a way as to make it appear that he
was conscientious. And while the disciples were searching for evidence to confirm the words of the Great Teacher, Judas would lead
them almost imperceptibly on another track. . . . In all that Christ
said to His disciples, there was something with which, in heart,
Judas disagreed. . . .

Yet Judas made no open opposition, nor seemed to question the
Savior's lessons. He made no outward murmur until the time of the
feast in Simon's house. When Mary anointed the Savior's feet, Judas
manifested his covetous disposition. At the reproof from Jesus his
very spirit seemed turned to gall. Wounded pride and desire for revenge broke down the barriers, and the greed so long indulged held
him in control. This will be the experience of everyone who persists
in tampering with sin. The elements of depravity that are not resisted
and overcome respond to Satan's temptation, and the soul is led captive at his will.[14]

UNITY IN DIVERSITY

And he ordained twelve, that they should be with him, and that he might send them forth to preach. Mark 3:14.

In these first disciples was presented a marked diversity. They were to be the world's teachers, and they represented widely varied types of character. There were Levi Matthew the publican, called from a life of business activity, and subservience to Rome; the zealot Simon, the uncompromising foe of the imperial authority; the impulsive, self-sufficient, warm-hearted Peter, with Andrew his brother; Judas the Judean, polished, capable, and mean-spirited; Philip and Thomas, faithful and earnest, yet slow of heart to believe; James the less and Jude, of less prominence among the brethren, but men of force, positive both in their faults and in their virtues; Nathanael, a child in sincerity and trust; and the ambitious, loving-hearted sons of Zebedee. . . .

Of the twelve disciples, four were to act a leading part, each in a distinct line. In preparation for this, Christ taught them, foreseeing all. James, destined to swift-coming death by the sword; John, longest of the brethren to follow his Master in labor and persecution; Peter, the pioneer in breaking through the barriers of ages, and teaching the heathen world; and Judas, in service capable of pre-eminence above his brethren, yet brooding in his soul purposes of whose ripening he little dreamed.[15]

In order successfully to carry forward the work to which they had been called, these disciples, differing so widely in natural characteristics, in training, and in habits of life, needed to come into unity of feeling, thought, and action. This unity it was Christ's object to secure. . . . The burden of His labor for them is expressed in His prayer to the Father, "that they all may be one; as thou, Father, art in me, and I in thee, that they also may be one in us" (John 17:21).[16]

In the apostles of our Lord there was nothing to bring glory to themselves. It was evident that the success of their labors was due only to God. The lives of these men, the characters they developed, and the mighty work that God wrought through them are a testimony to what He will do for all who are teachable and obedient.[17]

NONE WERE PERFECT

This priceless treasure we hold, so to speak, in a common earthenware jar—to show that the splendid power of it belongs to God and not to us. 2 Cor. 4:7, Phillips.

All the disciples had serious faults when Jesus called them to His service. Even John, who came into closest association with the meek and lowly One, was not himself naturally meek and yielding. He and his brother were called "the sons of thunder." While they were with Jesus, any slight shown to Him aroused their indignation and combativeness. Evil temper, revenge, the spirit of criticism, were all in the beloved disciple. He was proud, and ambitious to be first in the kingdom of God. But day by day, in contrast with his own violent spirit, he beheld the tenderness and forbearance of Jesus, and heard His lessons of humility and patience. He opened his heart to the divine influence, and became not only a hearer but a doer of the Savior's words. Self was hid in Christ. He learned to wear the yoke of Christ and to bear His burden.

Jesus reproved His disciples, He warned and cautioned them; but John and his brethren did not leave Him; they chose Jesus, notwithstanding the reproofs. The Savior did not withdraw from them because of their weakness and errors. They continued to the end to share His trials and to learn the lessons of His life. By beholding Christ, they became transformed in character. . . .

As His representatives among men, Christ does not choose angels who have never fallen, but human beings, men of like passions with those they seek to save. . . .

Having been in peril themselves, they are acquainted with the dangers and difficulties of the way, and for this reason are called to reach out for others in like peril. There are souls perplexed with doubt, burdened with infirmities, weak in faith, and unable to grasp the Unseen; but a friend whom they can see, coming to them in Christ's stead, can be a connecting link to fasten their trembling faith upon Christ.

We are to be laborers together with the heavenly angels in presenting Jesus to the world.[18]

DOUBTS AND QUESTIONS

Straightway Jesus spake unto them, saying, Be of good cheer; it is I; be not afraid. Matt. 14:27.

They [the disciples] "entered into a ship, and went over the sea toward Capernaum." They had left Jesus with dissatisfied hearts. . . . They murmured because they had not been permitted to proclaim Him king. They blamed themselves for yielding so readily to His command. . . .

Unbelief was taking possession of their minds and hearts. Love of honor had blinded them. . . . Would Christ never assert His authority as king? Why did not He who possessed such power reveal Himself in His true character, and make their way less painful? Why had He not saved John the Baptist from a violent death? Thus the disciples reasoned until they brought upon themselves great spiritual darkness. They questioned, Could Jesus be an impostor, as the Pharisees asserted?

The disciples had that day witnessed the wonderful works of Christ. It had seemed that heaven had come down to the earth. The memory of that precious, glorious day should have filled them with faith and hope. Had they, out of the abundance of their hearts, been conversing together in regard to these things, they would not have entered into temptation. . . . Their thoughts were stormy and unreasonable, and the Lord gave them something else to afflict their souls and occupy their minds. God often does this when men create burdens and troubles for themselves. . . .

A violent tempest had been stealing upon them, and they were unprepared for it. . . . They forgot their disaffection, their unbelief, their impatience. Everyone worked to keep the boat from sinking. . . . Until the fourth watch of the night they toiled at the oars. Then the weary men gave themselves up for lost. In storm and darkness the sea had taught them their own helplessness, and they longed for the presence of their Master.

Jesus had not forgotten them. . . . At the moment when they believe themselves lost, a gleam of light reveals a mysterious figure approaching them upon the waters. . . . Their beloved Master turns, His voice silences their fear, "Be of good cheer; it is I; be not afraid." [19]

SECRET INTERVIEW

He saved us, not because of deeds done by us in righteousness, but in virtue of his own mercy, by the washing of regeneration and renewal in the Holy Spirit. Titus 3:5, RSV.

Nicodemus held a high position of trust in the Jewish nation. He was highly educated, and possessed talents of no ordinary character, and he was an honored member of the national council. With others, he had been stirred by the teaching of Jesus. . . .

He greatly desired an interview with Jesus, but shrank from seeking Him openly. . . . He waited until the city was hushed in slumber, and then sought Him. . . .

"Rabbi," he said, "we know that thou art a teacher come from God." . . . His words were designed to express and to invite confidence; but they really expressed unbelief. He did not acknowledge Jesus to be the Messiah, but only a teacher sent from God. . . .

Jesus bent His eyes upon the speaker, as if reading his very soul. In His infinite wisdom He saw before Him a seeker after truth. . . . He came directly to the point, saying solemnly, yet kindly, "Verily, verily, I say unto thee, Except a man be born from above, he cannot see the kingdom of God" (John 3:3, margin). . . .

Nicodemus had heard the preaching of John the Baptist concerning repentance and baptism. . . . Yet the heart-searching message of the Baptist had failed to work in him conviction of sin. He was a strict Pharisee, and prided himself on his good works. He was widely esteemed for his benevolence and his liberality in sustaining the temple service, and he felt secure of the favor of God. He was startled at the thought of a kingdom too pure for him to see in his present state. . . .

By virtue of his birth as an Israelite he regarded himself as sure of a place in the kingdom of God. He felt that he needed no change. Hence his surprise at the Savior's words. He was irritated by their close application to himself. The pride of the Pharisee was struggling against the honest desire of the seeker after truth.[20]

AS THE WIND BLOWS

Jesus answered, Verily, verily, I say unto thee, Except a man be born of water and of the Spirit, he cannot enter into the kingdom of God. John 3:5.

Nicodemus was astonished as well as indignant at these words. He regarded himself as not only an intellectual, but a pious and religious man. . . . He could not harmonize this doctrine of conversion with his understanding of what constituted religion. He could not explain to his own satisfaction the science of conversion; but Jesus showed him, by a figure, that it could not be explained by any of his precise methods. Jesus pointed out to him the fact that he could not see the wind, yet he could discern its action. He might never be able to explain the process of conversion, but he would be able to discern its effect. He heard the sound of the wind which bloweth where it listeth, and he could see the result of its action. The operating agency was not revealed to view. . . . No human reasoning of the most learned man can define the operations of the Holy Spirit upon human minds and characters; yet they can see the effects upon the life and actions. . . .

He was not willing to admit truth, because he could not understand all that was connected with the operation of the power of God; and yet he accepted the facts of nature, although he could not explain or even comprehend them. Like other men of all ages, he was looking to forms and precise ceremonies as more essential to religion than the deep movings of the Spirit of God.[21]

We may have flattered ourselves, as did Nicodemus, that our life has been upright, that our moral character is correct, and think that we need not humble the heart before God, like the common sinner: but when the light from Christ shines into our souls, we shall see how impure we are; we shall discern the selfishness of motive, the enmity against God, that has defiled every act of life. Then we shall know that our own righteousness is indeed as filthy rags, and that the blood of Christ alone can cleanse us from the defilement of sin, and renew our hearts in His own likeness.[22]

BORN AGAIN

But he that doeth truth cometh to the light, that his deeds may be made manifest, that they are wrought in God. John 3:21.

Nicodemus had come to the Lord thinking to enter into a discussion with Him, but Jesus laid bare the foundation principles of truth. He said to Nicodemus, It is not theoretical knowledge you need so much as spiritual regeneration. You need not to have your curiosity satisfied, but to have a new heart. . . .

He [Nicodemus] saw that the most rigid obedience to the mere letter of the law as applied to the outward life could entitle no man to enter the kingdom of heaven. In the estimation of men, his life had been just and honorable; but in the presence of Christ he felt that his heart was unclean, and his life unholy. . . . As the Savior explained to him concerning the new birth, he longed to have this change wrought in himself. . . . Jesus answered the unspoken question: "As Moses lifted up the serpent in the wilderness, even so must the Son of man be lifted up: that whosoever believeth in Him should not perish, but have eternal life.". . .

Nicodemus received the lesson, and carried it with him. He searched the Scriptures in a new way, not for the discussion of a theory, but in order to receive life for the soul. He began to see the kingdom of heaven as he submitted himself to the leading of the Holy Spirit. . . .

For a time Nicodemus did not publicly acknowledge Christ, but he watched His life, and pondered His teachings. In the Sanhedrin council he repeatedly thwarted the schemes of the priests to destroy Him. . . .

After the Lord's ascension, when the disciples were scattered by persecution, Nicodemus came boldly to the front. He employed his wealth in sustaining the infant church that the Jews had expected to be blotted out at the death of Christ. In the time of peril he who had been so cautious and questioning was firm as a rock, encouraging the faith of the disciples, and furnishing means to carry forward the work of the gospel. He was scorned and persecuted by those who had paid him reverence in other days. He became poor in this world's goods; yet he faltered not in the faith which had its beginning in that night conference with Jesus.[23]

CONFRONTATION AT JACOB'S WELL

Whosoever drinketh of the water that I shall give him shall never thirst; but the water that I shall give him shall be in him a well of water springing up into everlasting life. John 4:14.

When Jesus sat down to rest at Jacob's well, He had come from Judea, where His ministry had produced little fruit. . . . He was faint and weary; yet He did not neglect the opportunity of speaking to one woman, though she was a stranger, an alien from Israel, and living in open sin.[24]

As the woman talked with Jesus, she was impressed with His words. . . . She realized her soul thirst, which the waters of the well of Sychar could never satisfy. Nothing that had hitherto come in contact with her had so awakened her to a higher need. Jesus had convinced her that He read the secrets of her life; yet she felt that He was her friend, pitying and loving her. While the very purity of His presence condemned her sin, He had spoken no word of denunciation, but had told her of His grace, that could renew the soul. . . .

Leaving her waterpot, she returned to the city, to carry the message to others. . . . With heart overflowing with gladness, she hastened on her way, to impart to others the precious light she had received.

"Come, see a man, which told me all things that ever I did," she said to the men of the city. "Is not this the Christ?" Her words touched their hearts. There was a new expression on her face, a change in her whole appearance. They were interested to see Jesus.[25]

As soon as she had found the Savior the Samaritan woman brought others to Him. She proved herself a more effective missionary than His own disciples. . . . Their thoughts were fixed upon a great work to be done in the future. They did not see that right around them was a harvest to be gathered. But through the woman whom they despised, a whole cityful were brought to hear the Savior. . . .

This woman represents the working of a practical faith in Christ. Every true disciple is born into the kingdom of God as a missionary. He who drinks of the living water becomes a fountain of life. The receiver becomes a giver.[26]

FROM DOUBT TO FAITH

Then said Jesus unto him, Except ye see signs and wonders, ye will not believe. John 4:48.

Like a flash of light, the Savior's words to the nobleman laid bare his heart. He saw that his motives in seeking Jesus were selfish. His vacillating faith appeared to him in its true character. In deep distress he realized that his doubt might cost the life of his son. He knew that he was in the presence of One who could read the thoughts, and to whom all things were possible. In an agony of supplication he cried, "Sir, come down ere my child die." His faith took hold upon Christ as did Jacob, when, wrestling with the Angel, he cried, "I will not let thee go, except thou bless me" (Gen. 32:26).

Like Jacob he prevailed. The Savior cannot withdraw from the soul that clings to Him, pleading its great need. "Go thy way," He said: "thy son liveth." The nobleman left the Savior's presence with a peace and joy he had never known before. Not only did he believe that his son would be restored, but . . . he trusted in Christ as the Redeemer. . . .

Like the afflicted father, we are often led to seek Jesus by the desire for some earthly good; and upon the granting of our request we rest our confidence in His love. The Savior longs to give us a greater blessing than we ask; and He delays the answer to our request that He may show us the evil of our own hearts, and our deep need of His grace. He desires us to renounce the selfishness that leads us to seek Him. Confessing our helplessness and bitter need, we are to trust ourselves wholly to His love.

The nobleman wanted to *see* the fulfillment of his prayer before he should believe; but he had to accept the word of Jesus that his request was heard and the blessing granted. This lesson we also have to learn.[27]

The day is just before us when Satan will . . . present numerous miracles to confirm the faith of all those who are seeking this kind of evidence. How terrible will be the situation of those who close their eyes to the light of truth and ask for miracles to establish them in deception![28]

"I AM NOT WORTHY"

Verily I say unto you, I have not found so great faith, no, not in Israel. Matt. 8:10.

The centurion did not question the Savior's power. . . . He had not seen the Savior, but the reports he heard had inspired him with faith. . . . In the teaching of Christ, as it had been reported to him, he found that which met the need of the soul. All that was spiritual within him responded to the Savior's words. But he felt unworthy to come into the presence of Jesus, and he appealed to the Jewish elders to make request for the healing of his servant.[29]

On the way to the centurion's home, Jesus receives a message from the officer himself, "Lord, trouble not thyself: for I am not worthy that thou shouldest enter under my roof." Still the Savior keeps on His way, and the centurion comes in person to complete the message, saying, "Neither thought I myself worthy to come unto thee," "but speak the word only, and my servant shall be healed. For I am a man under authority, having soldiers under me: and I say to this man, Go, and he goeth; and to another, Come, and he cometh; and to my servant, Do this, and he doeth it.". . .

"As thou hast believed," Christ said, "so be it done unto thee. And his servant was healed in the selfsame hour."

The Jewish elders had commended the centurion to Christ because of the favor he had shown to "our nation." He is worthy, they said, for "he hath built us a synagogue." But the centurion said of himself, "I am not worthy." [30]

His heart had been touched by the grace of Christ. He saw his own unworthiness; yet he feared not to ask help. He trusted not to his own goodness; his argument was his great need. His faith took hold upon Christ in His true character. He did not believe in Him merely as a worker of miracles, but as the friend and Savior of mankind.

It is thus that every sinner may come to Christ. . . . Renouncing all self-dependence, we may look to the cross of Calvary and say—

"In my hand no price I bring;
Simply to Thy cross I cling." [31]

GOD ABHORS CASTE

For there is no difference between the Jew and the Greek: for the same Lord over all is rich unto all that call upon him. For whosoever shall call upon the name of the Lord shall be saved. Rom. 10:12, 13.

"Behold, a Canaanitish woman came out from those borders, and cried, saying, Have mercy on me, O Lord, thou Son of David; my daughter is grievously vexed with a devil" (Matt. 15:22, RV). The people of this district were of the old Canaanite race. They were idolaters, and were despised and hated by the Jews. To this class belonged the woman who now came to Jesus. She was a heathen. . . .

Christ did not immediately reply to the woman's request. He received this representative of a despised race as the Jews would have done. . . . The woman urged her case with increased earnestness, bowing at Christ's feet, and crying, "Lord, help me.". . .

She yields at once to the divine influence of Christ, and has implicit faith in His ability to grant the favor she asks. She begs for the crumbs that fall from the Master's table. If she may have the privilege of a dog, she is willing to be regarded as a dog. She has no national or religious prejudice or pride to influence her course, and she immediately acknowledges Jesus as the Redeemer, and as being able to do all that she asks of Him.

The Savior is satisfied. He has tested her faith in Him. . . . Turning to her with a look of pity and love, He says, "O woman, great is thy faith: be it unto thee even as thou wilt." From that hour her daughter became whole. The demon troubled her no more. . . .

In faith the woman of Phoenicia flung herself against the barriers that had been piled up between Jew and Gentile. Against discouragement, regardless of appearances that might have led her to doubt, she trusted the Savior's love. It is thus that Christ desires us to trust in Him. The blessings of salvation are for every soul. Nothing but his own choice can prevent any man from becoming a partaker of the promise in Christ by the gospel.

Caste is hateful to God. He ignores everything of this character. In His sight the souls of all men are of equal value.[32]

IT HAS TO BE PERSONAL

If I may but touch his garment, I shall be whole. Matt. 9:21.

It was a poor woman who spoke these words—a woman who for twelve years had suffered from a disease that made her life a burden. She had spent all her means upon physicians and remedies, only to be pronounced incurable. But as she heard of the Great Healer, her hopes revived. . . . Again and again she had tried in vain to get near Him.[33]

She had begun to despair, when, in making His way through the multitude, He came near where she was. . . . But amid the confusion she could not speak to Him, nor catch more than a passing glimpse of His figure. . . . As He was passing, she reached forward, and succeeded in barely touching the border of His garment. But in that moment she knew that she was healed. In that one touch was concentrated the faith of her life, and instantly her pain and feebleness gave place to the vigor of perfect health.

With a grateful heart she then tried to withdraw from the crowd; but suddenly Jesus stopped. . . . The Savior could distinguish the touch of faith from the casual contact of the careless throng. Such trust should not be passed without comment. . . . Finding concealment vain, she came forward tremblingly, and cast herself at His feet. With grateful tears she told the story of her suffering, and how she had found relief. Jesus gently said, "Daughter, be of good comfort: thy faith hath made thee whole; go in peace." He gave no opportunity for superstition to claim healing virtue for the mere act of touching His garments. It was not through the outward contact with Him, but through the faith which took hold on His divine power, that the cure was wrought. . . .

So in spiritual things. To talk of religion in a casual way, to pray without soul hunger and living faith, avails nothing. A nominal faith in Christ, which accepts Him merely as the Savior of the world, can never bring healing to the soul. . . . It is not enough to believe *about* Christ; we must believe *in* Him. The only faith that will benefit us is that which embraces Him as a personal Savior; which appropriates His merits to ourselves.[34]

WHAT LACK I?

*And a certain ruler asked him, saying, Good Master, what shall
I do to inherit eternal life? Luke 18:18.*

The young man who asked Jesus what he should do that he might
have eternal life was answered: "Keep the commandments."[35]

The character of God is expressed in His law; and in order for you
to be in harmony with God, the principles of His law must be the
spring of your every action. . . .

To the words, "Keep the commandments," the young man answered, "Which?" . . . Christ was speaking of the law given from
Sinai. He mentioned several commandments from the second table
of the Decalogue. . . .

The young man answered without hesitation, "All these things
have I kept from my youth up; what lack I yet?" His conception of
the law was external and superficial. Judged by a human standard, he
had preserved an unblemished character. To a great degree his outward life had been free from guilt; he verily thought that his obedience had been without a flaw. Yet he had a secret fear that all was
not right between his soul and God. This prompted the question,
"What lack I yet?"

"If thou wilt be perfect," Christ said, "go and sell that thou hast,
and give to the poor, and thou shalt have treasure in heaven, and
come and follow Me. But when the young man heard that saying, he
went away sorrowful; for he had great possessions."

The lover of self is a transgressor of the law. This Jesus desired to
reveal to the young man, and He gave him a test that would make
manifest the selfishness of his heart. He showed him the plague spot
in his character. The young man desired no further enlightenment.
He had cherished an idol in the soul; the world was his god. He professed to have kept the commandments, but he was destitute of the
principle which is the very spirit and life of them all. He did not possess true love for God or man. This want was the want of everything
that would qualify him to enter the kingdom of heaven. In his love
of self and worldly gain he was out of harmony with the principles
of heaven.[36]

HE FAILED THE TEST

Then Jesus beholding him loved him, and said unto him, One thing thou lackest: go thy way, sell whatsoever thou hast, and give to the poor, and thou shalt have treasure in heaven: and come, take up the cross, and follow me. Mark 10:21.

Christ looked into the face of the young man, as if reading his life and searching his character. He loved him, and He hungered to give him that peace and grace and joy which would materially change his character. . . .

With what earnest, anxious longing, what soul hunger, did the Savior look at the young man, hoping that he would yield to the invitation of the Spirit of God! . . . The ruler was quick to discern all that Christ's words involved, and he became sad. . . . To give up his earthly treasure, that was seen, for the heavenly treasure, that was unseen, was too great a risk. He refused the offer of eternal life, and went away, and ever after the world was to receive his worship.

Thousands are passing through this ordeal, weighing Christ against the world; and many choose the world. Like the young ruler, they turn from the Savior, saying in their hearts, I will not have this Man as my leader. . . . All should consider what it means to desire heaven, and yet to turn away because of the conditions laid down. Think of what it means to say "No" to Christ. The ruler said, No, I cannot give You all. Do we say the same? . . .

The ruler's possessions were entrusted to him that he might prove himself a faithful steward; he was to dispense these goods for the blessing of those in need. So God now entrusts men with means, with talents and opportunities, that they may be His agents in helping the poor and the suffering. He who uses his entrusted gifts as God designs becomes a co-worker with the Savior. . . .

To those who, like the young ruler, are in high positions of trust and have great possessions, it may seem too great a sacrifice to give up all in order to follow Christ. But this is the rule of conduct for all who would become His disciples. Nothing short of obedience can be accepted. Self-surrender is the substance of the teachings of Christ.[37]

HE MADE THINGS RIGHT

For the Son of man is come to seek and to save that which was lost. Luke 19:10.

"The chief among the publicans," Zacchaeus, was a Jew, and detested by his countrymen. His rank and wealth were the reward of a calling they abhorred, and which was regarded as another name for injustice and extortion. Yet the wealthy customs officer was not altogether the hardened man of the world that he seemed. Beneath the appearance of worldliness and pride was a heart susceptible to divine influences.

Zacchaeus had heard of Jesus. . . . In this chief of the publicans was awakened a longing for a better life. . . . He felt that he was a sinner in the sight of God. Yet what he had heard of Jesus kindled hope in his heart. Repentance, reformation of life, was possible, even to him. . . . Zacchaeus began at once to follow the conviction that had taken hold upon him, and to make restitution to those whom he had wronged.

Already he had begun thus to retrace his steps, when the news sounded through Jericho that Jesus was entering the town. Zacchaeus determined to see Him. . . . In the presence of the multitude, "Zacchaeus stood, and said unto the Lord: Behold, Lord, the half of my goods I give to the poor; and if I have taken anything from any man by false accusation, I restore him fourfold. And Jesus said unto him, This day is salvation come to this house." [38]

There are those who have had very meager opportunities, who have walked in ways of error because they knew no better way, to whom beams of light will come. As the word of Christ came to Zacchaeus, "Today I must abide at thy house," so the word will come to them; and those who were supposed to be hardened sinners will be found to have hearts as tender as a child's because Christ has deigned to notice them. Many will come from the grossest error and sin, and will take the place of others who have had opportunities and privileges but have not prized them. They will be accounted the chosen of God, elect, precious; and when Christ shall come into His kingdom, they will stand next His throne. [39]

RICH MAN AND GOD

If the wicked restore the pledge, give again that he had robbed, walk in the statutes of life, without committing iniquity; he shall surely live, he shall not die. Eze. 33:15.

No sooner did Zacchaeus yield to the influence of the Holy Spirit than he cast aside every practice contrary to integrity. No repentance is genuine that does not work reformation. The righteousness of Christ is not a cloak to cover unconfessed and unforsaken sin. . . .

Every converted soul will, like Zacchaeus, signalize the entrance of Christ into his heart by an abandonment of the unrighteous practices that have marked his life. Like the chief publican, he will give proof of his sincerity by making restitution. . . .

If we have injured others through any unjust business transaction, . . . we should confess our wrong, and make restitution as far as lies in our power. It is right for us to restore not only that which we have taken, but all that it would have accumulated if put to a right and wise use during the time it has been in our possession.

To Zacchaeus the Savior said, "This day is salvation come to this house." Not only was Zacchaeus himself blessed, but all his household with him. . . . They had been shut out from the synagogues by the contempt of rabbis and worshipers; but now, the most favored household in all Jericho, they gathered in their own home about the divine Teacher, and heard for themselves the words of life.

It is when Christ is received as a personal Savior that salvation comes to the soul. Zacchaeus had received Jesus, not merely as a passing guest in his home, but as One to abide in the soul temple.[40]

When the rich young ruler had turned away from Jesus, the disciples had marveled at their Master's saying, "How hard is it for them that trust in riches to enter into the kingdom of God!" They had exclaimed one to another, "Who then can be saved?" Now they had a demonstration of the truth of Christ's words, "The things which are impossible with men are possible with God." They saw how, through the grace of God, a rich man could enter into the kingdom.[41]

SHE GAVE HER ALL

Believe me, this poor widow has put in more than all the others. For they have all put in what they can easily afford, but she in her poverty who needs so much, has given away everything, her whole living! Mark 12:43, 44, Phillips.

Jesus was in the court where were the treasure chests, and He watched those who came to deposit their gifts. Many of the rich brought large sums, which they presented with great ostentation. Jesus looked upon them sadly, but made no comment on their liberal offerings. Presently His countenance lighted as He saw a poor widow approach hesitatingly, as though fearful of being observed. . . . Watching her opportunity, she hurriedly threw in her two mites, and turned to hasten away. But in doing this she caught the eye of Jesus, which was fastened earnestly upon her.

The Savior called His disciples to Him, and bade them mark the widow's poverty. Then His words of commendation fell upon her ear. . . . Tears of joy filled her eyes as she felt that her act was understood and appreciated. . . . Jesus understood her motive. She believed the service of the temple to be of God's appointment, and she was anxious to do her utmost to sustain it. She did what she could, and her act was to be a monument to her memory through all time, and her joy in eternity. Her heart went with her gift; its value was estimated, not by the worth of the coin, but by the love to God and the interest in His work that had prompted the deed. . . .

The rich had bestowed from their abundance, many of them to be seen and honored by men. Their large donations had deprived them of no comfort, or even luxury; they had required no sacrifice, and could not be compared in value with the widow's mite. . . . Her example of self-sacrifice has acted and reacted upon thousands of hearts in every land and in every age. It has appealed to both the rich and the poor, and their offerings have swelled the value of her gift. God's blessing upon the widow's mite has made it the source of great results. So with every gift bestowed and every act performed with a sincere desire for God's glory. It is linked with the purposes of Omnipotence. Its results for good no man can measure.[42]

FRETTING AND FUSSING

The Lord answered, "Martha, Martha, you are fretting and fussing about so many things; but one thing is necessary. The part that Mary has chosen is best; and it shall not be taken away from her." Luke 10:41, 42, NEB.

As Christ gave His wonderful lessons, Mary sat at His feet, a reverent and devoted listener. On one occasion, Martha, perplexed with the care of preparing the meal, went to Christ, saying, "Lord, dost Thou not care that my sister hath left me to serve alone? bid her therefore that she help me." This was the time of Christ's first visit to Bethany. The Savior and His disciples had just made the toilsome journey on foot from Jericho. Martha was anxious to provide for their comfort, and in her anxiety she forgot the courtesy due to her Guest. . . .

The "one thing" that Martha needed was a calm, devotional spirit, a deeper anxiety for knowledge concerning the future, immortal life, and the graces necessary for spiritual advancement. She needed less anxiety for the things which pass away, and more for those things which endure forever. Jesus would teach His children to seize every opportunity of gaining that knowledge which will make them wise unto salvation. The cause of Christ needs careful, energetic workers. There is a wide field for the Marthas, with their zeal in active religious work. But let them first sit with Mary at the feet of Jesus. Let diligence, promptness, and energy be sanctified by the grace of Christ; then the life will be an unconquerable power for good.[43]

The reason why the youth, and even those of mature years, are so easily led into temptation and sin is that they do not study the word of God and meditate upon it as they should. The lack of firm, decided will power, which is manifest in life and character, results from neglect of the sacred instruction of God's word. They do not by earnest effort direct the mind to that which would inspire pure, holy thought and divert it from that which is impure and untrue. There are few who choose the better part, who sit at the feet of Jesus, as did Mary, to learn of the divine Teacher. Few treasure His words in the heart and practice them in the life.[44]

A GIFT OF LOVE

She hath done what she could. Mark 14:8.

Simon of Bethany was accounted a disciple of Jesus. He was one of the few Pharisees who had openly joined Christ's followers. He acknowledged Jesus as a teacher, and hoped that He might be the Messiah, but he had not accepted Him as a Savior. His character was not transformed; his principles were unchanged.

Simon had been healed of the leprosy, and it was this that had drawn him to Jesus. He desired to show his gratitude, and at Christ's last visit to Bethany he made a feast for the Savior and His disciples. . . . At the table the Savior sat with Simon . . . on one side, and Lazarus . . . on the other. Martha served at the table, but Mary was earnestly listening to every word from the lips of Jesus. In His mercy, Jesus had pardoned her sins, He had called forth her beloved brother from the grave, and Mary's heart was filled with gratitude. She had heard Jesus speak of His approaching death, and in her deep love and sorrow she had longed to show Him honor. At great personal sacrifice she had purchased an alabaster box of "ointment of spikenard, very costly," with which to anoint His body. But now many were declaring that He was about to be crowned king. Her grief was turned to joy, and she was eager to be first in honoring her Lord. Breaking her box of ointment, she poured its contents upon the head and feet of Jesus; then, as she knelt weeping, moistening them with her tears, she wiped His feet with her long, flowing hair. . . .

Judas looked upon this act with great displeasure. . . . He asked, "Why was not this ointment sold for three hundred pence, and given to the poor?" . . . The murmur passed round the table, "To what purpose is this waste? . . ." Mary heard the words of criticism. . . . She was about to shrink away, when the voice of her Lord was heard, "Let her alone; why trouble ye her?" . . . Lifting His voice above the murmur of criticism, He said, "She hath wrought a good work on me. For ye have the poor with you always, and whensoever ye will ye may do them good: but me ye have not always. She hath done what she could: she is come aforehand to anoint my body to the burying." [45]

305

THE FRAGRANCE LINGERS

Verily I say unto you, Wheresoever this gospel shall be preached throughout the whole world, this also that she hath done shall be spoken of for a memorial of her. Mark 14:9.

The fragrant gift which Mary had thought to lavish upon the dead body of the Savior she poured upon His living form. At the burial its sweetness could only have pervaded the tomb; now it gladdened His heart with the assurance of her faith and love. Joseph of Arimathea and Nicodemus offered not their gift of love to Jesus in His life. With bitter tears they brought their costly spices for His cold, unconscious form. The women who bore spices to the tomb found their errand in vain, for He had risen. But Mary, pouring out her love upon the Savior while He was conscious of her devotion, was anointing Him for the burial. And as He went down into the darkness of His great trial, He carried with Him the memory of that deed, an earnest of the love that would be His from His redeemed ones forever.

Many there are who bring their precious gifts for the dead. . . . Tenderness, appreciation, devotion, all are lavished upon one who sees not nor hears. Had these words been spoken when the weary spirit needed them so much, when the ear could hear and the heart could feel, how precious would have been their fragrance! . . .

Christ told Mary the meaning of her act. . . . He said, "she did it for my burial." As the alabaster box was broken, and filled the whole house with its fragrance, so Christ was to die, His body was to be broken; but He was to rise from the tomb, and the fragrance of His life was to fill the earth. . . . Looking into the future, the Savior spoke with certainty concerning His gospel. It was to be preached throughout the world. And as far as the gospel extended, Mary's gift would shed its fragrance, and hearts would be blessed through her unstudied act. Kingdoms would rise and fall; the names of monarchs and conquerors would be forgotten; but this woman's deed would be immortalized upon the pages of sacred history. Until time should be no more, that broken alabaster box would tell the story of the abundant love of God for a fallen race.[46]

NOTHING TOO COSTLY

For the love of Christ constraineth us. 2 Cor. 5:14.

Christ delighted in the earnest desire of Mary to do the will of her Lord. He accepted the wealth of pure affection which His disciples did not, would not, understand. The desire that Mary had to do this service for her Lord was of more value to Christ than all the precious ointment in the world, because it expressed her appreciation of the world's Redeemer. It was the love of Christ that constrained her. The matchless excellence of the character of Christ filled her soul. That ointment was a symbol of the heart of the giver. It was the outward demonstration of a love fed by heavenly streams until it overflowed.

The work of Mary was just the lesson the disciples needed to show them that the expression of their love for Him would be pleasing to Christ. He had been everything to them, and they did not realize that soon they would be deprived of His presence, that soon they could offer Him no token of their gratitude for His great love. The loneliness of Christ, separated from the heavenly courts, living the life of humanity, was never understood or appreciated by the disciples as it should have been. . . .

Their afterknowledge gave them a true sense of the many things they might have done for Jesus expressive of the love and gratitude of their hearts. . . . When Jesus was no longer with them, . . . they began to see how they might have shown Him attentions that would have brought gladness to His heart. They no longer cast blame upon Mary, but upon themselves. Oh, if they could have taken back their censuring, their presenting the poor as more worthy of the gift than was Christ! They felt the reproof keenly as they took from the cross the bruised body of their Lord.

The same want is evident in our world today. But few appreciate all that Christ is to them. If they did, the great love of Mary would be expressed, the anointing would be freely bestowed. The expensive ointment would not be called a waste. Nothing would be thought too costly to give for Christ, no self-denial or self-sacrifice too great to be endured for His sake.[47]

SIMON'S CHANGE OF HEART

Therefore thou art inexcusable, O man, whosoever thou art that judgest: for wherein thou judgest another, thou condemnest thyself; for thou that judgest doest the same things. Rom. 2:1.

Simon the host had been influenced by the criticism of Judas upon Mary's gift, and he was surprised at the conduct of Jesus. His Pharisaic pride was offended. He knew that many of his guests were looking upon Christ with distrust and displeasure. Simon said in his heart, "This Man, if He were a prophet, would have known who and what manner of woman this is that toucheth Him: for she is a sinner."

By curing Simon of leprosy, Christ had saved him from a living death. But now Simon questioned whether the Savior were a prophet. . . . Jesus knows nothing of this woman who is so free in her demonstrations, he thought, or He would not allow her to touch Him. . . .

As did Nathan with David, Christ concealed His home thrust under the veil of a parable. He threw upon His host the burden of pronouncing sentence upon himself. Simon had led into sin the woman he now despised. She had been deeply wronged by him. . . . But Simon felt himself more righteous than Mary, and Jesus desired him to see how great his guilt really was. He would show him that his sin was greater than hers, as much greater as a debt of five hundred pence exceeds a debt of fifty pence. . . .

Simon's coldness and neglect toward the Savior showed how little he appreciated the mercy he had received. He had thought he honored Jesus by inviting Him to his house. But he now saw himself as he really was. . . . His religion had been a robe of Pharisaism. . . . While Mary was a sinner pardoned, he was a sinner unpardoned. The rigid rule of justice he had desired to enforce against her condemned him.

Simon was touched by the kindness of Jesus in not openly rebuking him before the guests. He had not been treated as he desired Mary to be treated. . . . Stern denunciation would have hardened Simon against repentance, but patient admonition convinced him of his error. He saw the magnitude of the debt which he owed his Lord. His pride was humbled, he repented, and the proud Pharisee became a lowly, self-sacrificing disciple.[48]

CHRIST SEES OUR POSSIBILITIES

I tell you, Simon, that her sins, many as they are, are forgiven; for she has shown me so much love. But the man who has little to be forgiven has only a little love to give. Luke 7:47, Phillips.

Mary had been looked upon as a great sinner, but Christ knew the circumstances that had shaped her life. He might have extinguished every spark of hope in her soul, but He did not. It was He who had lifted her from despair and ruin. Seven times she had heard His rebuke of the demons that controlled her heart and mind. She had heard His strong cries to the Father in her behalf. She knew how offensive is sin to His unsullied purity, and in His strength she had overcome.

When to human eyes her case appeared hopeless, Christ saw in Mary capabilities for good. He saw the better traits of her character. The plan of redemption has invested humanity with great possibilities, and in Mary these possibilities were to be realized. Through His grace she became a partaker of the divine nature. The one who had fallen, and whose mind had been a habitation of demons, was brought very near to the Savior in fellowship and ministry. It was Mary who sat at His feet and learned of Him. It was Mary who poured upon His head the precious anointing oil, and bathed His feet with her tears. Mary stood beside the cross, and followed Him to the sepulcher. Mary was first at the tomb after His resurrection. It was Mary who first proclaimed a risen Savior.

Jesus knows the circumstances of every soul. You may say, I am sinful, very sinful. You may be; but the worse you are, the more you need Jesus. He turns no weeping, contrite one away. He does not tell to any all that He might reveal, but He bids every trembling soul take courage. Freely will He pardon all who come to Him for forgiveness and restoration. . . . He is today standing at the altar of incense, presenting before God the prayers of those who desire His help.

The souls that turn to Him for refuge, Jesus lifts above the accusing and the strife of tongues. No man or evil angel can impeach these souls. Christ unites them to His own divine-human nature. They stand beside the great Sin Bearer, in the light proceeding from the throne of God.[49]

PETER LOOKED BACK

O thou of little faith, wherefore didst thou doubt? Matt. 14:31.

Looking unto Jesus, Peter walks securely; but as in self-satisfaction he glances back toward his companions in the boat, his eyes are turned from the Savior. The wind is boisterous. The waves roll high. . . . For a moment Christ is hidden from his view, and his faith gives way. He begins to sink. But while the billows talk with death, Peter lifts his eyes from the angry waters and, fixing them upon Jesus, cries, "Lord, save me." Immediately Jesus grasps the outstretched hand, saying, "O thou of little faith, wherefore didst thou doubt?"

Walking side by side, Peter's hand in that of his Master, they stepped into the boat together. But Peter was now subdued and silent. He had no reason to boast over his fellows, for through unbelief and self-exaltation he had very nearly lost his life. When he turned his eyes from Jesus, his footing was lost, and he sank amid the waves.

When trouble comes upon us, how often we are like Peter! We look upon the waves, instead of keeping our eyes fixed upon the Savior. Our footsteps slide, and the proud waters go over our souls. Jesus did not bid Peter come to Him that he should perish; He does not call us to follow Him, and then forsake us. . . .

In this incident on the sea He desired to reveal to Peter his own weakness—to show that his safety was in constant dependence upon divine power. Amid the storms of temptation he could walk safely only as in utter self-distrust he should rely upon the Savior. It was on the point where he thought himself strong that Peter was weak; and not until he discerned his weakness could he realize his need of dependence upon Christ. Had he learned the lesson that Jesus sought to teach him in that experience on the sea, he would not have failed when the great test came upon him.

Day by day God instructs His children. By the circumstances of the daily life He is preparing them to act their part upon that wider stage to which His providence has appointed them. It is the issue of the daily test that determines their victory or defeat in life's great crisis.[50]

PETER SPEAKS UP

He saith unto them, But whom say ye that I am? And Simon Peter answered and said, Thou art the Christ, the Son of the living God. Matt. 16:15, 16.

From the first, Peter had believed Jesus to be the Messiah. Many others who had been convicted by the preaching of John the Baptist, and had accepted Christ, began to doubt as to John's mission when he was imprisoned and put to death; and they now doubted that Jesus was the Messiah, for whom they had looked so long. . . . But Peter and his companions turned not from their allegiance. The vacillating course of those who praised yesterday and condemned today did not destroy the faith of the true follower of the Savior. . . .

Peter had expressed the faith of the twelve. Yet the disciples were still far from understanding Christ's mission. The opposition and misrepresentation of the priests and rulers, while it could not turn them away from Christ, still caused them great perplexity. . . . From time to time precious rays of light from Jesus shone upon them, yet often they were like men groping among shadows. But on this day, before they were brought face to face with the great trial of their faith, the Holy Spirit rested upon them in power. For a little time their eyes were turned away from "the things which are seen," to behold "the things which are not seen" (2 Cor. 4:18). Beneath the guise of humanity they discerned the glory of the Son of God. . . .

The truth which Peter had confessed is the foundation of the believer's faith. It is that which Christ Himself has declared to be eternal life. But the possession of this knowledge was no ground for self-glorification. Through no wisdom or goodness of his own had it been revealed to Peter. Never can humanity, of itself, attain to a knowledge of the divine. "It is as high as heaven; what canst thou do? deeper than hell; what canst thou know?" (Job 11:8). Only the spirit of adoption can reveal to us the deep things of God, which "eye hath not seen, nor ear heard, neither have entered into the heart of man." "God hath revealed them unto us by His Spirit; for the Spirit searcheth all things, yea, the deep things of God" (1 Cor. 2:9, 10).[1]

UNDER SATAN'S POWER

But he turned, and said unto Peter, Get thee behind me, Satan: thou art an offence unto me: for thou savourest not the things that be of God, but those that be of men. Matt. 16:23.

Satan is ever intruding himself between the soul of man and God. . . . This lesson in regard to Peter needs to be studied carefully.[2]

Peter did not desire to see the cross in the work of Christ. The impression which his words would make was directly opposed to that which Christ desired to make on the minds of His followers, and the Savior was moved to utter one of the sternest rebukes that ever fell from His lips. . . .

Satan was trying to discourage Jesus, and turn Him from His mission; and Peter, in his blind love, was giving voice to the temptation. The prince of evil was the author of the thought. His instigation was behind that impulsive appeal. . . . He was seeking to fix Peter's gaze upon the earthly glory, that he might not behold the cross to which Jesus desired to turn his eyes. And through Peter, Satan was again pressing the temptation upon Jesus. But the Savior heeded it not; His thought was for His disciple. Satan had interposed between Peter and his Master, that the heart of the disciple might not be touched at the vision of Christ's humiliation for him. The words of Christ were spoken, not to Peter, but to the one who was trying to separate him from his Redeemer. "Get thee behind Me, Satan." No longer interpose between Me and My erring servant. Let Me come face to face with Peter, that I may reveal to him the mystery of My love.

It was to Peter a bitter lesson, and one which he learned but slowly, that the path of Christ on earth lay through agony and humiliation. The disciple shrank from fellowship with his Lord in suffering. But in the heat of the furnace fire he was to learn its blessing. Long afterward, when his active form was bowed with the burden of years and labors, he wrote, "Beloved, think it not strange concerning the fiery trial which is to try you, as though some strange thing happened unto you: but rejoice, inasmuch as ye are partakers of Christ's sufferings; that, when His glory shall be revealed, ye may be glad also with exceeding joy" (1 Peter 4:12, 13).[3]

PETER LEARNED HIS LESSON

And the Lord said, Simon, Simon, behold, Satan hath desired to have you, that he may sift you as wheat: but I have prayed for thee, that thy faith fail not: and when thou art converted, strengthen thy brethren. Luke 22:31, 32.

Bold, aggressive, and self-confident, quick to perceive and forward to act, prompt in retaliation yet generous in forgiving, Peter often erred, and often received reproof. Nor were his warmhearted loyalty and devotion to Christ the less decidedly recognized and commended. Patiently, with discriminating love, the Savior dealt with His impetuous disciple, seeking to check his self-confidence, and to teach him humility, obedience, and trust. But only in part was the lesson learned. . . . Over and over again was given the warning, "Thou shalt . . . deny that thou knowest me." It was the grieved, loving heart of the disciple that spoke out in the avowal, "Lord, I am ready to go with thee, both into prison, and to death.". . .

When in the judgment hall the words of denial had been spoken; when Peter's love and loyalty, awakened under the Savior's glance of pity and love and sorrow, had sent him forth to the garden where Christ had wept and prayed; when his tears of remorse dropped upon the sod that had been moistened with the blood drops of His agony—then the Savior's words, "I have prayed for thee" . . . were a stay to his soul. Christ, though foreseeing his sin, had not abandoned him to despair.

If the look that Jesus cast upon him had spoken condemnation instead of pity; if in foretelling the sin He had failed of speaking hope, how dense would have been the darkness that encompassed Peter! . . .

He who could not spare His disciple the anguish left him not alone to its bitterness. His is a love that fails not nor forsakes. Human beings, themselves given to evil, are prone to deal untenderly with the tempted and the erring. They cannot read the heart, they know not its struggle and pain. Of the rebuke that is love, of the blow that wounds to heal, of the warning that speaks hope, they have need to learn. . . .

A miracle of divine tenderness was Peter's transformation. It is a life lesson to all who seek to follow in the steps of the Master Teacher.[4]

313

A FOND MOTHER'S REQUEST

To him that overcometh will I grant to sit with me in my throne, even as I also overcame, and am set down with my Father in his throne. Rev. 3:21.

James and John presented through their mother a petition requesting that they might be permitted to occupy the highest positions of honor in Christ's kingdom. Notwithstanding Christ's repeated instruction concerning the nature of His kingdom, these young disciples still cherished the hope for a Messiah who would take His throne and kingly power in accordance with the desires of men. . . .

But the Savior answered, "Ye know not what ye ask. Are ye able to drink of the cup that I shall drink of, and to be baptized with the baptism that I am baptized with?" They recalled His mysterious words pointing to trial and suffering, yet answered confidently, "We are able." They would count it highest honor to prove their loyalty by sharing all that was to befall their Lord.

"Ye shall drink indeed of My cup, and be baptized with the baptism that I am baptized with," Christ declared. . . . James and John were to be sharers with their Master in suffering—the one, destined to swift-coming death by the sword; the other, longest of all the disciples to follow his Master in labor and reproach and persecution. "But to sit on my right hand, and on my left," He continued, "is not mine to give, but it shall be given to them for whom it is prepared of my Father.". . .

In the kingdom of God, position is not gained through favoritism. It is not earned, nor is it received through an arbitrary bestowal. It is the result of character. The crown and the throne are the tokens of a condition attained—tokens of self-conquest through the grace of our Lord Jesus Christ. . . .

The one who stands nearest to Christ will be he who has drunk most deeply of His spirit of self-sacrificing love—love that "vaunteth not itself, . . . seeketh not her own, is not easily provoked, thinketh no evil"—love that moves the disciple, as it moved our Lord, to give all, to live and labor and sacrifice even unto death, for the saving of humanity.[5]

BELOVED DISCIPLE

We love him, because he first loved us. 1 John 4:19.

John is distinguished above the other apostles as "the disciple whom Jesus loved" (John 21:20). . . . He received many tokens of the Savior's confidence and love. He was one of the three permitted to witness Christ's glory upon the mount of transfiguration and His agony in Gethsemane, and it was to his care that our Lord confided His mother in those last hours of anguish upon the cross.[6]

John's was a nature that longed for love, for sympathy and companionship. He pressed close to Jesus, sat by His side, leaned upon His breast. As a flower the sun and dew, so did he drink in the divine light and life.[7]

The depth and fervor of John's affection for his Master was not the cause of Christ's love for him, but the effect of that love. John desired to become like Jesus, and under the transforming influence of the love of Christ he did become meek and lowly. Self was hid in Jesus. Above all his companions, John yielded himself to the power of that wondrous life. . . . John knew the Savior by an experimental knowledge. His Master's lessons were graven on his soul. When he testified of the Savior's grace, his simple language was eloquent with the love that pervaded his whole being.

It was John's deep love for Christ which led him always to desire to be close by His side. The Savior loved all the Twelve, but John's was the most receptive spirit. He was younger than the others, and with more of the child's confiding trust he opened his heart to Jesus. Thus he came more into sympathy with Christ, and through him the Savior's deepest spiritual teaching was communicated to the people. . . .

John could talk of the Father's love as no other of the disciples could. He revealed to his fellow men that which he felt in his own soul, representing in his character the attributes of God. . . . The beauty of holiness which had transformed him shone with a Christlike radiance from his countenance. In adoration and love he beheld the Savior until likeness to Christ and fellowship with Him became his one desire, and in his character was reflected the character of his Master.[8]

JOHN AND JUDAS—A CONTRAST

He that saith he abideth in him ought himself also so to walk, even as he walked. 1 John 2:6.

In the life of the disciple John true sanctification is exemplified. During the years of his close association with Christ, he was often warned and cautioned by the Savior; and these reproofs he accepted. As the character of the Divine One was manifested to him, John saw his own deficiencies, and was humbled by the revelation. . . . The power and tenderness, the majesty and meekness, the strength and patience, that he saw in the daily life of the Son of God, filled his soul with admiration. He yielded his resentful, ambitious temper to the molding power of Christ, and divine love wrought in him a transformation of character.

In striking contrast to the sanctification worked out in the life of John is the experience of his fellow disciple, Judas. . . . John warred earnestly against his faults; but Judas violated his conscience and yielded to temptation, fastening upon himself more securely his habits of evil. . . .

John and Judas are representatives of those who profess to be Christ's followers. Both these disciples had the same opportunities to study and follow the divine Pattern. Both were closely associated with Jesus and were privileged to listen to His teaching. Each possessed serious defects of character; and each had access to the divine grace that transforms character. But while one in humility was learning of Jesus, the other revealed that he was not a doer of the word, but a hearer only. One, daily dying to self and overcoming sin, was sanctified through the truth; the other, resisting the transforming power of grace and indulging selfish desires, was brought into bondage to Satan.

Such transformation of character as is seen in the life of John is ever the result of communion with Christ. There may be marked defects in the character of an individual, yet when he becomes a true disciple of Christ, the power of divine grace transforms and sanctifies him. Beholding as in a glass the glory of the Lord, he is changed from glory to glory, until he is like Him whom he adores.[9]

ENSLAVED BY MONEY

Then one of the twelve, called Judas Iscariot, went unto the chief priests, and said unto them, What will ye give me, and I will deliver him unto you? And they covenanted with him for thirty pieces of silver. Matt. 26:14, 15.

Judas had naturally a strong love for money; but he had not always been corrupt enough to do such a deed as this. He had fostered the evil spirit of avarice until it had become the ruling motive of his life. The love of mammon overbalanced his love for Christ. Through becoming the slave of one vice he gave himself to Satan. . . .

Judas was highly regarded by the disciples, and had great influence over them. He himself had a high opinion of his own qualifications, and looked upon his brethren as greatly inferior to him in judgment and ability. They did not see their opportunities, he thought, and take advantage of circumstances. The church would never prosper with such shortsighted men as leaders. Peter was impetuous; he would move without consideration. John, who was treasuring up the truths that fell from Christ's lips, was looked upon by Judas as a poor financier. Matthew, whose training had taught him accuracy in all things, was very particular in regard to honesty, and he was ever contemplating the words of Christ, and became so absorbed in them that, as Judas thought, he could not be trusted to do sharp, farseeing business. Thus Judas summed up all the disciples, and flattered himself that the church would often be brought into perplexity and embarrassment if it were not for his ability as a manager.[10]

The history of Judas presents the sad ending of a life that might have been honored of God. Had Judas died before his last journey to Jerusalem he would have been regarded as a man worthy of a place among the twelve, and one who would be greatly missed. The abhorrence which has followed him through the centuries would not have existed but for the attributes revealed at the close of his history. But it was for a purpose that his character was laid open to the world. It was to be a warning to all who, like him, should betray sacred trusts. . . . For thirty pieces of silver—the price of a slave—he sold the Lord of glory to ignominy and death.[11]

A CHANCE FOR ALL

Not every one that saith unto me, Lord, Lord, shall enter into the kingdom of heaven; but he that doeth the will of my Father which is in heaven. Matt. 7:21.

Not all who profess to be workers for Christ are true disciples. Among those who bear His name, and who are even numbered with His workers, are some who do not represent Him in character. . . . Till the end of time there will be tares among the wheat. . . .

In His mercy and long-suffering, God bears patiently with the perverse and even the falsehearted. Among Christ's chosen apostles was Judas the traitor. Should it then be a cause of surprise or discouragement that there are falsehearted ones among His workers today? If He who reads the heart could bear with him who He knew was to be His betrayer, with what patience should we bear with those at fault.

And not all, even of those who appear most faulty, are like Judas. Peter, impetuous, hasty, and self-confident, often appeared to far greater disadvantage than Judas did. He was oftener reproved by the Savior. But what a life of service and sacrifice was his! What a testimony does it bear to the power of God's grace![12]

Christ connected Judas and impulsive Peter with Himself, not because Judas was covetous and Peter passionate, but that they might learn of Him, their great Teacher, and become, like Him, unselfish, meek, and lowly of heart. He saw good material in both these men. Judas possessed financial ability and would have been of value to the church had he taken home to his heart the lessons which Christ was giving by rebuking all selfishness, fraud, and avarice, even in the little matters of life.[13]

The world has no right to doubt the truth of Christianity because there are unworthy members in the church, nor should Christians become disheartened because of these false brethren. How was it with the early church? Ananias and Sapphira joined themselves to the disciples. Simon Magus was baptized. . . . Judas Iscariot was numbered with the apostles. The Redeemer does not want to lose one soul; His experience with Judas is recorded to show His long patience with perverse human nature; and He bids us bear with it as He has borne.[14]

ONLY JESUS KNEW

The Son of man goeth as it is written of him: but woe unto that man by whom the Son of man is betrayed! it had been good for that man if he had not been born. Matt. 26:24.

The disciples knew nothing of the purpose of Judas. Jesus alone could read his secret. Yet He did not expose him. Jesus hungered for his soul. . . . His heart was crying, How can I give thee up? The constraining power of that love was felt by Judas. When the Savior's hands were bathing those soiled feet, and wiping them with the towel, the heart of Judas thrilled through and through with the impulse then and there to confess his sin. But he would not humble himself. He hardened his heart against repentance; and the old impulses, for the moment put aside, again controlled him. Judas was now offended at Christ's act in washing the feet of His disciples. If Jesus could so humble Himself, he thought, He could not be Israel's king. All hope of worldly honor in a temporal kingdom was destroyed. Judas was satisfied that there was nothing to be gained by following Christ. . . . He was possessed by a demon, and he resolved to complete the work he had agreed to do in betraying his Lord.[15]

Judas the betrayer was present at the sacramental service. He received from Jesus the emblems of His broken body and His spilled blood. He heard the words, "This do in remembrance of Me." And sitting there in the very presence of the Lamb of God, the betrayer brooded upon his own dark purposes, and cherished his sullen, revengeful thoughts.[16]

At the Passover supper Jesus proved His divinity by revealing the traitor's purpose. He tenderly included Judas in the ministry to the disciples. But the last appeal of love was unheeded. Then the case of Judas was decided, and the feet that Jesus had washed went forth to the betrayer's work.[17]

Until this step was taken, Judas had not passed beyond the possibility of repentance. But when he left the presence of his Lord and his fellow disciples, the final decision had been made. He had passed the boundary line.[18]

How many today are, like Judas, betraying their Lord?[19]

A SLOW STUDENT

Jesus saith unto him, Have I been so long time with you, and yet hast thou not known me, Philip? he that hath seen me hath seen the Father; and how sayest thou then, Shew us the Father? John 14:9.

At the head of one of the groups into which the apostles are divided stands the name of Philip. He was the first disciple to whom Jesus addressed the distinct command, "Follow me.". . . He had listened to the teaching of John the Baptist, and had heard his announcement of Christ as the Lamb of God. Philip was a sincere seeker for truth, but he was slow of heart to believe. . . . Though Christ had been proclaimed by the voice from heaven as the Son of God, to Philip He was "Jesus of Nazareth, the son of Joseph" (John 1:45). Again, when the five thousand were fed, Philip's lack of faith was shown. It was to test him that Jesus questioned, "Whence shall we buy bread, that these may eat?" . . . Again, in those last hours before the crucifixion, the words of Philip were such as to discourage faith. . . . So slow of heart, so weak in faith, was that disciple who for three years had been with Jesus.[20]

He wished Christ to reveal the Father in bodily form; but in Christ God had already revealed Himself. Is it possible, Christ said, that after walking with Me, hearing My words, seeing the miracle of feeding the five thousand, of healing the sick of the dread disease leprosy, of bringing the dead to life, of raising Lazarus, who was a prey to death, whose body had indeed seen corruption, you do not know Me? Is it possible that you do not discern the Father in the works that He does by Me? . . . God cannot be seen in external form by any human being. Christ alone can represent the Father to humanity.[21]

In happy contrast to Philip's unbelief was the childlike trust of Nathanael. He was a man of intensely earnest nature, one whose faith took hold upon unseen realities. Yet Philip was a student in the school of Christ, and the divine Teacher bore patiently with his unbelief and dullness. When the Holy Spirit was poured out upon the disciples, Philip became a teacher after the divine order. He knew whereof he spoke, and he taught with an assurance that carried conviction to the hearers.[22]

ON ENEMY GROUND

Wherefore let him that thinketh he standeth take heed lest he fall. 1 Cor. 10:12.

When Christ on the eve of His betrayal forewarned His disciples, "All ye shall be offended because of me this night," Peter confidently declared, "Although all shall be offended, yet will not I" (Mark 14:27, 29). Peter did not know his own danger. Self-confidence misled him. He thought himself able to withstand temptation; but in a few short hours the test came, and with cursing and swearing he denied his Lord.[23]

Peter had not designed that his real character should be known. In assuming an air of indifference he had placed himself on the enemy's ground, and he became an easy prey to temptation. If he had been called to fight for his Master, he would have been a courageous soldier; but when the finger of scorn was pointed at him, he proved himself a coward. Many who do not shrink from active warfare for their Lord are driven by ridicule to deny their faith. By associating with those whom they should avoid, they place themselves in the way of temptation. They invite the enemy to tempt them, and are led to say and do that of which under other circumstances they would never have been guilty. The disciple of Christ who in our day disguises his faith through dread of suffering or reproach denies his Lord as really as did Peter in the judgment hall.[24]

When the crowing of the cock reminded him of the words of Christ, surprised and shocked at what he had just done he turned and looked at his Master. At that moment Christ looked at Peter, and beneath that grieved look, in which compassion and love for him were blended, Peter understood himself. He went out and wept bitterly. That look of Christ's broke his heart. Peter had come to the turning point, and bitterly did he repent his sin. . . . Now his self-confidence was gone. Never again were the old boastful assertions repeated. . . .

It was through self-sufficiency that Peter fell; and it was through repentance and humiliation that his feet were again established. In the record of his experience every repenting sinner may find encouragement.[25]

CONVERTED AT LAST

He saith unto him the third time, Simon, son of Jonas, lovest thou me? John 21:17.

This heart-searching question was necessary in the case of Peter, and it is necessary in our case. The work of restoration can never be thorough unless the roots of evil are reached. Again and again the shoots have been clipped, while the root of bitterness has been left to spring up and defile many; but the very depth of the hidden evil must be reached. . . .

When, the third time, Christ said to Peter, "Lovest thou me?" the probe reached the soul center. Self-judged, Peter fell upon the Rock, saying, "Lord, thou knowest all things; thou knowest that I love thee."

This is the work before every soul who has dishonored God, and grieved the heart of Christ, by a denial of truth and righteousness. If the tempted soul endures the trying process, and self does not awake to life to feel hurt and abused under the test, that probing knife reveals that the soul is indeed dead to self, but alive unto God.

Some assert that if a soul stumbles and falls, he can never regain his position; but the case before us contradicts this. . . . In committing to his stewardship the souls for whom He had given His life, Christ gave to Peter the strongest evidence of His confidence in his restoration. And he was commissioned to feed not only the sheep, but the lambs—a broader and more delicate work than had hitherto been appointed him.[26]

Peter was now humble enough to understand the words of Christ, and without further questioning, the once restless, boastful, self-confident disciple became subdued and contrite. He followed his Lord indeed—the Lord he had denied. The thought that Christ had not denied and rejected him was to Peter a light and comfort and blessing. He felt that he could be crucified from choice, but it must be with his head downward. And he who was so close a partaker of Christ's sufferings will also be a partaker of His glory when He shall "sit upon the throne of his glory."[27]

CAIAPHAS

Rend your heart, and not your garments, and turn unto the Lord your God. Joel 2:13.

It was the custom among the Jews for the garments to be rent at the death of friends, but this custom the priests were not to observe. . . . Everything worn by the priest was to be whole and without blemish. By those beautiful official garments was represented the character of the great antitype, Jesus Christ. Nothing but perfection, in dress and attitude, in word and spirit, could be acceptable to God. He is holy, and His glory and perfection must be represented by the earthly service. . . . Finite man might rend his own heart by showing a contrite and humble spirit. This God would discern. But no rent must be made in the priestly robes, for this would mar the representation of heavenly things.[28]

When Christ declared Himself the Son of God, Caiaphas, in pretended horror, rent his robe, and accused the Holy One of Israel of blasphemy.[29]

He had done the very thing that the Lord had commanded should not be done. Standing under the condemnation of God, he pronounced sentence on Christ as a blasphemer. . . . The priestly robe he rent in order to impress the people with his horror of the sin of blasphemy covered a heart full of wickedness.[30]

How different was the true High Priest from the false and corrupted Caiaphas. Christ stood before the false high priest, pure and undefiled, without a taint of sin. Christ mourned for the transgression of every human being. He bore even the guiltiness of Caiaphas, knowing the hypocrisy that dwelt in his soul, while for pretense he rent his robe. Christ did not rend His robe, but His soul was rent. His garment of human flesh was rent as He hung on the cross, the sin-bearer of the race.[31]

Many today who claim to be Christians are in danger of rending their garments, making an outward show of repentance, when their hearts are not softened nor subdued. This is why so many continue to make failures in the Christian life. An outward appearance of sorrow is shown for wrong, but their repentance is not that which needs not to be repented of.[32]

PILATE

When Pilate realized that nothing more could be done but that there would soon be a riot, he took a bowl of water and washed his hands before the crowd, saying: "I take no responsibility for the death of this man. You must see to that yourselves." Matt. 27:24, Phillips.

If at the first Pilate had stood firm, refusing to condemn a man whom he found guiltless, he would have broken the fatal chain that was to bind him in remorse and guilt as long as he lived. Had he carried out his convictions of right, the Jews would not have presumed to dictate to him. Christ would have been put to death, but the guilt would not have rested upon Pilate. But Pilate had taken step after step in the violation of his conscience. He had excused himself from judging with justice and equity, and he now found himself almost helpless in the hands of the priests and rulers. His wavering and indecision proved his ruin.[33]

In fear and self-condemnation Pilate looked upon the Savior. In the vast sea of upturned faces, His alone was peaceful. About His head a soft light seemed to shine. Pilate said in his heart, He is a God. Turning to the multitude, he declared, I am clear of His blood. Take ye Him, and crucify Him. But . . . I pronounce Him a just man. May He whom He claims as His Father judge you and not me for this day's work. Then to Jesus he said, Forgive me for this act; I cannot save You. . . .

Pilate longed to deliver Jesus. But he saw that he could not do this, and yet retain his own position and honor. Rather than lose his worldly power, he chose to sacrifice an innocent life. How many, to escape loss or suffering, in like manner sacrifice principle. Conscience and duty point one way, and self-interest points another. . . .

Pilate yielded to the demands of the mob. Rather than risk losing his position, he delivered Jesus up to be crucified. But . . . the very thing he dreaded afterward came upon him. His honors were stripped from him, he was cast down from his high office, and, stung by remorse and wounded pride, not long after the crucifixion he ended his own life. So all who compromise with sin will gain only sorrow and ruin. "There is a way which seemeth right unto a man, but the end thereof are the ways of death" (Prov. 14:12).[34]

THE CROSS BEARER

And as they led him away, they laid hold upon one Simon, a Cyrenian, coming out of the country, and on him they laid the cross, that he might bear it after Jesus. Luke 23:26.

Jesus had hardly passed the gate of Pilate's house when the cross which had been prepared for Barabbas was brought out and laid upon His bruised and bleeding shoulders. He had borne His burden but a few rods, when, from loss of blood and excessive weariness and pain, He fell fainting to the ground. When He revived, the cross was again placed upon His shoulders, and He was forced forward. He staggered on for a few steps, bearing His heavy load, and then fell as one lifeless to the ground. The priests and rulers felt no compassion for their suffering victim, but they saw that it was impossible for Him to carry the instrument of torture farther. They were puzzled to find anyone who would humiliate himself to bear the cross to the place of execution.[35]

The crowd that followed the Savior to Calvary taunted and reviled Him because He could not carry the wooden cross. They all saw the weak and staggering steps of Christ, but compassion did not reveal itself in the hearts of those who had advanced from one step to another in their abuse and torture of the Son of God. . . .

A stranger, Simon, a Cyrenian, coming to the city from the country, hears the crowd pass the taunts and ribaldry; he hears the contemptuous repetition, "Make way for the King of the Jews." He stops in astonishment at the scene, and as he expresses his compassion in words and deeds, they seize him and compel him to lift the cross which is too heavy for Christ to bear. . . . That wooden cross borne by him to Calvary was the means of Simon taking upon himself the cross of Christ from choice, to ever cheerfully stand beneath its burden. His compulsory companionship with Christ in bearing His cross to Calvary, in beholding the sad and dreadful work and the spectators beneath the cross, was the means of drawing his heart to Jesus. Every word from the lips of Christ was graven upon his soul. . . . And the heart of Simon believed.[36]

"REMEMBER ME"

And he said unto Jesus, Lord, remember me when thou comest into thy kingdom. Luke 23:42.

To Jesus in His agony on the cross there came one gleam of comfort. It was the prayer of the penitent thief. . . . This man was not a hardened criminal; he had been led astray by evil associations. . . . He had seen and heard Jesus, and had been convicted by His teaching, but he had been turned away from Him by the priests and rulers. Seeking to stifle conviction, he had plunged deeper and deeper into sin, until he was arrested, tried as a criminal, and condemned to die on the cross.

In the judgment hall and on the way to Calvary he had been in company with Jesus. He had heard Pilate declare, "I find no fault in Him" (John 19:4). He had marked His godlike bearing, and His pitying forgiveness of His tormentors. . . . The conviction comes back to him that this is the Christ. Turning to his fellow criminal, he says, "Dost not thou fear God, seeing thou art in the same condemnation?" The dying thieves have no longer anything to fear from man. But upon one of them presses the conviction that there is a God to fear, a future to cause him to tremble. And now, all sin-polluted as it is, his life history is about to close. . . .

When condemned for his crime, the thief had become hopeless and despairing; but strange, tender thoughts now spring up. He calls to mind all he has heard of Jesus. . . . The Holy Spirit illuminates his mind, and little by little the chain of evidence is joined together. In Jesus, bruised, mocked, and hanging upon the cross, he sees the Lamb of God, that taketh away the sin of the world. Hope is mingled with anguish in his voice as the helpless, dying soul casts himself upon a dying Savior. "Lord, remember me," he cries, "when Thou comest into Thy kingdom."

Quickly the answer came. Soft and melodious the tone, full of love, compassion, and power the words: Verily I say unto thee today, Thou shalt be with Me in paradise. . . . To the penitent thief came the perfect peace of acceptance with God.[37]

SECRET FRIENDS NO LONGER

Joseph of Arimathaea, being a disciple of Jesus, but secretly for fear of the Jews, besought Pilate that he might take away the body of Jesus: and Pilate gave him leave. He came therefore, and took the body of Jesus. And there came also Nicodemus, which at the first came to Jesus by night, and brought a mixture of myrrh and aloes, about an hundred pound weight. John 19:38, 39.

Neither Joseph nor Nicodemus had openly accepted the Savior while He was living. They knew that such a step would exclude them from the Sanhedrin, and they hoped to protect Him by their influence in its councils. For a time they had seemed to succeed; but the wily priests, seeing their favor to Christ, had thwarted their plans. In their absence Jesus had been condemned and delivered to be crucified. Now that He was dead, they no longer concealed their attachment to Him. While the disciples feared to show themselves openly as His followers, Joseph and Nicodemus came boldly to their aid. . . .

Nicodemus, when he saw Jesus lifted up on the cross, remembered His words spoken by night in the Mount of Olives: "As Moses lifted up the serpent in the wilderness, even so must the Son of man be lifted up: that whosoever believeth in Him should not perish, but have eternal life" (John 3:14, 15).

On that Sabbath, when Christ lay in the grave, Nicodemus had opportunity for reflection. A clearer light now illuminated his mind, and the words which Jesus had spoken to him were no longer mysterious. He felt that he had lost much by not connecting himself with the Savior during His life. Now he recalled the events of Calvary. The prayer of Christ for His murderers and His answer to the petition of the dying thief spoke to the heart of the learned councilor. Again he looked upon the Savior in His agony; again he heard that last cry, "It is finished," spoken like the words of a conqueror. Again he beheld the reeling earth, the darkened heavens, the rent veil, the shivered rocks, and his faith was forever established.

The very event that destroyed the hopes of the disciples convinced Joseph and Nicodemus of the divinity of Jesus. Their fears were overcome by the courage of a firm and unwavering faith.[38]

THOMAS THE DOUBTER

Jesus saith unto him, Thomas, because thou hast seen me, thou hast believed: blessed are they that have not seen, and yet have believed. John 20:29.

When Jesus first met the disciples in the upper chamber [following His resurrection], Thomas was not with them. He heard the reports of the others, and received abundant proof that Jesus had risen; but gloom and unbelief filled his heart. . . . He was determined not to believe, and for a whole week he brooded over his wretchedness, which seemed all the darker in contrast with the hope and faith of his brethren. . . . He ardently loved his Lord, but he had allowed jealousy and unbelief to take possession of his mind and heart.[39]

[He] firmly and self-confidently affirmed that he would not believe unless he should put his fingers in the prints of the nails and his hand in the side where the cruel spear was thrust. . . .

When Jesus again met with His disciples, Thomas was with them. . . . And Jesus gave him the evidence which he had desired.[40]

His heart leaped for joy, and he cast himself at the feet of Jesus crying, "My Lord and my God." Jesus accepted his acknowledgment, but gently reproved his unbelief. . . .

Many who, like Thomas, wait for all cause of doubt to be removed will never realize their desire. They gradually become confirmed in unbelief. . . .

In His treatment of Thomas, Jesus gave a lesson for His followers. His example shows how we should treat those whose faith is weak, and who make their doubts prominent. Jesus did not overwhelm Thomas with reproach, nor did He enter into controversy with him. He revealed Himself to the doubting one. Thomas had been most unreasonable in dictating the conditions of his faith, but Jesus, by His generous love and consideration, broke down all the barriers. Unbelief is seldom overcome by controversy. . . . But let Jesus, in His love and mercy, be revealed as the crucified Savior, and from many once unwilling lips will be heard the acknowledgment of Thomas, "My Lord and my God."[41]

RELIGIOUS LIBERTY

But Peter and John answered and said unto them, Whether it be right in the sight of God to hearken unto you more than unto God, judge ye. For we cannot but speak the things which we have seen and heard. Acts 4:19, 20.

On the day following the healing of the cripple [Acts 3], Annas and Caiaphas, with the other dignitaries of the temple, met together for the trial, and the prisoners [Peter and John] were brought before them. In that very room and before some of those very men, Peter had shamefully denied his Lord. This came distinctly to his mind as he appeared for his own trial. He now had an opportunity of redeeming his cowardice. . . .

But the Peter who denied Christ in the hour of His greatest need was impulsive and self-confident, differing widely from the Peter who was brought before the Sanhedrin for examination. Since his fall he had been converted. He was no longer proud and boastful, but modest and self-distrustful. He was filled with the Holy Spirit, and by the help of this power he was resolved to remove the stain of his apostasy by honoring the name he had once disowned.[42]

The principle for which the disciples stood so fearlessly when, in answer to the command not to speak any more in the name of Jesus, they declared, "Whether it be right in the sight of God to hearken unto you more than unto God, judge ye," is the same that the adherents of the gospel struggled to maintain in the days of the Reformation. . . .

This principle we in our day are firmly to maintain. The banner of truth and religious liberty held aloft by the founders of the gospel church and by God's witnesses during the centuries that have passed since then, has, in this last conflict, been committed to our hands. . . . We are to recognize human government as an ordinance of divine appointment, and teach obedience to it as a sacred duty, within its legitimate sphere. But when its claims conflict with the claims of God, we must obey God rather than men. God's word must be recognized as above all human legislation. A "Thus saith the Lord" is not to be set aside for a "Thus saith the church" or a "Thus saith the state." The crown of Christ is to be lifted above the diadems of earthly potentates.[43]

MISHANDLING GOD'S GOODS

When thou shalt vow a vow unto the Lord thy God, thou shalt not slack to pay it: for the Lord thy God will surely require it of thee. Deut. 23:21.

The brief but terrible history of Ananias and Sapphira is traced by the pen of inspiration for the benefit of all who profess to be the followers of Christ. This important lesson has not rested with sufficient weight upon the minds of our people. . . . This one marked evidence of God's retributive justice is fearful, and should lead all to fear and tremble to repeat sins which brought such a punishment. . . .

Ananias and his wife Sapphira had the privilege of hearing the gospel preached by the apostles. . . . While under the direct influence of the Spirit of God, they made a pledge to give to the Lord certain lands; but when they were no longer under this heavenly influence, the impression was less forcible, and they began to question and draw back from fulfilling the pledge which they had made. . . . Covetousness was first cherished; then, ashamed to have their brethren know that their selfish souls grudged that which they had solemnly dedicated and pledged to God, deception was practiced. . . . When convicted of their falsehood, their punishment was instant death.[44]

Not to the early church only, but to all future generations, this example of God's hatred of covetousness, fraud, and hypocrisy was given as a danger signal. . . . When the heart is stirred by the influence of the Holy Spirit, and a vow is made to give a certain amount, the one who vows has no longer any right to the consecrated portion. Promises of this kind made to men would be looked upon as binding; are those not more binding that are made to God? . . .

Many spend money lavishly in self-gratification. Men and women consult their pleasure and gratify their taste, while they bring to God, almost unwillingly, a stinted offering. They forget that God will one day demand a strict account of how His goods have been used, and that He will no more accept the pittance they hand into the treasury than He accepted the offering of Ananias and Sapphira.[45]

MARTYRED FOR CHRIST

And all that sat in the council, looking stedfastly on him, saw his face as it had been the face of an angel. Acts 6:15.

Stephen, the foremost of the seven deacons, was a man of deep piety and broad faith. . . . He was very active in the cause of Christ and boldly proclaimed his faith. Learned rabbis and doctors of the law engaged in public discussion with him, confidently expecting an easy victory. But "they were not able to resist the wisdom and the spirit by which he spake.". . .

As the priests and rulers saw the power that attended the preaching of Stephen, they were filled with bitter hatred. . . . [They] seized Stephen and brought him before the Sanhedrin council for trial. . . .

Saul of Tarsus was present and took a leading part against Stephen. He brought the weight of eloquence and the logic of the rabbis to bear upon the case, to convince the people that Stephen was preaching delusive and dangerous doctrines; but in Stephen he met one who had a full understanding of the purpose of God in the spreading of the gospel to other nations. . . .

In the cruel faces about him the prisoner read his fate; but he did not waver. For him the fear of death was gone. For him the enraged priests and the excited mob had no terror. The scene before him faded from his vision. To him the gates of heaven were ajar, and, looking in, he saw the glory of the courts of God, and Christ, as if just risen from His throne, standing ready to sustain His servant.[46]

In every age God's chosen messengers have been reviled and persecuted, yet through their affliction the knowledge of God has been spread abroad. . . . When the noble and eloquent Stephen was stoned to death . . . there was no loss to the cause of the gospel. The light of heaven that glorified his face, the divine compassion breathed in his dying prayer, were as a sharp arrow of conviction to the bigoted Sanhedrist who stood by, and Saul, the persecuting Pharisee, became a chosen vessel to bear the name of Christ before Gentiles and kings and the children of Israel.[47]

JUST FOR ONE MAN

And the angel of the Lord spake unto Philip, saying, Arise, and go toward the south unto the way that goeth down from Jerusalem unto Gaza, which is desert. And he arose and went. Acts 8:26, 27.

Notice how much effort was put forth for just one man, an Ethiopian.[48]

This Ethiopian was a man of good standing and of wide influence. God saw that when converted he would give others the light he had received and would exert a strong influence in favor of the gospel. Angels of God were attending this seeker for light, and he was being drawn to the Savior. By the ministration of the Holy Spirit the Lord brought him into touch with one who could lead him to the light.

Philip was directed to go to the Ethiopian and explain to him the prophecy that he was reading. "Go near," the Spirit said, "and join thyself to this chariot." . . . The man's heart thrilled with interest as the Scriptures were explained to him; and when the disciple had finished, he was ready to accept the light given. He did not make his high worldly position an excuse for refusing the gospel. . . .

This Ethiopian represented a large class who need to be taught by such missionaries as Philip—men who will hear the voice of God and go where He sends them. There are many who are reading the Scriptures who cannot understand their true import. All over the world men and women are looking wistfully to heaven. Prayers and tears and inquiries go up from souls longing for light, for grace, for the Holy Spirit. Many are on the verge of the kingdom, waiting only to be gathered in.

An angel guided Philip to the one who was seeking for light and who was ready to receive the gospel, and today angels will guide the footsteps of those workers who will allow the Holy Spirit to sanctify their tongues and refine and ennoble their hearts.[49]

He who sent Philip to the Ethiopian councilor, Peter to the Roman centurion, and the little Israelitish maiden to the help of Naamah, the Syrian captain, sends men and women and youth today as His representatives to those in need of divine help and guidance.[50]

THE FIRST DORCAS

*Now there was at Joppa a certain disciple named Tabitha,
which by interpretation is called Dorcas: this woman was full of
good works and almsdeeds which she did. Acts 9:36.*

At Joppa, which was near Lydda, there lived a woman named
Dorcas, whose good deeds had made her greatly beloved. She was a
worthy disciple of Jesus, and her life was filled with acts of kindness.
She knew who needed comfortable clothing and who needed sympathy, and she freely ministered to the poor and the sorrowful. . . .

"And it came to pass in those days, that she was sick, and died."
. . . Hearing that Peter was at Lydda, the believers sent messengers
to him. . . . "When he was come, they brought him into the upper
chamber: and all the widows stood by him weeping, and showing
the coats and garments which Dorcas made, while she was with
them.". . .

The apostle's heart was touched with sympathy as he beheld their
sorrow. Then, directing that the weeping friends be sent from the
room, he kneeled down and prayed fervently to God to restore
Dorcas to life and health. . . . Dorcas had been of great service to the
church, and God saw fit to bring her back from the land of the
enemy, that her skill and energy might still be a blessing to others,
and also that by this manifestation of His power the cause of Christ
might be strengthened.[51]

Let the children and youth learn from the Bible how God has honored the work of the everyday toiler. . . . Let them read of Jesus the
carpenter, and Paul the tent-maker, who with the toil of the craftsman
linked the highest ministry, human and divine. Let them read of the
lad whose five loaves were used by the Savior in that wonderful miracle for the feeding of the multitude; of Dorcas the seamstress, called
back from death, that she might continue to make garments for the
poor; of the wise woman described in the Proverbs, who "seeketh
wool and flax, and worketh willingly with her hands"; . . . who
"stretcheth out her hand to the poor; yea, . . . reacheth forth her
hands to the needy." . . .

Of such a one, God says: "She shall be praised. Give her of the
fruit of her hands; and let her own works praise her in the gates."[52]

NO NATIONAL BARRIERS

Thy prayers and thine alms are come up for a memorial before God. And now send men to Joppa, and call for one Simon, whose surname is Peter: he lodgeth with one Simon a tanner, whose house is by the sea side: he shall tell thee what thou oughtest to do. Acts10: 4-6.

The explicitness of these directions, in which was named even the occupation of the man with whom Peter was staying, shows that Heaven is acquainted with the history and business of men in every station of life. God is familiar with the experience and work of the humble laborer, as well as with that of the king upon his throne.[53]

My heart is made very tender as I read of the interest manifested by the Lord in Cornelius. Cornelius was a man in high position, an officer in the Roman army, but he was walking in strict accordance with all the light he had received. The Lord sent a special message from heaven to him, and by another message directed Peter to visit him and give him light.[54]

Cornelius was gladly obedient to the vision.[55]

Thus was the gospel brought to those who had been strangers and foreigners, making them fellow citizens with the saints, and members of the household of God. The conversion of Cornelius and his household was but the first fruits of a harvest to be gathered in. From this household a wide-spread work of grace was carried on in that heathen city.

Today God is seeking for souls among the high as well as the lowly. There are many like Cornelius, men whom the Lord desires to connect with His work in the world. Their sympathies are with the Lord's people, but the ties that bind them to the world hold them firmly. It requires moral courage for them to take their position for Christ. Special efforts should be made for these souls, who are in so great danger, because of their responsibilities and associations.[56]

From the story of Cornelius we learn that God will lead every one who is willing to be led. He led Cornelius. He drew out His servant's heart in prayer. He prepared him to receive the light of His truth, and he chose to enlighten the mind of Cornelius through the agency of one who had already received light from above.[57]

TO ALL THE WORLD

Peter began: "I now see how true it is that God has no favourites, but that in every nation the man who is godfearing and does what is right is acceptable to him." Acts 10:34, 35, NEB.

Peter . . . was called by God to take the gospel to Cornelius. . . .

As yet none of the disciples had preached the gospel to the Gentiles. In their minds the middle wall of partition, broken down by the death of Christ, still existed, and their labors had been confined to the Jews, for they had looked upon the Gentiles as excluded from the blessings of the gospel. Now the Lord was seeking to teach Peter the world-wide extent of the divine plan. . . .

How carefully the Lord worked to overcome the prejudice against the Gentiles that had been so firmly fixed in Peter's mind by his Jewish training! By the vision of the sheet and its contents He sought to divest the apostle's mind of this prejudice and to teach the important truth that in heaven there is no respect of persons; that Jew and Gentile are alike precious in God's sight; that through Christ the heathen may be made partakers of the blessings and privileges of the gospel. . . .

It was with reluctance at every step that he [Peter] undertook the duty laid upon him but he dared not disobey. . . . As Peter pointed those present [Cornelius and his kinsmen and friends] to Jesus as the sinner's only hope, he himself understood more fully the meaning of the vision he had seen, and his heart glowed with the spirit of the truth that he was presenting. . . .

When the brethren in Judea heard that Peter had gone to the house of a Gentile and preached to those assembled, they were surprised and offended. They feared that such a course, which looked to them presumptuous, would have the effect of counteracting his own teaching. . . .

Peter laid the whole matter before them. . . . Convinced that Peter's course was in direct fulfillment of the plan of God, and that their prejudices and exclusiveness were utterly contrary to the spirit of the gospel, they glorified God, saying, "Then hath God also to the Gentiles granted repentance unto life." [58]

ANGEL PROTECTORS

And when Peter was come to himself, he said, Now I know of a surety, that the Lord hath sent his angel, and hath delivered me out of the hand of Herod. Acts 12:11.

The day of Peter's execution was at last appointed, but still the prayers of the believers ascended to heaven; and while all their energies and sympathies were called out in fervent appeals for help, angels of God were watching over the imprisoned apostle. . . .

Herod on this occasion had taken double precautions. To prevent all possibility of release, Peter had been put under the charge of sixteen soldiers, who, in different watches, guarded him day and night. In his cell, he was placed between two soldiers, and was bound by two chains, each chain being fastened to the wrist of one of the soldiers. He was unable to move without their knowledge. With the prison doors securely fastened, and a strong guard before them, all chance of rescue or escape through human means was cut off. But man's extremity is God's opportunity. . . . Herod was lifting his hand against Omnipotence, and he was to be utterly defeated. By the putting forth of His might, God was about to save the precious life that the Jews were plotting to destroy. . . . A mighty angel is sent from heaven to rescue Peter.[59]

The principalities and powers of heaven are watching the warfare which, under apparently discouraging circumstances, God's servants are carrying on. New conquests are being achieved, new honors won, as the Christians, rallying round the banner of their Redeemer, go forth to fight the good fight of faith. All the heavenly angels are at the service of the humble, believing people of God; and as the Lord's army of workers here below sing their songs of praise, the choir above join with them in ascribing praise to God and to His Son. . . .

Every true child of God has the co-operation of heavenly beings. Invisible armies of light and power attend the meek and lowly ones who believe and claim the promises of God. Cherubim and seraphim, and angels that excel in strength, stand at God's right hand, "all ministering spirits, sent forth to minister for them who shall be heirs of salvation."[60]

LINKED WITH HEAVEN

The angel of the Lord encampeth round about them that fear him, and delivereth them. Ps. 34:7.

The experience of Philip, directed by an angel from heaven to go to the place where he met one seeking for truth; of Cornelius, visited by an angel with a message from God; of Peter, in prison and condemned to death, led by an angel forth to safety—all show the closeness of the connection between heaven and earth.

To the worker for God the record of these angel visits should bring strength and courage. Today, as verily as in the days of the apostles, heavenly messengers are passing through the length and breadth of the land, seeking to comfort the sorrowing, to protect the impenitent, to win the hearts of men to Christ. We cannot see them personally; nevertheless they are with us, guiding, directing, protecting.

Heaven is brought near to earth by that mystic ladder, the base of which is firmly planted on the earth, while the topmost round reaches the throne of the Infinite. Angels are constantly ascending and descending this ladder of shining brightness, bearing the prayers of the needy and distressed to the Father above, and bringing blessing and hope, courage and help, to the children of men. These angels of light create a heavenly atmosphere about the soul, lifting us toward the unseen and the eternal. We cannot behold their forms with our natural sight. . . . The spiritual ear alone can hear the harmony of heavenly voices. . . .

God commissions His angels to save His chosen ones from calamity, to guard them from "the pestilence that walketh in darkness" and "the destruction that wasteth at noonday."

Again and again have angels talked with men as a man speaketh with a friend, and led them to places of security. Again and again have the encouraging words of angels renewed the drooping spirits of the faithful and, carrying their minds above the things of earth, caused them to behold by faith the white robes, the crowns, the palm branches of victory, which overcomers will receive when they surround the great white throne.[61]

337

AT THE DAMASCUS GATE

And as he journeyed, he came near Damascus: and suddenly there shined round about him a light from heaven: and he fell to the earth, and heard a voice saying unto him, Saul, Saul, why persecutest thou me? Acts 9:3, 4.

With the faith and experience of the Galilean disciples who had companied with Jesus were united, in the work of the gospel, the fiery vigor and intellectual power of a rabbi of Jerusalem. A Roman citizen, born in a Gentile city; a Jew, not only by descent but by lifelong training, patriotic devotion, and religious faith; educated in Jerusalem by the most eminent of the rabbis, and instructed in all the laws and traditions of the fathers, Saul of Tarsus shared to the fullest extent the pride and the prejudices of his nation. While still a young man, he became an honored member of the Sanhedrin. He was looked upon as a man of promise, a zealous defender of the ancient faith.

In the theological schools of Judea the word of God had been set aside for human speculations; it was robbed of its power by the interpretations and traditions of the rabbis. . . . With their fierce hatred of their Roman oppressors, they cherished the determination to recover by force of arms their national supremacy. The followers of Jesus, whose message of peace was so contrary to their schemes of ambition, they hated and put to death. In this persecution, Saul was one of the most bitter and relentless actors. . . .

At the gate of Damascus the vision of the Crucified One changed the whole current of his life. The persecutor became a disciple, the teacher a learner. The days of darkness spent in solitude at Damascus were as years in his experience. The Old Testament Scriptures stored in his memory were his study, and Christ his teacher.[62]

Paul did not think that he made any real sacrifice when he exchanged Phariseeism for the gospel of Jesus Christ. . . . When Paul found that he was in a wrong path, he linked himself, according to divine light, with a people he had thought he must wipe from the earth. . . . He taught Christ and lived Christ, and suffered martyrdom for Christ's sake.[63]

SAUL TO PAUL

And he trembling and astonished said, Lord, what wilt thou have me to do? And the Lord said unto him, Arise, and go into the city, and it shall be told thee what thou must do. Acts 9:6.

In the wonderful conversion of Paul we see the miraculous power of God. . . . Jesus, whose name of all others he most hated and despised, revealed Himself to Paul for the purpose of arresting his mad yet honest career, that He might make this most unpromising instrument a chosen vessel to bear the gospel to the Gentiles. . . . The light of heavenly illumination had taken away Paul's eyesight; but Jesus, the Great Healer of the blind, does not restore it. He answers the question of Paul in these words: "Arise, and go into the city, and it shall be told thee what thou must do." Jesus could not only have healed Paul of his blindness, but He could have forgiven his sins and told him his duty by marking out his future course. From Christ all power and mercies were to flow; but He did not give Paul an experience, in his conversion to truth, independent of His church recently organized upon the earth.

The marvelous light given Paul upon that occasion astonished and confounded him. He was wholly subdued. This part of the work man could not do for Paul, but there was a work still to be accomplished which the servants of Christ could do. Jesus directs him to His agents in the church for a further knowledge of duty. Thus He gives authority and sanction to His organized church. Christ had done the work of revelation and conviction, and now Paul was in a condition to learn of those whom God had ordained to teach the truth. Christ directs Paul to His chosen servants, thus placing him in connection with His church. The very men whom Paul was purposing to destroy were to be his instructors in the very religion that he had despised and persecuted. . . .

An angel is sent to Ananias, directing him to go to a certain house where Saul is praying to be instructed in what he is to do next. . . . In Christ's stead Ananias touches his eyes that they may receive sight; in Christ's stead he lays his hands upon him, prays in Christ's name, and Saul receives the Holy Ghost.[64]

339

ARABIAN INTERLUDE

Neither went I up to Jerusalem to them which were apostles before me; but I went into Arabia, and returned again unto Damascus. Gal. 1:17.

Paul's life was in peril, and he received a commission from God to leave Damascus for a time. He went into Arabia; and there, in comparative solitude, he had ample opportunity for communion with God and for contemplation. He wished to be alone with God, to search his own heart, to deepen his repentance, and to prepare himself by prayer and study to engage in a work which appeared to him too great and too important for him to undertake. He was an apostle, not chosen of men, but chosen of God, and his work was plainly stated to be among the Gentiles.

While in Arabia he did not communicate with the apostles; he sought God earnestly with all his heart, determining not to rest till he knew for a certainty that his repentance was accepted and his great sin pardoned. He would not give up the conflict until he had the assurance that Jesus would be with him in his coming ministry. He was ever to carry about with him in the body the marks of Christ's glory, in his eyes, which had been blinded by the heavenly light, and he desired also to bear with him constantly the assurance of Christ's sustaining grace. Paul came into close connection with Heaven, and Jesus communed with him, and established him in his faith bestowing upon him His wisdom and grace.[65]

All who are under the training of God need the quiet hour for communion with their own hearts, with nature, and with God. . . . They need to have a personal experience in obtaining a knowledge of the will of God. We must individually hear Him speaking to the heart. When every other voice is hushed, and in quietness we wait before Him, the silence of the soul makes more distinct the voice of God. . . . Amidst the hurrying throng, and the strain of life's intense activities, he who is thus refreshed will be surrounded with an atmosphere of light and peace. He will receive a new endowment of both physical and mental strength. His life will breathe out a fragrance, and will reveal a divine power that will reach men's hearts.[66]

340

PAUL EXALTS THE CROSS

For I determined not to know any thing among you, save Jesus Christ, and him crucified. . . . And my speech and my preaching was not with enticing words of man's wisdom, but in demonstration of the Spirit and of power. 1 Cor. 2:2-4.

It had been Paul's custom to adopt an oratorical style in his preaching. He was a man fitted to speak before kings, before the great and learned men of Athens, and his intellectual acquirements were often of value to him in preparing the way for the gospel. He tried to do this in Athens, meeting eloquence with eloquence, philosophy with philosophy, and logic with logic; but he failed to meet with the success he had hoped for. His after-sight led him to understand that there was something needed above human wisdom. . . . He must receive his power from a higher source. In order to convict and convert sinners, the Spirit of God must come into his work and sanctify every spiritual development.[1]

To Paul the cross was the one object of supreme interest. Ever since he had been arrested in his career of persecution against the followers of the crucified Nazarene he had never ceased to glory in the cross. . . . He knew by personal experience that when a sinner once beholds the love of the Father, as seen in the sacrifice of His Son, and yields to the divine influence, a change of heart takes place, and henceforth Christ is all and in all.

At the time of his conversion, Paul was inspired with a longing desire to help his fellow men to behold Jesus of Nazareth as the Son of the living God, mighty to transform and to save. Henceforth his life was wholly devoted to an effort to portray the love and power of the Crucified One. . . . The apostle's efforts were not confined to public speaking; there were many who could not have been reached in that way. . . . He visited the sick and the sorrowing, comforted the afflicted, and lifted up the oppressed. And in all that he said and did he magnified the name of Jesus. . . .

Paul realized that his sufficiency was not in himself, but in the presence of the Holy Spirit, whose gracious influence filled his heart. . . . Self was hidden; Christ was revealed and exalted.[2]

341

GOSPEL TENTMAKER

In all things I have kept myself from being burdensome unto you, and so will I keep myself. 2 Cor. 11:9.

Paul was a tentmaker, and he supported himself by working at his trade. While working thus, he spoke of the gospel to those with whom he came in contact, and turned many souls from error to truth. He lost no opportunity of speaking of the Savior, or of helping those in trouble.[3]

The history of the apostle Paul is a constant testimony that manual labor cannot be degrading, that it is not inconsistent with true greatness and elevation of human or Christian character. Those toilworn hands, he deemed, detracted nothing from the force of his pathetic appeals, sensible, intelligent, and eloquent. . . . Those toilworn hands as he presented them before the people bore testimony that he was not chargeable to any man for his support. . . . At times he also supported his fellow workers, himself suffering from hunger in order to relieve the necessities of others. He shared his earnings with Luke, and helped Timothy obtain the necessary equipment for his journey.[4]

Paul set an example against the sentiment, then gaining influence in the church, that the gospel could be proclaimed successfully only by those who were wholly freed from the necessity of physical toil. He illustrated in a practical way what might be done by consecrated laymen in many places where the people were unacquainted with the truths of the gospel. His course inspired many humble toilers with a desire to do what they could to advance the cause of God, while at the same time they supported themselves in daily labor. . . .

While some with special talents are chosen to devote all their energies to the work of teaching and preaching the gospel, many others, upon whom human hands have never been laid in ordination, are called to act an important part in soulsaving. . . . The self-sacrificing servant of God who labors untiringly in word and doctrine, carries on his heart a heavy burden. . . . His wages do not influence him in his labor. . . . From heaven he received his commission, and to heaven he looks for his recompense when the work entrusted to him is done.[5]

PROFITABLE BONFIRE

And many that believed came, and confessed, and shewed their deeds. Many of them also which used curious arts brought their books together, and burned them before all men. Acts 19:18, 19.

By burning their books on magic, the Ephesian converts showed that the things in which they had once delighted they now abhorred. It was by and through magic that they had especially offended God and imperiled their souls; and it was against magic that they showed such indignation. . . . By retaining these books the disciples would have exposed themselves to temptation; by selling them they would have placed temptation in the way of others. They had renounced the kingdom of darkness, and to destroy its power they did not hesitate at any sacrifice. Thus truth triumphed over men's prejudices and their love of money. . . . The influence of what had taken place was more widespread than even Paul realized. From Ephesus the news was widely circulated, and a strong impetus was given to the cause of Christ. Long after the apostle himself had finished his course, these scenes lived in the memory of men and were the means of winning converts to the gospel.

It is fondly supposed that heathen superstitions have disappeared before the civilization of the twentieth century. But the word of God and the stern testimony of facts declare that sorcery is practiced in this age as verily as in the days of the old-time magicians. The ancient system of magic is, in reality, the same as what is now known as modern spiritualism. Satan is finding access to thousands of minds by presenting himself under the guise of departed friends. . . .

The magicians of heathen times have their counterpart in the spiritualistic mediums, the clairvoyants, and the fortunetellers of today. . . . Could the veil be lifted from before our eyes, we should see evil angels employing all their arts to deceive and to destroy. Wherever an influence is exerted to cause men to forget God, there Satan is exercising his bewitching power. . . . The apostle's admonition to the Ephesian church should be heeded by the people of God today: "Have no fellowship with the unfruitful works of darkness, but rather reprove them." [6]

343

WHILE YOU ARE YOUNG

Don't let people look down on you because you are young; see that they look up to you because you are an example to them in your speech and behavior, in your love and faith and sincerity. 1 Tim. 4:12, Phillips.

He [Timothy] was a mere lad when chosen by God as a teacher; but so fixed were his principles by a correct education that he was fitted for this important position. He bore his responsibilities with Christlike meekness. He was faithful, steadfast, and true, and Paul selected him to be his companion in labor and travel. Lest Timothy should meet with slights because of his youthfulness, Paul wrote to him, "Let no man despise thy youth." He could safely do this, because Timothy was not self-sufficient, but continually sought guidance.

There are many youth who move from impulse rather than from judgment. But Timothy inquired at every step, "Is this the way of the Lord?" He had no specially brilliant talents, but he consecrated all his abilities to the service of God, and this made his work valuable. The Lord found in him a mind that He could mold and fashion for the indwelling of the Holy Spirit.

God will use the youth today as He used Timothy, if they will submit to His guidance. It is your privilege to be God's missionaries. He calls upon you to work for your companions. Seek out those you know to be in danger, and in the love of Christ try to help them. How are they to know the Savior unless they see His virtues in His followers?[7]

The highest aim of our youth should not be to strain after something novel. There was none of this in the mind and work of Timothy. They should bear in mind that, in the hands of the enemy of all good, knowledge alone may be a power to destroy them. It was a very intellectual being, one who occupied a high position among the angelic throng, that finally became a rebel; and many a mind of superior intellectual attainments is now being led captive by his power. The youth should place themselves under the teaching of the Holy Scriptures, and weave them into their daily thoughts and practical life. Then they will possess the attributes classed as highest in the heavenly courts.[8]

"FROM A CHILD"

From a child thou hast known the holy scriptures, which are able to make thee wise unto salvation through faith which is in Christ Jesus. 2 Tim. 3:15.

We see the advantage that Timothy had in a correct example of piety and true godliness. Religion was the atmosphere of his home. The manifest spiritual power of the piety in the home kept him pure in speech, and free from all corrupting sentiments.[9]

God had commanded the Hebrews to teach their children His requirements and to make them acquainted with all His dealings with their fathers. This was one of the special duties of every parent—one that was not to be delegated to another. In the place of stranger lips the loving hearts of the father and mother were to give instruction to their children. Thoughts of God were to be associated with all the events of daily life. The mighty works of God in the deliverance of His people and the promises of the Redeemer to come were to be often recounted in the homes of Israel. . . . The great truths of God's providence and of the future life were impressed on the young mind. It was trained to see God alike in the scenes of nature and the words of revelation. The stars of heaven, the trees and flowers of the field, the lofty mountains, the rippling brooks—all spoke of the Creator. The solemn service of sacrifice and worship at the sanctuary and the utterances of the prophets were a revelation of God.

Such was the training of Moses in the lowly cabin home in Goshen; of Samuel, by the faithful Hannah; of David, in the hill dwelling at Bethlehem; of Daniel, before the scenes of the captivity separated him from the home of his fathers. Such, too, was the early life of Christ at Nazareth; such the training by which the child Timothy learned from the lips of his grandmother Lois, and his mother Eunice, the truths of Holy Writ.[10]

Parents, there is a great work for you to do for Jesus. . . . Satan seeks to bind the children to himself as with bands of steel, and you can attain success in bringing them to Jesus only through determined personal effort.[11]

ALL THAT A SON COULD BE

Do your best to present yourself to God as one approved, a workman who has no need to be ashamed, rightly handling the word of truth. 2 Tim. 2:15, RSV.

Paul loved Timothy, his "own son in the faith" (1 Tim. 1:2). The great apostle often drew the younger disciple out, questioning him in regard to Scripture history, and as they traveled from place to place, he carefully taught him how to do successful work.[12]

The affection between Paul and Timothy began with Timothy's conversion; and the tie had strengthened as they had shared the hopes, the perils, and the toils of missionary life, till they seemed to be as one. The disparity in their ages and the difference in their characters made their love for each other more earnest. The ardent, zealous, indomitable spirit of Paul found repose and comfort in the mild, yielding, retiring disposition of Timothy. The faithful ministration and tender love of this tried companion had brightened many a dark hour in the apostle's life. . . . All that a son could be to a loved and honored father, the youthful Timothy was to the tried and lonely Paul.[13]

Paul loved Timothy because Timothy loved God. His intelligent knowledge of experimental piety and of the truth gave him distinction and influence. The piety and influence of his home life was not of a cheap order, but pure, sensible, and uncorrupted by false sentiments. . . . The Word of God was the rule which guided Timothy. . . . Impressions of the highest possible order were kept before his mind. His home instructors cooperated with God in educating this young man to bear the burdens that were to come upon him at an early age.[14]

In his work, Timothy constantly sought Paul's advice and instruction. He did not move from impulse, but exercised consideration and calm thought. . . . The Holy Spirit found in him one who could be molded and fashioned as a temple for the indwelling of the divine Presence.

As the lessons of the Bible are wrought into the daily life, they have a deep and lasting influence upon the character. These lessons Timothy learned and practiced.[15]

PASSING THE TORCH

I charge thee therefore before God, and the Lord Jesus Christ, who shall judge the quick and the dead at his appearing and his kingdom; preach the word; be instant in season, out of season; reprove, rebuke, exhort with all longsuffering and doctrine. 2 Tim. 4:1, 2.

In this his last letter to Timothy, Paul held up before the younger worker a high ideal, pointing out the duties devolving on him as a minister of Christ. . . . Paul bids him preach the word, not the sayings and customs of men; to be ready to witness for God whenever opportunity should present itself—before large congregations and private circles, by the way and at the fireside, to friends and to enemies, whether in safety or exposed to hardship and peril, reproach and loss.

Fearing that Timothy's mild, yielding disposition might lead him to shun an essential part of his work, Paul exhorted him to be faithful in reproving sin and even to rebuke with sharpness those who were guilty of gross evils. Yet he was to do this "with all long-suffering and doctrine." He was to reveal the patience and love of Christ. . . .

To hate and reprove sin, and at the same time to show pity and tenderness for the sinner, is a difficult attainment. The more earnest our own efforts to attain to holiness of heart and life, the more acute will be our perception of sin and the more decided our disapproval of any deviation from the right. We must guard against undue severity toward the wrongdoer, but we must also be careful not to lose sight of the exceeding sinfulness of sin. There is need of showing Christlike patience and love for the erring one, but there is also danger of showing so great toleration for his error that he will look upon himself as undeserving of reproof. . . .

With the growing contempt for God's law there is an increasing distaste for religion, an increase of pride, love of pleasure, disobedience to parents, and self-indulgence; and thoughtful minds everywhere are anxiously inquiring, What can be done to correct these alarming evils? The answer is found in Paul's exhortation to Timothy, "Preach the word." In the Bible are found the only safe principles of action. It is a transcript of the will of God, an expression of divine wisdom.[16]

347

THIS DROPOUT MADE GOOD

Pick up Mark and bring him with you, for I find him a useful assistant. 2 Tim. 4:11, NEB.

Mark's mother was a convert to the Christian religion, and her home at Jerusalem was an asylum for the disciples. . . . Mark proposed to Paul and Barnabas that he should accompany them on their missionary tour. He felt the favor of God in his heart and longed to devote himself entirely to the work of the gospel ministry. . . .

Their way was toilsome; they encountered hardships and privations, and were beset with dangers on every side. . . . But Paul and Barnabas had learned to trust God's power to deliver. Their hearts were filled with fervent love for perishing souls. As faithful shepherds in search of the lost sheep, they gave no thought to their own ease and convenience. Forgetful of self, they faltered not when weary, hungry, and cold. They had in view but one object—the salvation of those who had wandered far from the fold. . . .

Mark, overwhelmed with fear and discouragement, wavered for a time in his purpose to give himself wholeheartedly to the Lord's work. Unused to hardships, he was disheartened by the perils and privations of the way. . . . He had yet to learn to face danger and persecution and adversity with a brave heart. As the apostles advanced, and still greater difficulties were apprehended, Mark was intimidated and, losing all courage, refused to go farther and returned to Jerusalem.

This desertion caused Paul to judge Mark unfavorably, and even severely, for a time. Barnabas, on the other hand, was inclined to excuse him because of his inexperience. He felt anxious that Mark should not abandon the ministry, for he saw in him qualifications that would fit him to be a useful worker for Christ. In after years his solicitude in Mark's behalf was richly rewarded, for the young man gave himself unreservedly to the Lord and to the work of proclaiming the gospel message in difficult fields. Under the blessing of God, and the wise training of Barnabas, he developed into a valuable worker. Paul was afterward reconciled to Mark and received him as a fellow laborer.[17]

MARK AND DEMAS

Love not the world, neither the things that are in the world. If any man love the world, the love of the Father is not in him. 1 John 2:15.

Among Paul's assistants at Rome were many of his former companions and fellow workers. Luke, "the beloved physician," . . . was with him still. . . . Demas and Mark were also with him. . . .

Since the earlier years of his profession of faith, Mark's Christian experience had deepened. As he had studied more closely the life and death of Christ he had obtained clearer views of the Savior's mission, its toils and conflicts. Reading in the scars in Christ's hands and feet the marks of His service for humanity, and the length to which self-abnegation leads to save the lost and perishing, Mark had become willing to follow the Master in the path of self-sacrifice. Now, sharing the lot of Paul the prisoner, he understood better than ever before that it is infinite gain to win Christ, infinite loss to win the world and lose the soul for whose redemption the blood of Christ was shed. In the face of severe trial and adversity, Mark continued steadfast, a wise and beloved helper of the apostle.

Demas, steadfast for a time, afterward forsook the cause of Christ. In referring to this, Paul wrote, "Demas hath forsaken me, having loved this present world" (2 Tim. 4:10). For worldly gain, Demas bartered every high and noble consideration. How shortsighted the exchange! Possessing only worldly wealth or honor, Demas was poor indeed, however much he might proudly call his own; while Mark, choosing to suffer for Christ's sake, possessed eternal riches, being accounted in heaven an heir of God and a joint heir with His Son.[18]

If we would permit our minds to dwell more upon Christ and the heavenly world, we should find a powerful stimulus and support in fighting the battles of the Lord. Pride and love of the world will lose their power as we contemplate the glories of that better land so soon to be our home. Beside the loveliness of Christ, all earthly attractions will seem of little worth.[19]

MASTER AND SERVANT

Not now as a servant, but above a servant, a brother beloved, specially to me, but how much more unto thee, both in the flesh, and in the Lord? Philemon 16.

Among those who gave their hearts to God through the labors of Paul in Rome was Onesimus, a pagan slave who had wronged his master, Philemon, a Christian believer in Colosse, and had escaped to Rome. In the kindness of his heart, Paul sought to relieve the poverty and distress of the wretched fugitive and then endeavored to shed the light of truth into his darkened mind. Onesimus listened to the words of life, confessed his sins, and was converted to the faith of Christ. . . . Paul . . . counseled him to return without delay to Philemon; beg his forgiveness, and plan for the future. The apostle promised to hold himself responsible for the sum of which Philemon had been robbed. . . . It was a severe test for this servant thus to deliver himself up to the master he had wronged; but he had been truly converted, and he did not turn aside from this duty. . . .

Paul's letter to Philemon shows the influence of the gospel upon the relation between master and servant. Slaveholding was an established institution throughout the Roman Empire, and both masters and slaves were found in most of the churches for which Paul labored. . . .

It was not the apostle's work to overturn arbitrarily or suddenly the established order of society. To attempt this would be to prevent the success of the gospel. But he taught principles which struck at the very foundation of slavery and which, if carried into effect, would surely undermine the whole system. . . . When converted, the slave became a member of the body of Christ, and as such was to be loved and treated as a brother, a fellow heir with his master to the blessings of God and the privileges of the gospel. On the other hand, servants were to perform their duties, "not with eyeservice, as men pleasers; but as the servants of Christ, doing the will of God from the heart" (Eph. 6:6).

Christianity makes a strong bond of union between master and slave, king and subject. . . . They have been washed in the same blood, quickened by the same Spirit; and they are made one in Christ Jesus.[20]

350

THE RACE BEFORE US

Let us lay aside every weight, and the sin which doth so easily beset us, and let us run with patience the race that is set before us, looking unto Jesus the author and finisher of our faith. Heb. 12:1, 2.

In the epistle to the Hebrews is pointed out the singlehearted purpose that should characterize the Christian's race for eternal life. . . . Envy, malice, evil thinking, evilspeaking, covetousness—these are weights that the Christian must lay aside if he would run successfully the race for immortality. Every habit or practice that leads into sin and brings dishonor upon Christ must be put away, whatever the sacrifice. . . . "Know ye not," Paul asked, "that they which run in a race run all, but one receiveth the prize?" However eagerly and earnestly the runners might strive, the prize could be awarded to but one. . . .

Such is not the case in the Christian warfare. Not one who complies with the conditions will be disappointed at the end of the race. . . . The race is not to the swift, nor the battle to the strong. The weakest saint, as well as the strongest, may wear the crown of immortal glory. . . .

That he might not run uncertainly or at random in the Christian race, Paul subjected himself to severe training. The words, "I keep under my body," literally mean to beat back by severe discipline the desires, impulses, and passions. . . .

It was this singlehearted purpose to win the race for eternal life that Paul longed to see revealed in the lives of the Corinthian believers. He knew that in order to reach Christ's ideal for them, they had before them a life struggle from which there would be no release. He entreated them to strive lawfully, day by day seeking for piety and moral excellence. He pleaded with them to lay aside every weight and to press forward to the goal of perfection in Christ.[21]

In view of the issue at stake, nothing is small that will help or hinder. Every act casts its weight into the scale that determines life's victory or defeat. And the reward given to those who win will be in proportion to the energy and earnestness with which they have striven.[22]

A VOICE OF GLADNESS

Rejoice in the Lord alway: and again I say, Rejoice. Phil. 4:4.

The great apostle Paul was firm where duty and principle were at stake; but courtesy was a marked trait of his character, and this gave him access to the highest class of society. Paul never doubted the ability of God or His willingness to give him the grace he needed to live the life of a Christian. . . . He does not live under a cloud of doubt, groping his way in the mist and darkness of uncertainty, complaining of hardship and trials. A voice of gladness, strong with hope and courage, sounds all along the line down to our time. Paul had a healthful religious experience. The love of Christ was his grand theme, and the constraining power that governed him.

When in the most discouraging circumstances, which would have had a depressing influence upon halfway Christians, he is firm of heart, full of courage and hope and cheer. . . . The same hope and cheerfulness is seen when he is upon the deck of the ship, the tempest beating about him, the ship going to pieces. He gives orders to the commander of the ship and preserves the lives of all on board. Although a prisoner, he is really the master of the ship, the freest and happiest man on board. . . .

When before kings and dignitaries of the earth, who held his life in their hands, he quailed not; for he had given his life to God, and it was hid in Christ. He softened, by his courtesy, the hearts of these men in power, men of fierce temper, wicked and corrupt though they were in heart and life. . . . Propriety of deportment, the grace of true politeness, marked all his conduct. When he stretched out his hand, as was his custom in speaking, the clanking chains caused him no shame or embarrassment. He looked upon them as tokens of honor, and rejoiced that he could suffer for the word of God and the testimony of Jesus Christ. . . . His reasoning was so clear and convincing that it made the profligate king tremble. . . . Grace, like an angel of mercy, makes his voice heard sweet and clear, repeating the story of the cross, the matchless love of Jesus.[23]

TOWARD THE MARK

This one thing I do, forgetting those things which are behind, and reaching forth unto those things which are before, I press toward the mark for the prize of the high calling of God in Christ Jesus. Phil. 3:13, 14.

Paul did many things. He was a wise teacher. His many letters are full of instructive lessons setting forth correct principles. He worked with his hands, for he was a tent-maker, and in this way earned his daily bread. . . . He carried a heavy burden for the churches. He strove most earnestly to present their errors before them, that they might correct them, and not be deceived and led away from God. He was always seeking to help them in their difficulties; and yet he declares, "One thing I do." . . . The responsibilities of his life were many, yet he kept always before him this "one thing." The constant sense of the presence of God constrained him to keep his eye ever looking unto Jesus, the Author and Finisher of his faith.[24]

The great purpose that constrained Paul to press forward in the face of hardship and difficulty should lead every Christian worker to consecrate himself wholly to God's service. Worldly attractions will be presented to draw his attention from the Savior, but he is to press on toward the goal, showing to the world, to angels, and to men that the hope of seeing the face of God is worth all the effort and sacrifice that the attainment of this hope demands.[25]

The lowliest disciple of Christ may become an inhabitant of heaven, an heir of God to an inheritance incorruptible, and that fadeth not away. O that every one might make choice of the heavenly gift, become an heir of God to that inheritance whose title is secure from any destroyer, world without end! Oh, choose not the world, but choose the better inheritance! Press, urge your way toward the mark for the prize of your high calling in Christ Jesus.[26]

Soon we shall witness the coronation of our King. Those whose lives have been hidden with Christ, those who on this earth have fought the good fight of faith, will shine forth with the Redeemer's glory in the kingdom of God.[27]

TO CAESAR

I stand at Caesar's judgment seat, where I ought to be judged. . . . For if I be an offender, or have committed any thing worthy of death, I refuse not to die: but if there be none of these things whereof these accuse me, no man may deliver me unto them. I appeal unto Caesar. Acts 25:10, 11.

Once more, because of hatred born of bigotry and self-righteousness, a servant of God was driven to turn for protection to the heathen. It was this same hatred that forced the prophet Elijah to flee for succor to the widow of Sarepta; and that forced the heralds of the gospel to turn from the Jews to proclaim their message to the Gentiles. And this hatred the people of God living in this age have yet to meet. Among many of the professing followers of Christ there is the same pride, formalism, and selfishness, the same spirit of oppression, that held so large a place in the Jewish heart. . . . In the great crisis through which they are soon to pass, the faithful servants of God will encounter the same hardness of heart, the same cruel determination, the same unyielding hatred.

All who in that evil day would fearlessly serve God according to the dictates of conscience will need courage, firmness, and a knowledge of God and His word; for those who are true to God will be persecuted, their motives will be impugned, their best efforts misinterpreted, and their names cast out as evil. Satan will work with all his deceptive power to influence the heart and becloud the understanding, to make evil appear good, and good evil. . . .

God desires His people to prepare for the soon-coming crisis. . . . Those only who have brought their lives into conformity to the divine standard will stand firm at that time of test and trial. When secular rulers unite with ministers of religion to dictate in matters of conscience, then it will be seen who really fear and serve God. When the darkness is deepest, the light of a godlike character will shine the brightest. . . . And while the enemies of truth are on every side, watching the Lord's servants for evil, God will watch over them for good. He will be to them as the shadow of a great rock in a weary land.[28]

DIVINE BODYGUARD

At my first answer no man stood with me, but all men forsook me. . . . Notwithstanding the Lord stood with me, and strengthened me; that by me the preaching might be fully known, and that all the Gentiles might hear. 2 Tim. 4:16, 17.

When Paul was summoned to appear before the emperor Nero for trial, it was with the near prospect of certain death. . . . Among the Christians at Rome, there was not one who came forward to stand by him in that trying hour. . . . Paul before Nero—how striking the contrast! . . . The name of Nero made the world tremble. To incur his displeasure was to lose property, liberty, life; and his frown was more to be dreaded than a pestilence.

Without money, without friends, without counsel, the aged prisoner stood before Nero—the countenance of the emperor bearing the shameful record of the passions that raged within; the face of the accused telling of a heart at peace with God.[29]

How could Nero, a capricious, passionate, licentious tyrant, be expected to understand or appreciate the character and motives of this son of God? . . . The results of opposite systems of education stood that day contrasted—a life of unbounded self-indulgence and a life of entire self-sacrifice. Here were the representatives of two theories of life—all-absorbing selfishness, which counts nothing too valuable to be sacrificed for momentary gratification, and self-denying endurance, ready to give up life itself, if need be, for the good of others. . . .

The people and the judges looked at him in surprise. They had been present at many trials, and had looked upon many a criminal; but never had they seen a man wear a look of such holy calmness. . . . His words struck a chord that vibrated in the hearts even of the most hardened. Truth, clear and convincing, overthrew error. . . . The words spoken on this occasion were destined to shake nations. . . .

Faithful among the faithless, loyal among the disloyal, he stands as God's representative, and his voice is as a voice from heaven. . . . His words are as a shout of victory above the roar of battle.[30]

A GOOD FIGHT

I have fought a good fight, I have finished my course, I have kept the faith: henceforth there is laid up for me a crown of righteousness, which the Lord, the righteous judge, shall give me at that day: and not to me only, but unto all them also that love his appearing. 2 Tim. 4:7, 8.

Through his long term of service, Paul had never faltered in his allegiance to his Savior. Wherever he was—whether before scowling Pharisees, or Roman authorities; before the furious mob at Lystra, or the convicted sinners in the Macedonian dungeon; whether reasoning with the panic-stricken sailors on the shipwrecked vessel, or standing alone before Nero to plead for his life—he had never been ashamed of the cause he was advocating. The one great purpose of his Christian life had been to serve Him whose name had once filled him with contempt; and from this purpose no opposition or persecution had been able to turn him aside.[31]

Paul's life was an exemplification of the truths he taught, and herein lay his power. His heart was filled with a deep, abiding sense of his responsibility, and he labored in close communion with Him who is the fountain of justice, mercy, and truth. . . . The love of the Savior was the undying motive that upheld him in his conflicts with self and in his struggles against evil as in the service of Christ he pressed forward against the unfriendliness of the world and the opposition of his enemies.

What the church needs in these days of peril is an army of workers who, like Paul, have educated themselves for usefulness, who have a deep experience in the things of God, and who are filled with earnestness and zeal. Sanctified, self-sacrificing men are needed; men who will not shun trial and responsibility; men who are brave and true; men in whose hearts Christ is formed "the hope of glory," and who with lips touched with holy fire will "preach the word.". . .

Will our young men accept the holy trust at the hands of their fathers? Are they preparing to fill the vacancies made by the death of the faithful? Will the apostle's charge be heeded, the call to duty be heard, amidst the incitements to selfishness and ambition that allure the youth?[32]

"LOVE ONE ANOTHER"

Herein is love, not that we loved God, but that he loved us, and sent his Son to be the propitiation for our sins. Beloved, if God so loved us, we ought also to love one another. 1 John 4:10, 11.

After the ascension of Christ, John stands forth as a faithful, earnest laborer for the Master. . . . The love for Christ which glowed in his heart led him to put forth earnest, untiring labor for his fellow men, especially for his brethren in the Christian church.

Christ had bidden the first disciples love one another as He had loved them. . . . After the descent of the Holy Spirit, when the disciples went forth to proclaim a living Savior, their one desire was the salvation of souls. They rejoiced in the sweetness of communion with saints. They were tender, thoughtful, self-denying, willing to make any sacrifice for the truth's sake. In their daily association with one another, they revealed the love that Christ had enjoined upon them. . . .

But gradually a change came. The believers began to look for defects in others. . . . They lost sight of the Savior and His love. . . . John, realizing that brotherly love was waning in the church, urged upon believers the constant need of this love. . . . It is not the opposition of the world that most endangers the church of Christ. It is the evil cherished in the hearts of believers that works their most grievous disaster and most surely retards the progress of God's cause. There is no surer way of weakening spirituality than by cherishing envy, suspicion, faultfinding, and evil surmising. On the other hand, the strongest witness that God has sent His Son into the world is the existence of harmony and union among men of varied dispositions who form His church. . . .

Unbelievers are watching to see if the faith of professed Christians is exerting a sanctifying influence upon their lives; and they are quick to discern the defects in character, the inconsistencies in action. . . . Christians are all members of one family, all children of the same heavenly Father, with the same blessed hope of immortality. Very close and tender should be the tie that binds them together. . . . "Let us not love in word," the apostle writes, "but in deed and in truth." [33]

PERILS WITHIN AND WITHOUT

Beloved, believe not every spirit, but try the spirits whether they are of God: because many false prophets are gone out into the world. 1 John 4:1.

As the years went by and the number of believers grew, John labored with increasing fidelity and earnestness for his brethren. The times were full of peril for the church. Satanic delusions existed everywhere. By misrepresentation and falsehood the emissaries of Satan sought to arouse opposition against the doctrines of Christ, and in consequence dissensions and heresies were imperiling the church. . . . Thus many were being led into the mazes of skepticism and delusion.

John was filled with sadness as he saw these poisonous errors creeping into the church. He saw the dangers to which the church was exposed, and he met the emergency with promptness and decision. The epistles of John breathe the spirit of love. It seems as if he wrote with a pen dipped in love. But when he came in contact with those who were breaking the law of God, yet claiming that they were living without sin, he did not hesitate to warn them of their fearful deception. . . .

We are authorized to hold in the same estimation as did the beloved disciple those who claim to abide in Christ while living in transgression of God's law. There exist in these last days evils similar to those that threatened the prosperity of the early church; and the teachings of the apostle John on these points should be carefully heeded. . . . While we are to love the souls for whom Christ died, we are to make no compromise with evil. We are not to unite with the rebellious and call this charity. God requires His people in this age of the world to stand for the right as unflinchingly as did John in opposition to soul-destroying errors. . . .

He declared what he knew, what he had seen and heard. . . . Out of the abundance of a heart overflowing with love for the Savior he spoke; and no power could stay his words. . . .

So may every true believer be able, through his own experience, to "set to his seal that God is true" (John 3:33). He can bear witness to that which he has seen and heard and felt of the power of Christ.[34]

PURE IN HEART AND LIFE

And every man that hath this hope in him purifieth himself, even as he is pure. 1 John 3:3.

John was a teacher of holiness, and in his letters to the church he laid down unerring rules for the conduct of Christians. . . . He taught that the Christian must be pure in heart and life. Never should he be satisfied with an empty profession. As God is holy in His sphere, so fallen man, through faith in Christ, is to be holy in his sphere. . . .

There are those who profess holiness, who declare that they are wholly the Lord's, who claim a right to the promises of God, while refusing to render obedience to His commandments. These transgressors of the law claim everything that is promised to the children of God; but this is presumption on their part, for John tells us that true love for God will be revealed in obedience to all His commandments. It is not enough to believe the theory of truth, to make a profession of faith in Christ. . . . "He that saith, I know him, and keepeth not his commandments," John wrote, "is a liar, and the truth is not in him.". . .

John did not teach that salvation was to be earned by obedience; but that obedience was the fruit of faith and love. . . . If we abide in Christ, if the love of God dwells in the heart, our feelings, our thoughts, our actions, will be in harmony with the will of God. . . .

There are many who, though striving to obey God's commandments, have little peace or joy. This lack in their experience is the result of a failure to exercise faith. They walk as it were in a salt land, a parched wilderness. They claim little, when they might claim much; for there is no limit to the promises of God. Such ones do not correctly represent the sanctification that comes through obedience to the truth. The Lord would have all His sons and daughters happy, peaceful, and obedient. Through the exercise of faith the believer comes into possession of these blessings. Through faith, every deficiency of character may be supplied, every defilement cleansed, every fault corrected, every excellence developed.[35]

BEYOND THE GLOOM TO GLORY

Yea, and all that will live godly in Christ Jesus shall suffer persecution. 2 Tim. 3:12.

In the experience of the apostle John under persecution, there is a lesson of wonderful strength and comfort for the Christian. God does not prevent the plottings of wicked men, but He causes their devices to work for good to those who in trial and conflict maintain their faith and loyalty. . . .

It is the work of faith to rest in God in the darkest hour, to feel, however sorely tried and tempest-tossed, that our Father is at the helm. The eye of faith alone can look beyond the things of time to estimate aright the worth of the eternal riches.

Jesus does not present to His followers the hope of attaining earthly glory and riches, of living a life free from trial. Instead He calls upon them to follow Him in the path of self-denial and reproach. He who came to redeem the world was opposed by the united forces of evil. . . . So it will be with all who will live godly in Christ Jesus. Persecution and reproach await all who are imbued with the Spirit of Christ. . . .

In all ages Satan has persecuted the people of God. He has tortured them and put them to death, but in dying they became conquerors. They bore witness to the power of One mightier than Satan. Wicked men may torture and kill the body, but they cannot touch the life that is hid with Christ in God. They can incarcerate men and women in prison walls, but they cannot bind the spirit.

Through trial and persecution the glory—the character—of God is revealed in His chosen ones. . . . They follow Christ through sore conflicts; they endure self-denial and experience bitter disappointments; but thus they learn the guilt and woe of sin, and they look upon it with abhorrence. Being partakers of Christ's sufferings, they can look beyond the gloom to the glory, saying, "I reckon that the sufferings of this present time are not worthy to be compared with the glory which shall be revealed in us" (Rom. 8:18).[36]

THE LAST OF THE TWELVE

Blessed are ye, when men shall revile you, and persecute you, and shall say all manner of evil against you falsely, for my sake. Rejoice, and be exceeding glad: for great is your reward in heaven: for so persecuted they the prophets which were before you. Matt. 5:11, 12.

John lived to be very old. He witnessed the destruction of Jerusalem and the ruin of the stately temple. The last survivor of the disciples who had been intimately connected with the Savior, his message had great influence in setting forth the fact that Jesus was the Messiah, the Redeemer of the world. . . .

The rulers of the Jews were filled with bitter hatred against John for his unwavering fidelity to the cause of Christ. They declared that their efforts against the Christians would avail nothing so long as John's testimony kept ringing in the ears of the people. In order that the miracles and teachings of Jesus might be forgotten, the voice of the bold witness must be silenced.

John was accordingly summoned to Rome to be tried for his faith. Here before the authorities the apostle's doctrines were misstated. False witnesses accused him of teaching seditious heresies. . . . John answered for himself in a clear and convincing manner. . . . But the more convincing his testimony, the deeper was the hatred of his opposers. The emperor Domitian was filled with rage. He could neither dispute the reasoning of Christ's faithful advocate, nor match the power that attended his utterance of truth; yet he determined that he would silence his voice.

John was cast into a caldron of boiling oil; but the Lord preserved the life of His faithful servant, even as He preserved the three Hebrews in the fiery furnace. As the words were spoken, Thus perish all who believe in that deceiver, Jesus Christ of Nazareth, John declared, My Master patiently submitted to all that Satan and his angels could devise to humiliate and torture Him. He gave His life to save the world. I am honored in being permitted to suffer for His sake. I am a weak, sinful man. Christ was holy, harmless, undefiled. He did no sin, neither was guile found in His mouth. These words had their influence, and John was removed from the caldron by the very men who had cast him in.[37]

SHUT AWAY WITH GOD

Fear none of those things which thou shalt suffer: behold, the devil shall cast some of you into prison, that ye may be tried; . . . be thou faithful unto death, and I will give thee a crown of life. Rev. 2:10.

By the emperor's decree John was banished to the Isle of Patmos, condemned "for the word of God, and for the testimony of Jesus Christ" (Rev. 1:9). Here, his enemies thought, his influence would no longer be felt, and he must finally die of hardship and distress.

Patmos, a barren, rocky island in the Aegean Sea, had been chosen by the Roman government as a place of banishment for criminals; but to the servant of God this gloomy abode became the gate of heaven. Here, shut away from the busy scenes of life, and from the active labors of former years, he had the companionship of God and Christ and the heavenly angels, and from them he received instruction for the church for all future time. . . . Among the cliffs and rocks of Patmos, John held communion with his Maker. He reviewed his past life, and at thought of the blessings he had received, peace filled his heart. . . .

In his isolated home John was able to study more closely than ever before the manifestations of divine power as recorded in the book of nature and in the pages of inspiration. . . . In former years his eyes had been greeted by the sight of forest-covered hills, green valleys, and fruitful plains; and in the beauties of nature it had ever been his delight to trace the wisdom and skill of the Creator. He was now surrounded by scenes that to many would appear gloomy and uninteresting; but to John it was otherwise. While his surroundings might be desolate and barren, the blue heavens that bent above him were as bright and beautiful as the skies above his loved Jerusalem. In the wild, rugged rocks, in the mysteries of the deep, in the glories of the firmament, he read important lessons. All bore the message of God's power and glory. . . .

By the rocks he was reminded of Christ, the Rock of his strength, in whose shelter he could hide without fear. From the exiled apostle on rocky Patmos there went up the most ardent longing of soul after God, the most fervent prayers.[38]

KEEP YOUR ARMOR ON

And even to your old age I am he; and even to hoar hairs will I carry you: I have made, and I will bear; even I will carry, and will deliver you. Isa. 46:4.

The history of John affords a striking illustration of the way in which God can use aged workers. When John was exiled to the Isle of Patmos, there were many who thought him to be past service, an old and broken reed, ready to fall at any time. But the Lord saw fit to use him still. Though banished from the scenes of his former labor, he did not cease to bear witness to the truth. Even in Patmos he made friends and converts. His was a message of joy, proclaiming a risen Savior. . . .

The most tender regard should be cherished for those whose life interest has been bound up with the work of God. These aged workers have stood faithful amid storm and trial. They may have infirmities, but they still possess talents that qualify them to stand in their place in God's cause. Though worn, and unable to bear the heavier burdens that younger men can and should carry, the counsel they can give is of the highest value.

They may have made mistakes, but from their failures they have learned to avoid errors and dangers, and are they not therefore competent to give wise counsel? They have borne test and trial, and though they have lost some of their vigor, the Lord does not lay them aside. He gives them special grace and wisdom. . . . The Lord desires the younger laborers to gain wisdom, strength, and maturity by association with these faithful men. . . .

As those who have spent their lives in the service of Christ draw near to the close of their earthly ministry, they will be impressed by the Holy Spirit to recount the experiences they have had in connection with the work of God. The record of His wonderful dealings with His people, of His great goodness in delivering them from trial, should be repeated to those newly come to the faith. God desires the old and tried laborers to stand in their place, doing their part to save men and women from being swept downward by the mighty current of evil. He desires them to keep the armor on till He bids them lay it down.[39]

"HITHERTO HATH THE LORD HELPED US"

O give thanks unto the Lord; call upon his name: make known his deeds among the people. Sing unto him, sing psalms unto him: talk ye of all his wondrous works. Ps. 105:1, 2.

The dealings of God with His people should be often repeated. How frequently were the waymarks set up by the Lord in His dealings with ancient Israel! Lest they should forget the history of the past, He commanded Moses to frame these events into song, that parents might teach them to their children. They were to gather up memorials and to lay them up in sight. Special pains were taken to preserve them, that when the children should inquire concerning these things, the whole story might be repeated. Thus the providential dealings and the marked goodness and mercy of God in His care and deliverance of His people were kept in mind. We are exhorted to "call to remembrance the former days, in which, after ye were illuminated, ye endured a great fight of afflictions" (Heb. 10:32). For His people in this generation the Lord has wrought as a wonder-working God. . . . We need often to recount God's goodness and to praise Him for His wonderful works.[40]

Let us not cast away our confidence, but have firm assurance, firmer than ever before. "Hitherto hath the Lord helped us," and He will help us to the end (1 Sam. 7:12). Let us look to the monumental pillars, reminders of what the Lord has done to comfort us and to save us from the hand of the destroyer. Let us keep fresh in our memory all the tender mercies that God has shown us—the tears He has wiped away, the pains He has soothed, the anxieties removed, the fears dispelled, the wants supplied, the blessings bestowed—thus strengthening ourselves for all that is before us through the remainder of our pilgrimage.

We cannot but look forward to new perplexities in the coming conflict, but we may look on what is past as well as on what is to come, and say, "Hitherto hath the Lord helped us." "As thy days, so shall thy strength be" (Deut. 33:25). The trial will not exceed the strength that shall be given us to bear it. Then let us take up our work just where we find it, believing that whatever may come, strength proportionate to the trial will be given.[41]

TO GOD BE THE GLORY

From the rising of the sun unto the going down of the same the Lord's name is to be praised. Ps.113:3.

The Bible has little to say in praise of men. Little space is given to recounting the virtues of even the best men who have ever lived. This silence is not without purpose; it is not without a lesson. All the good qualities that men possess are the gift of God; their good deeds are performed by the grace of God through Christ. Since they owe all to God the glory of whatever they are or do belongs to Him alone; they are but instruments in His hands. More than this—as all the lessons of Bible history teach—it is a perilous thing to praise or exalt men; for if one comes to lose sight of his entire dependence on God, and to trust to his own strength, he is sure to fall. Man is contending with foes who are stronger than he. . . . It is impossible for us in our own strength to maintain the conflict; and whatever diverts the mind from God, whatever leads to self-exaltation or to self-dependence, is surely preparing the way for our overthrow. The tenor of the Bible is to inculcate distrust of human power and to encourage trust in divine power.[42]

The truly converted soul is illuminated from on high. . . . His words, his motives, his actions, may be misinterpreted and falsified; but he does not mind it because he has greater interests at stake. . . . He is not ambitious for display; he does not crave the praise of men. His hope is in heaven, and he keeps straight on, with his eye fixed on Jesus. He does right because it is right.[43]

By their good works, Christ's followers are to bring glory, not to themselves, but to Him through whose grace and power they have wrought. It is through the Holy Spirit that every good work is accomplished, and the Spirit is given to glorify, not the receiver, but the Giver. When the light of Christ is shining in the soul, the lips will be filled with praise and thanksgiving to God. Your prayers, your performance of duty, your benevolence, your self-denial, will not be the theme of your thought or conversation. Jesus will be magnified, self will be hidden, and Christ will appear as all in all.[44]

NOBLE EXAMPLES

The righteous also shall hold on his way, and he that hath clean hands shall be stronger and stronger. Job 17:9.

Sacred history presents many illustrations of the results of true education. It presents many noble examples of men whose characters were formed under divine direction, men whose lives were a blessing to their fellow men and who stood in the world as representatives of God. Among these are Joseph and Daniel, Moses, Elisha, and Paul—the greatest statesmen, the wisest legislator, one of the most faithful of reformers, and except Him who spoke as never man spake, the most illustrious teacher that this world has known.

In early life, just as they were passing from youth to manhood, Joseph and Daniel were separated from their homes and carried as captives to heathen lands. Especially was Joseph subject to the temptations that attend great changes of fortune. In his father's home a tenderly cherished child; in the house of Potiphar a slave, then a confidant and companion; a man of affairs, educated by study, observation, contact with men; in Pharaoh's dungeon a prisoner of state, condemned unjustly, without hope of vindication or prospect of release; called at a great crisis to the leadership of the nation—what enabled him to preserve his integrity? . . .

Loyalty to God, faith in the Unseen, was Joseph's anchor. In this lay the hiding of his power. . . .

By their wisdom and justice, by the purity and benevolence of their daily life, by their devotion to the interests of the people—and they idolaters—Joseph and Daniel proved themselves true to the principles of their early training, true to Him whose representative they were. . . .

What a lifework was that of these noble Hebrews! . . .

The same mighty truths that were revealed through these men, God desires to reveal through the youth and the children of today. The history of Joseph and Daniel is an illustration of what He will do for those who yield themselves to Him and with the whole heart seek to accomplish His purpose.[45]

"ALL THINGS THROUGH CHRIST"

What time I am afraid, I will trust in thee. Ps. 56:3.

Only the sense of God's presence can banish the fear that, for the timid child, would make life a burden. Let him fix in his memory the promise, "The angel of the Lord encampeth round about them that fear him, and delivereth them" (Ps. 34:7). Let him read that wonderful story of Elisha in the mountain city, and, between him and the hosts of armed foemen, a mighty encircling band of heavenly angels. Let him read how to Peter, in prison and condemned to death, God's angel appeared; how, past the armed guards, the massive doors and great iron gateway with their bolts and bars, the angel led God's servant forth in safety. Let him read of that scene on the sea, when to the tempest-tossed soldiers and seamen, worn with labor and watching and long fasting, Paul the prisoner, on his way to trial and execution, spoke those grand words of courage and hope: "Be of good cheer: for there shall be no loss of any man's life among you. . . . For there stood by me this night the angel of God, whose I am, and whom I serve, saying, Fear not, Paul; thou must be brought before Caesar: and, lo, God hath given thee all them that sail with thee." In the faith of this promise Paul assured his companions, "There shall not an hair fall from the head of any of you." So it came to pass. Because there was in that ship one man through whom God could work, the whole shipload of heathen soldiers and sailors was preserved. "They escaped all safe to land" (Acts 27:22-24, 34, 44).

These things were not written merely that we might read and wonder, but that the same faith which wrought in God's servants of old might work in us. In no less marked a manner than He wrought then will He work now wherever there are hearts of faith to be channels of His power.

Let the self-distrustful, whose lack of self-reliance leads them to shrink from care and responsibility, be taught reliance upon God. Thus many a one who otherwise would be but a cipher in the world, perhaps only a helpless burden, will be able to say with the apostle Paul, "I can do all things through Christ which strengtheneth me" (Phil. 4:13).[46]

WE NEED NOT DESPAIR

For a just man falleth seven times, and riseth up again: but the wicked shall fall into mischief. Prov. 24:16.

The pen of inspiration, true to its task, tells us of the sins that overcame Noah, Lot, Moses, Abraham, David, and Solomon, and that even Elijah's strong spirit sank under temptation during his fearful trial. Jonah's disobedience and Israel's idolatry are faithfully recorded. Peter's denial of Christ, the sharp contention of Paul and Barnabas, the failings and infirmities of the prophets and apostles, are all laid bare. . . . There before us lie the lives of the believers, with all their faults and follies, which are intended as a lesson to all the generations following them. If they had been without foible they would have been more than human, and our sinful natures would despair of ever reaching such a point of excellence. But seeing where they struggled and fell, where they took heart again and conquered through the grace of God, we are encouraged, and led to press over the obstacles that degenerate nature places in our way.

God has ever been faithful to punish crime. He sent His prophets to warn the guilty, denounce their sins, and pronounce judgment upon them. . . .

We need just such lessons as the Bible gives us, for with the revelation of sin is recorded the retribution which follows. The sorrow and penitence of the guilty, and the wailing of the sin-sick soul, come to us from the past, telling us that man was then, as now, in need of the pardoning mercy of God. . . .

Bible history stays the fainting heart with the hope of God's mercy. We need not despair when we see that others have struggled through discouragements like our own, have fallen into temptations even as we have done, and yet have recovered their ground and been blessed of God. The words of inspiration comfort and cheer the erring soul. Although the patriarchs and apostles were subject to human frailties, yet through faith they obtained a good report, fought their battles in the strength of the Lord, and conquered gloriously. Thus may we trust in the virtue of the atoning sacrifice and be overcomers in the name of Jesus.[47]

GOD REMEMBERS HIS OWN

Woe to the inhabiters of the earth and of the sea! for the devil is come down unto you, having great wrath, because he knoweth that he hath but a short time. Rev. 12:12.

In all ages God's appointed witnesses have exposed themselves to reproach and persecution for the truth's sake. Joseph was maligned and persecuted. . . . David, the chosen messenger of God, was hunted like a beast of prey by his enemies. . . . Stephen was stoned because he preached Christ and Him crucified. Paul was imprisoned, beaten with rods, stoned, and finally put to death. . . . John was banished to the Isle of Patmos "for the word of God, and for the testimony of Jesus Christ."

These examples of human steadfastness bear witness to the faithfulness of God's promises—of His abiding presence and sustaining grace. They testify to the power of faith to withstand the powers of the world.[48]

The season of distress and anguish before us will require a faith that can endure weariness, delay, and hunger—a faith that will not faint though severely tried.[49]

Many of all nations and of all classes, high and low, rich and poor, black and white, will be cast into the most unjust and cruel bondage. The beloved of God pass weary days, bound in chains, shut in by prison bars, sentenced to be slain, some apparently left to die of starvation in dark and loathsome dungeons. . . . No human hand is ready to lend them help.

Will the Lord forget His people in this trying hour? Did He forget faithful Noah when judgments were visited upon the antediluvian world? Did He forget Lot when the fire came down from heaven to consume the cities of the plain? . . . Did He forget Elijah when the oath of Jezebel threatened him with the fate of the prophets of Baal? Did He forget Jeremiah in the dark and dismal pit of his prison house? Did He forget the three worthies in the fiery furnace? or Daniel in the den of lions? . . .

Though enemies may thrust them into prison, yet dungeon walls cannot cut off the communication between their souls and Christ. One who sees their every weakness, who is acquainted with every trial, is above all earthly powers; and angels will come to them in lonely cells, bringing light and peace from heaven.[50]

FIRST THINGS FIRST

But seek ye first the kingdom of God, and his righteousness; and all these things shall be added unto you. Matt. 6:33.

This promise will never fail. We cannot enjoy the favor of God unless we comply with the conditions upon which His favor is bestowed. By so doing there will come to us that peace, contentment, and wisdom that the world can neither give nor take away. . . . A humble mind and a grateful heart will elevate us above petty trials and real difficulties. The less earnest, energetic, and vigilant we are in the service of the Master, the more will the mind dwell upon self, magnifying molehills into mountains of difficulty. . . .

The burden of God's work, laid upon Moses, made him a man of power. While keeping, for so many years, the flocks of Jethro, he gained an experience that taught him true humility. . . . The command to deliver Israel seemed overwhelming; but, in the fear of God, Moses accepted the trust. Mark the result: He did not bring the work down to his deficiency; but in the strength of God he put forth the most earnest efforts to elevate and sanctify himself for his sacred mission.

Moses would never have been prepared for his position of trust had he waited for God to do the work for him. Light from heaven will come to those who feel the need of it, and who seek for it as for hidden treasures. But if we sink down into a state of inactivity, willing to be controlled by Satan's power, God will not send His inspiration to us. Unless we exert to the utmost the powers which He has given us, we shall ever remain weak and inefficient. Much prayer and the most vigorous exercise of the mind are necessary if we would be prepared to do the work which God would entrust to us. Many never attain to the position which they might occupy, because they wait for God to do for them that which He has given them power to do for themselves. All who are fitted for usefulness in this life must be trained by the severest mental and moral discipline, and then God will assist them by combining divine power with human effort. . . .

Wrong habits are not overcome by a single effort. Only through long and severe struggle is self mastered.[51]

GOD'S PLAN FOR ME

For the Lord of hosts hath purposed, and who shall disannul it? and his hand is stretched out, and who shall turn it back? Isa. 14:27.

Each actor in history stands in his lot and place; for God's great work after His own plan will be carried out by men who have prepared themselves to fill positions for good or evil. In opposition to righteousness, men become instruments of unrighteousness. But they are not forced to take this course of action. They need not become instruments of unrighteousness, any more than Cain needed to. . . .

Men of all characters, righteous and unrighteous, will stand in their several positions in God's plan. With the characters they have formed, they will act their part in the fulfillment of history. In a crisis, just at the right moment, they will stand in the places they have prepared themselves to fill. Believers and unbelievers will fall into line as witnesses to confirm truth that they themselves do not comprehend. All will cooperate in accomplishing the purposes of God, just as did Annas, Caiaphas, Pilate, and Herod. In putting Christ to death, the priests thought they were carrying out their own purposes, but unconsciously and unintentionally they were fulfilling the purpose of God.[52]

God looks into the tiny seed that He Himself has formed, and sees wrapped within it the beautiful flower, the shrub, or the lofty, wide-spreading tree. So does He see the possibilities in every human being. We are here for a purpose. God has given us His plan for our life, and He desires us to reach the highest standard of development. . . .

He desires the youth to cultivate every power of their being, and to bring every faculty into active exercise. . . . Let them look to Christ as the pattern after which they are to be fashioned. The holy ambition that He revealed in His life they are to cherish—an ambition to make the world better for their having lived in it. This is the work to which they are called.[53]

You want now to . . . so relate yourself to society and to life that you may answer the purpose of God in your creation.[54]

KEY TO ABBREVIATIONS

AA	*Acts of the Apostles, The*
AH	*Adventist Home, The*
1BC	Ellen G. White Comments in *The Seventh-day Adventist Bible Commentary*, vol. 1 (2BC, etc., for vols. 2-7)
CD	*Counsels on Diet and Foods*
CG	*Child Guidance*
COL	*Christ's Object Lessons*
CSW	*Counsels on Sabbath School Work*
CT	*Counsels to Parents, Teachers, and Students*
DA	*Desire of Ages, The*
Ed	*Education*
EW	*Early Writings*
FE	*Fundamentals of Christian Education*
GC	*Great Controversy, The*
GW	*Gospel Workers*
IHP	*In Heavenly Places*
Letter	Ellen G. White letter
MB	*Thoughts From the Mount of Blessing*
MH	*Ministry of Healing, The*
ML	*My Life Today*
MS	Ellen G. White manuscript
MYP	*Messages to Young People*
PK	*Prophets and Kings*
PP	*Patriarchs and Prophets*
RH	*Review and Herald*
SC	*Steps to Christ*
SD	*Sons and Daughters of God*
3SG	*Spiritual Gifts*, vol. 3
4SG	*Spiritual Gifts*, vol. 4
4SG-a	*Spiritual Gifts*, vol. 4, part a
SL	*Sanctified Life, The*
1SM	*Selected Messages*, book 1
2SM	*Selected Messages*, book 2
2SP	*Spirit of Prophecy, The*, vol. 2
SR	*Story of Redemption, The*
ST	*Signs of the Times*
SW	*Southern Watchman*
1T	*Testimonies for the Church*, vol. 1 (2T, etc., for vols. 2-9)
Te	*Temperance*
Und. MS	Undated Ellen G. White manuscript
YI	*Youth's Instructor*

SOURCE REFERENCES

January
1. 4T 9-11
2. *Ibid.*, 11-15
3. PP 84
4. Ed 254, 255
5. *Ibid.*, 146-148
6. PP 44, 45
7. SR 21
8. *Ibid.*, 21, 22
9. AH 27
10. PP 48-51
11. *Ibid.*, 46
12. *Ibid.*, 52-55
13. *Ibid.*, 56, 57
14. 1BC 1084
15. *Ibid.*, 1083
16. PP 58-60
17. Ed 26, 27
18. 1BC 1085
19. Letter 91, 1900
20. ST, Jan. 30, 1879
21. 3T 138, 139
22. 1BC 1082
23. PP 61
24. ST, Feb. 6, 1879
25. GC 644-648
26. PP 71, 72
27. *Ibid.*, 72, 73
28. 1BC 1086
29. MS 77, 1897
30. 2T 92
31. CSW 112, 113
32. PP 77-81
33. GC 543
34. COL 200
35. PP 84, 85
36. RH, Dec. 3, 1889
37. MS 16, 1887
38. ST, Oct. 30, 1879
39. 2T, 121, 122
40. 5T 535
41. GW 52
42. 6BC 1097, 1098
43. COL 129, 130
44. ML 14
45. COL 332
46. GW 53
47. Ed 127
48. PP 90, 91

49. *Ibid.*, 95, 96
50. *Ibid.*, 91
51. 4SG-a 154-156
52. PP 90, 91
53. 1BC 1090
54. *Ibid.*, 1089
55. MS 16, 1898
56. MS 31a, 1898
57. Letter 73a, 1896
58. MS 88, 1897
59. MS 16, 1895
60. MS 29, 1911
61. 3SG 63, 64
62. SR 62
63. PP 338
64. MS 161, 1897
65. PP 95
66. *Ibid.*, 97
67. MS 161, 1897

FEBRUARY
1. PP 92-95
2. 3SG 61
3. SR 64
4. 3SG 59, 60
5. PP 95
6. *Ibid.*, 97, 98
7. Letter 108, 1896
8. PP 98
9. *Ibid.*, 98, 99
10. ST, Apr. 10, 1901
11. PP 99, 100
12. *Ibid.*, 103
13. *Ibid.*, 102
14. *Ibid.*, 118-124
15. 8T 213, 214
16. PP 119, 120
17. 8T 215
18. PP 125-127
19. *Ibid.*, 128, 129
20. *Ibid.*, 129-131
21. *Ibid.*, 132, 133
22. *Ibid.*, 133
23. 4T 110
24. PP 174
25. 2SM 355
26. Letter 144, 1902
27. MS 22, 1904
28. 5T 548

29. PP 138
30. 6T 341, 342
31. PP 139, 140
32. 6T 342
33. PP 158
34. *Ibid.*, 162-165
35. 5T 233, 234
36. 2SM 354
37. PP 161, 162
38. *Ibid.*, 168-170
39. *Ibid.*, 147
40. 4T 144, 145
41. 3T 368
42. PP 171-175
43. *Ibid.*, 175, 176
44. *Ibid.*, 175
45. *Ibid.*, 133, 134
46. *Ibid.*, 177-179
47. *Ibid.*, 178
48. 2T 38
49. 1BC 1094, 1095
50. *Ibid.*, 1095
51. SR 88, 89
52. PP 180
53. *Ibid.*, 180, 181
54. SC 23
55. PP 183-187
56. *Ibid.*, 187, 188

MARCH
1. PP 188, 189
2. MB 144
3. PP 196, 197
4. MB 144
5. PP 201, 202
6. *Ibid.*, 202, 203
7. *Ibid.*, 198, 201
8. *Ibid.*, 207, 208
9. *Ibid.*, 208-210
10. 1BC 1096
11. PP 213, 214
12. *Ibid.*, 214, 217
13. Letter 3, 1879
14. PP 217, 218
15. 1BC 1097
16. PP 218
17. *Ibid.*, 222
18. 5T 321
19. 6T 219

20. PP 222, 223
21. *Ibid.*, 239, 240
22. 1BC 1097, 1098
23. Ed 61
24. PP 243, 244
25. Ed 62
26. PP 245, 246
27. FE 342-344
28. PP 247
29. FE 345-347
30. 4T 343-345
31. 5T 651, 652
32. Ed 62
33. PP 248-251
34. *Ibid.*, 251-256
35. 1BC 1100
36. *Ibid.*, 1099, 1100
37. PP 268, 269
38. Letter 31, 1891
39. 1BC 1100
40. PP 281, 282
41. COL 286, 287
42. PP 282, 283
43. 6T 404
44. PP 290
45. *Ibid.*, 288, 289
46. *Ibid.*, 293
47. *Ibid.*, 292, 293
48. 2T 106-108
49. PP 299
50. CT 59, 60
51. 1BC 1108
52. Letter 60, 1907
53. CT 60
54. 1BC 1108

APRIL
1. PP 316, 317
2. *Ibid.*, 320, 323
3. 4T 531-533
4. PP 359, 360
5. *Ibid.*, 361, 362
6. Te 149
7. 3T 293-295
8. 1BC 1102
9. PP 382
10. *Ibid.*, 378
11. *Ibid.*, 382, 384
12. *Ibid.*, 382-386
13. *Ibid.*, 384, 385
14. 4T 148-151
15. 5T 378-383

16. 2SM 369
17. PP 402-404
18. 4T 369, 370
19. PP 419-421
20. *Ibid.*, 479, 480
21. *Ibid.*, 439, 440
22. *Ibid.*, 439-441
23. GC 529, 530
24. PP 451, 452
25. RH, May 17, 1887
26. 2BC 993
27. *Ibid.*, 993, 994
28. *Ibid.*, 994
29. *Ibid.*, 994, 995
30. *Ibid.*, 995
31. *Ibid.*, 995, 996
32. *Ibid.*, 996
33. *Ibid.*, 997
34. 4T 493-495
35. MS 12, 1893
36. 2BC 998
37. *Ibid.*, 996, 997
38. PP 497, 498
39. 1SM 352
40. PP 505-507
41. *Ibid.*, 511-513
42. *Ibid.*, 513, 514
43. *Ibid.*, 521-524
44. *Ibid.*, 546, 547
45. 2BC 1003

MAY
1. PP 548, 549
2. 2BC 1003
3. PP 549, 550
4. 2BC 1003
5. PP 555,556
6. 2BC 1004, 1005
7. MS 18, 1887
8. CD 218, 219
9. PP 561
10. Te 233, 234
11. MH 372
12. PP 562, 563
13. *Ibid.*, 567, 568
14. *Ibid.*, 564-566
15. 2BC 1007
16. PP 566
17. 2BC 1007
18. *Ibid.*
19. *Ibid.*, 1006
20. *Ibid.*, 1007

21. PP 566, 567
22. 2BC 1007, 1008
23. PP 569, 570
24. 2BC 1008
25. PP 572, 573
26. MH 371, 372
27. 2BC 1008, 1009
28. PP 575-578
29. 4T 516, 517
30. 2BC 1009
31. PP 578
32. *Ibid.*, 577
33. *Ibid.*, 582
34. 4T 200
35. PP 578, 579
36. Letter 144, 1906
37. 2BC 1009, 1010
38. PP 573, 574
39. 2BC 1021
40. PP 590, 591
41. 4SG 65, 66
42. PP 607
43. 2BC 1013
44. *Ibid.*, 1014
45. *Ibid.*, 1013, 1014
46. PP 636
47. *Ibid.*, 608
48. 2BC 1013
49. *Ibid.*, 1016, 1017
50. PP 616, 618
51. 2BC 1014
52. PP 618
53. 2BC 1014, 1015
54. *Ibid.*, 1015
55. PP 623
56. SD 208
57. PP 624, 625
58. *Ibid.*, 625, 626
59. *Ibid.*, 627, 628
60. *Ibid.*, 628, 629
61. *Ibid.*, 629, 630
62. Letter 12a, 1893

JUNE
1. PP 631, 634
2. 4SG-a 78, 79
3. 2BC 1018
4. PP 638
5. Ed 266
6. PP 643, 644
7. *Ibid.*, 644-646
8. 3T 218, 219

9. PP 645
10. 3T 219
11. PP 647
12. 3T 219
13. PP 648
14. 2BC 1019
15. PP 657, 658
16. *Ibid.,* 658, 659
17. 2BC 1022
18. MS 17, 1891
19. *Ibid.*
20. PP 666, 667
21. MS 17, 1891
22. 2BC 1021, 1022
23. PP 668
24. 2BC 1022
25. PP 676-681
26. 2BC 1022, 1023
27. *Ibid.,* 1022
28. PP 686, 687
29. *Ibid.,* 681, 682
30. 2BC 1019
31. *Ibid.,* 1017
32. PP 695, 696
33. Ed 157
34. PP 696
35. *Ibid.,* 705, 706
36. *Ibid.,* 717, 718
37. *Ibid.,* 718-720
38. *Ibid.,* 720, 721
39. 2BC 1023
40. PP 722-724
41. 3BC 1147
42. PP 724
43. *Ibid.,* 729-730
44. 4SG-a 89
45. PP 731
46. Letter 6, 1880
47. PP 737, 738
48. *Ibid.,* 740, 741
49. *Ibid.,* 742-744
50. *Ibid.,* 750-753
51. 3BC 1148
52. 1T 422, 423
53. PP 754

JULY
1. PK 32, 33
2. Ed 152, 153
3. FE 498
4. 3BC 1128
5. Letter 104, 1902

6. PK 30, 31
7. 2BC 1026
8. PK 31
9. 2BC 1026
10. *Ibid.*
11. PK 33, 34
12. 2BC 1031
13. PK 54
14. 2BC 1031
15. PK 55, 56
16. MS 40, 1898
17. 2BC 1031
18. 2BC 1030
19. PK 59, 60
20. 2BC 1031
21. PK 70-74
22. PK 76-78
23. 2BC 1031, 1032
24. Letter 8b, 1891
25. 2SM 174-176
26. PK 66, 67
27. MS 47, 1898
28. 2BC 1032, 1033
29. PK 88-94
30. *Ibid.,* 102-105
31. *Ibid.,* 110, 111
32. *Ibid.,* 115, 116
33. 2BC 1033
34. PK 119-122
35. *Ibid.,* 129-132
36. 1T 173, 174
37. 6T 345-348
38. PK 133-142
39. 5T 526, 527
40. 2BC 1034
41. 5T 527, 528
42. GC 583, 584
43. *Ibid.,* 583
44. *Ibid.,* 582
45. PK 155-158
46. 2BC 1034, 1035
47. *Ibid.,* 1035
48. PK 159-166
49. *Ibid.,* 167-173
50. *Ibid.,* 170, 171
51. *Ibid.,* 173-175
52. *Ibid.,* 198-202
53. *Ibid.,* 202
54. SD 199
55. *Ibid.,* 198

AUGUST
1. PK 209-212
2. *Ibid.,* 217, 218
3. *Ibid.,* 219, 220
4. *Ibid.,* 219
5. *Ibid.,* 221-227
6. *Ibid.,* 228
7. Ed 60, 61
8. PK 231-234
9. *Ibid.,* 235-237
10. *Ibid.,* 240-243
11. *Ibid.,* 244, 245
12. MH 473
13. 2T 309, 310
14. MH 473, 474
15. PK 263, 264
16. 2SM 271, 272
17. PK 265-274
18. *Ibid.,* 275-278
19. 5T 749-751
20. 4BC 1140
21. *Ibid.*
22. *Ibid.,* 1139
23. *Ibid.*
24. *Ibid.,* 1141
25. PK 314-320
26. *Ibid.,* 367-370
27. *Ibid.,* 407, 408
28. *Ibid.,* 419-421
29. 4T 174, 175
30. PK 425, 426
31. *Ibid.,* 350-362
32. *Ibid.,* 340-342
33. MH 231, 232
34. PK 346-348
35. ST, Oct. 1, 1902
36. PK 384-388
37. 3BC 1139
38. *Ibid.*
39. *Ibid.*
40. PK 600, 601
41. Ed 263
42. 3BC 1140
43. PK 605, 606
44. MYP 243
45. Ed 57
46. *Ibid.,* 54, 55
47. MYP 243
48. PK 486, 487
49. YI, June 25, 1903
50. YI, July 9, 1903
51. PK 487-489

SEPTEMBER

1. PK 494-502
2. SD 216
3. Letter 90, 1894
4. PK 508-513
5. RH, Sept. 8, 1896
6. PK 520, 521
7. *Ibid.,* 546-548
8. 1T 295, 296
9. PK 543-545
10. *Ibid.,* 554, 555
11. RH, Feb. 9, 1897
12. 4BC 1175
13. PK 557-559
14. 4BC 1170
15. PK 594, 595
16. *Ibid.,* 608, 609
17. *Ibid.,* 623-626
18. 3BC 1134
19. PK 609-616
20. *Ibid.,* 628-632
21. SW, Mar. 15, 1904
22. 3BC 1136
23. PK 637
24. 3BC 1137
25. *Ibid.*
26. PK 638-640
27. *Ibid.,* 641-645
28. *Ibid.,* 647-652
29. 3BC 1135
30. PK 659, 660
31. *Ibid.,* 675-768
32. MH 379
33. CG 23
34. 2SP 47
35. DA 100, 101
36. GW 54, 55
37. 3T 61-63
38. DA 178, 179
39. 5BC 1115
40. 8T 333
41. DA 181,182
42. CT 445
43. FE 123
44. 4T 108, 109
45. DA 214-218
46. *Ibid.,* 223-225
47. *Ibid.,* 219, 220
48. *Ibid.*

OCTOBER

1. DA 139-142

2. 1SM 414, 415
3. 6T 37, 38
4. DA 249, 250
5. *Ibid.,* 297
6. *Ibid.,* 272, 273
7. *Ibid.,* 273
8. ST, June 23, 1898
9. DA 275
10. *Ibid.,* 293-295
11. *Ibid.,* 295
12. 6T 264, 265
13. Ed 91
14. DA 719, 720
15. Ed 85, 86
16. *Ibid.,* 86
17. DA 250
18. *Ibid.,* 295-297
19. *Ibid.,* 380, 381
20. *Ibid.,* 167-171
21. RH, May 5, 1896
22. SC 28, 29
23. DA 171-177
24. *Ibid.,* 194
25. *Ibid.,* 189, 191
26. *Ibid.,* 195
27. DA 198-200
28. Ev 594
29. DA 315
30. MH 63-65
31. DA 317
32. DA 399-403
33. MH 59
34. DA 343-347
35. 4T 219, 220
36. COL 391, 392
37. DA 519-523
38. *Ibid.,* 552-555
39. COL 236
40. DA 555, 556
41. *Ibid.,* 555
42. *Ibid.,* 614-616
43. *Ibid.,* 525
44. MH 458
45. DA 557-560
46. *Ibid.,* 560, 563
47. *Ibid.,* 564, 565
48. *Ibid.,* 566-568
49. *Ibid.,* 568
50. *Ibid.,* 381, 382

NOVEMBER

1. DA 411, 412

2. Letter 65, 1894
3. DA 415, 416
4. Ed 88-91
5. AA 541-543
6. AA 539
7. Ed 87
8. AA 544, 545
9. *Ibid.,* 557-559
10. DA 716, 717
11. *Ibid.,* 716
12. MH 493
13. 4T 486
14. COL 72, 73
15. DA 645
16. *Ibid.,* 653
17. *Ibid.,* 720
18. *Ibid.,* 654, 655
19. 5BC 1102
20. DA 292, 293
21. 5BC 1141, 1142
22. DA 293
23. COL 152
24. DA 712
25. COL 152-155
26. 5BC 1152
27. *Ibid.*
28. DA 708, 709
29. 5BC 1104
30. *Ibid.,* 1105
31. *Ibid.*
32. *Ibid.,* 1104, 1105
33. DA 732
34. *Ibid.,* 738
35. Und. MS 127
36. MS 103, 1897
37. DA 749-751
38. *Ibid.,* 773-776
39. *Ibid.,* 806, 807
40. EW 188
41. DA 807, 808
42. AA 62, 63
43. *Ibid.,* 68, 69
44. 4T 462, 463
45. AA 74, 75
46. *Ibid.,* 97-101
47. MB 33, 34
48. 8T 57
49. AA 107-109
50. MH 473
51. AA 131, 132
52. Ed 217
53. AA 133, 134

54. 6T 79
55. AA 134
56. *Ibid.,* 139, 140
57. IHP 322
58. AA 132-142
59. *Ibid.,* 145, 146
60. *Ibid.,* 154
61. AA 152, 153
62. Ed 64, 65
63. MS 41, 1894
64. 3T 429-433
65. SR 274, 275
66. MH 58

DECEMBER
1. 6BC 1084
2. AA 245-251
3. Letter 107, 1904
4. Letter 103, 1900
5. AA 355, 356
6. *Ibid.,* 288-290
7. 7BC 915
8. YI, May 5, 1898

9. 7BC 919
10. PP 592
11. 1SM 319
12. AA 204
13. 7BC 917
14. *Ibid.,* 918
15. AA 205
16. *Ibid.,* 501-506
17. *Ibid.,* 166-170
18. *Ibid.,* 454, 455
19. SL 91
20. AA 456-460
21. *Ibid.,* 312-315
22. *Ibid.,* 313, 314
23. ST, Nov. 6, 1879
24. Letter 135, 1897
25. AA 484
26. FE 235
27. 9T 287
28. AA 430-432
29. *Ibid.,* 492-494
30. ST, Dec. 5, 1906
31. AA 500

32. *Ibid.,* 507, 508
33. *Ibid.,* 546-551
34. *Ibid.,* 553-556
35. *Ibid.,* 559-564
36. *Ibid.,* 574-577
37. *Ibid.,* 569, 570
38. *Ibid.,* 570-572
39. *Ibid.,* 572-574
40. 6T 364, 365
41. SC 125
42. PP 717
43. 5T 569
44. MB 80, 81
45. Ed 51-57
46. *Ibid.,* 255, 256
47. 4T 12-15
48. AA 575
49. GC 621
50. *Ibid.,* 626, 627
51. 4T 610-612
52. RH, June 12, 1900
53. MH 397, 398
54. MYP 36

INDEX OF BIBLE CHARACTERS

378

SCRIPTURE INDEX

380

383